Cheeky Brat

Mitsubachi Miyuki

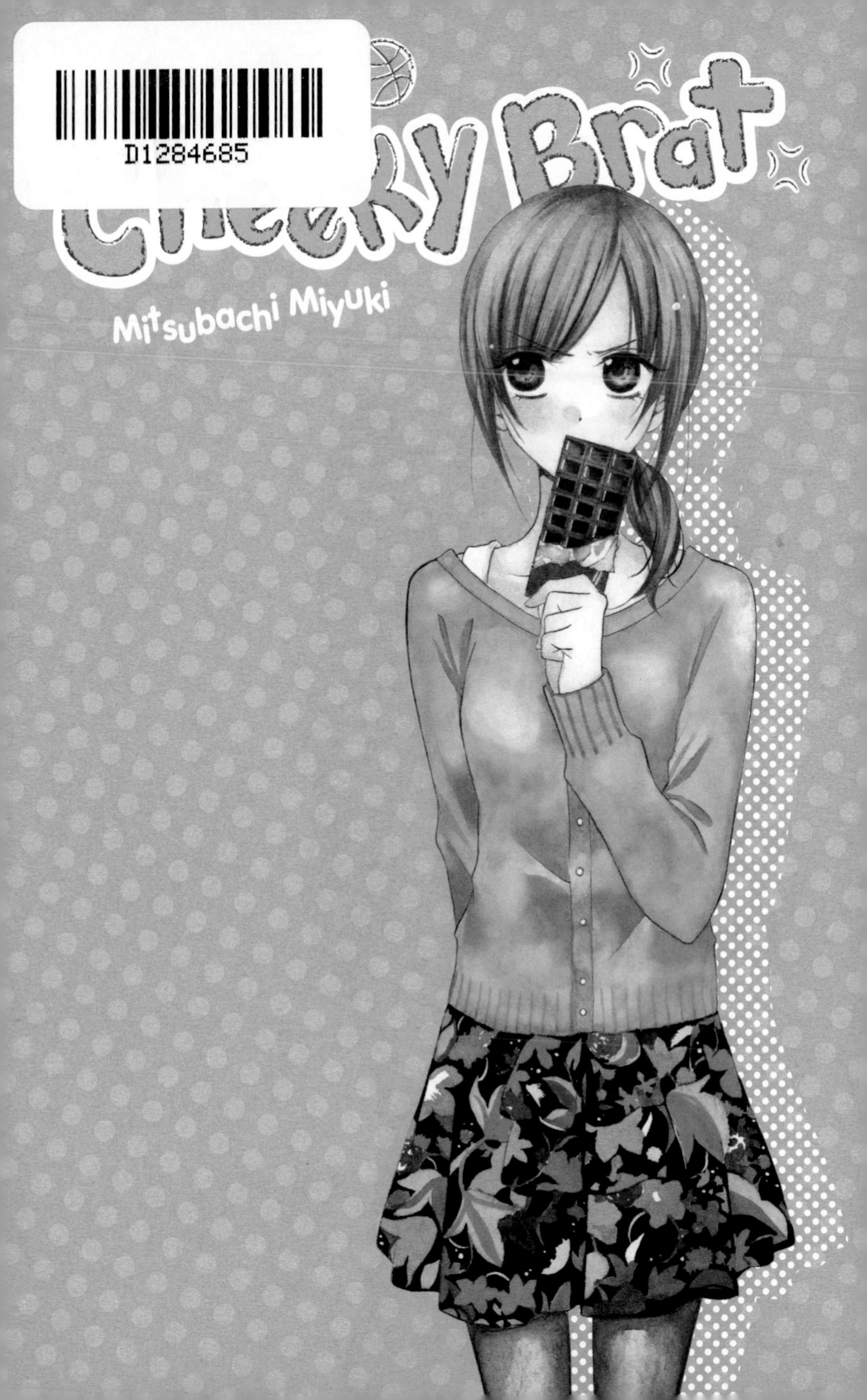

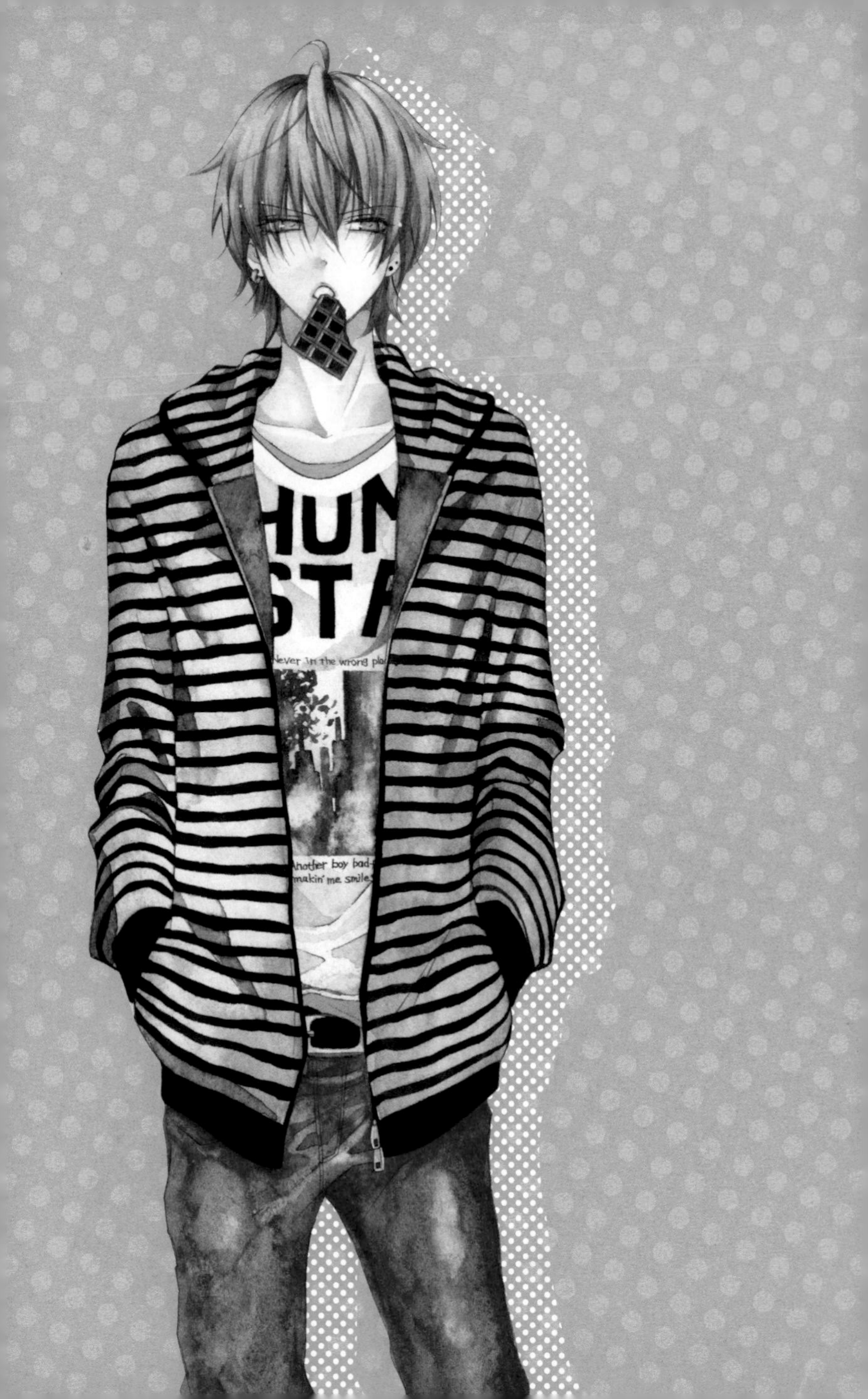
Never in the wrong
Another boy bad-
makin' me smiles

Cheeky Brat

Mitsubachi Miyuki

1

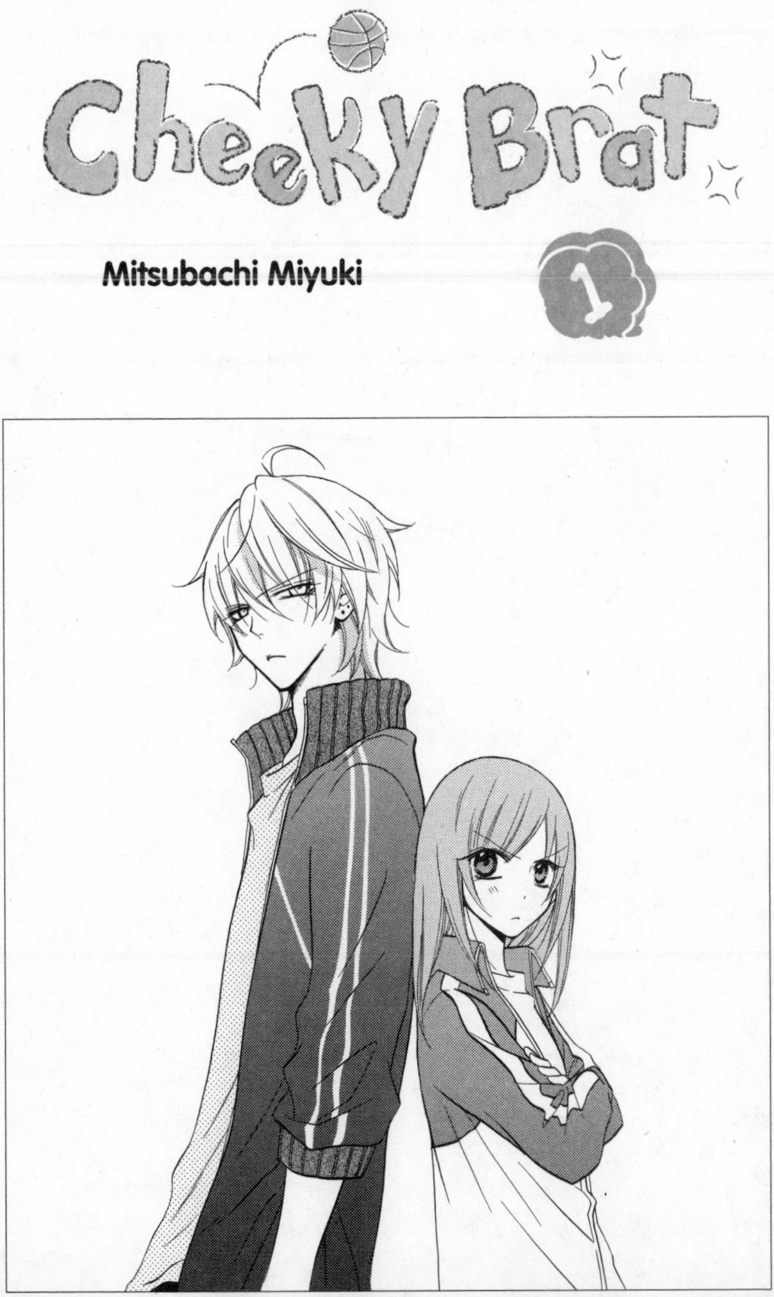

Cheeky Brat

1

Contents

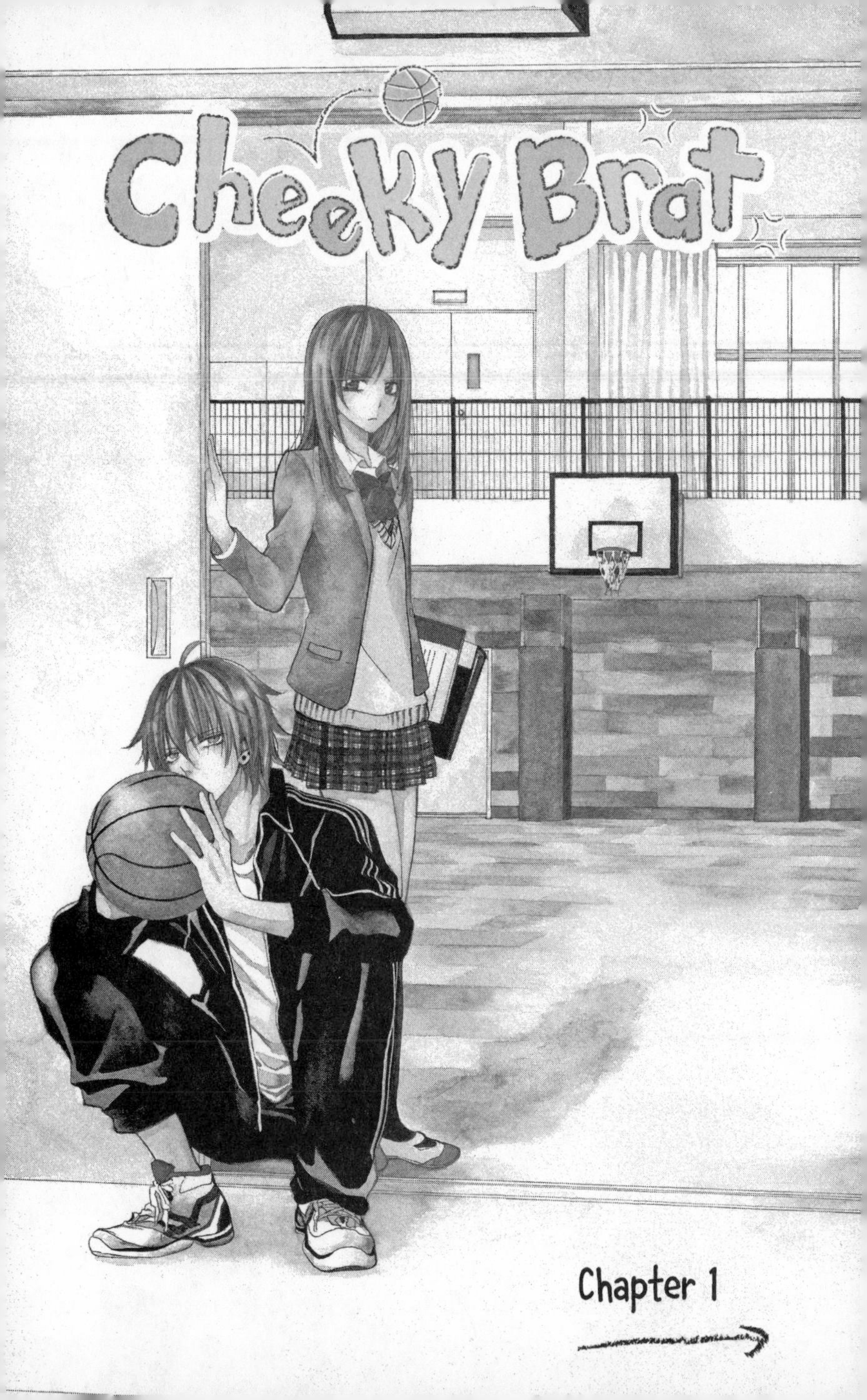
Cheeky Brat
Chapter 1

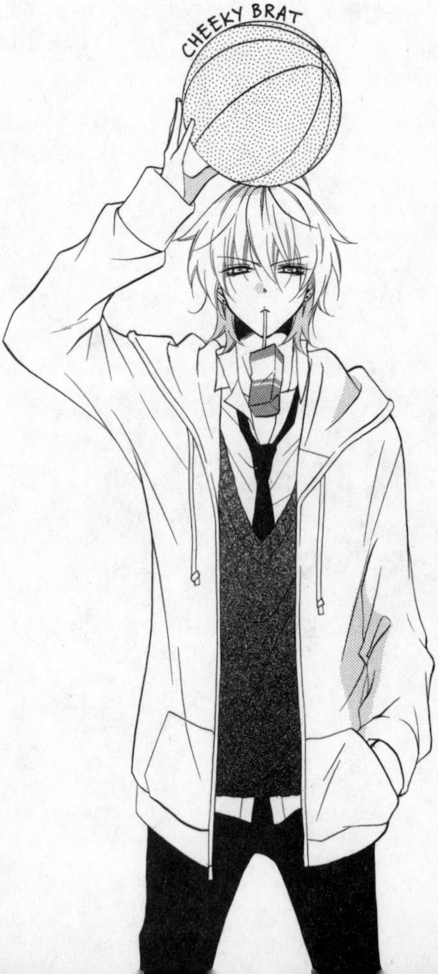
CHEEKY BRAT

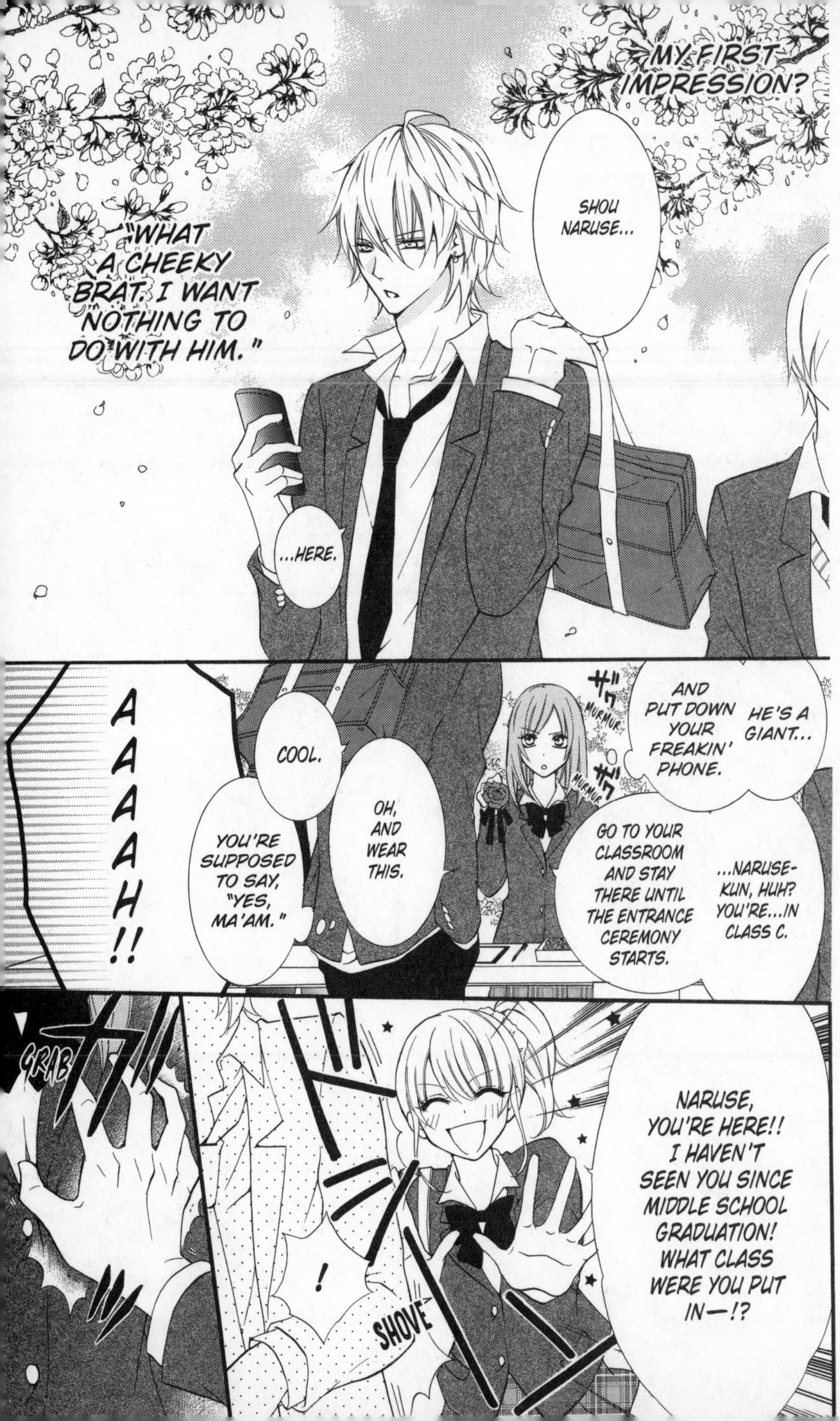
MY FIRST IMPRESSION?
SHOU NARUSE...
"WHAT A CHEEKY BRAT. I WANT NOTHING TO DO WITH HIM."
...HERE.
HE'S A GIANT...
AND PUT DOWN YOUR FREAKIN' PHONE.
MURMUR
MURMUR
...NARUSE-KUN, HUH? YOU'RE...IN CLASS C.
GO TO YOUR CLASSROOM AND STAY THERE UNTIL THE ENTRANCE CEREMONY STARTS.
OH, AND WEAR THIS.
COOL.
YOU'RE SUPPOSED TO SAY, "YES, MA'AM."
AAAAAH!!
NARUSE, YOU'RE HERE!! I HAVEN'T SEEN YOU SINCE MIDDLE SCHOOL GRADUATION! WHAT CLASS WERE YOU PUT IN—!?
!
SHOVE
GRAB

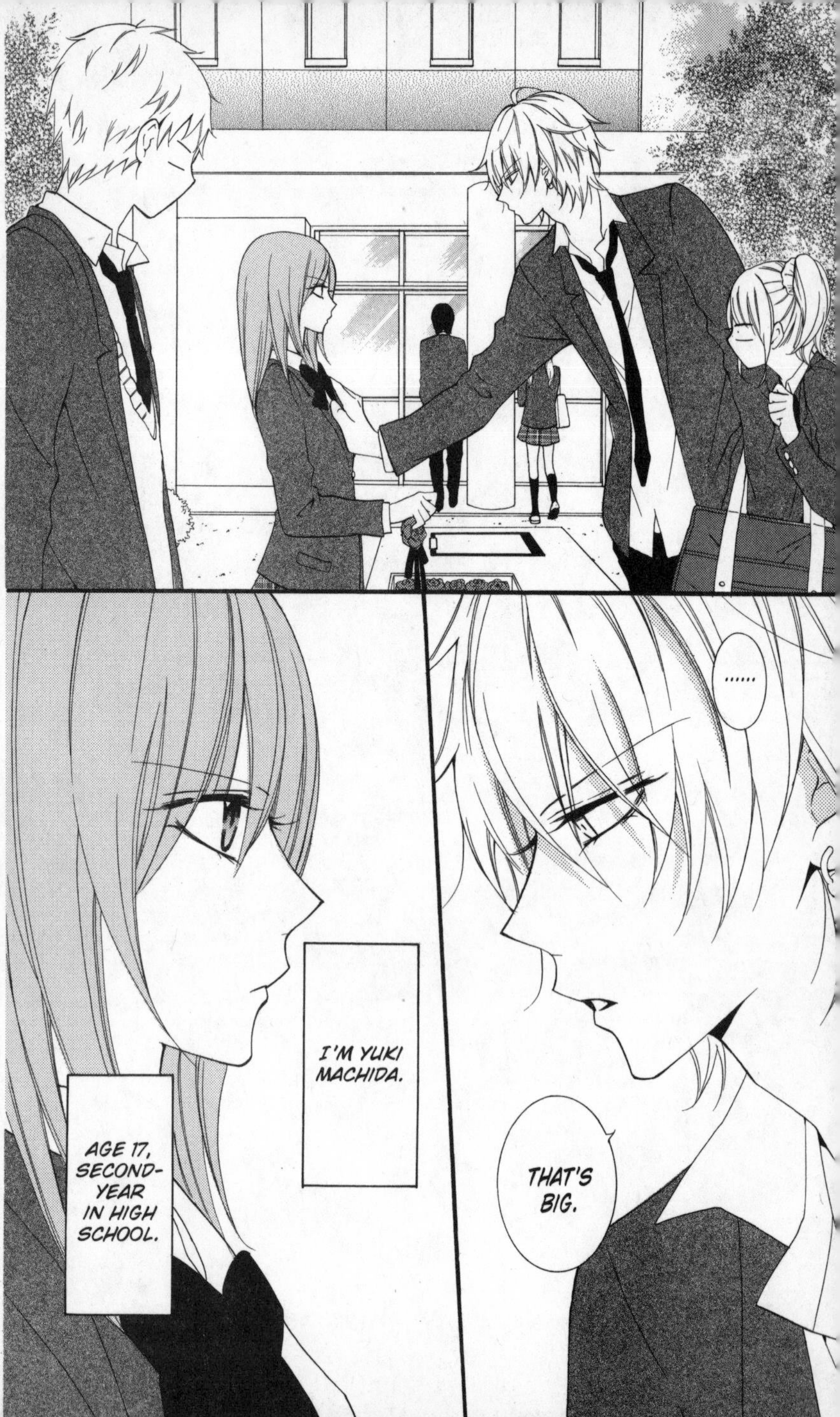
......
THAT'S BIG.
I'M YUKI MACHIDA.
AGE 17, SECOND-YEAR IN HIGH SCHOOL.

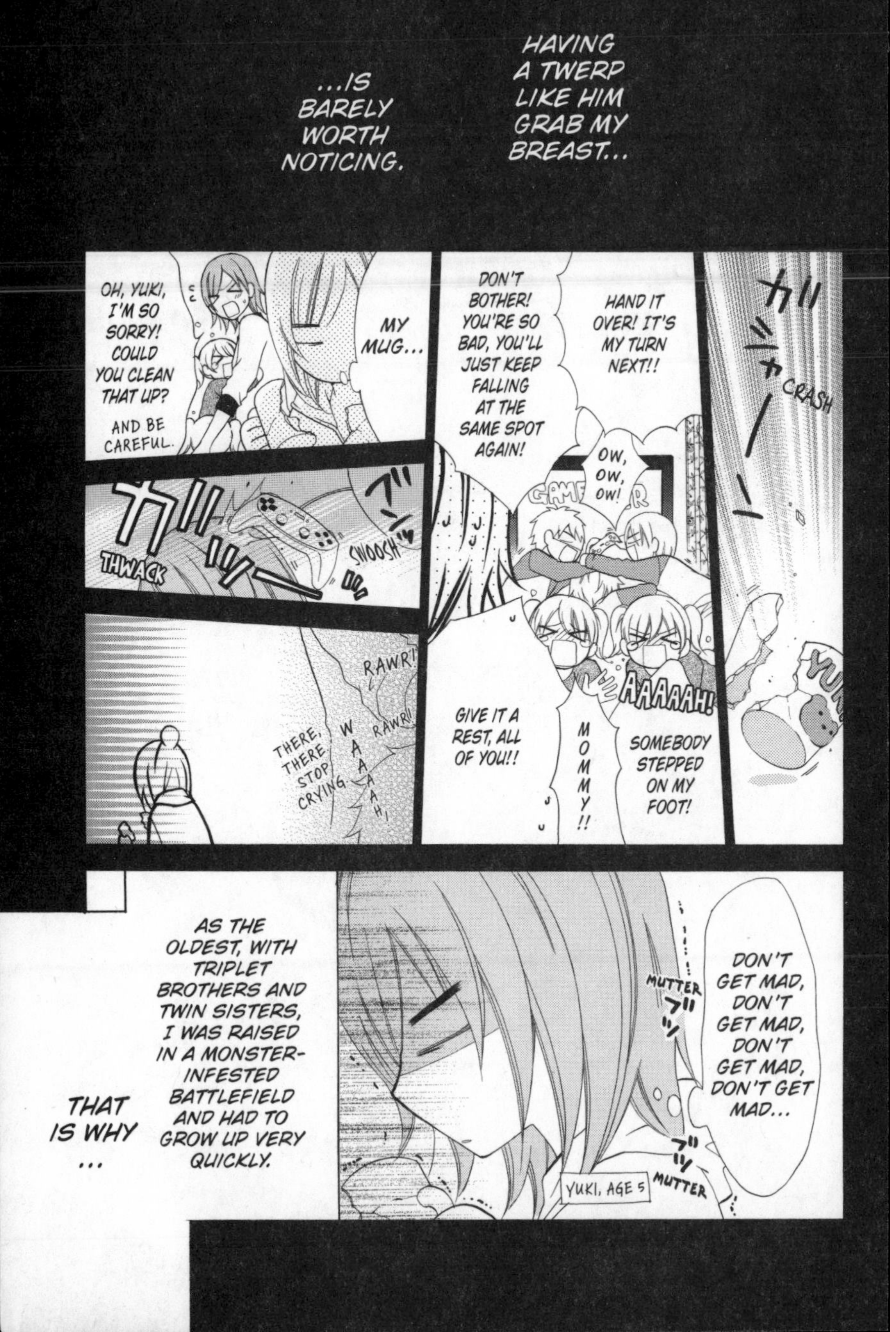
HAVING A TWERP LIKE HIM GRAB MY BREAST...
...IS BARELY WORTH NOTICING.
CRASH
HAND IT OVER! IT'S MY TURN NEXT!!
DON'T BOTHER! YOU'RE SO BAD, YOU'LL JUST KEEP FALLING AT THE SAME SPOT AGAIN!
OW, OW, OW!
AAAAAH!
SOMEBODY STEPPED ON MY FOOT!
MOMMY!!
GIVE IT A REST, ALL OF YOU!!
MY MUG...
OH, YUKI, I'M SO SORRY! COULD YOU CLEAN THAT UP?
AND BE CAREFUL.
SWOOSH
THWACK
RAWR!
RAWR!
WAAAAAH!
THERE, THERE STOP CRYING
DON'T GET MAD, DON'T GET MAD, DON'T GET MAD, DON'T GET MAD...
MUTTER
MUTTER
YUKI, AGE 5
AS THE OLDEST, WITH TRIPLET BROTHERS AND TWIN SISTERS, I WAS RAISED IN A MONSTER-INFESTED BATTLEFIELD AND HAD TO GROW UP VERY QUICKLY.
THAT IS WHY ...

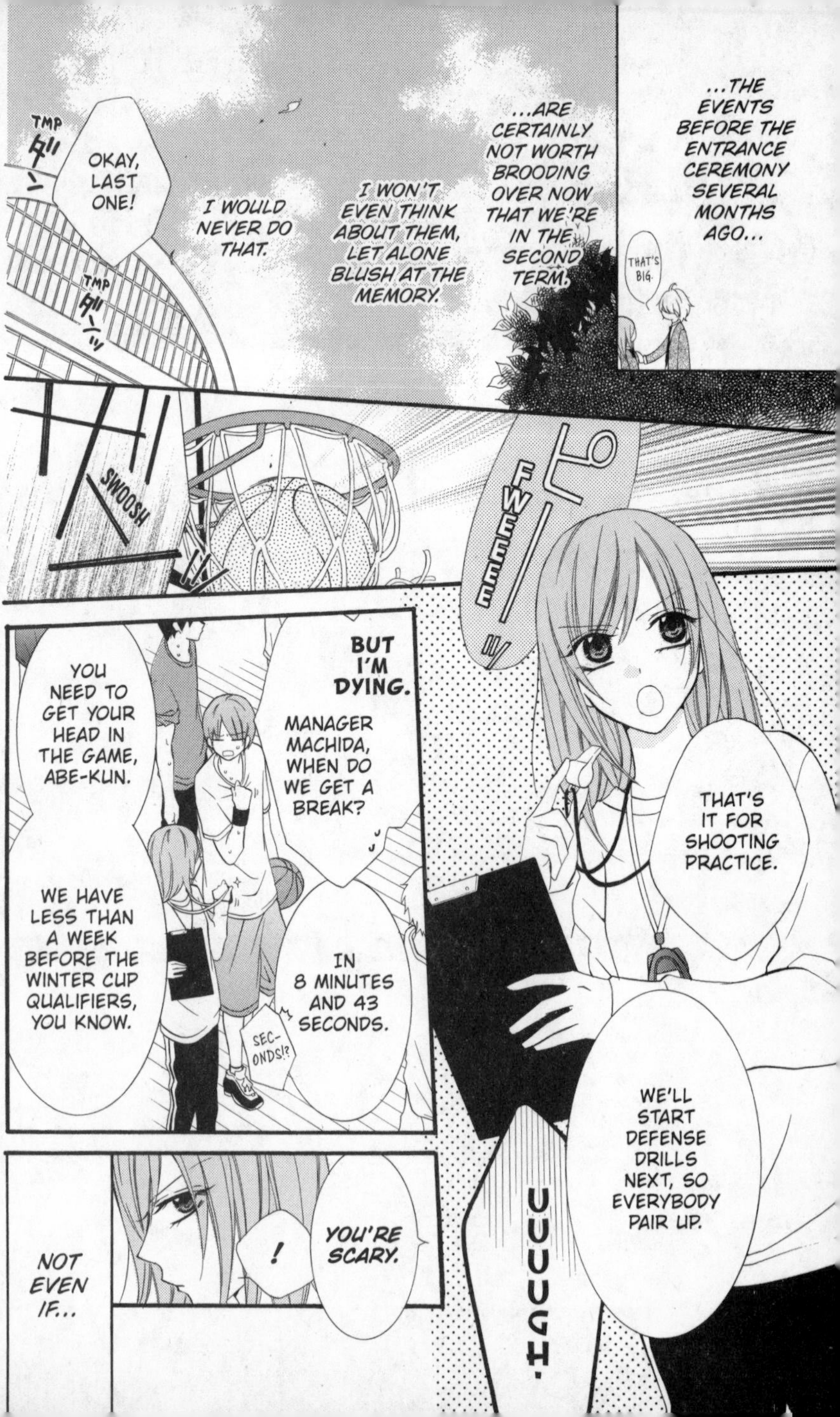
...THE EVENTS BEFORE THE ENTRANCE CEREMONY SEVERAL MONTHS AGO...
THAT'S BIG.
...ARE CERTAINLY NOT WORTH BROODING OVER NOW THAT WE'RE IN THE SECOND TERM.
I WON'T EVEN THINK ABOUT THEM, LET ALONE BLUSH AT THE MEMORY.
I WOULD NEVER DO THAT.
TMP
OKAY, LAST ONE!
TMP
SWOOSH
FWEEEE
THAT'S IT FOR SHOOTING PRACTICE.
WE'LL START DEFENSE DRILLS NEXT, SO EVERYBODY PAIR UP.
UUUUGH.
BUT I'M DYING.
MANAGER MACHIDA, WHEN DO WE GET A BREAK?
IN 8 MINUTES AND 43 SECONDS.
SEC-ONDS!?
YOU NEED TO GET YOUR HEAD IN THE GAME, ABE-KUN.
WE HAVE LESS THAN A WEEK BEFORE THE WINTER CUP QUALIFIERS, YOU KNOW.
YOU'RE SCARY.
!
NOT EVEN IF...

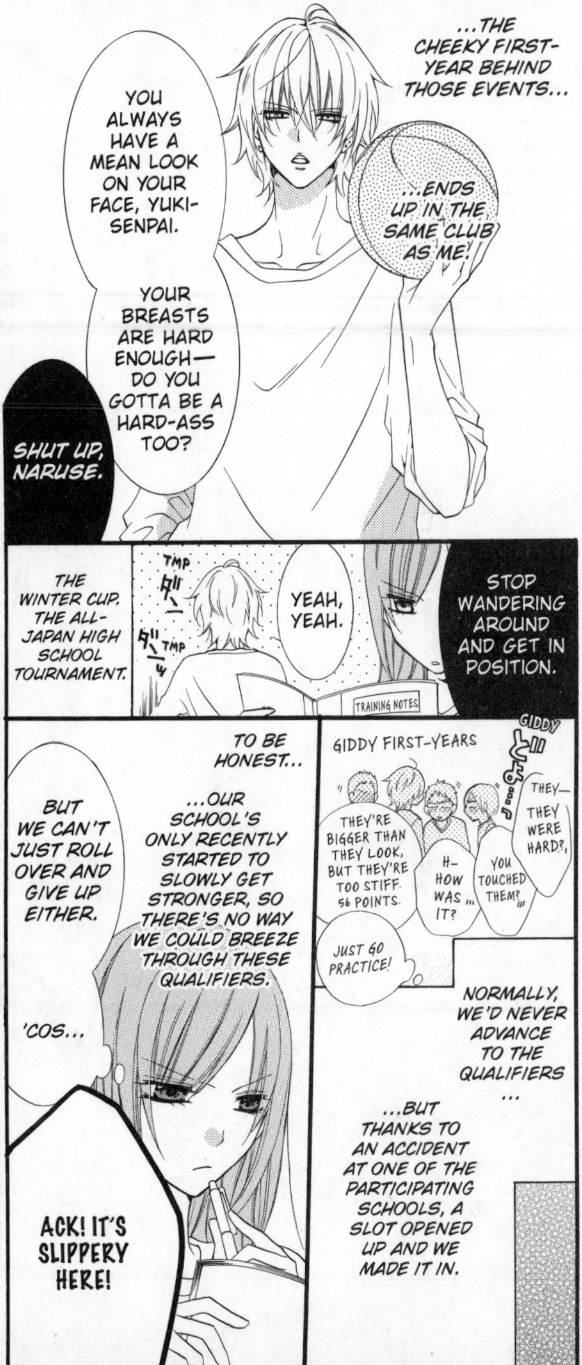
...THE CHEEKY FIRST-YEAR BEHIND THOSE EVENTS...
...ENDS UP IN THE SAME CLUB AS ME.
YOU ALWAYS HAVE A MEAN LOOK ON YOUR FACE, YUKI-SENPAI.
YOUR BREASTS ARE HARD ENOUGH—DO YOU GOTTA BE A HARD-ASS TOO?
SHUT UP, NARUSE.
STOP WANDERING AROUND AND GET IN POSITION.
YEAH, YEAH.
TMP
TMP
TRAINING NOTES
THE WINTER CUP. THE ALL-JAPAN HIGH SCHOOL TOURNAMENT.
GIDDY
GIDDY FIRST-YEARS
THEY— THEY WERE HARD?
YOU TOUCHED THEM?
H-HOW WAS IT?
THEY'RE BIGGER THAN THEY LOOK, BUT THEY'RE TOO STIFF. 56 POINTS.
JUST GO PRACTICE!
NORMALLY, WE'D NEVER ADVANCE TO THE QUALIFIERS...
...BUT THANKS TO AN ACCIDENT AT ONE OF THE PARTICIPATING SCHOOLS, A SLOT OPENED UP AND WE MADE IT IN.
TO BE HONEST...
...OUR SCHOOL'S ONLY RECENTLY STARTED TO SLOWLY GET STRONGER, SO THERE'S NO WAY WE COULD BREEZE THROUGH THESE QUALIFIERS.
BUT WE CAN'T JUST ROLL OVER AND GIVE UP EITHER.
'COS...
ACK! IT'S SLIPPERY HERE!

01

VOLUME 1

Hello and nice to meet you. I am Mitsubachi Miyuki.

Thank you very much for picking up *Cheeky Brat*.

This series started out as a 40-page one-shot that I wrote for the magazine *Hana to Yume* (that version isn't in this book).

I hadn't done a high school romance in ages, so for me, it was a lot of fun. I liked the story a lot, so I put everything into drawing those 40 pages, all the while thinking, "Aww, when this one-shot is over, I won't get to draw Yuki and Naruse anymore."

But then—I was blessed with the happy opportunity to draw both of them a lot. Now, unbelievably, I can present them to the world in a full volume of manga. Thank you very, very much.

And this series gave me my beyond-beyond-unbelievable colored chapter title page, and the beyond-beyond-beyond-unbelievable opportunity to draw a cover for *Hana to Yume*.

THANK YOU SO, SO MUCH!!!

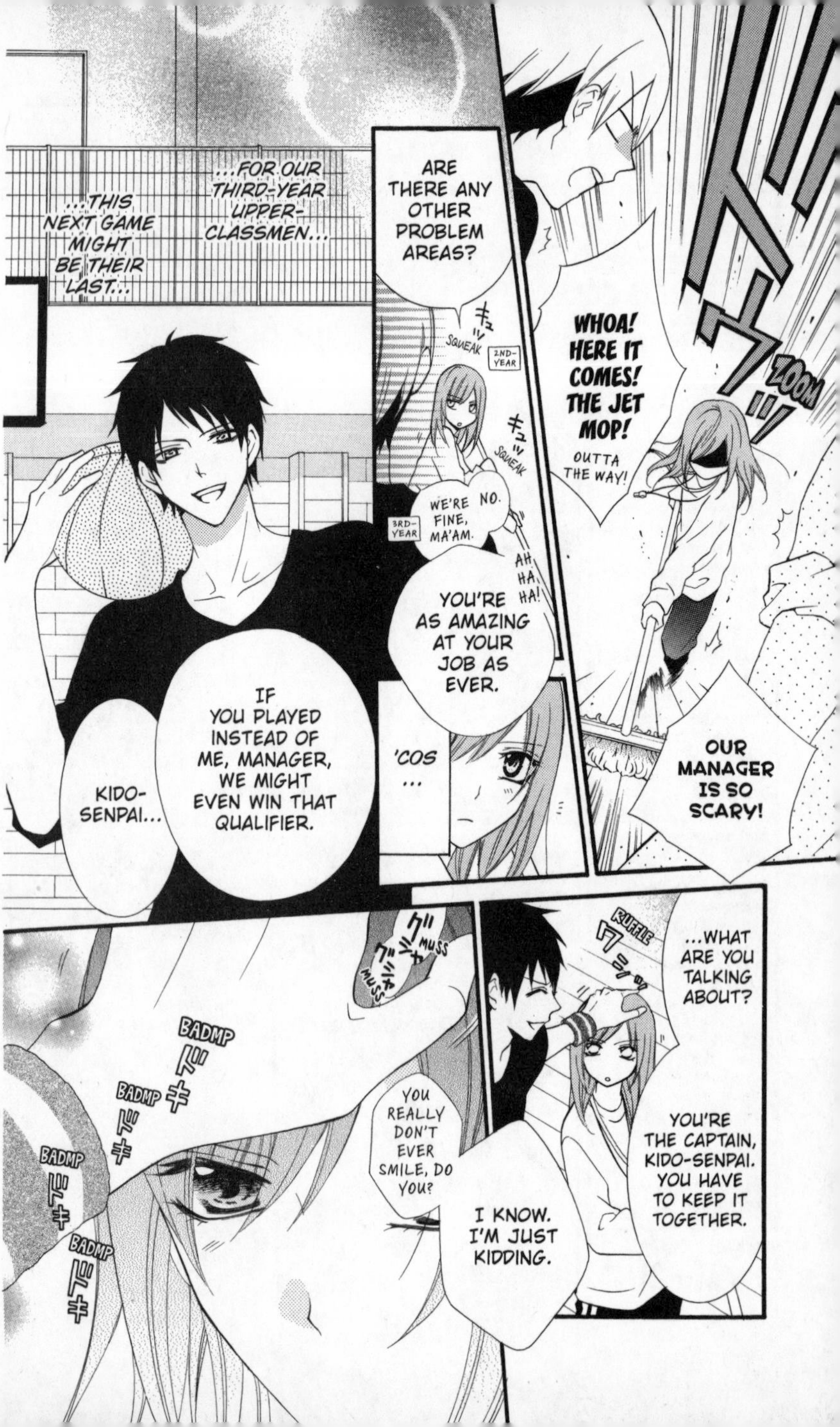
WHOA! HERE IT COMES! THE JET MOP!
OUTTA THE WAY!
ZOOM
OUR MANAGER IS SO SCARY!
ARE THERE ANY OTHER PROBLEM AREAS?
SQUEAK
2ND-YEAR
SQUEAK
NO.
WE'RE FINE, MA'AM.
3RD-YEAR
AH HA HA!
YOU'RE AS AMAZING AT YOUR JOB AS EVER.
'COS ...
...FOR OUR THIRD-YEAR UPPER-CLASSMEN...
...THIS NEXT GAME MIGHT BE THEIR LAST...
IF YOU PLAYED INSTEAD OF ME, MANAGER, WE MIGHT EVEN WIN THAT QUALIFIER.
KIDO-SENPAI...
RUFFLE
...WHAT ARE YOU TALKING ABOUT?
YOU'RE THE CAPTAIN, KIDO-SENPAI. YOU HAVE TO KEEP IT TOGETHER.
I KNOW. I'M JUST KIDDING.
YOU REALLY DON'T EVER SMILE, DO YOU?
MUSS
MUSS
BADMP
BADMP
BADMP
BADMP

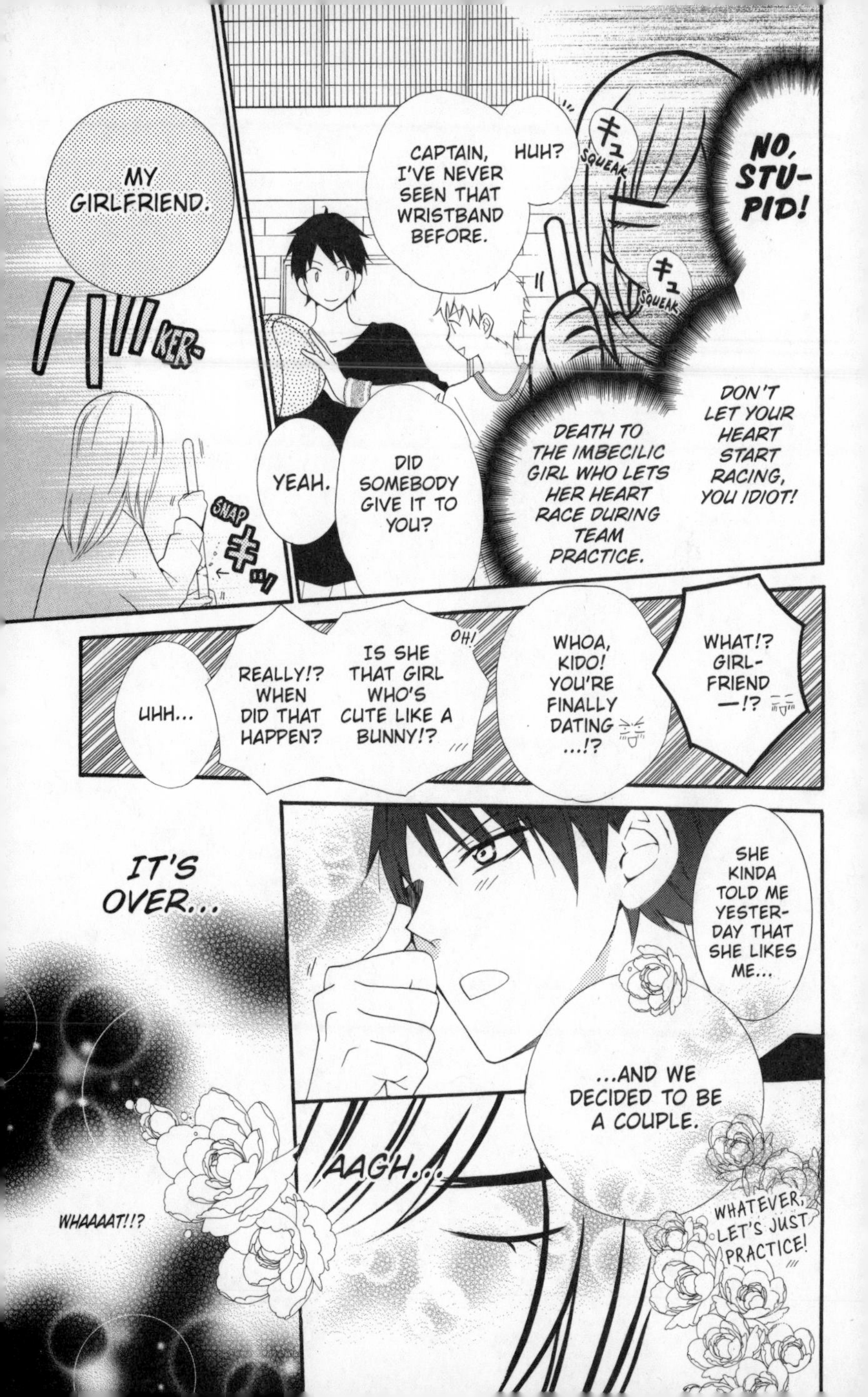
NO, STU-PID!
キュ SQUEAK
キュ SQUEAK
HUH?
CAPTAIN, I'VE NEVER SEEN THAT WRISTBAND BEFORE.
DON'T LET YOUR HEART START RACING, YOU IDIOT!
DEATH TO THE IMBECILIC GIRL WHO LETS HER HEART RACE DURING TEAM PRACTICE.
DID SOMEBODY GIVE IT TO YOU?
YEAH.
MY GIRLFRIEND.
KER-
SNAP
キ
WHAT!? GIRL-FRIEND—!?
WHOA, KIDO! YOU'RE FINALLY DATING ...!?
OH!
IS SHE THAT GIRL WHO'S CUTE LIKE A BUNNY!?
REALLY!? WHEN DID THAT HAPPEN?
UHH...
SHE KINDA TOLD ME YESTER-DAY THAT SHE LIKES ME...
...AND WE DECIDED TO BE A COUPLE.
WHATEVER, LET'S JUST PRACTICE!
AAGH...
IT'S OVER...
WHAAAAT!!?

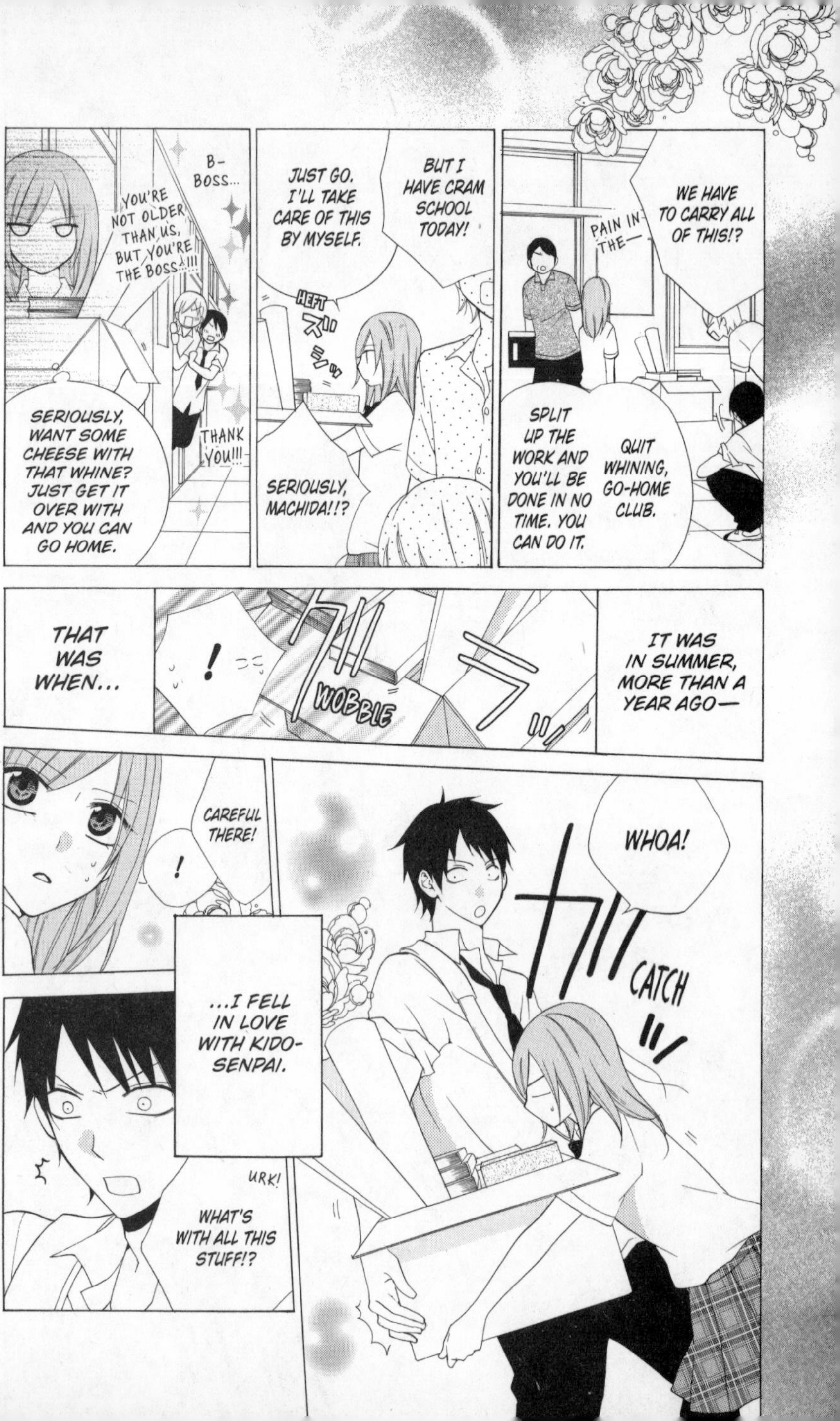
WE HAVE TO CARRY ALL OF THIS!?
PAIN IN THE—
QUIT WHINING, GO-HOME CLUB.
SPLIT UP THE WORK AND YOU'LL BE DONE IN NO TIME. YOU CAN DO IT.
BUT I HAVE CRAM SCHOOL TODAY!
JUST GO. I'LL TAKE CARE OF THIS BY MYSELF.
HEFT
SERIOUSLY, MACHIDA!!?
B-BOSS...
YOU'RE NOT OLDER THAN US, BUT YOU'RE THE BOSS♪!!!
THANK YOU!!!
SERIOUSLY, WANT SOME CHEESE WITH THAT WHINE? JUST GET IT OVER WITH AND YOU CAN GO HOME.
IT WAS IN SUMMER, MORE THAN A YEAR AGO—
!
WOBBLE
THAT WAS WHEN...
WHOA!
CATCH
...I FELL IN LOVE WITH KIDO-SENPAI.
CAREFUL THERE!
!
URK!
WHAT'S WITH ALL THIS STUFF!?

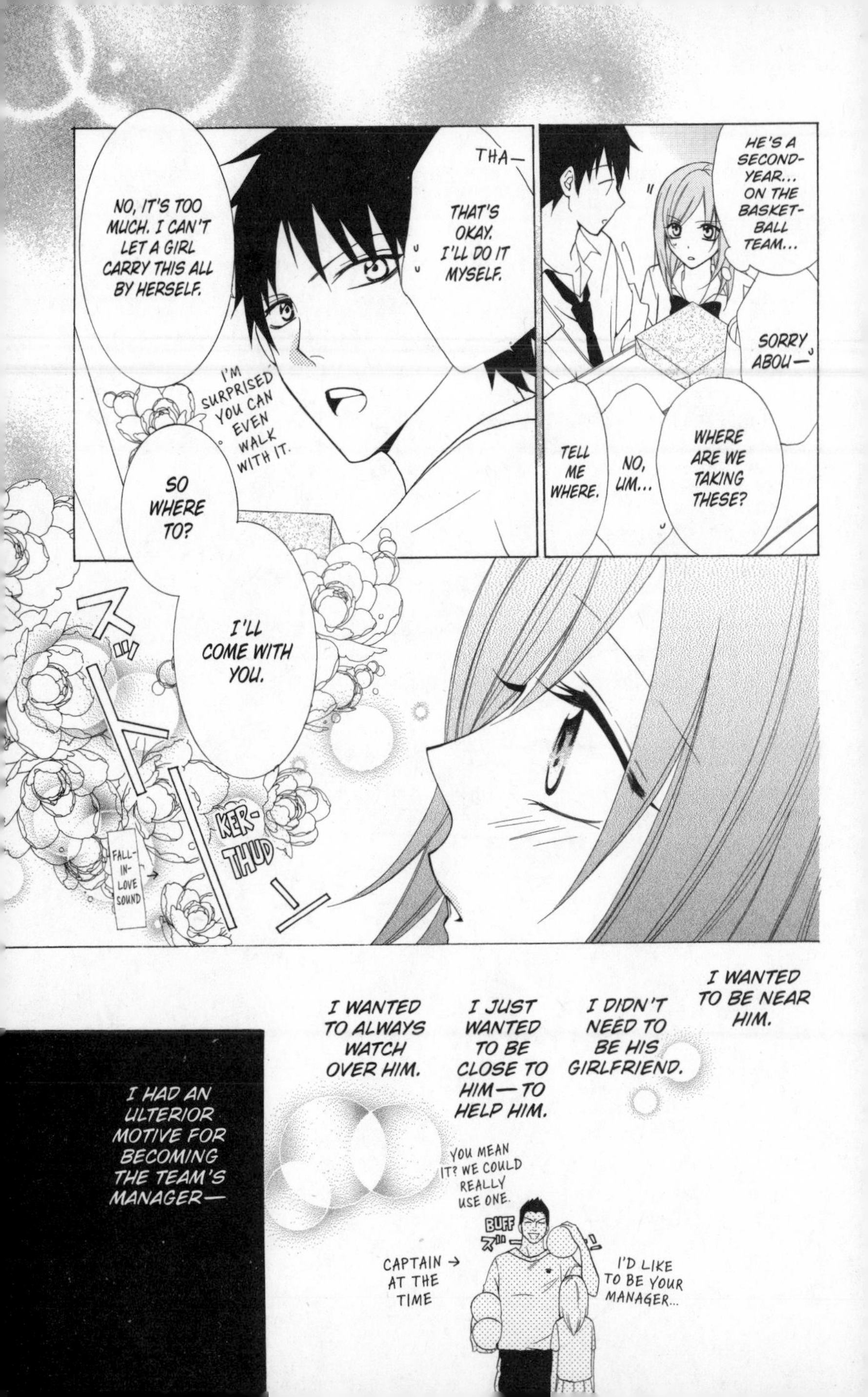
HE'S A SECOND-YEAR... ON THE BASKETBALL TEAM...
SORRY ABOU—
WHERE ARE WE TAKING THESE?
NO, UM...
TELL ME WHERE.
THA—
THAT'S OKAY. I'LL DO IT MYSELF.
NO, IT'S TOO MUCH. I CAN'T LET A GIRL CARRY THIS ALL BY HERSELF.
I'M SURPRISED YOU CAN EVEN WALK WITH IT.
SO WHERE TO?
I'LL COME WITH YOU.
KER-THUD
FALL-IN-LOVE SOUND
I WANTED TO BE NEAR HIM.
I DIDN'T NEED TO BE HIS GIRLFRIEND.
I JUST WANTED TO BE CLOSE TO HIM—TO HELP HIM.
I WANTED TO ALWAYS WATCH OVER HIM.
I'D LIKE TO BE YOUR MANAGER...
BUFF
YOU MEAN IT? WE COULD REALLY USE ONE.
CAPTAIN AT THE TIME
I HAD AN ULTERIOR MOTIVE FOR BECOMING THE TEAM'S MANAGER—

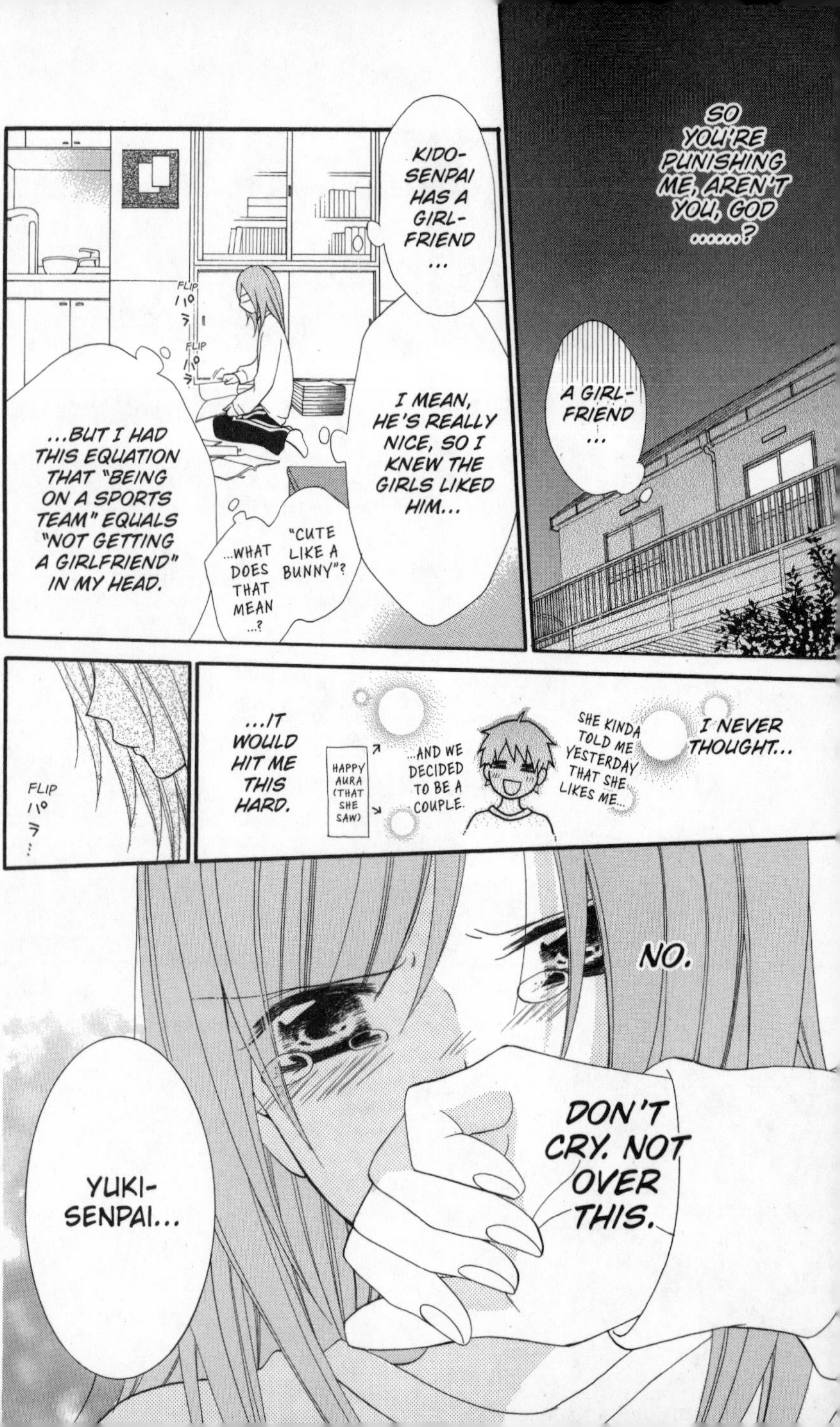
SO YOU'RE PUNISHING ME, AREN'T YOU, GOD ......?
A GIRL-FRIEND...
KIDO-SENPAI HAS A GIRL-FRIEND...
I MEAN, HE'S REALLY NICE, SO I KNEW THE GIRLS LIKED HIM...
FLIP
FLIP
...BUT I HAD THIS EQUATION THAT "BEING ON A SPORTS TEAM" EQUALS "NOT GETTING A GIRLFRIEND" IN MY HEAD.
"CUTE LIKE A BUNNY"?
...WHAT DOES THAT MEAN...?
I NEVER THOUGHT...
SHE KINDA TOLD ME YESTERDAY THAT SHE LIKES ME...
...AND WE DECIDED TO BE A COUPLE.
HAPPY AURA (THAT SHE SAW)
...IT WOULD HIT ME THIS HARD.
FLIP...
NO.
DON'T CRY. NOT OVER THIS.
YUKI-SENPAI...

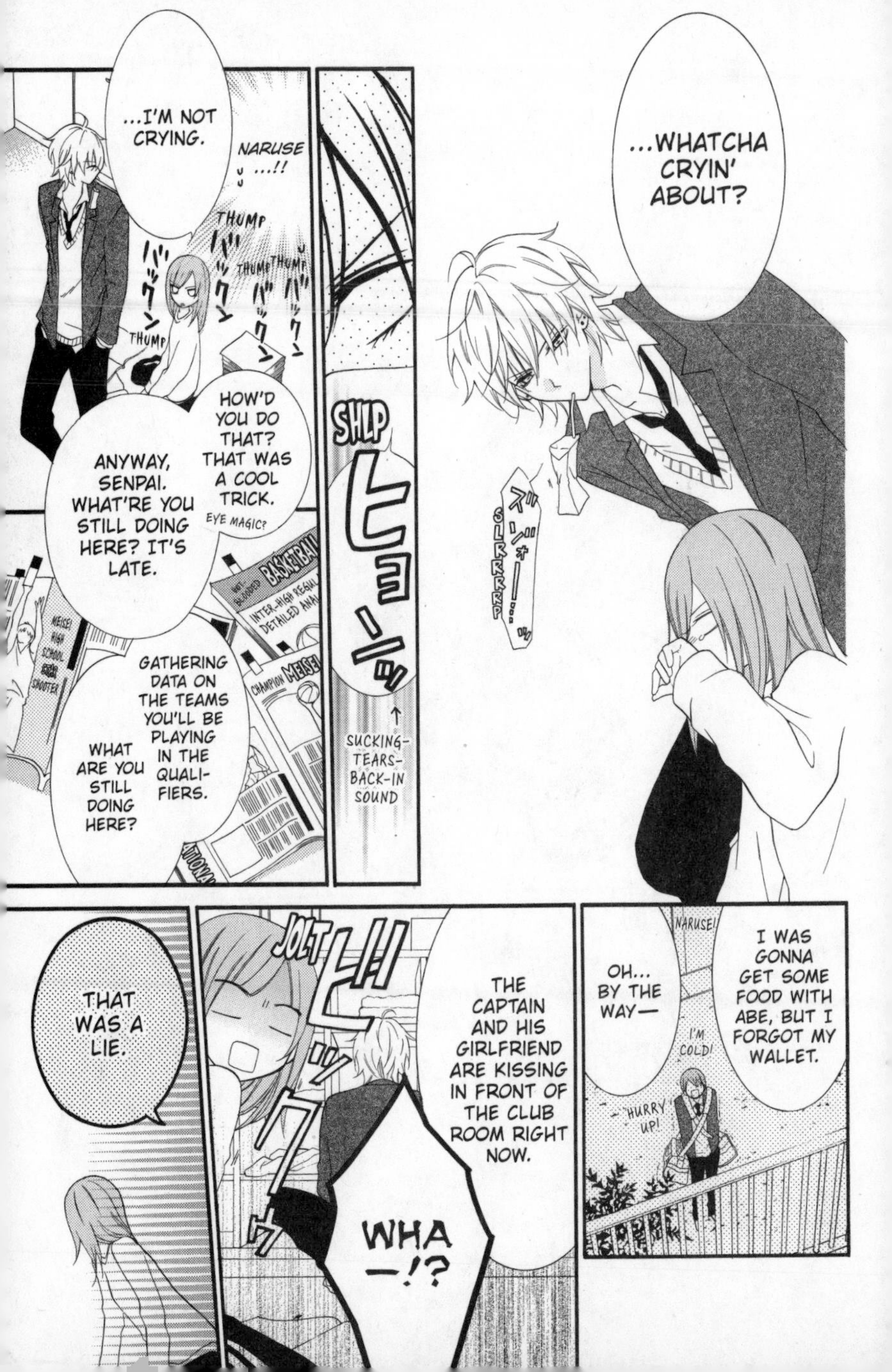
...WHATCHA CRYIN' ABOUT?
SLRRRRP
SHLP
SUCKING-TEARS-BACK-IN SOUND
...I'M NOT CRYING.
NARUSE ...!!
THUMP THUMP THUMP THUMP
HOW'D YOU DO THAT? THAT WAS A COOL TRICK.
EYE MAGIC?
ANYWAY, SENPAI. WHAT'RE YOU STILL DOING HERE? IT'S LATE.
GATHERING DATA ON THE TEAMS YOU'LL BE PLAYING IN THE QUALIFIERS.
WHAT ARE YOU STILL DOING HERE?
HOT-BLOODED BASKETBALL
CHAMPION MEISEI
MEISEI HIGH SCHOOL STAR SHOOTER
NARUSE!
I WAS GONNA GET SOME FOOD WITH ABE, BUT I FORGOT MY WALLET.
I'M COLD!
HURRY UP!
OH... BY THE WAY—
THE CAPTAIN AND HIS GIRLFRIEND ARE KISSING IN FRONT OF THE CLUB ROOM RIGHT NOW.
JOLT
WHA—!?
THAT WAS A LIE.

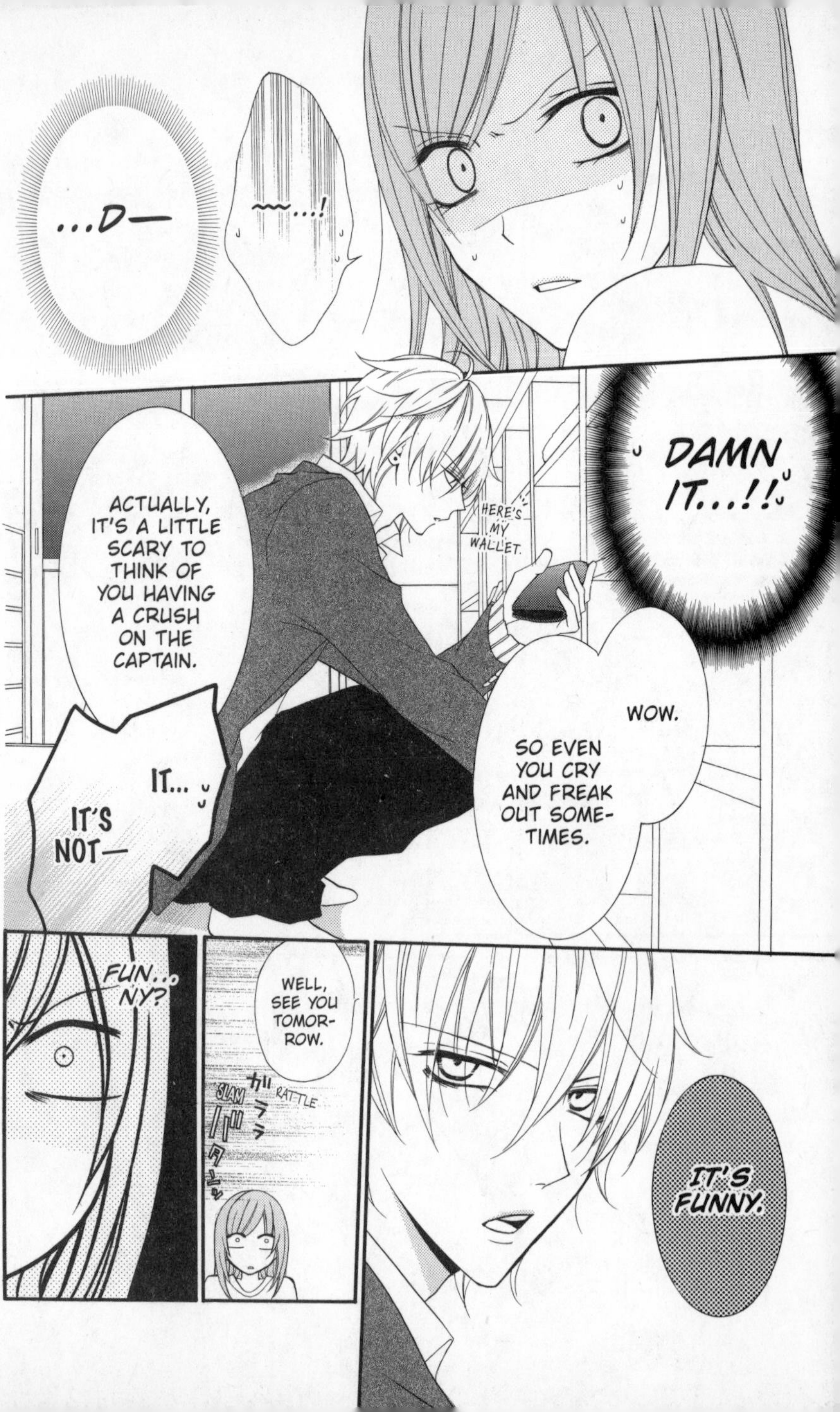
~~...!
...D—
DAMN IT...!!
HERE'S MY WALLET.
ACTUALLY, IT'S A LITTLE SCARY TO THINK OF YOU HAVING A CRUSH ON THE CAPTAIN.
WOW.
SO EVEN YOU CRY AND FREAK OUT SOME-TIMES.
IT...
IT'S NOT—
IT'S FUNNY.
WELL, SEE YOU TOMOR-ROW.
RATTLE
SLAM
FUN... NY?

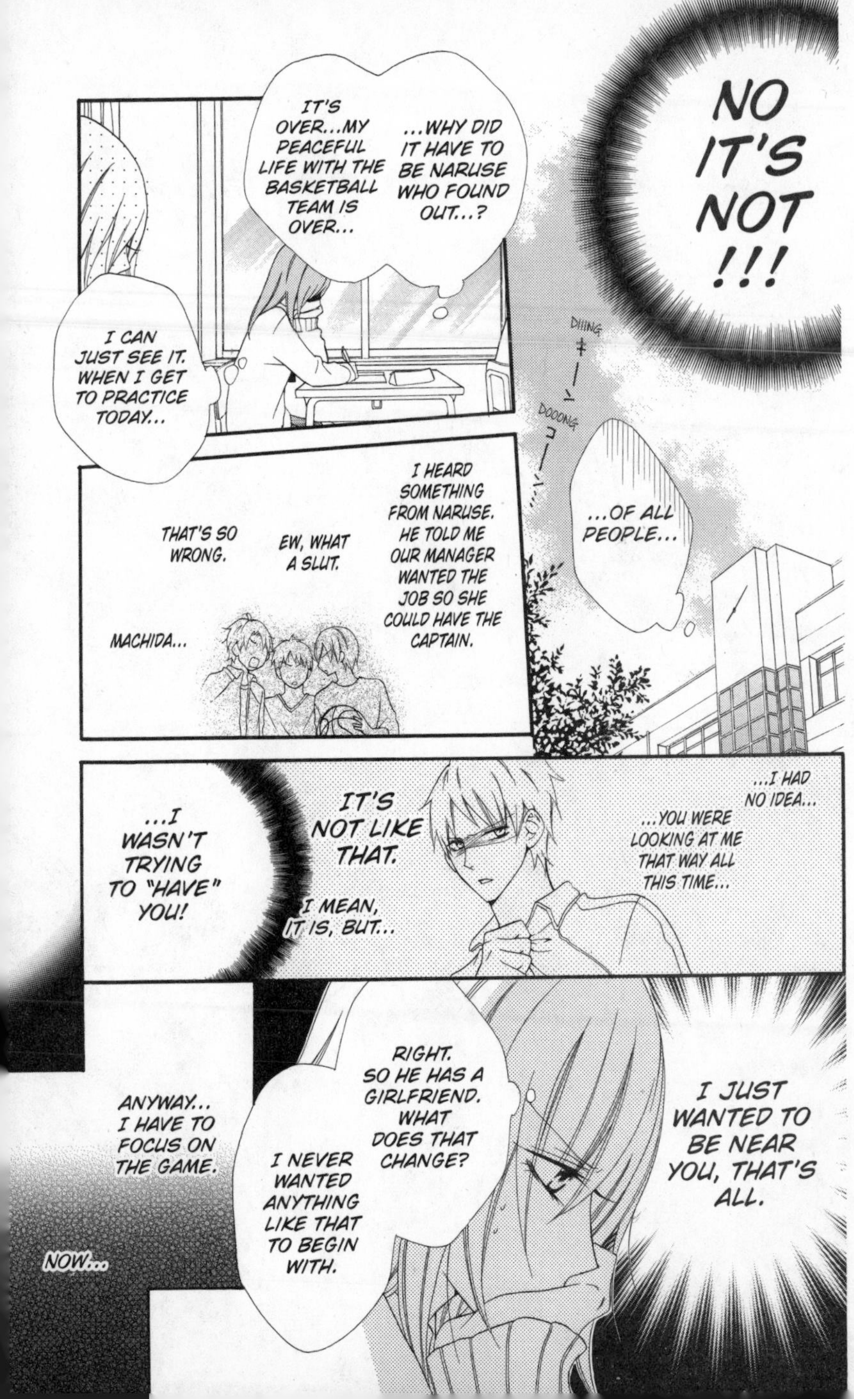
NO IT'S NOT!!!
DIIING
DOOONG
...OF ALL PEOPLE...
IT'S OVER...MY PEACEFUL LIFE WITH THE BASKETBALL TEAM IS OVER... ...WHY DID IT HAVE TO BE NARUSE WHO FOUND OUT...?
I CAN JUST SEE IT. WHEN I GET TO PRACTICE TODAY...
I HEARD SOMETHING FROM NARUSE. HE TOLD ME OUR MANAGER WANTED THE JOB SO SHE COULD HAVE THE CAPTAIN.
EW, WHAT A SLUT.
THAT'S SO WRONG.
MACHIDA...
...I HAD NO IDEA...
...YOU WERE LOOKING AT ME THAT WAY ALL THIS TIME...
IT'S NOT LIKE THAT.
I MEAN, IT IS, BUT...
...I WASN'T TRYING TO "HAVE" YOU!
I JUST WANTED TO BE NEAR YOU, THAT'S ALL.
RIGHT. SO HE HAS A GIRLFRIEND. WHAT DOES THAT CHANGE?
I NEVER WANTED ANYTHING LIKE THAT TO BEGIN WITH.
ANYWAY... I HAVE TO FOCUS ON THE GAME.
NOW...

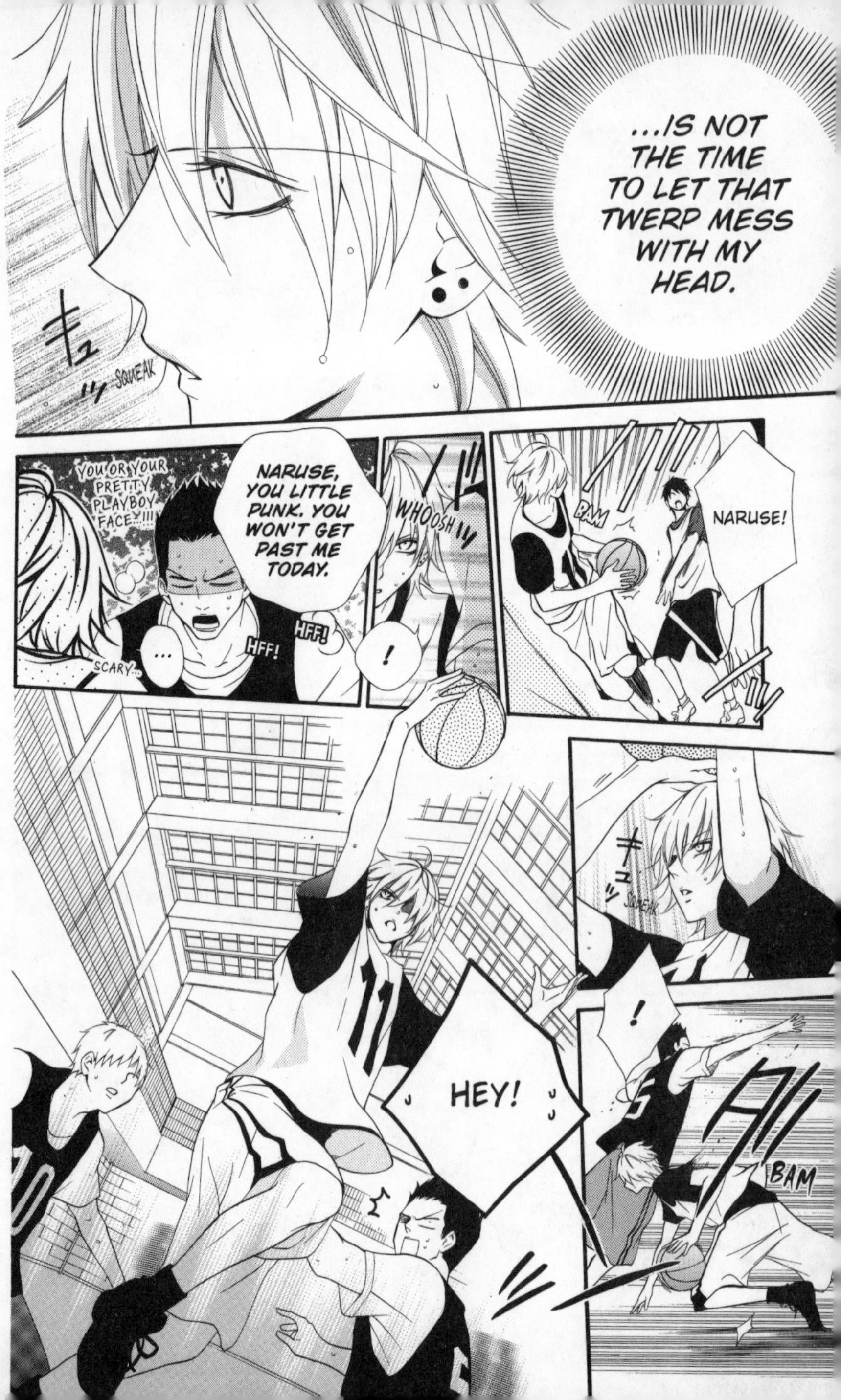
...IS NOT THE TIME TO LET THAT TWERP MESS WITH MY HEAD.
SQUEAK
NARUSE!
BAM
WHOOSH
!
NARUSE, YOU LITTLE PUNK. YOU WON'T GET PAST ME TODAY.
YOU OR YOUR PRETTY PLAYBOY FACE...!!!
HFF!
HFF!
...
SCARY...
SQUEAK
!
BAM
HEY!

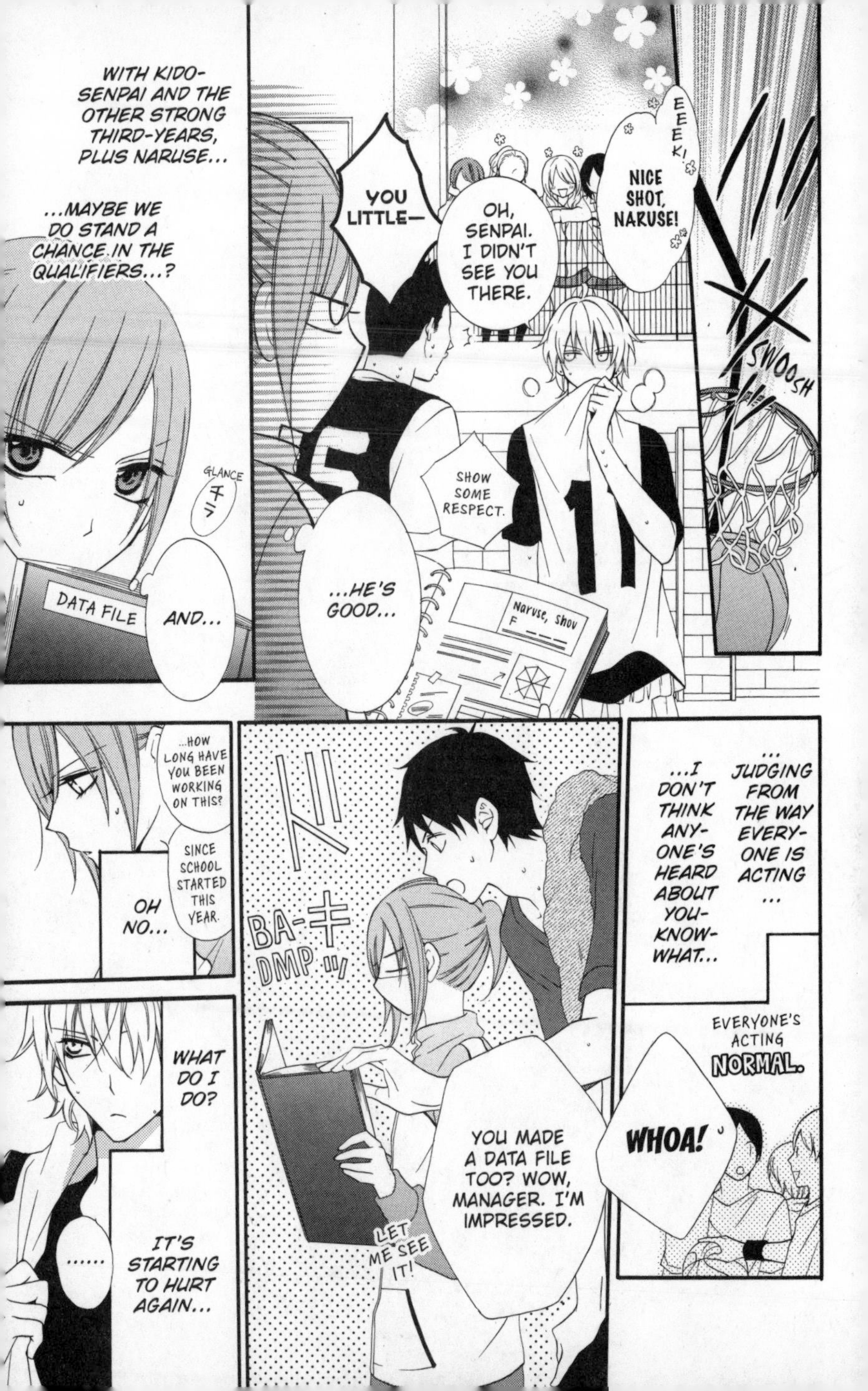
SWOOSH
EEEK!
NICE SHOT, NARUSE!
OH, SENPAI. I DIDN'T SEE YOU THERE.
YOU LITTLE—
SHOW SOME RESPECT.
WITH KIDO-SENPAI AND THE OTHER STRONG THIRD-YEARS, PLUS NARUSE...
...MAYBE WE DO STAND A CHANCE IN THE QUALIFIERS...?
GLANCE
チラ
...HE'S GOOD...
Naruse, Shou
F
DATA FILE
AND...
...JUDGING FROM THE WAY EVERYONE IS ACTING...
...I DON'T THINK ANYONE'S HEARD ABOUT YOU-KNOW-WHAT...
EVERYONE'S ACTING NORMAL.
WHOA!
BA-DMP
YOU MADE A DATA FILE TOO? WOW, MANAGER. I'M IMPRESSED.
LET ME SEE IT!
...HOW LONG HAVE YOU BEEN WORKING ON THIS?
SINCE SCHOOL STARTED THIS YEAR.
OH NO...
WHAT DO I DO?
......
IT'S STARTING TO HURT AGAIN...

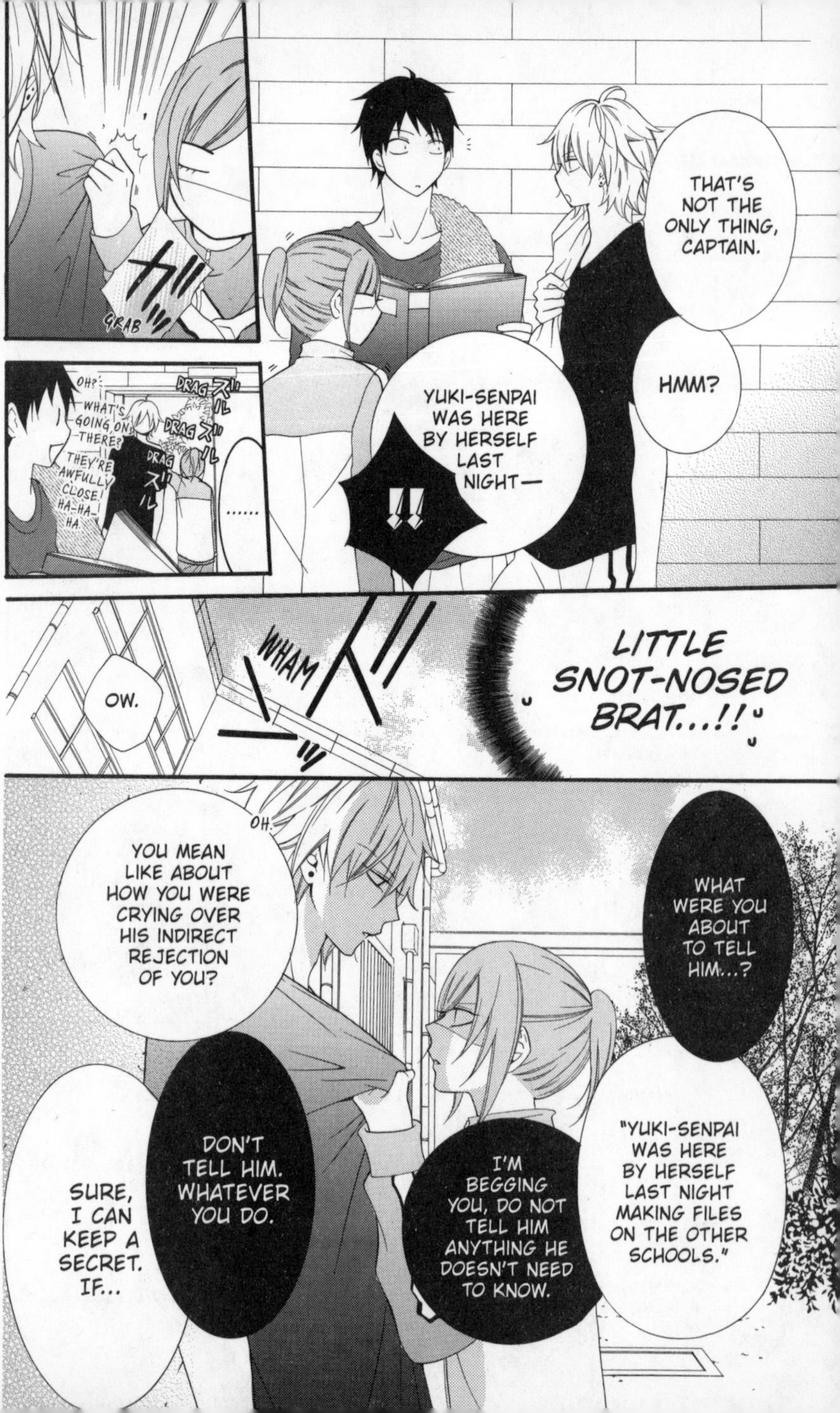
THAT'S NOT THE ONLY THING, CAPTAIN.
HMM?
YUKI-SENPAI WAS HERE BY HERSELF LAST NIGHT—
!!
GRAB
OH? WHAT'S GOING ON THERE? THEY'RE AWFULLY CLOSE! HA-HA-HA.
DRAG
DRAG
DRAG
......
LITTLE SNOT-NOSED BRAT...!!
WHAM
OW.
WHAT WERE YOU ABOUT TO TELL HIM...?
OH.
YOU MEAN LIKE ABOUT HOW YOU WERE CRYING OVER HIS INDIRECT REJECTION OF YOU?
"YUKI-SENPAI WAS HERE BY HERSELF LAST NIGHT MAKING FILES ON THE OTHER SCHOOLS."
I'M BEGGING YOU, DO NOT TELL HIM ANYTHING HE DOESN'T NEED TO KNOW.
DON'T TELL HIM. WHATEVER YOU DO.
SURE, I CAN KEEP A SECRET. IF...

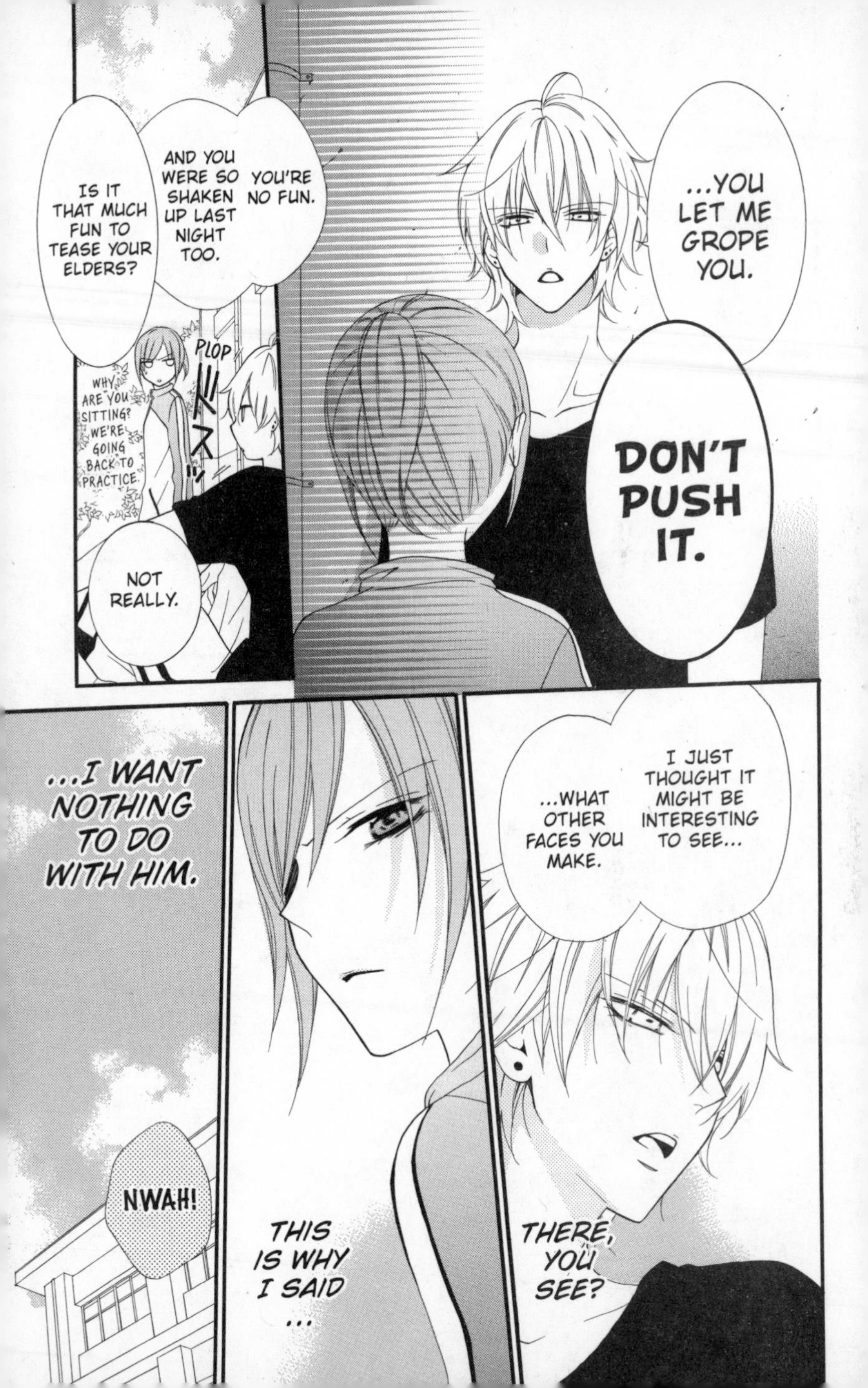
...YOU LET ME GROPE YOU.
DON'T PUSH IT.
YOU'RE NO FUN.
AND YOU WERE SO SHAKEN UP LAST NIGHT TOO.
IS IT THAT MUCH FUN TO TEASE YOUR ELDERS?
PLOP
WHY ARE YOU SITTING? WE'RE GOING BACK TO PRACTICE.
NOT REALLY.
I JUST THOUGHT IT MIGHT BE INTERESTING TO SEE...
...WHAT OTHER FACES YOU MAKE.
THERE, YOU SEE?
THIS IS WHY I SAID ...
...I WANT NOTHING TO DO WITH HIM.
NWAH!

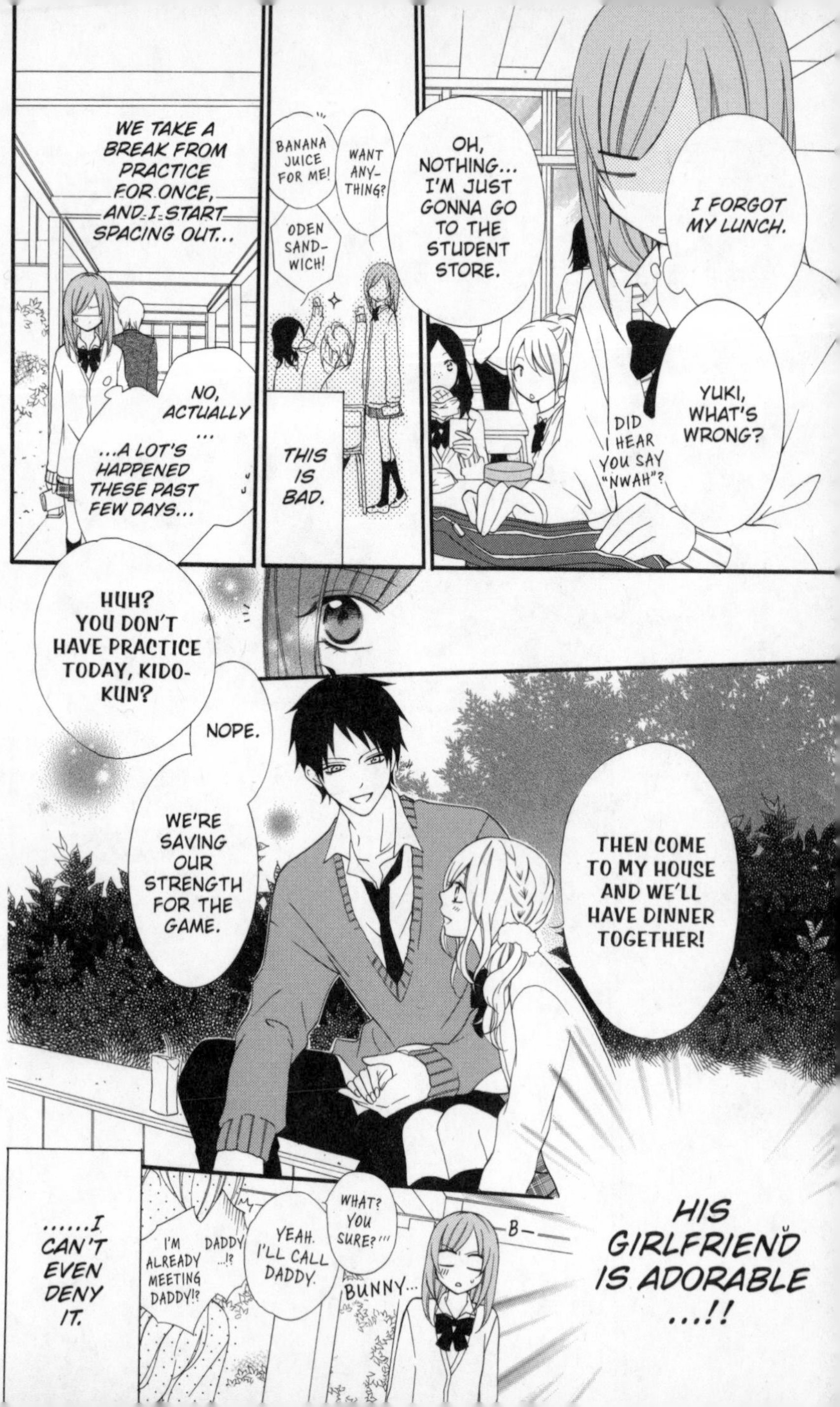
I FORGOT MY LUNCH.
YUKI, WHAT'S WRONG?
DID I HEAR YOU SAY "NWAH"?
OH, NOTHING... I'M JUST GONNA GO TO THE STUDENT STORE.
WANT ANY-THING?
BANANA JUICE FOR ME!
ODEN SAND-WICH!
THIS IS BAD.
WE TAKE A BREAK FROM PRACTICE FOR ONCE, AND I START SPACING OUT...
NO, ACTUALLY...
...A LOT'S HAPPENED THESE PAST FEW DAYS...
HUH? YOU DON'T HAVE PRACTICE TODAY, KIDO-KUN?
NOPE.
WE'RE SAVING OUR STRENGTH FOR THE GAME.
THEN COME TO MY HOUSE AND WE'LL HAVE DINNER TOGETHER!
HIS GIRLFRIEND IS ADORABLE ...!!
B—
BUNNY...
WHAT? YOU SURE?
YEAH. I'LL CALL DADDY.
DADDY ...!?
I'M ALREADY MEETING DADDY!?
......I CAN'T EVEN DENY IT.

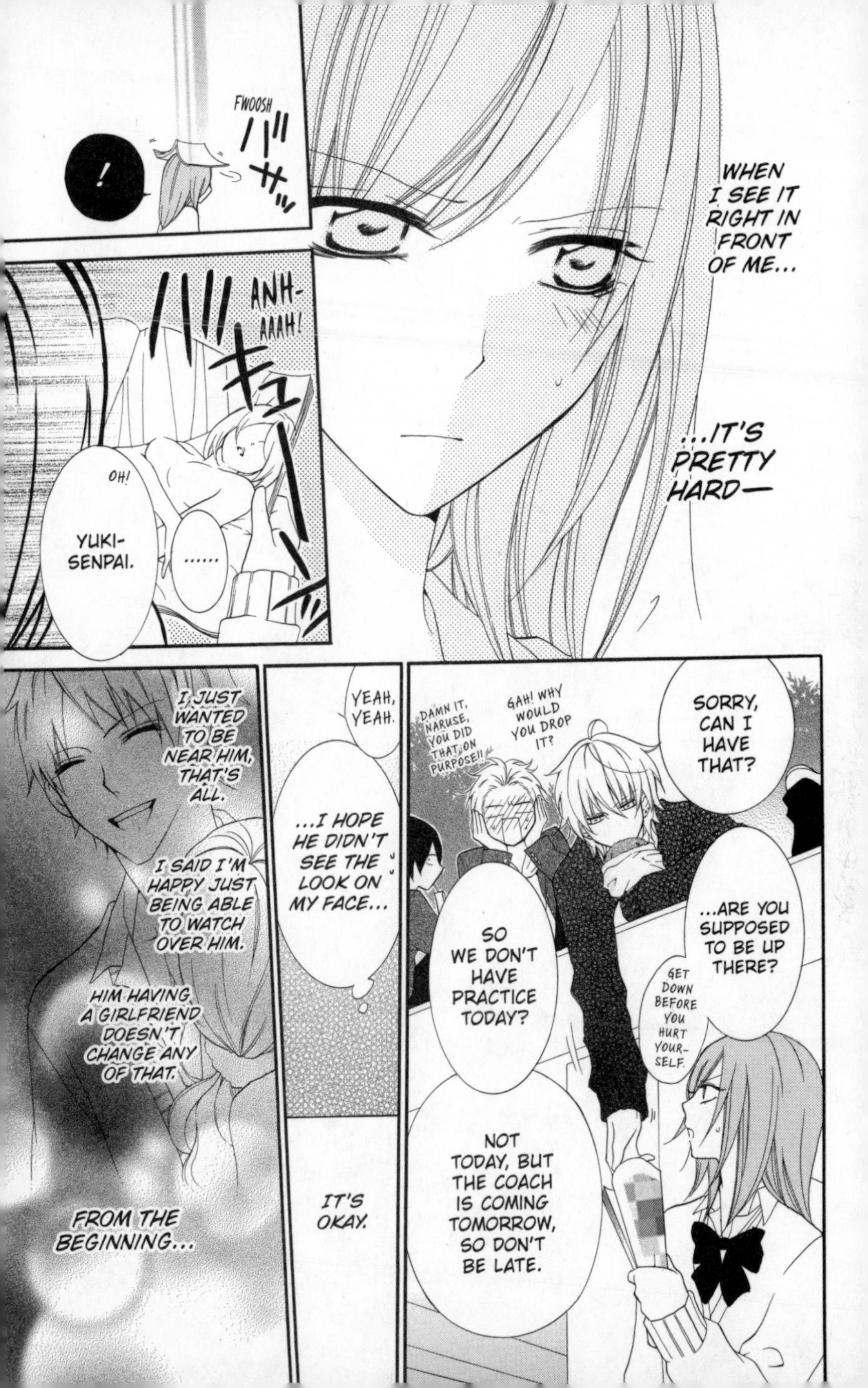
WHEN I SEE IT RIGHT IN FRONT OF ME...
...IT'S PRETTY HARD—
FWOOSH
!
ANH-AAAH!
OH!
YUKI-SENPAI.
......
SORRY, CAN I HAVE THAT?
GAH! WHY WOULD YOU DROP IT?
DAMN IT, NARUSE, YOU DID THAT ON PURPOSE!!
...ARE YOU SUPPOSED TO BE UP THERE?
GET DOWN BEFORE YOU HURT YOURSELF.
SO WE DON'T HAVE PRACTICE TODAY?
NOT TODAY, BUT THE COACH IS COMING TOMORROW, SO DON'T BE LATE.
YEAH, YEAH.
...I HOPE HE DIDN'T SEE THE LOOK ON MY FACE...
IT'S OKAY.
I JUST WANTED TO BE NEAR HIM, THAT'S ALL.
I SAID I'M HAPPY JUST BEING ABLE TO WATCH OVER HIM.
HIM HAVING A GIRLFRIEND DOESN'T CHANGE ANY OF THAT.
FROM THE BEGINNING...

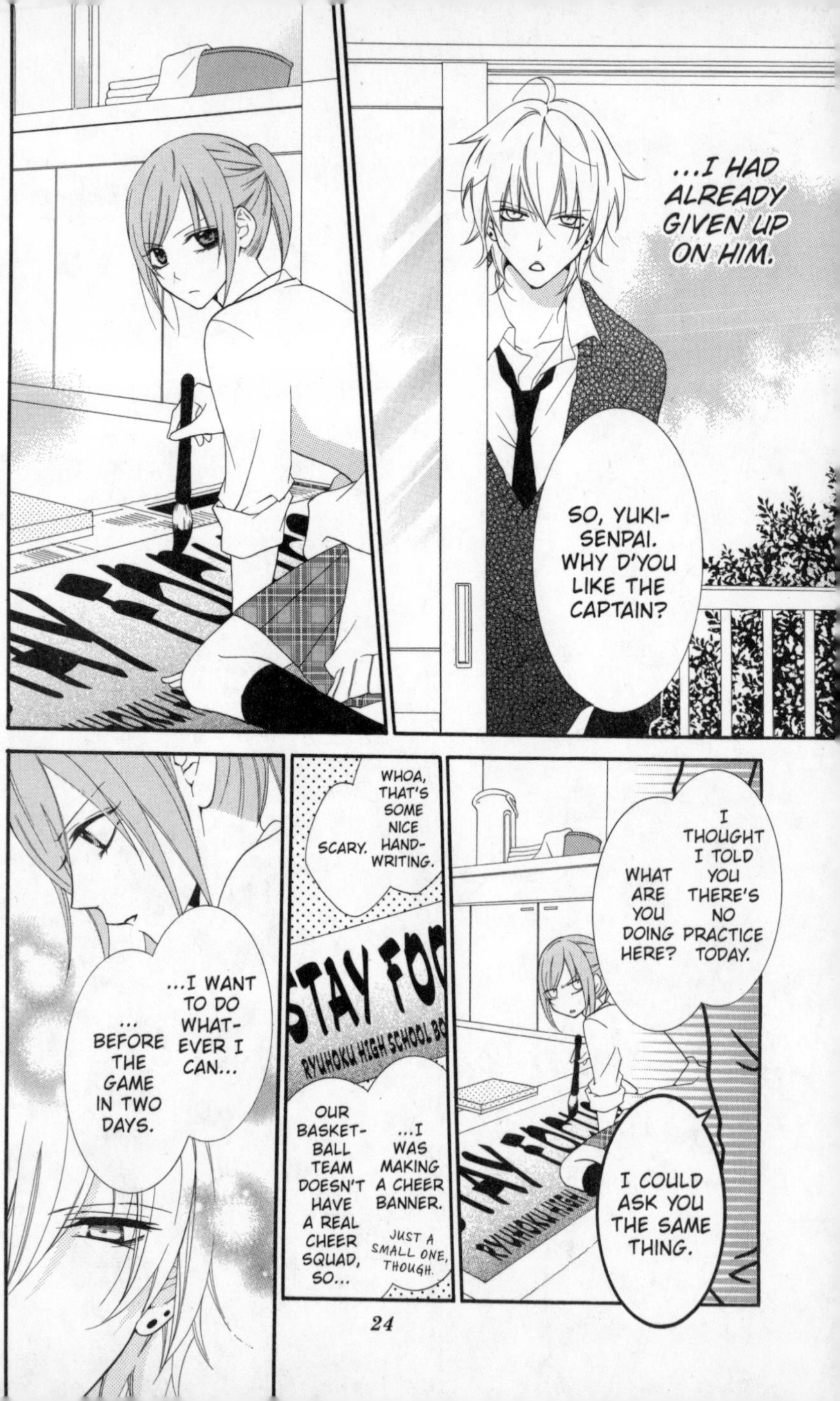
...I HAD ALREADY GIVEN UP ON HIM.
SO, YUKI-SENPAI. WHY D'YOU LIKE THE CAPTAIN?
I THOUGHT I TOLD YOU THERE'S NO PRACTICE TODAY.
WHAT ARE YOU DOING HERE?
I COULD ASK YOU THE SAME THING.
WHOA, THAT'S SOME NICE HAND-WRITING.
SCARY.
...I WAS MAKING A CHEER BANNER.
OUR BASKET-BALL TEAM DOESN'T HAVE A REAL CHEER SQUAD, SO...
JUST A SMALL ONE, THOUGH.
...I WANT TO DO WHAT-EVER I CAN...
...BEFORE THE GAME IN TWO DAYS.

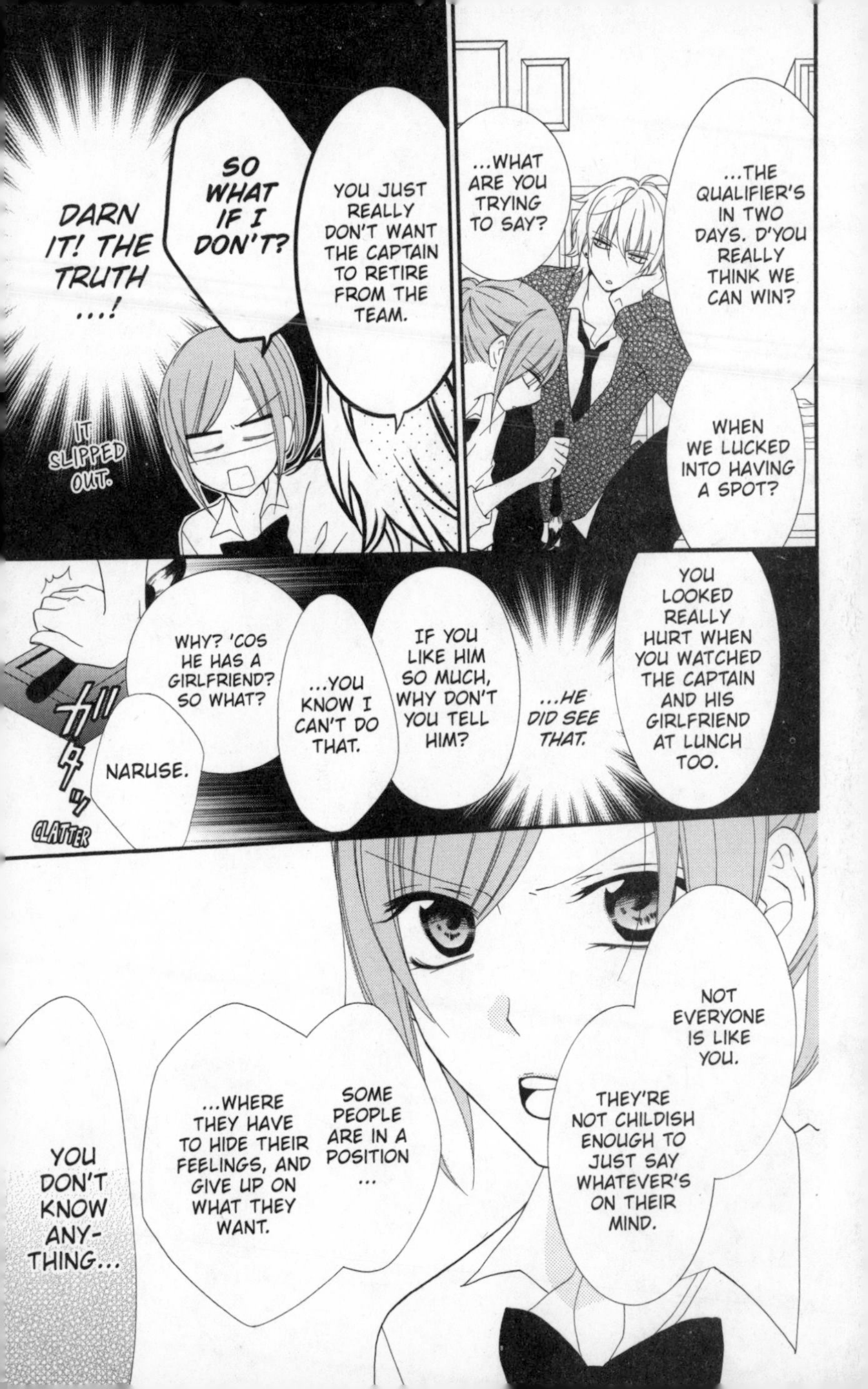
...THE QUALIFIER'S IN TWO DAYS. D'YOU REALLY THINK WE CAN WIN?
WHEN WE LUCKED INTO HAVING A SPOT?
...WHAT ARE YOU TRYING TO SAY?
YOU JUST REALLY DON'T WANT THE CAPTAIN TO RETIRE FROM THE TEAM.
SO WHAT IF I DON'T?
DARN IT! THE TRUTH...!
IT SLIPPED OUT.
YOU LOOKED REALLY HURT WHEN YOU WATCHED THE CAPTAIN AND HIS GIRLFRIEND AT LUNCH TOO.
...HE DID SEE THAT.
IF YOU LIKE HIM SO MUCH, WHY DON'T YOU TELL HIM?
...YOU KNOW I CAN'T DO THAT.
WHY? 'COS HE HAS A GIRLFRIEND? SO WHAT?
NARUSE.
ガタッ
CLATTER
NOT EVERYONE IS LIKE YOU.
THEY'RE NOT CHILDISH ENOUGH TO JUST SAY WHATEVER'S ON THEIR MIND.
SOME PEOPLE ARE IN A POSITION...
...WHERE THEY HAVE TO HIDE THEIR FEELINGS, AND GIVE UP ON WHAT THEY WANT.
YOU DON'T KNOW ANYTHING...

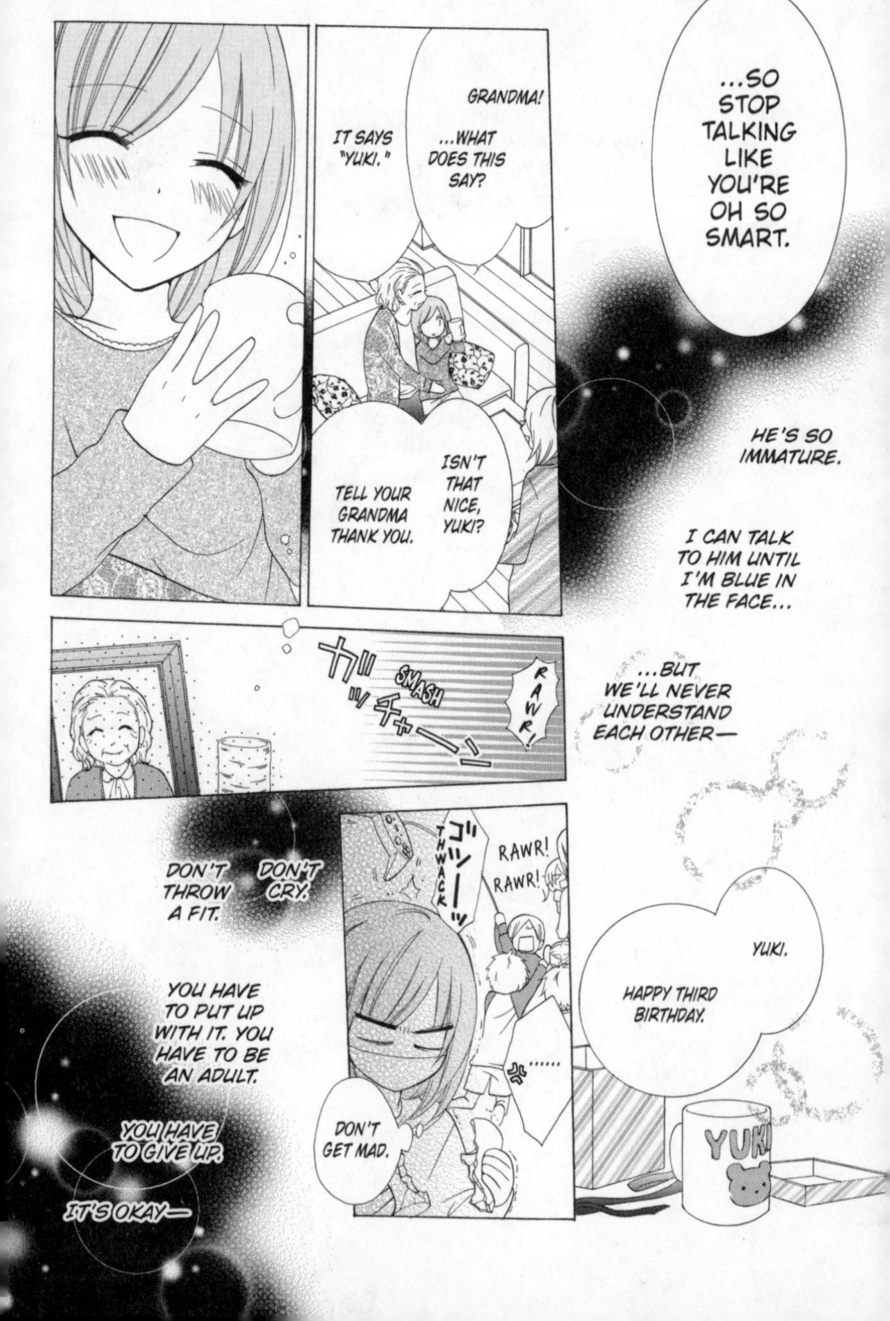
...SO STOP TALKING LIKE YOU'RE OH SO SMART.
HE'S SO IMMATURE.
I CAN TALK TO HIM UNTIL I'M BLUE IN THE FACE...
...BUT WE'LL NEVER UNDERSTAND EACH OTHER—
GRANDMA!
...WHAT DOES THIS SAY?
IT SAYS "YUKI."
ISN'T THAT NICE, YUKI?
TELL YOUR GRANDMA THANK YOU.
RAWR!
ガッチャーン
SMASH
YUKI.
HAPPY THIRD BIRTHDAY.
RAWR!
RAWR!
ゴツーッ
THWACK
......
DON'T GET MAD.
DON'T CRY.
DON'T THROW A FIT.
YOU HAVE TO PUT UP WITH IT. YOU HAVE TO BE AN ADULT.
YOU HAVE TO GIVE UP.
IT'S OKAY—
YUKI

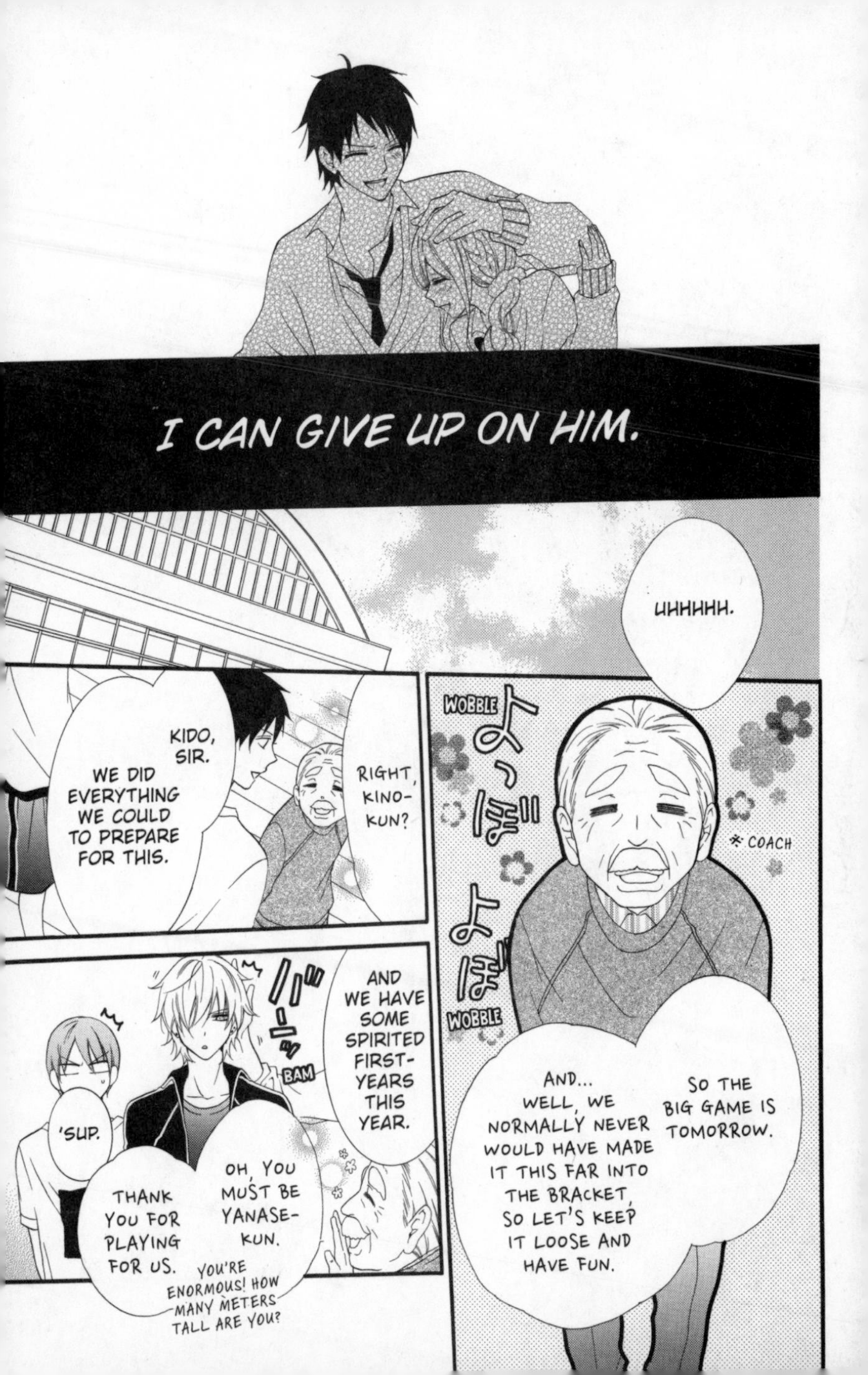
I CAN GIVE UP ON HIM.
UHHHHH.
WOBBLE
よっぼよぼ
WOBBLE
※COACH
SO THE BIG GAME IS TOMORROW.
AND... WELL, WE NORMALLY NEVER WOULD HAVE MADE IT THIS FAR INTO THE BRACKET, SO LET'S KEEP IT LOOSE AND HAVE FUN.
RIGHT, KINO-KUN?
KIDO, SIR.
WE DID EVERYTHING WE COULD TO PREPARE FOR THIS.
AND WE HAVE SOME SPIRITED FIRST-YEARS THIS YEAR.
BAM
OH, YOU MUST BE YANASE-KUN.
YOU'RE ENORMOUS! HOW MANY METERS TALL ARE YOU?
THANK YOU FOR PLAYING FOR US.
'SUP.

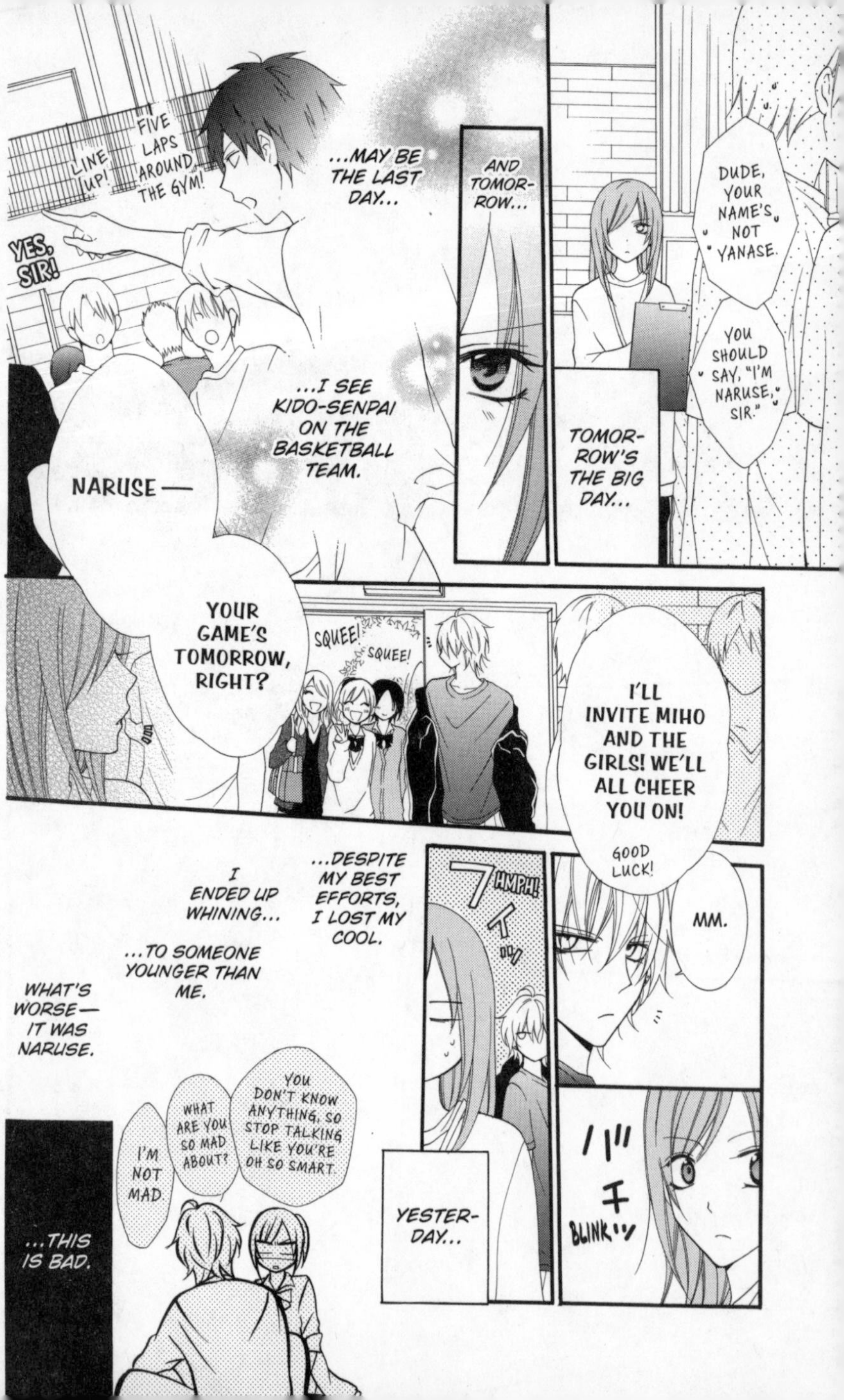

DUDE, YOUR NAME'S NOT YANASE.
YOU SHOULD SAY, "I'M NARUSE, SIR."
TOMORROW'S THE BIG DAY...
AND TOMORROW...
...MAY BE THE LAST DAY...
FIVE LAPS AROUND THE GYM!
LINE UP!
YES, SIR!
...I SEE KIDO-SENPAI ON THE BASKETBALL TEAM.
NARUSE—
YOUR GAME'S TOMORROW, RIGHT?
I'LL INVITE MIHO AND THE GIRLS! WE'LL ALL CHEER YOU ON!
SQUEE!
SQUEE!
GOOD LUCK!
MM.
HMPH!
BLINK
YESTERDAY...
...DESPITE MY BEST EFFORTS, I LOST MY COOL.
I ENDED UP WHINING...
...TO SOMEONE YOUNGER THAN ME.
WHAT'S WORSE—IT WAS NARUSE.
YOU DON'T KNOW ANYTHING, SO STOP TALKING LIKE YOU'RE OH SO SMART.
WHAT ARE YOU SO MAD ABOUT?
I'M NOT MAD.
...THIS IS BAD.

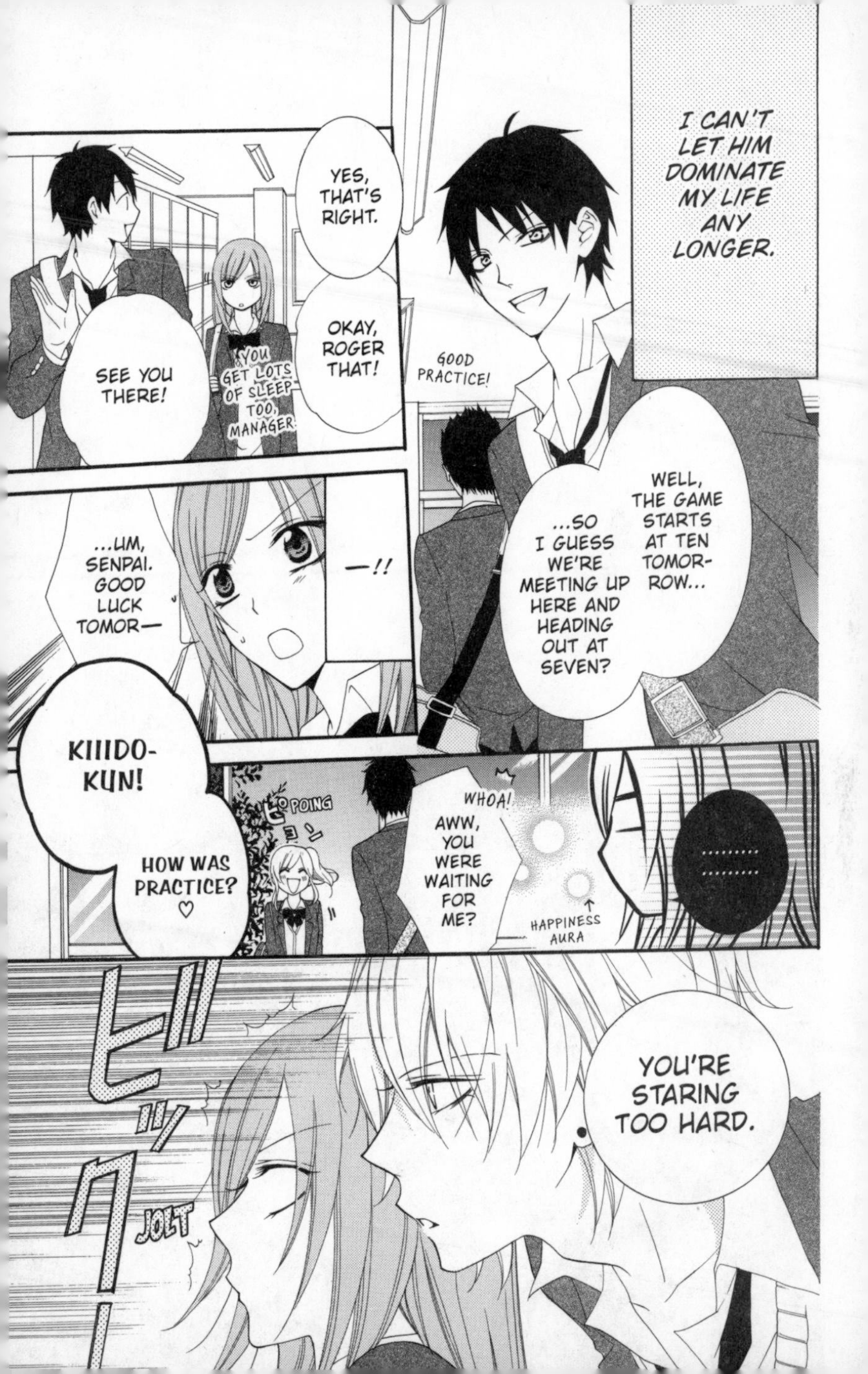
I CAN'T LET HIM DOMINATE MY LIFE ANY LONGER.
GOOD PRACTICE!
WELL, THE GAME STARTS AT TEN TOMORROW...
...SO I GUESS WE'RE MEETING UP HERE AND HEADING OUT AT SEVEN?
YES, THAT'S RIGHT.
OKAY, ROGER THAT!
YOU GET LOTS OF SLEEP TOO, MANAGER!
SEE YOU THERE!
...UM, SENPAI. GOOD LUCK TOMOR—
KIIIDO-KUN!
—!!
......
......
HAPPINESS AURA
WHOA!
AWW, YOU WERE WAITING FOR ME?
POING
HOW WAS PRACTICE? ♡
YOU'RE STARING TOO HARD.
JOLT

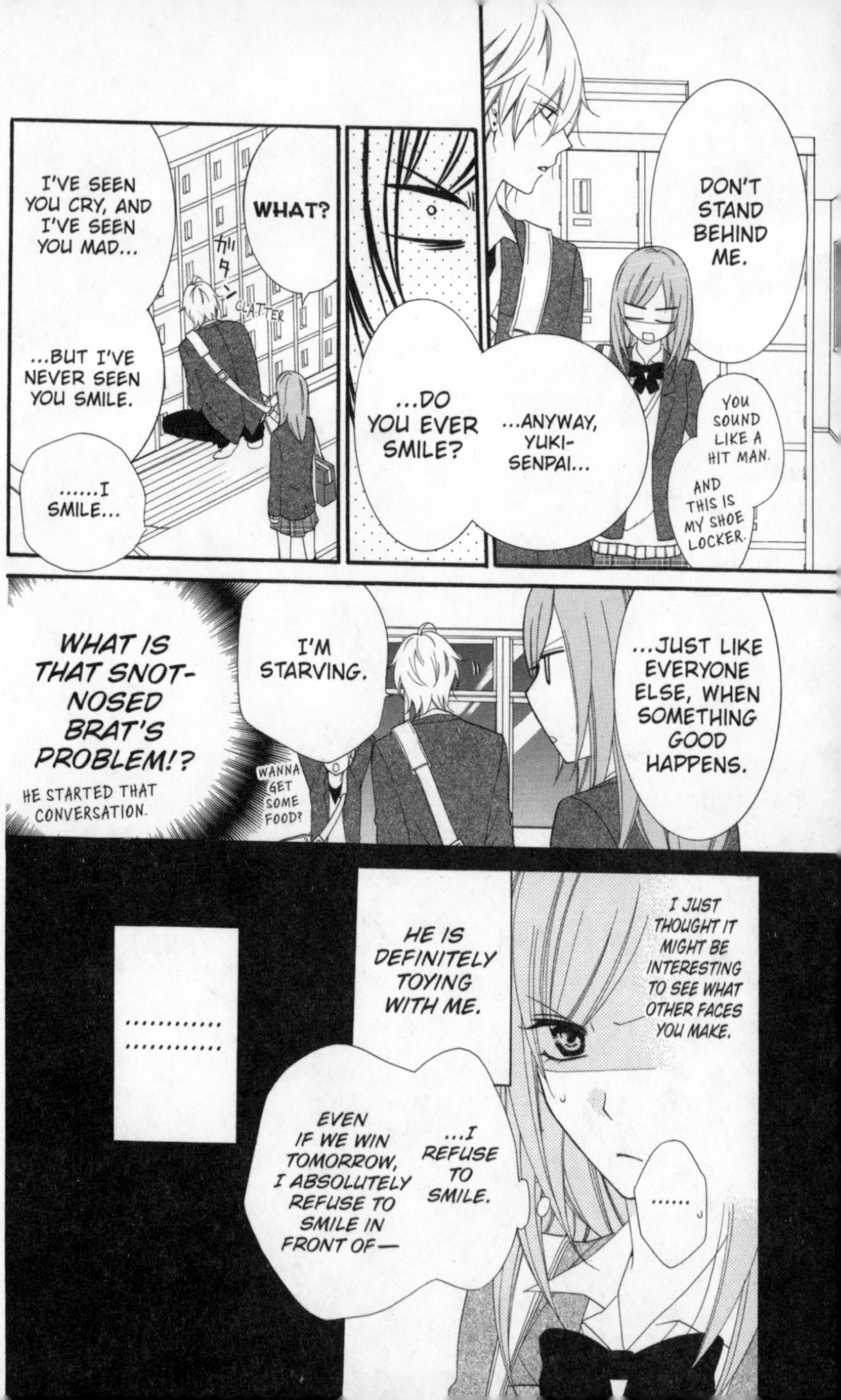
DON'T STAND BEHIND ME.
YOU SOUND LIKE A HIT MAN.
AND THIS IS MY SHOE LOCKER.
...ANYWAY, YUKI-SENPAI...
...DO YOU EVER SMILE?
WHAT?
CLATTER
I'VE SEEN YOU CRY, AND I'VE SEEN YOU MAD...
...BUT I'VE NEVER SEEN YOU SMILE.
......I SMILE...
...JUST LIKE EVERYONE ELSE, WHEN SOMETHING GOOD HAPPENS.
I'M STARVING.
WANNA GET SOME FOOD?
WHAT IS THAT SNOT-NOSED BRAT'S PROBLEM!?
HE STARTED THAT CONVERSATION.
I JUST THOUGHT IT MIGHT BE INTERESTING TO SEE WHAT OTHER FACES YOU MAKE.
HE IS DEFINITELY TOYING WITH ME.
......
...I REFUSE TO SMILE.
EVEN IF WE WIN TOMORROW, I ABSOLUTELY REFUSE TO SMILE IN FRONT OF—
....
....

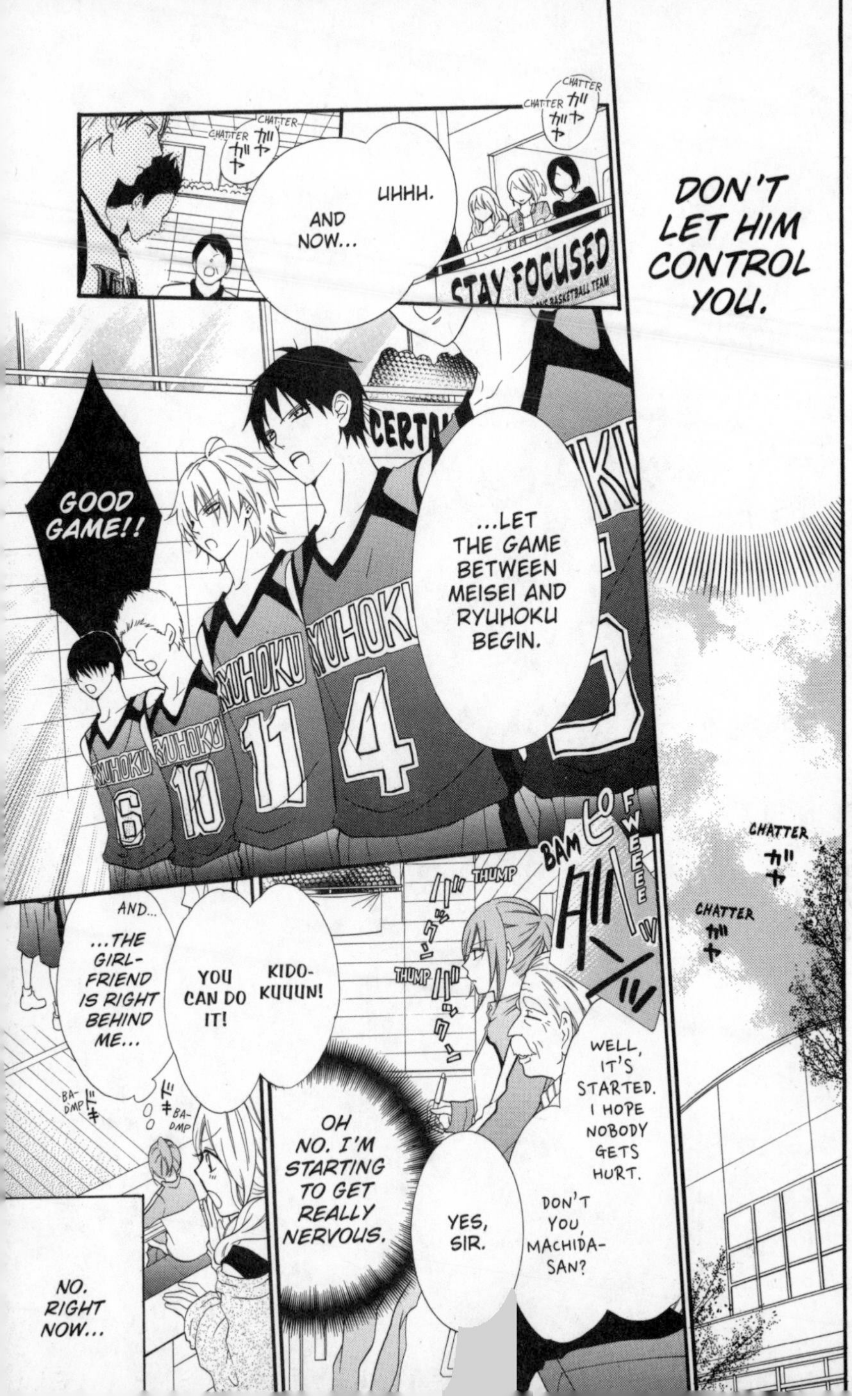

DON'T LET HIM CONTROL YOU.
CHATTER
CHATTER
CHATTER ガヤ CHATTER ガヤガヤ
CHATTER ガヤ CHATTER ガヤ
STAY FOCUSED
BASKETBALL TEAM
UHHH.
AND NOW...
...LET THE GAME BETWEEN MEISEI AND RYUHOKU BEGIN.
GOOD GAME!!
BAM
FWEEEE
THUMP
THUMP
WELL, IT'S STARTED. I HOPE NOBODY GETS HURT.
DON'T YOU, MACHIDA-SAN?
YES, SIR.
OH NO. I'M STARTING TO GET REALLY NERVOUS.
KIDO-KUUUN!
YOU CAN DO IT!
AND...
...THE GIRL-FRIEND IS RIGHT BEHIND ME...
BA-DMP
BA-DMP
NO. RIGHT NOW...

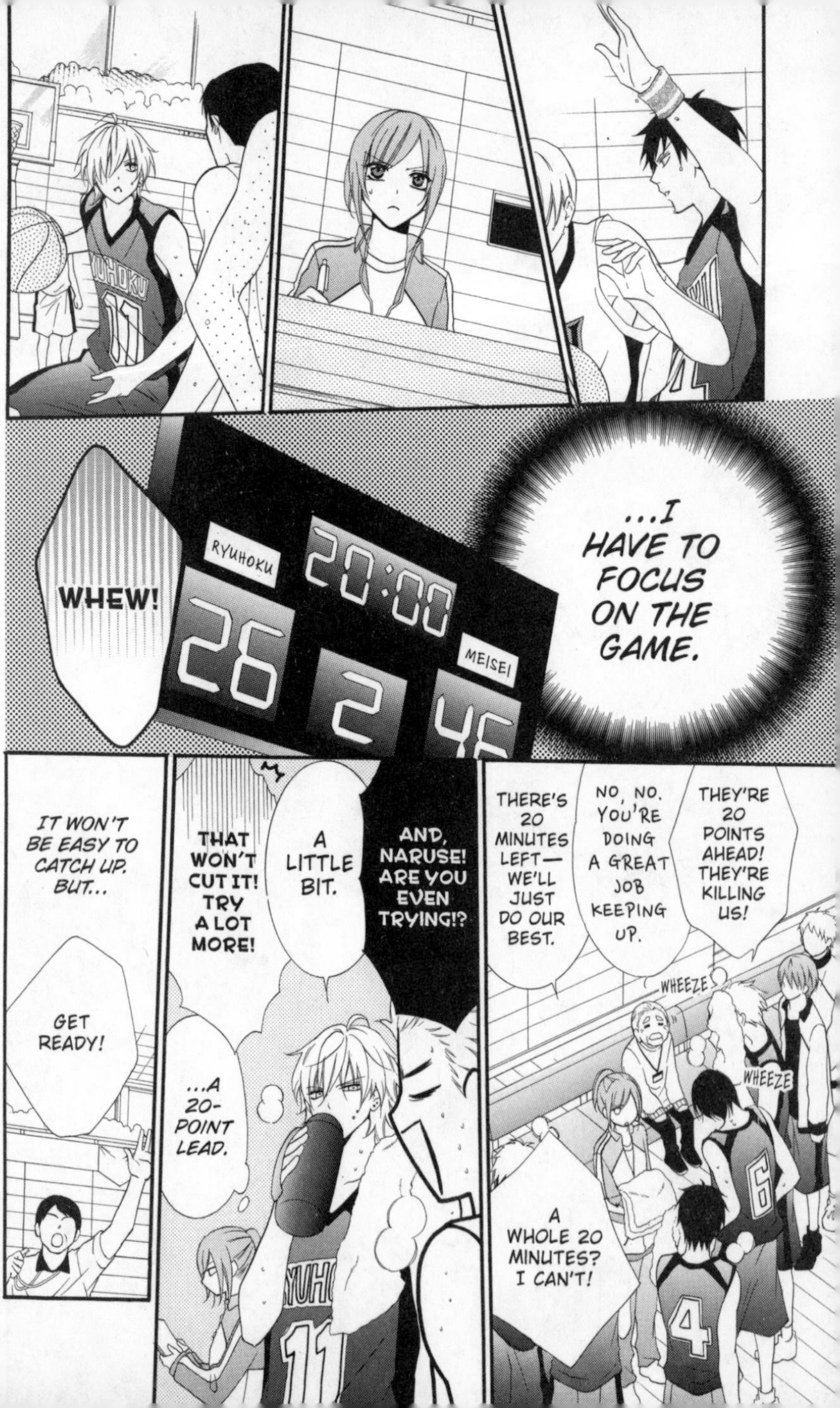
...I HAVE TO FOCUS ON THE GAME.
RYUHOKU
20:00
26
2
MEISEI
46
WHEW!
THEY'RE 20 POINTS AHEAD! THEY'RE KILLING US!
NO, NO. YOU'RE DOING A GREAT JOB KEEPING UP.
THERE'S 20 MINUTES LEFT— WE'LL JUST DO OUR BEST.
WHEEZE
WHEEZE
A WHOLE 20 MINUTES? I CAN'T!
AND, NARUSE! ARE YOU EVEN TRYING!?
A LITTLE BIT.
THAT WON'T CUT IT! TRY A LOT MORE!
...A 20-POINT LEAD.
IT WON'T BE EASY TO CATCH UP. BUT...
GET READY!

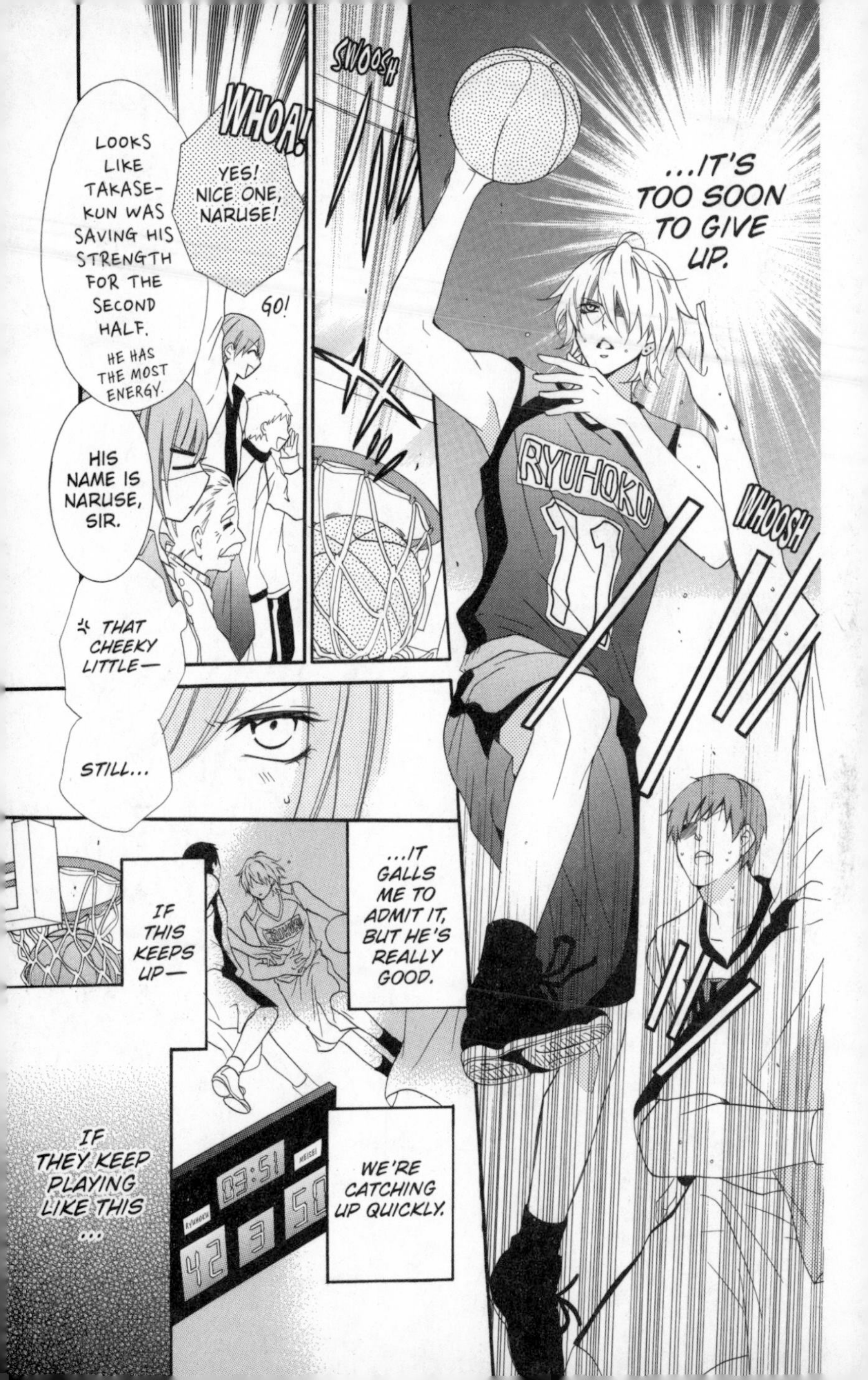
...IT'S TOO SOON TO GIVE UP.
WHOOSH
RYUHOKU 11
SWOOSH
WHOA!
YES! NICE ONE, NARUSE!
LOOKS LIKE TAKASE-KUN WAS SAVING HIS STRENGTH FOR THE SECOND HALF.
GO!
HE HAS THE MOST ENERGY.
HIS NAME IS NARUSE, SIR.
THAT CHEEKY LITTLE—
STILL...
...IT GALLS ME TO ADMIT IT, BUT HE'S REALLY GOOD.
IF THIS KEEPS UP—
WE'RE CATCHING UP QUICKLY.
IF THEY KEEP PLAYING LIKE THIS...
03:51
MEISEI
50
42
3

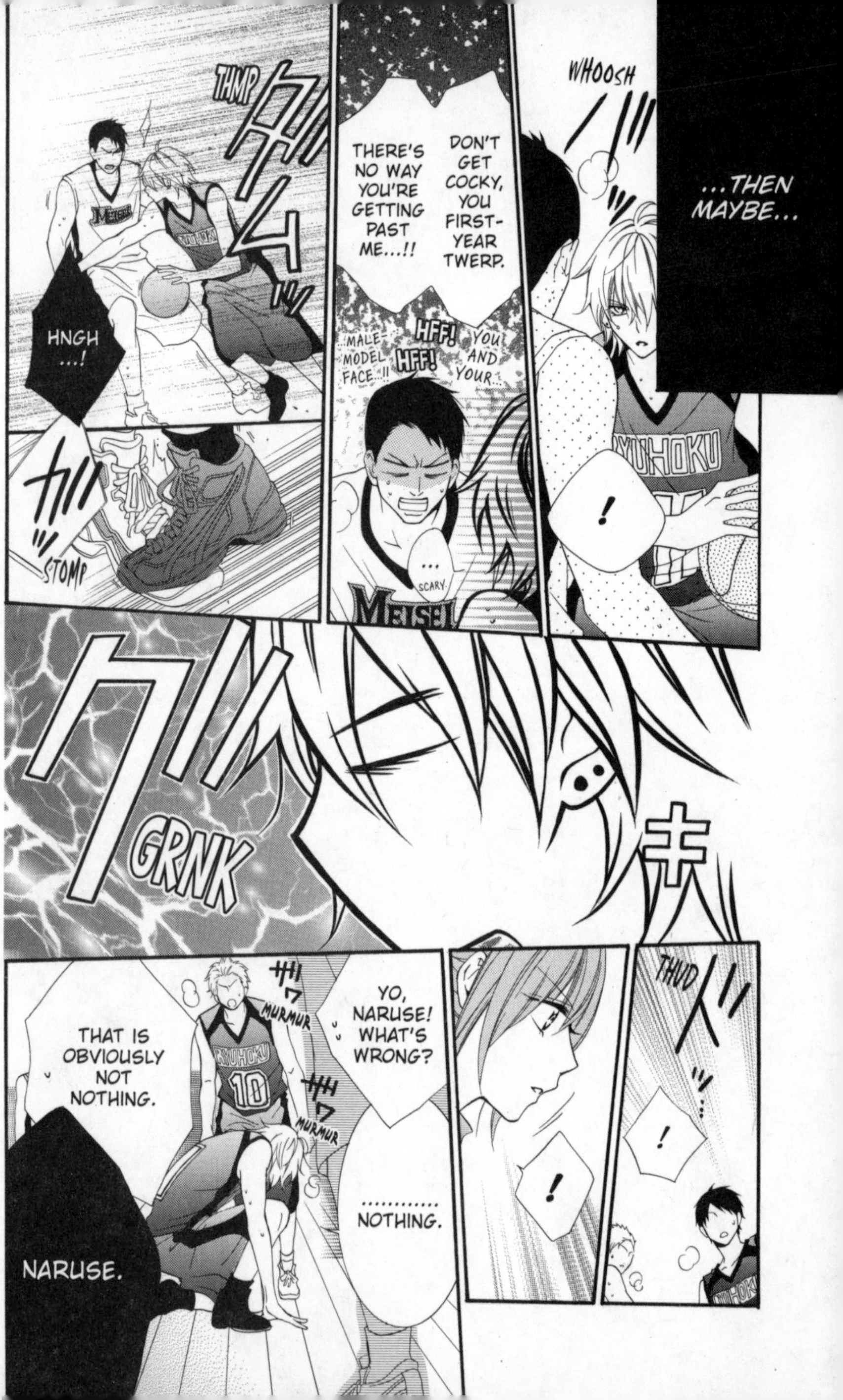
...THEN MAYBE...
WHOOSH
!
DON'T GET COCKY, YOU FIRST-YEAR TWERP.
THERE'S NO WAY YOU'RE GETTING PAST ME...!!
YOU AND YOUR...
HFF! HFF!
...MALE-MODEL FACE...!!
... SCARY.
THMP
HNGH ...!
STOMP
GRNK
THUD
!
!
YO, NARUSE! WHAT'S WRONG?
MURMUR
MURMUR
.... NOTHING.
THAT IS OBVIOUSLY NOT NOTHING.
NARUSE.

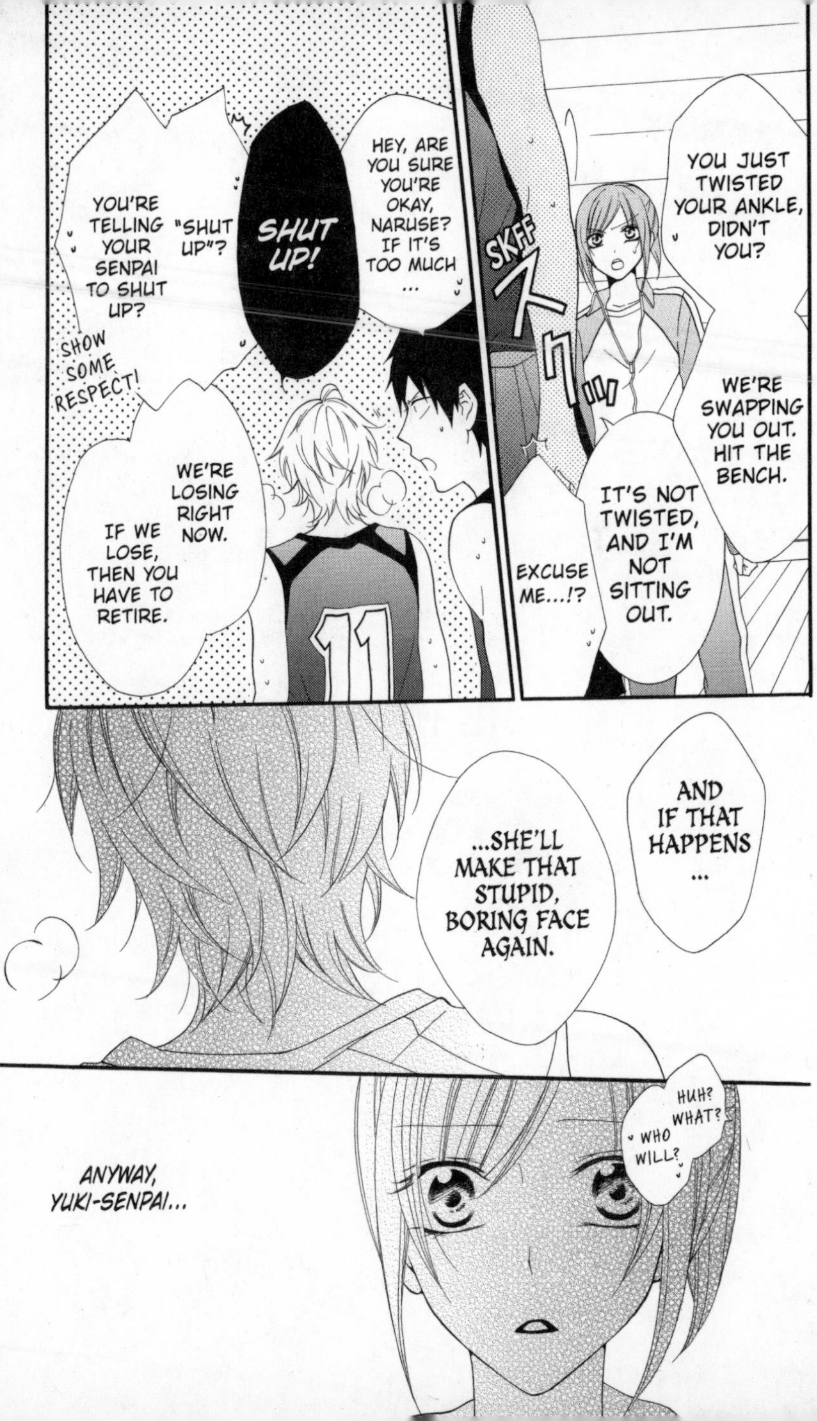
YOU JUST TWISTED YOUR ANKLE, DIDN'T YOU?
WE'RE SWAPPING YOU OUT. HIT THE BENCH.
SKFF
IT'S NOT TWISTED, AND I'M NOT SITTING OUT.
EXCUSE ME...!?
HEY, ARE YOU SURE YOU'RE OKAY, NARUSE? IF IT'S TOO MUCH ...
SHUT UP!
"SHUT UP"?
YOU'RE TELLING YOUR SENPAI TO SHUT UP?
SHOW SOME RESPECT!
WE'RE LOSING RIGHT NOW.
IF WE LOSE, THEN YOU HAVE TO RETIRE.
AND IF THAT HAPPENS ...
...SHE'LL MAKE THAT STUPID, BORING FACE AGAIN.
HUH? WHAT? WHO WILL?
ANYWAY, YUKI-SENPAI...

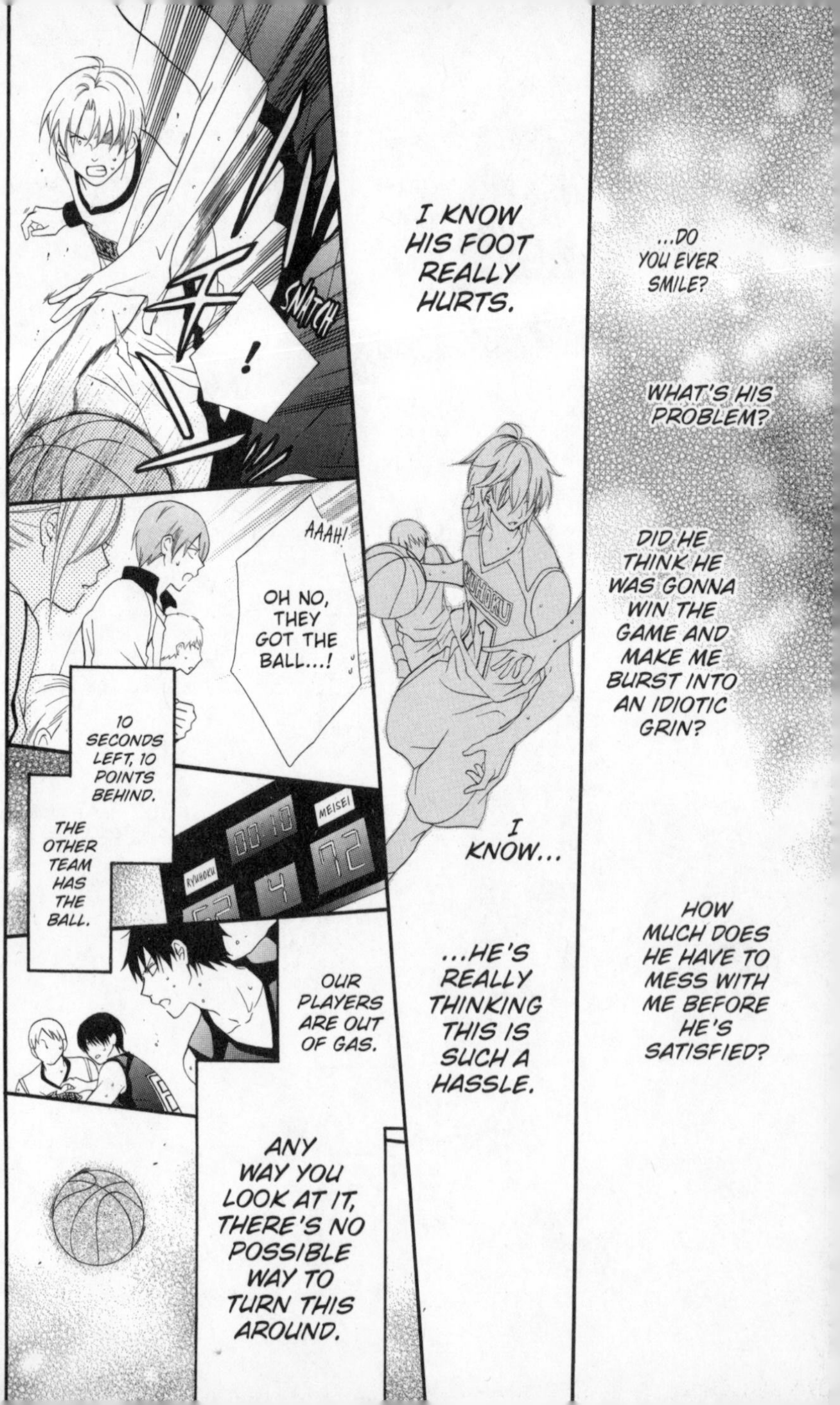
...DO YOU EVER SMILE?
WHAT'S HIS PROBLEM?
DID HE THINK HE WAS GONNA WIN THE GAME AND MAKE ME BURST INTO AN IDIOTIC GRIN?
HOW MUCH DOES HE HAVE TO MESS WITH ME BEFORE HE'S SATISFIED?
I KNOW HIS FOOT REALLY HURTS.
I KNOW...
...HE'S REALLY THINKING THIS IS SUCH A HASSLE.
SNATCH
!
AAAH!
OH NO, THEY GOT THE BALL...!
10 SECONDS LEFT, 10 POINTS BEHIND.
THE OTHER TEAM HAS THE BALL.
MEISEI
RYUHOKU
OUR PLAYERS ARE OUT OF GAS.
ANY WAY YOU LOOK AT IT, THERE'S NO POSSIBLE WAY TO TURN THIS AROUND.

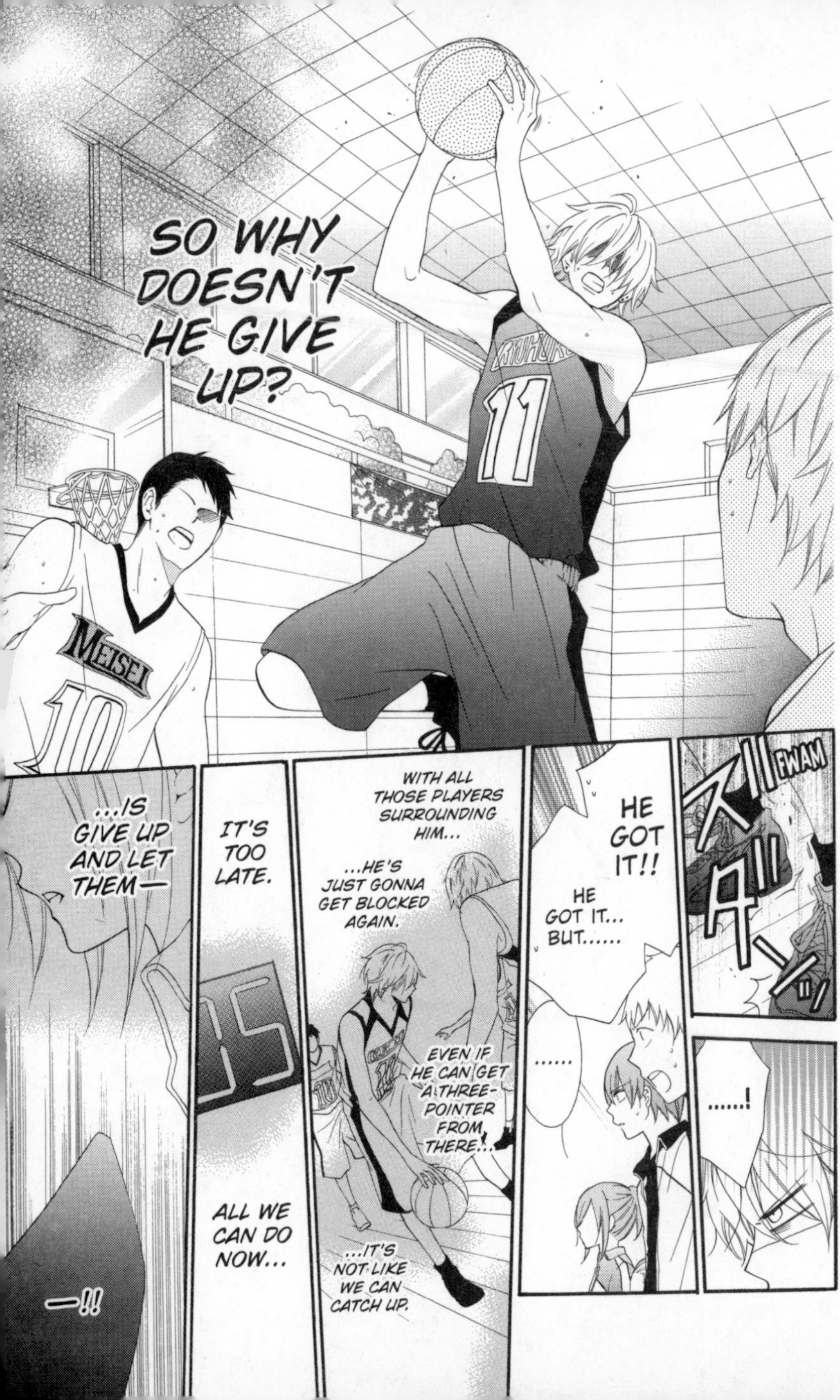
SO WHY DOESN'T HE GIVE UP?
FWAM
HE GOT IT!!
HE GOT IT... BUT......
......
......!
WITH ALL THOSE PLAYERS SURROUNDING HIM...
...HE'S JUST GONNA GET BLOCKED AGAIN.
EVEN IF HE CAN GET A THREE-POINTER FROM THERE...
...IT'S NOT LIKE WE CAN CATCH UP.
IT'S TOO LATE.
ALL WE CAN DO NOW...
...IS GIVE UP AND LET THEM—
—!!

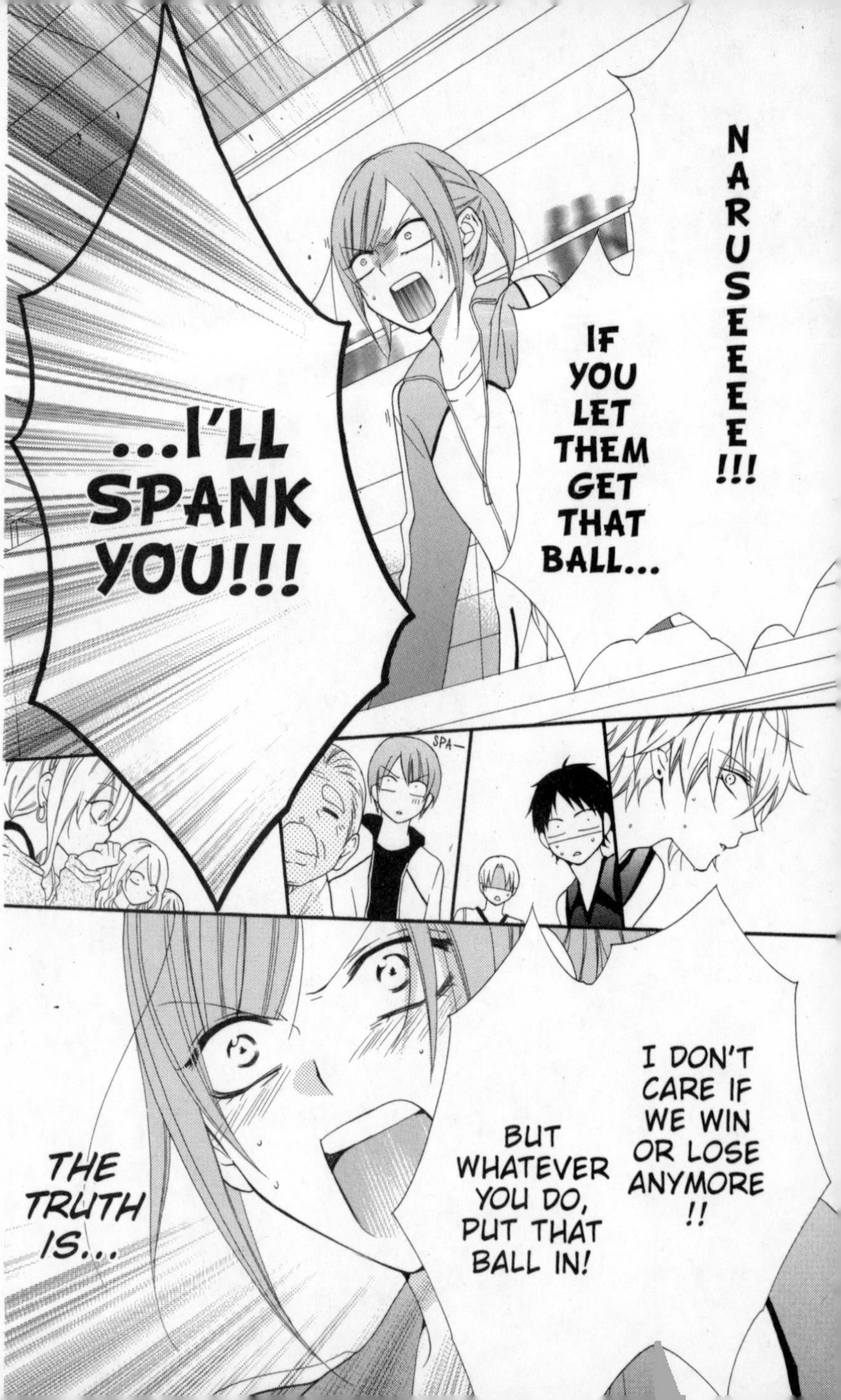
NARUSEEEE!!!
IF YOU LET THEM GET THAT BALL...
...I'LL SPANK YOU!!!
SPA—
I DON'T CARE IF WE WIN OR LOSE ANYMORE!!
BUT WHATEVER YOU DO, PUT THAT BALL IN!
THE TRUTH IS...

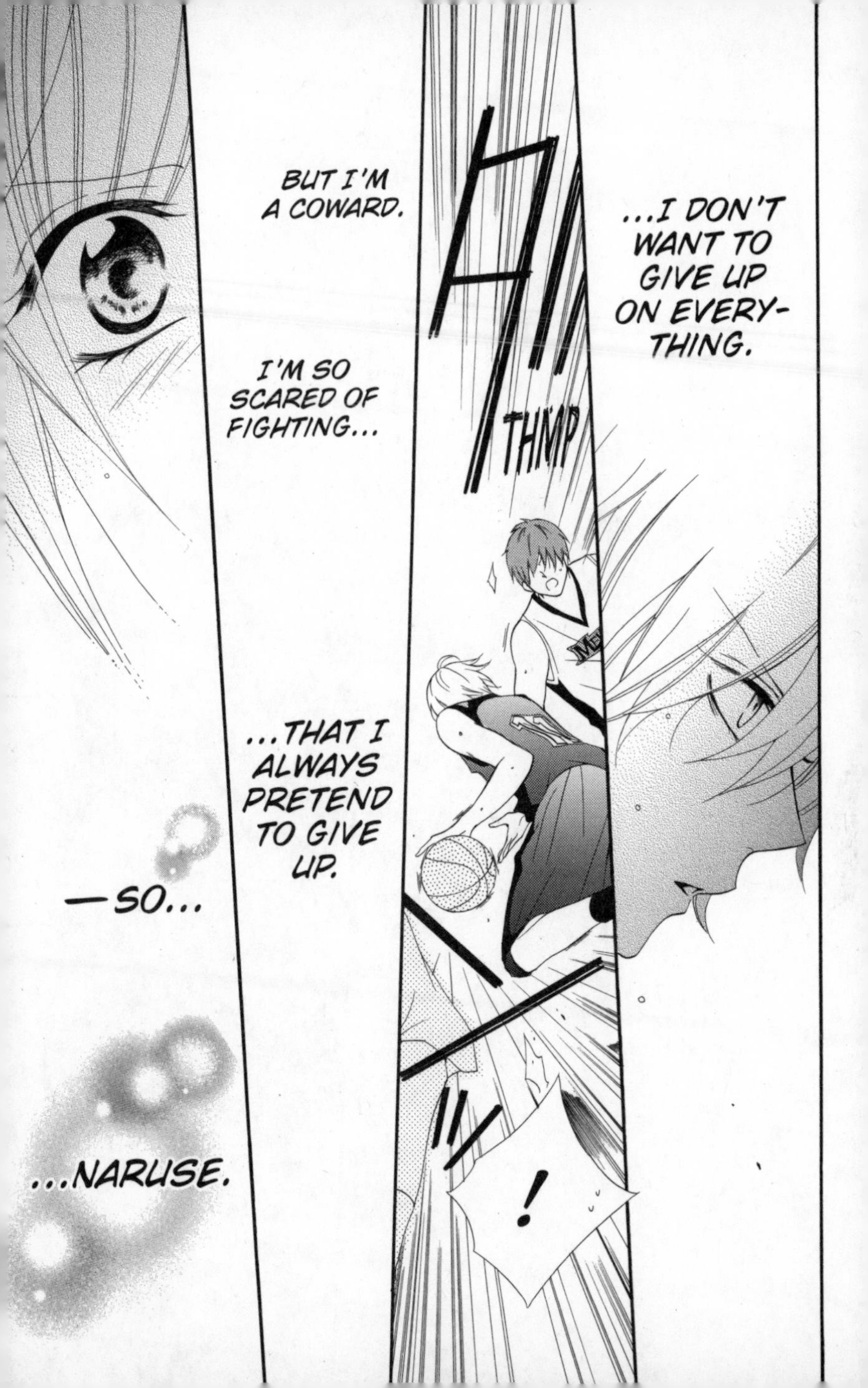
...I DON'T WANT TO GIVE UP ON EVERY-THING.
THMP
!
BUT I'M A COWARD.
I'M SO SCARED OF FIGHTING...
...THAT I ALWAYS PRETEND TO GIVE UP.
—SO...
...NARUSE.

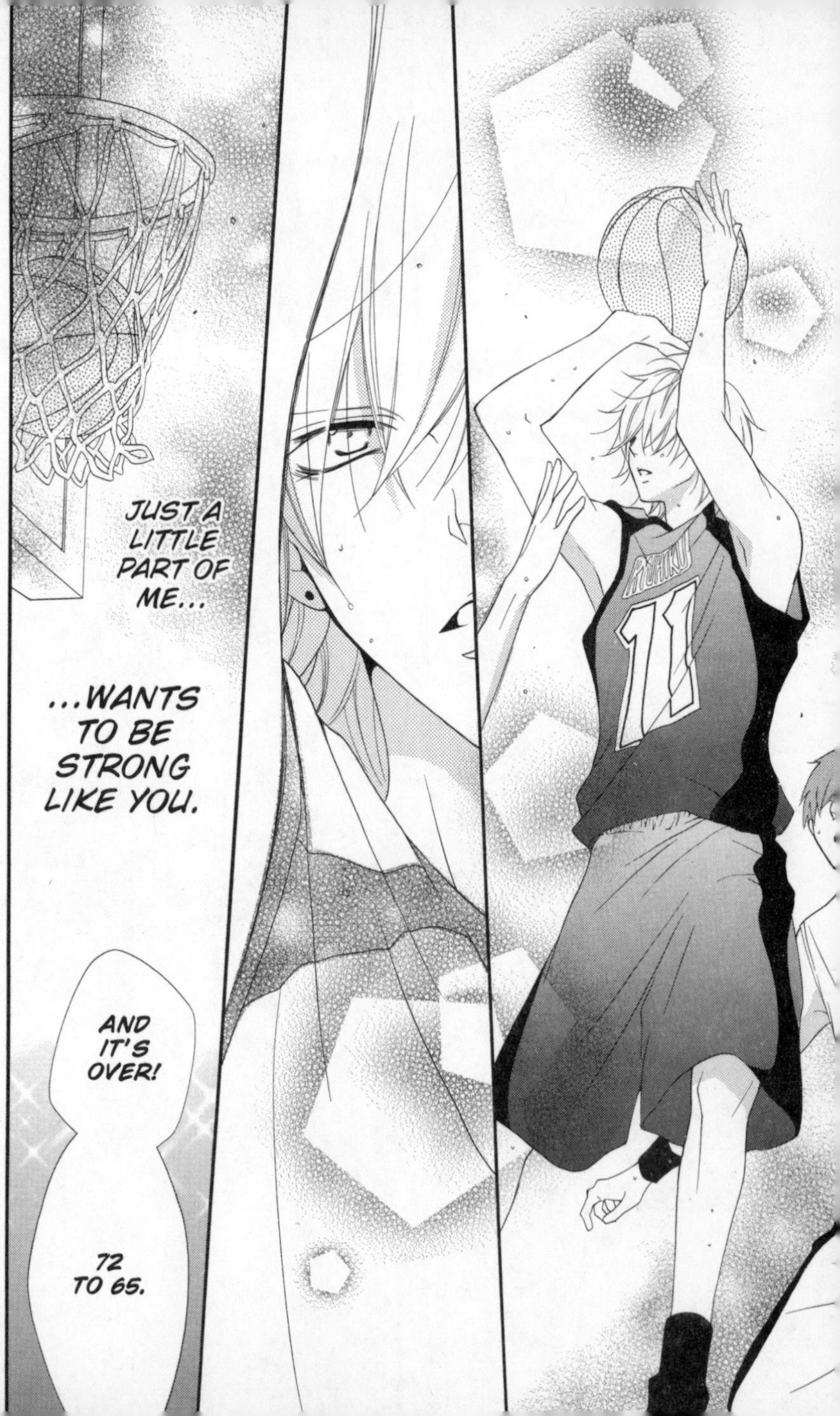
JUST A LITTLE PART OF ME...
...WANTS TO BE STRONG LIKE YOU.
AND IT'S OVER!
72 TO 65.

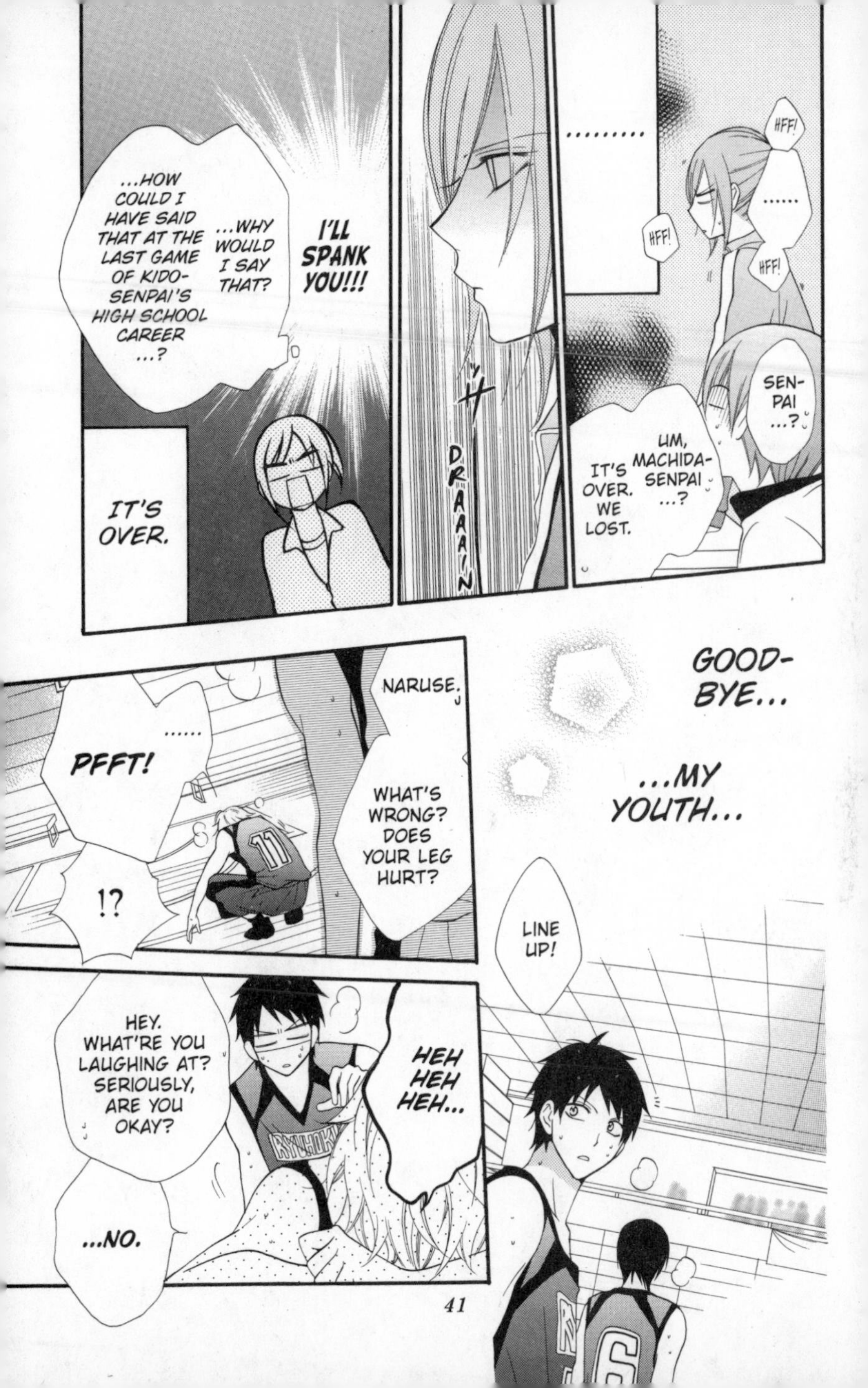
....
HFF!
......
HFF!
HFF!
SEN-PAI ...?
UM, MACHIDA-SENPAI ...?
IT'S OVER. WE LOST.
DRAAAAIN
I'LL SPANK YOU!!!
...WHY WOULD I SAY THAT?
...HOW COULD I HAVE SAID THAT AT THE LAST GAME OF KIDO-SENPAI'S HIGH SCHOOL CAREER ...?
IT'S OVER.
GOOD-BYE...
...MY YOUTH...
LINE UP!
NARUSE.
WHAT'S WRONG? DOES YOUR LEG HURT?
......
PFFT!
!?
HEH HEH HEH...
HEY. WHAT'RE YOU LAUGHING AT? SERIOUSLY, ARE YOU OKAY?
...NO.

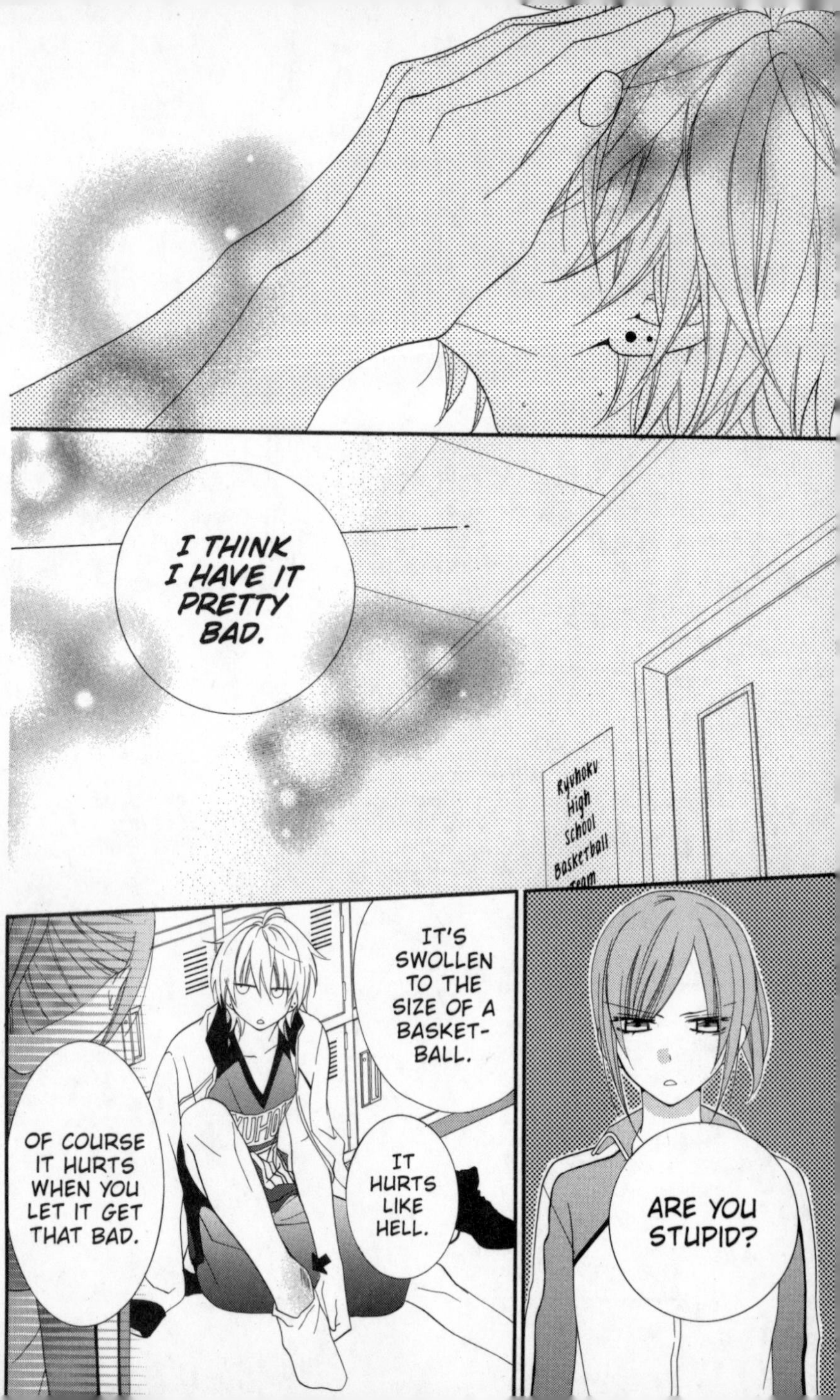
I THINK I HAVE IT PRETTY BAD.
Ryuhoku High School Basketball
ARE YOU STUPID?
IT'S SWOLLEN TO THE SIZE OF A BASKET-BALL.
IT HURTS LIKE HELL.
OF COURSE IT HURTS WHEN YOU LET IT GET THAT BAD.

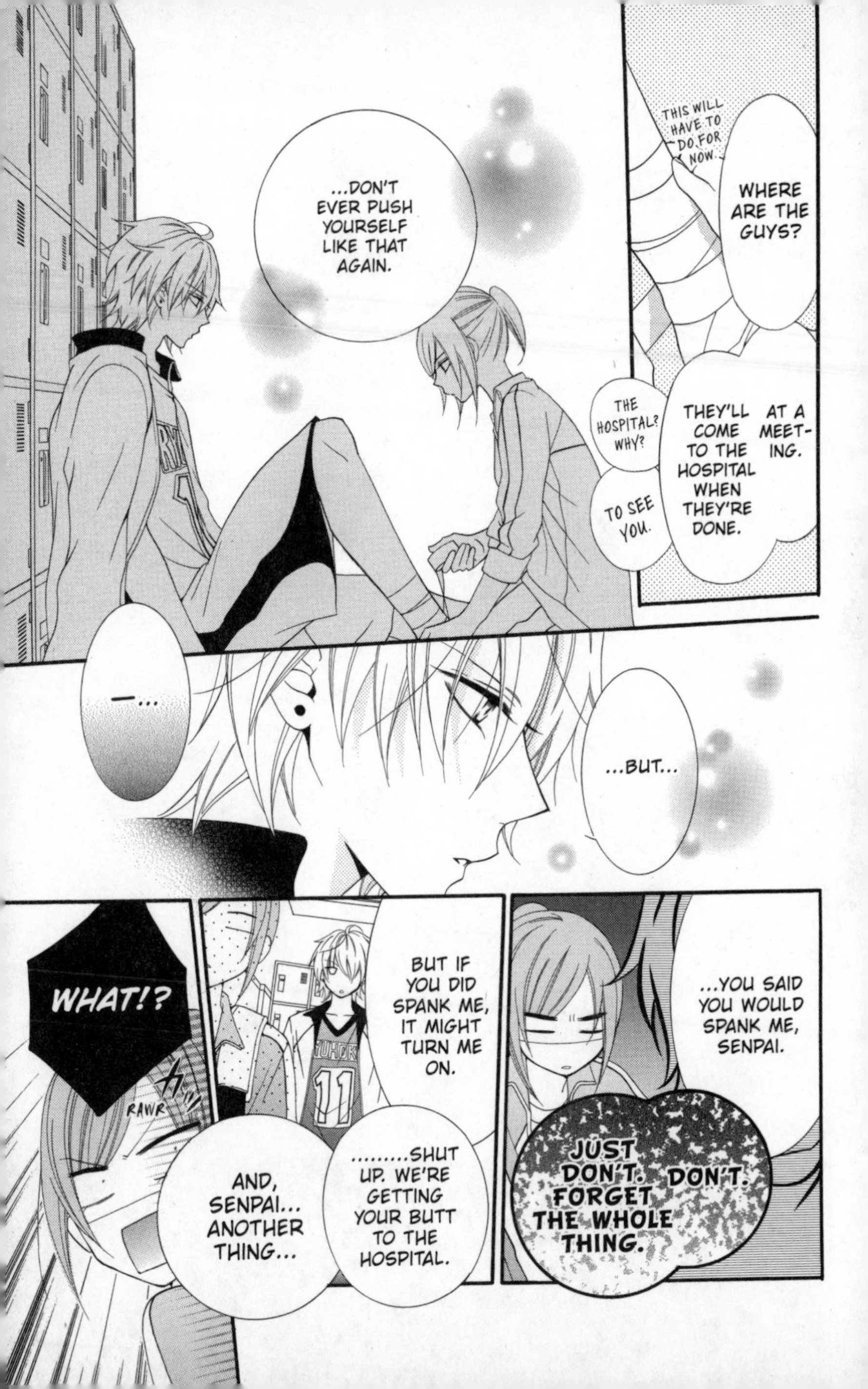
THIS WILL HAVE TO DO FOR NOW.
WHERE ARE THE GUYS?
AT A MEETING.
THEY'LL COME TO THE HOSPITAL WHEN THEY'RE DONE.
THE HOSPITAL? WHY?
TO SEE YOU.
...DON'T EVER PUSH YOURSELF LIKE THAT AGAIN.
...BUT...
—...
...YOU SAID YOU WOULD SPANK ME, SENPAI.
DON'T.
JUST DON'T. FORGET THE WHOLE THING.
BUT IF YOU DID SPANK ME, IT MIGHT TURN ME ON.
.........SHUT UP. WE'RE GETTING YOUR BUTT TO THE HOSPITAL.
WHAT!?
RAWR
AND, SENPAI... ANOTHER THING...

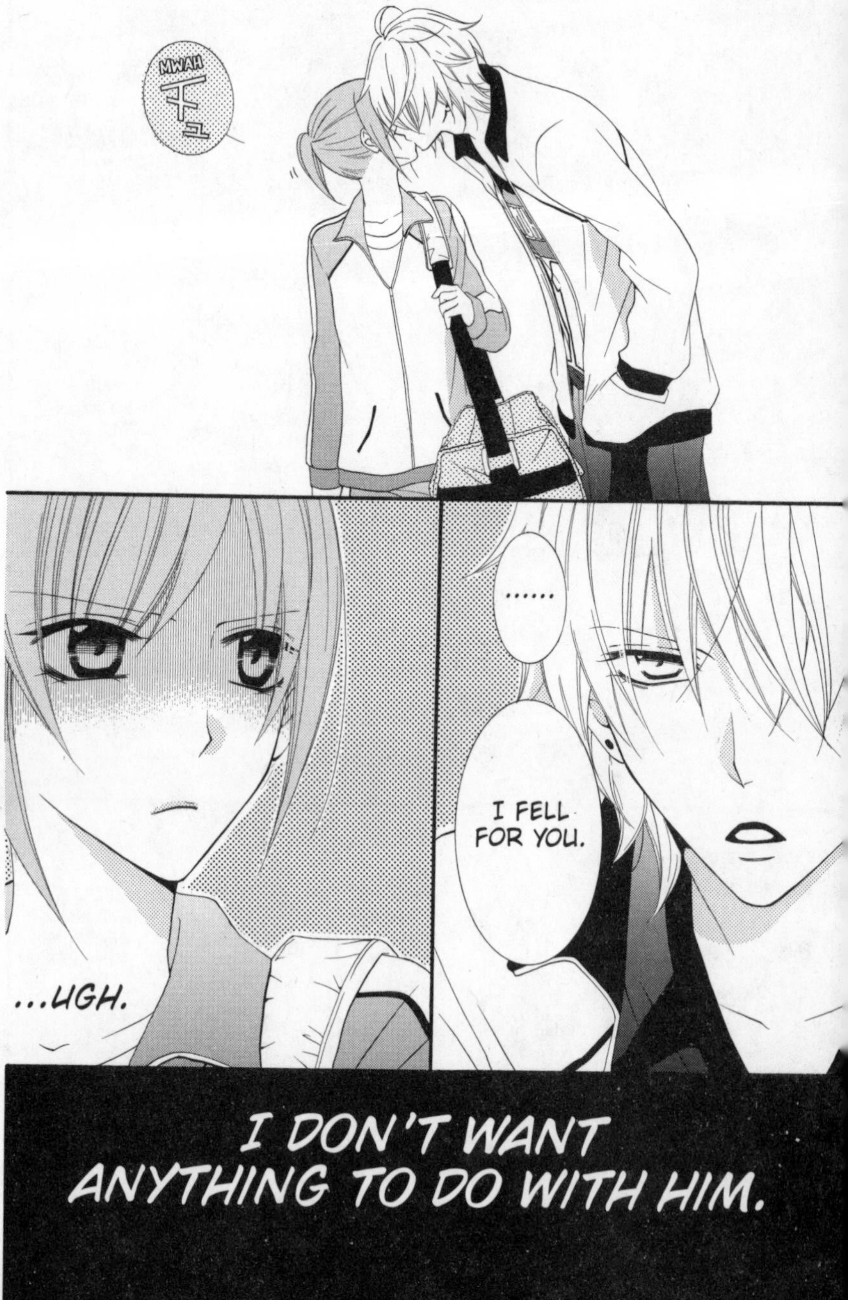
MWAH
チュ
......
I FELL FOR YOU.
...UGH.
I DON'T WANT ANYTHING TO DO WITH HIM.

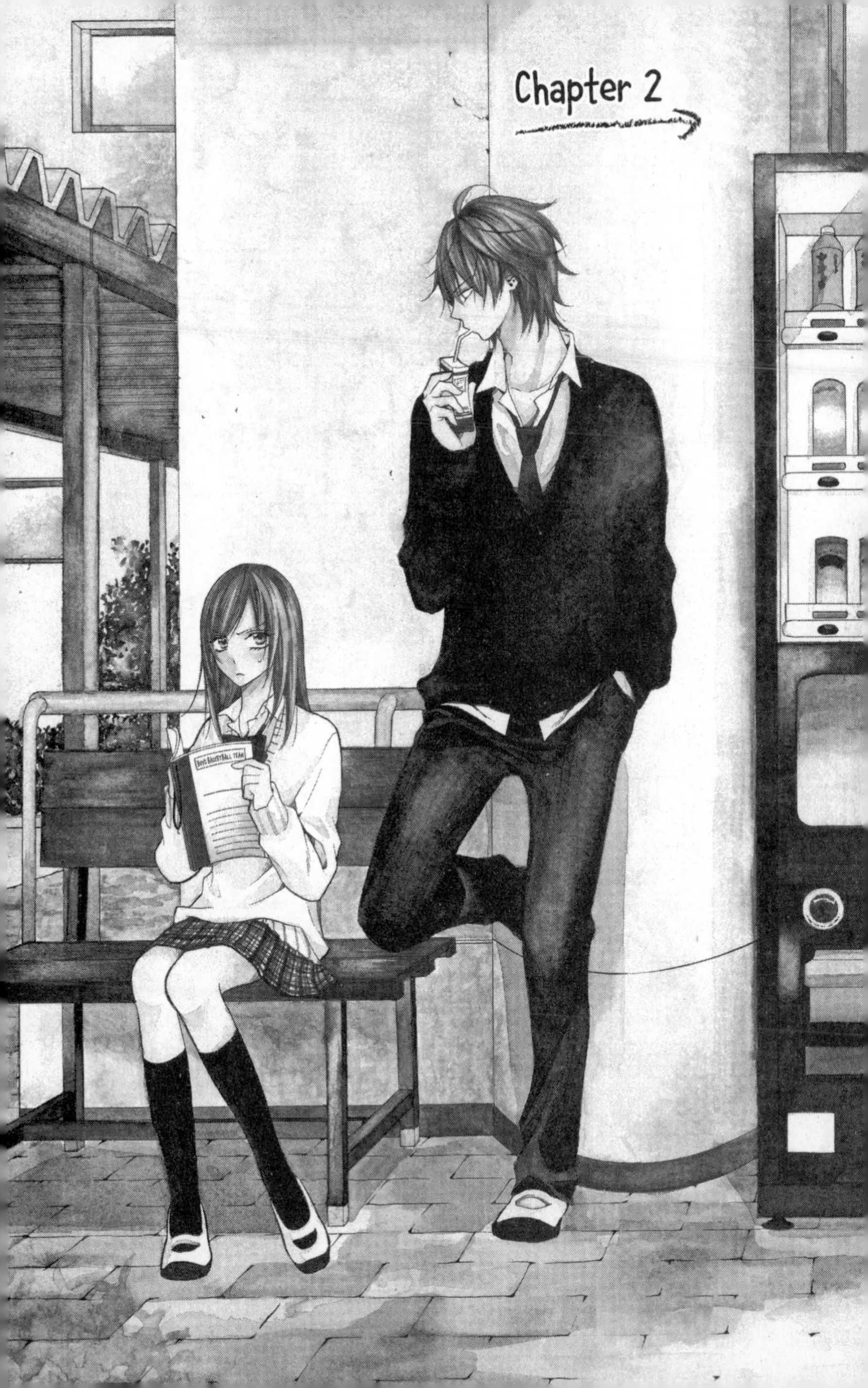
Chapter 2
BOYS BASKETBALL TEAM

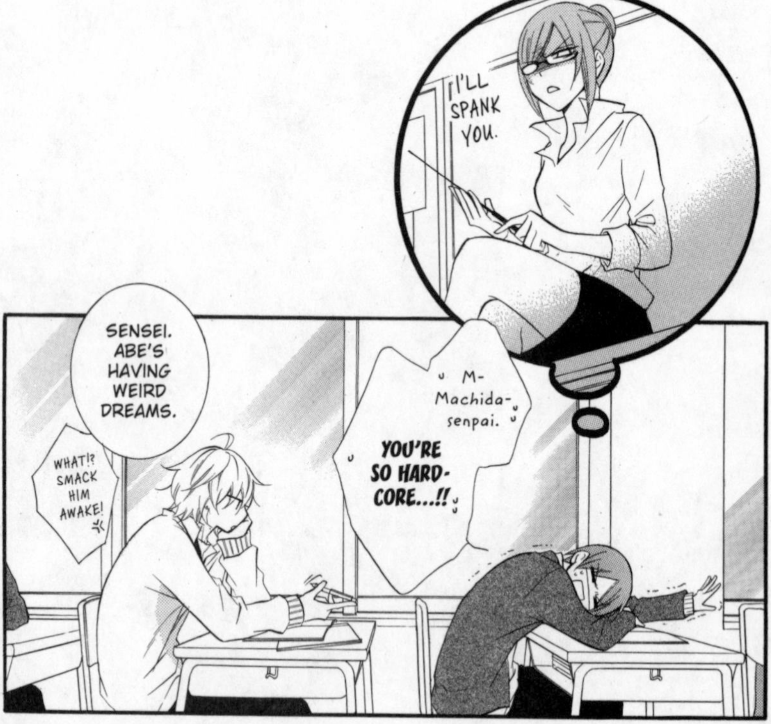
I'LL SPANK YOU.
M-Machida-senpai.
YOU'RE SO HARD-CORE...!!
SENSEI. ABE'S HAVING WEIRD DREAMS.
WHAT!? SMACK HIM AWAKE!

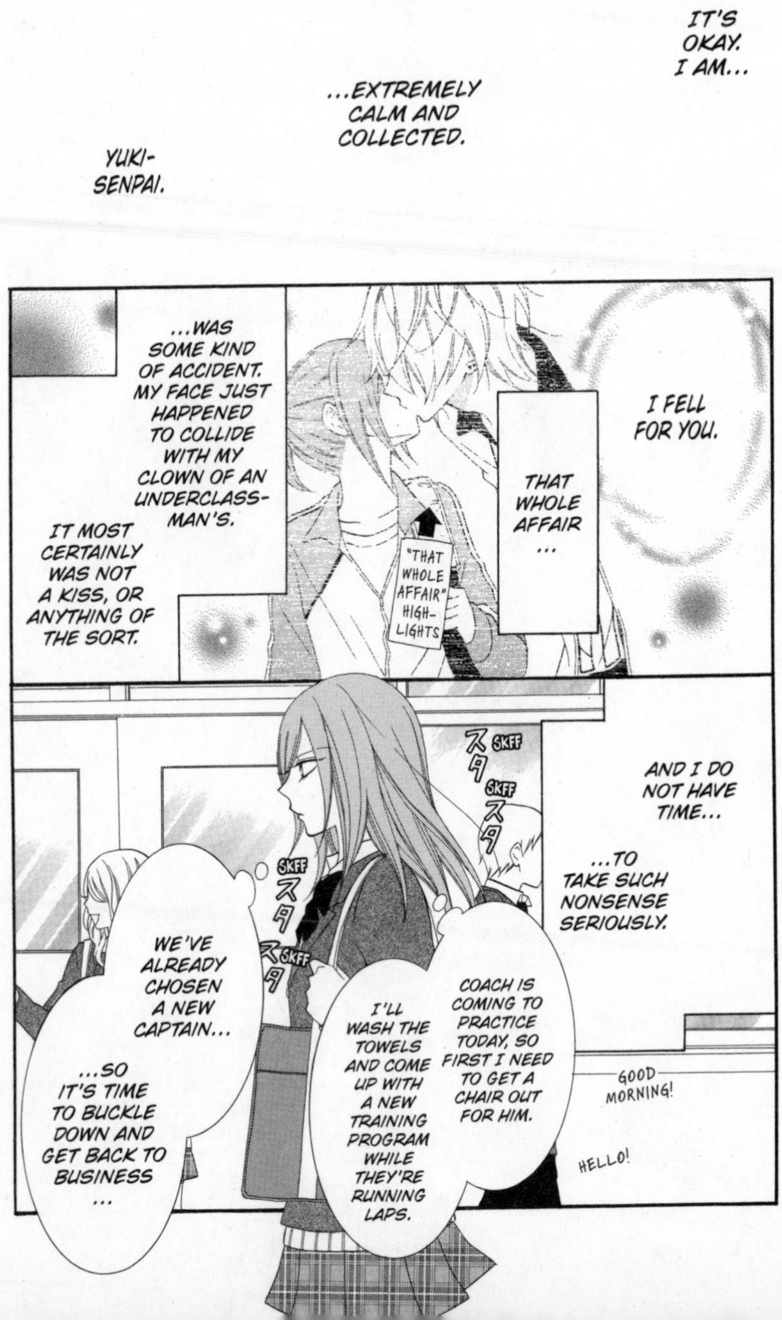
IT'S OKAY. I AM...
...EXTREMELY CALM AND COLLECTED.
YUKI-SENPAI.
I FELL FOR YOU.
THAT WHOLE AFFAIR...
"THAT WHOLE AFFAIR" HIGHLIGHTS
...WAS SOME KIND OF ACCIDENT. MY FACE JUST HAPPENED TO COLLIDE WITH MY CLOWN OF AN UNDERCLASSMAN'S.
IT MOST CERTAINLY WAS NOT A KISS, OR ANYTHING OF THE SORT.
AND I DO NOT HAVE TIME...
...TO TAKE SUCH NONSENSE SERIOUSLY.
スタ SKFF
SKFF スタ
GOOD MORNING!
HELLO!
COACH IS COMING TO PRACTICE TODAY, SO FIRST I NEED TO GET A CHAIR OUT FOR HIM.
I'LL WASH THE TOWELS AND COME UP WITH A NEW TRAINING PROGRAM WHILE THEY'RE RUNNING LAPS.
SKFF スタ
スタ SKFF
WE'VE ALREADY CHOSEN A NEW CAPTAIN...
...SO IT'S TIME TO BUCKLE DOWN AND GET BACK TO BUSINESS...

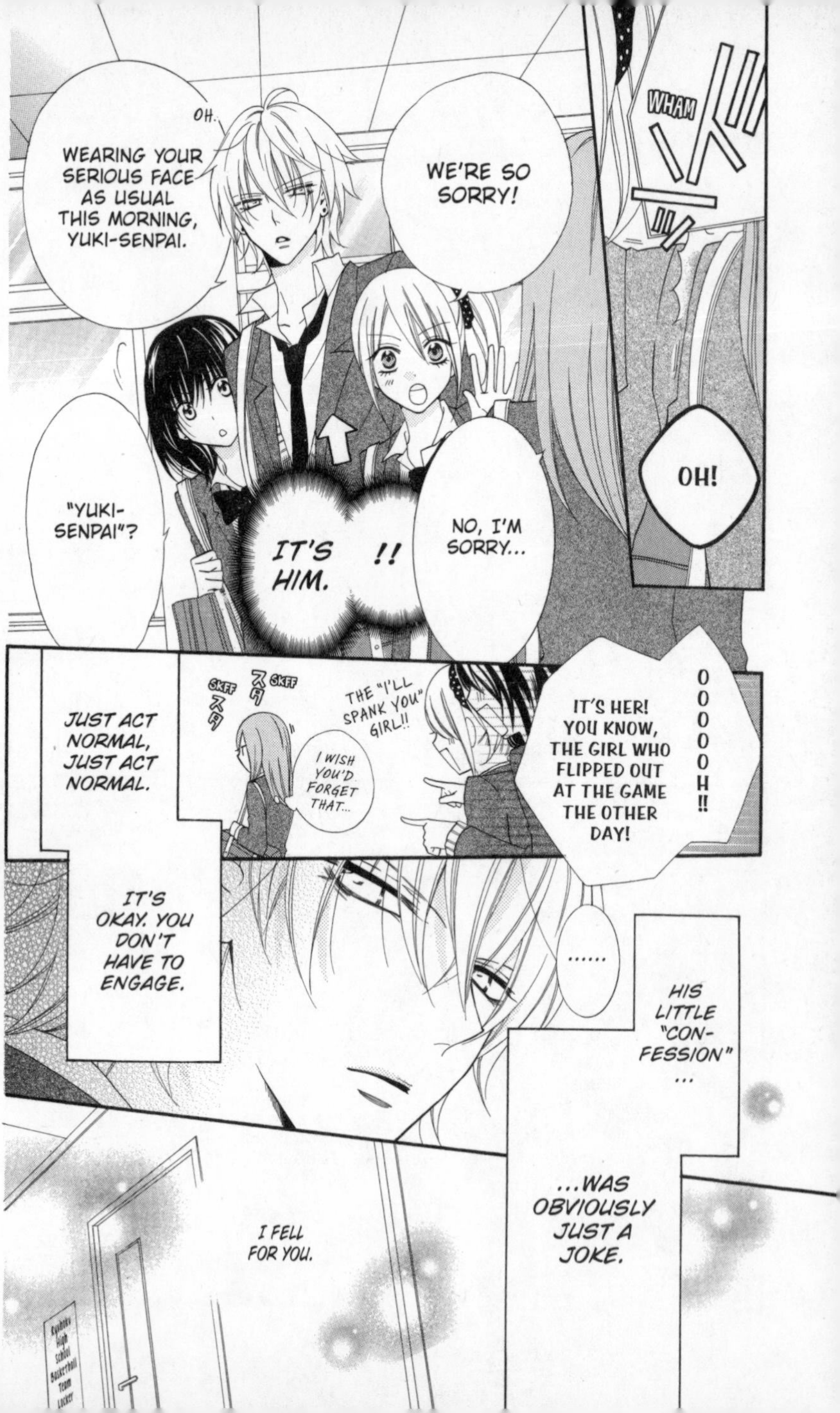
WHAM
OH!
WE'RE SO SORRY!
OH.
WEARING YOUR SERIOUS FACE AS USUAL THIS MORNING, YUKI-SENPAI.
NO, I'M SORRY...
IT'S HIM. !!
"YUKI-SENPAI"?
OOOOOOOH!!
IT'S HER! YOU KNOW, THE GIRL WHO FLIPPED OUT AT THE GAME THE OTHER DAY!
THE "I'LL SPANK YOU" GIRL!!
I WISH YOU'D FORGET THAT...
SKFF
SKFF
JUST ACT NORMAL, JUST ACT NORMAL.
......
IT'S OKAY. YOU DON'T HAVE TO ENGAGE.
HIS LITTLE "CON-FESSION"...
...WAS OBVIOUSLY JUST A JOKE.
I FELL FOR YOU.
High School Basketball Team Locker

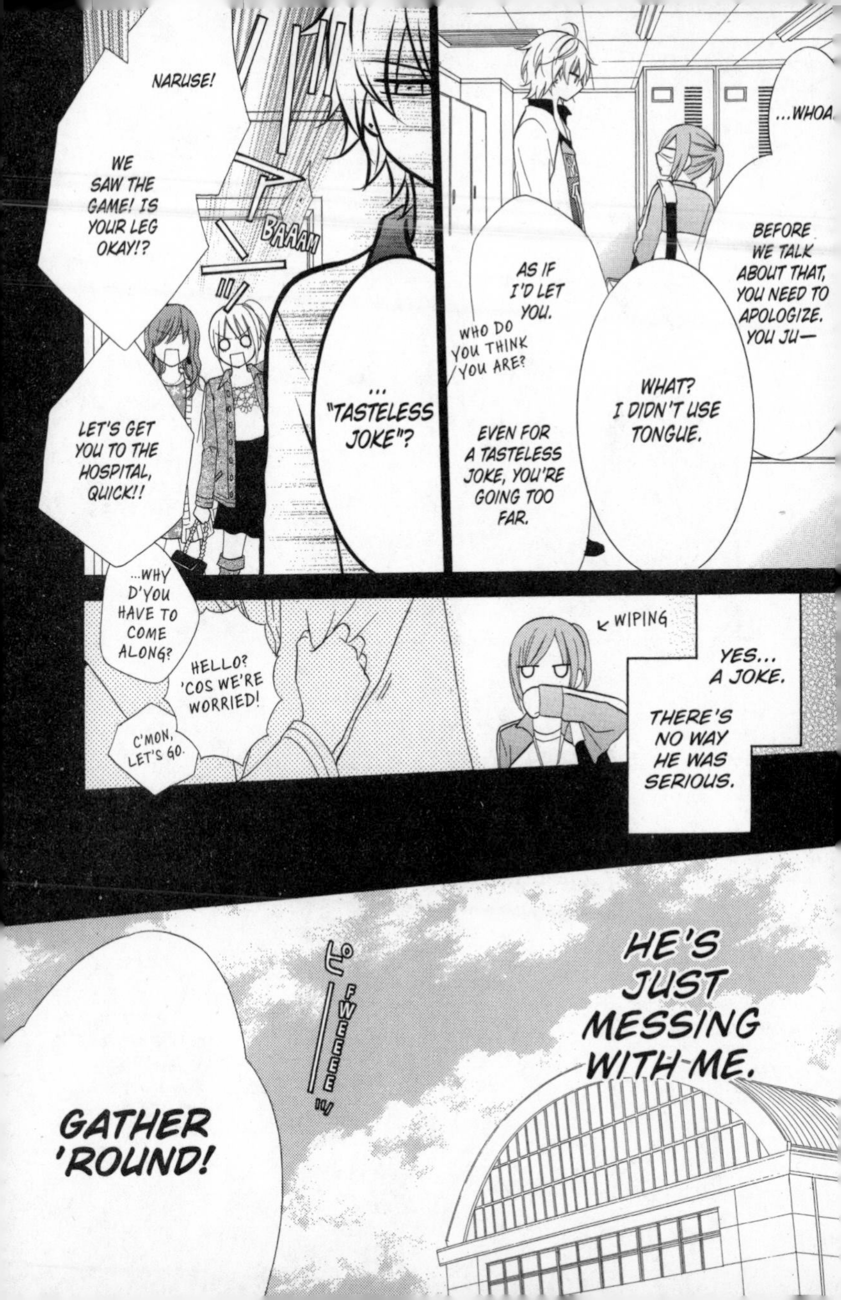
...WHOA.
BEFORE WE TALK ABOUT THAT, YOU NEED TO APOLOGIZE. YOU JU—
AS IF I'D LET YOU.
WHO DO YOU THINK YOU ARE?
WHAT? I DIDN'T USE TONGUE.
EVEN FOR A TASTELESS JOKE, YOU'RE GOING TOO FAR.
... "TASTELESS JOKE"?
BAAAM
NARUSE!
WE SAW THE GAME! IS YOUR LEG OKAY!?
LET'S GET YOU TO THE HOSPITAL, QUICK!!
WIPING
YES... A JOKE.
THERE'S NO WAY HE WAS SERIOUS.
...WHY D'YOU HAVE TO COME ALONG?
HELLO? 'COS WE'RE WORRIED!
C'MON, LET'S GO.
HE'S JUST MESSING WITH ME.
ピー
FWEEEE
GATHER 'ROUND!

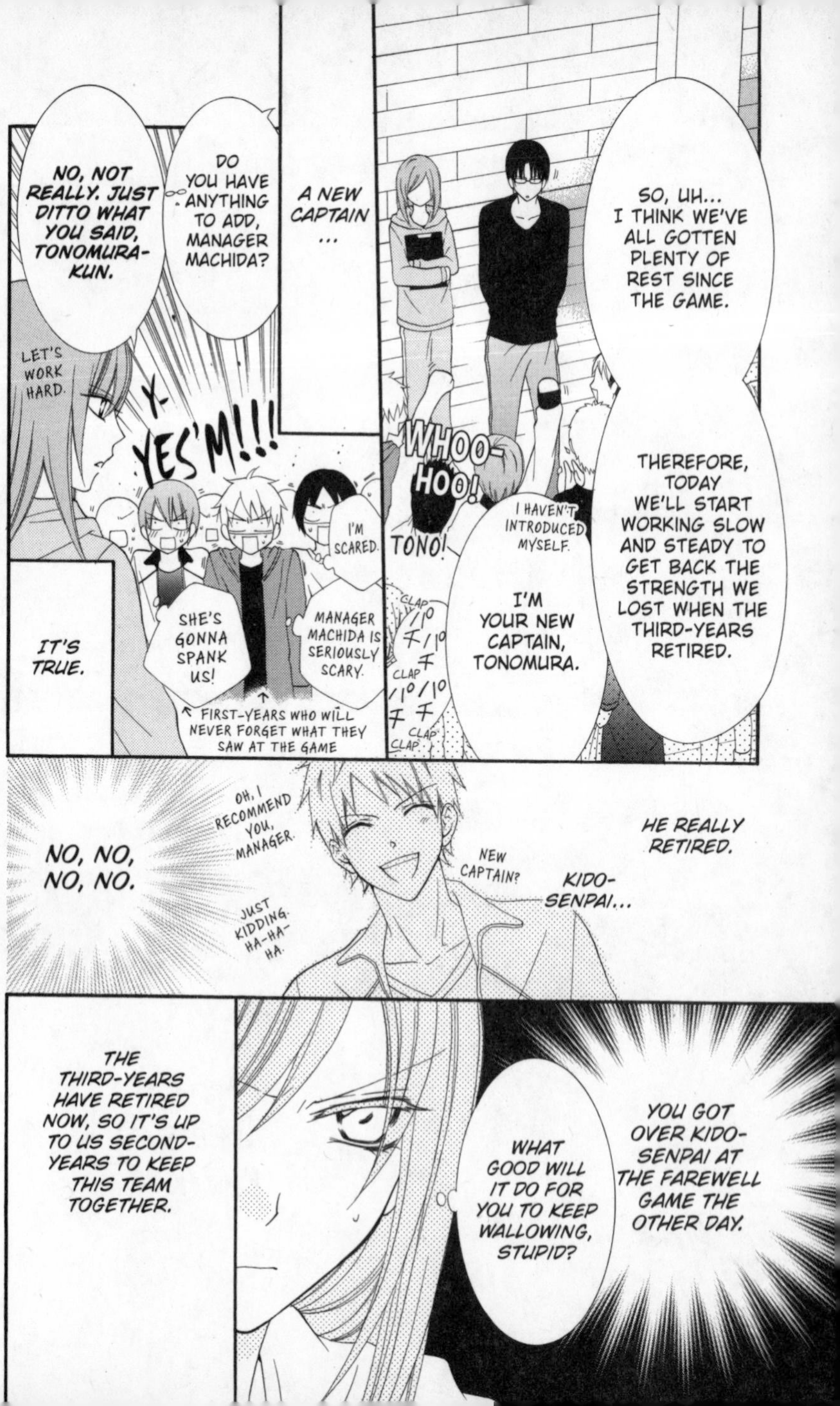
SO, UH... I THINK WE'VE ALL GOTTEN PLENTY OF REST SINCE THE GAME.
THEREFORE, TODAY WE'LL START WORKING SLOW AND STEADY TO GET BACK THE STRENGTH WE LOST WHEN THE THIRD-YEARS RETIRED.
I HAVEN'T INTRODUCED MYSELF.
I'M YOUR NEW CAPTAIN, TONOMURA.
WHOO-HOO!
TONO!
CLAP CLAP CLAP CLAP
A NEW CAPTAIN ...
DO YOU HAVE ANYTHING TO ADD, MANAGER MACHIDA?
NO, NOT REALLY. JUST DITTO WHAT YOU SAID, TONOMURA-KUN.
LET'S WORK HARD.
Y-YES'M!!!
I'M SCARED.
MANAGER MACHIDA IS SERIOUSLY SCARY.
SHE'S GONNA SPANK US!
FIRST-YEARS WHO WILL NEVER FORGET WHAT THEY SAW AT THE GAME
IT'S TRUE.
HE REALLY RETIRED.
KIDO-SENPAI...
NEW CAPTAIN?
OH, I RECOMMEND YOU, MANAGER.
JUST KIDDING. HA-HA-HA.
NO, NO, NO, NO.
YOU GOT OVER KIDO-SENPAI AT THE FAREWELL GAME THE OTHER DAY.
WHAT GOOD WILL IT DO FOR YOU TO KEEP WALLOWING, STUPID?
THE THIRD-YEARS HAVE RETIRED NOW, SO IT'S UP TO US SECOND-YEARS TO KEEP THIS TEAM TOGETHER.

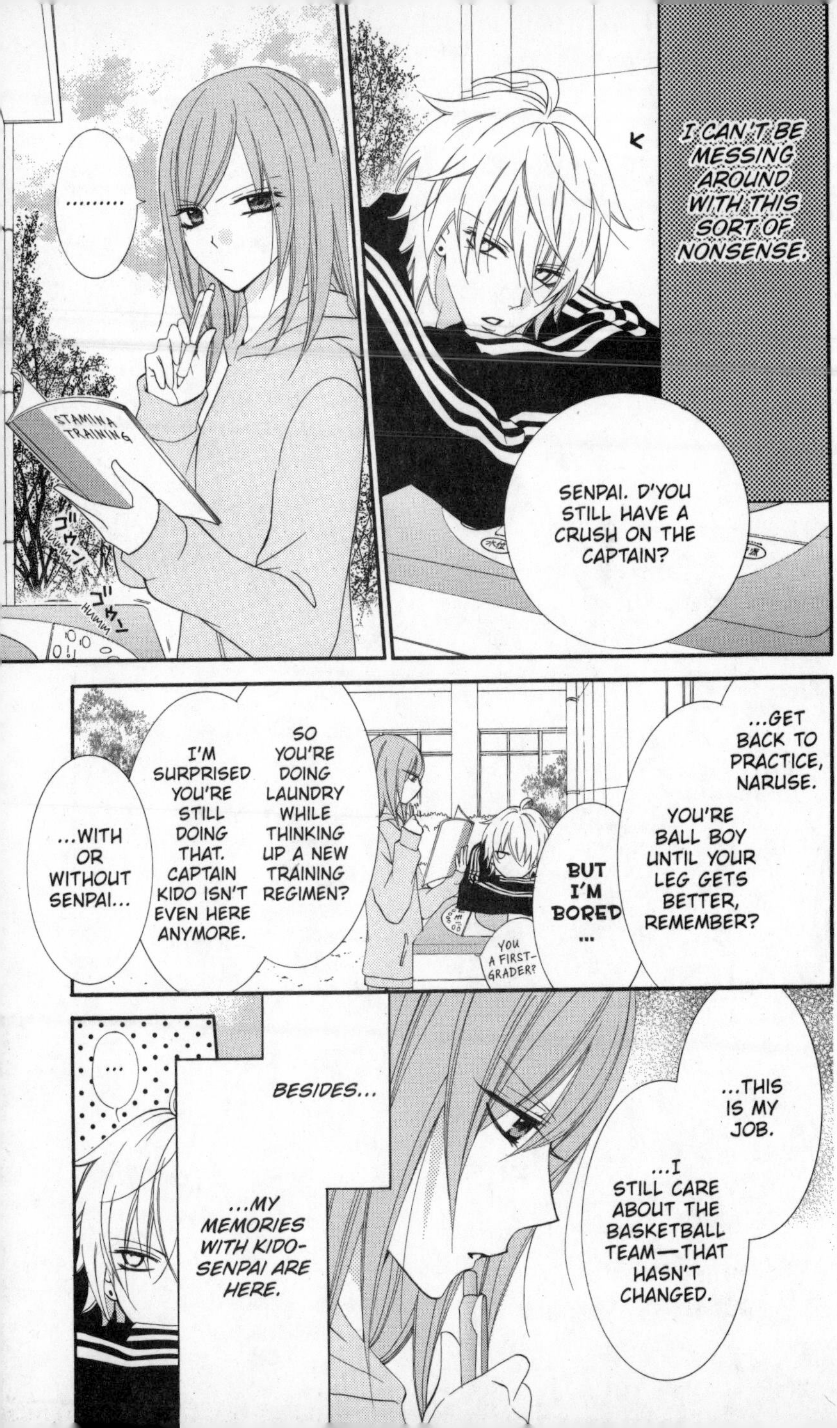
I CAN'T BE MESSING AROUND WITH THIS SORT OF NONSENSE.
SENPAI. D'YOU STILL HAVE A CRUSH ON THE CAPTAIN?
....
STAMINA TRAINING
HUMMM
HUMMM
...GET BACK TO PRACTICE, NARUSE.
YOU'RE BALL BOY UNTIL YOUR LEG GETS BETTER, REMEMBER?
BUT I'M BORED...
YOU A FIRST-GRADER?
SO YOU'RE DOING LAUNDRY WHILE THINKING UP A NEW TRAINING REGIMEN?
I'M SURPRISED YOU'RE STILL DOING THAT. CAPTAIN KIDO ISN'T EVEN HERE ANYMORE.
...WITH OR WITHOUT SENPAI...
...THIS IS MY JOB.
...I STILL CARE ABOUT THE BASKETBALL TEAM—THAT HASN'T CHANGED.
BESIDES...
...MY MEMORIES WITH KIDO-SENPAI ARE HERE.
...

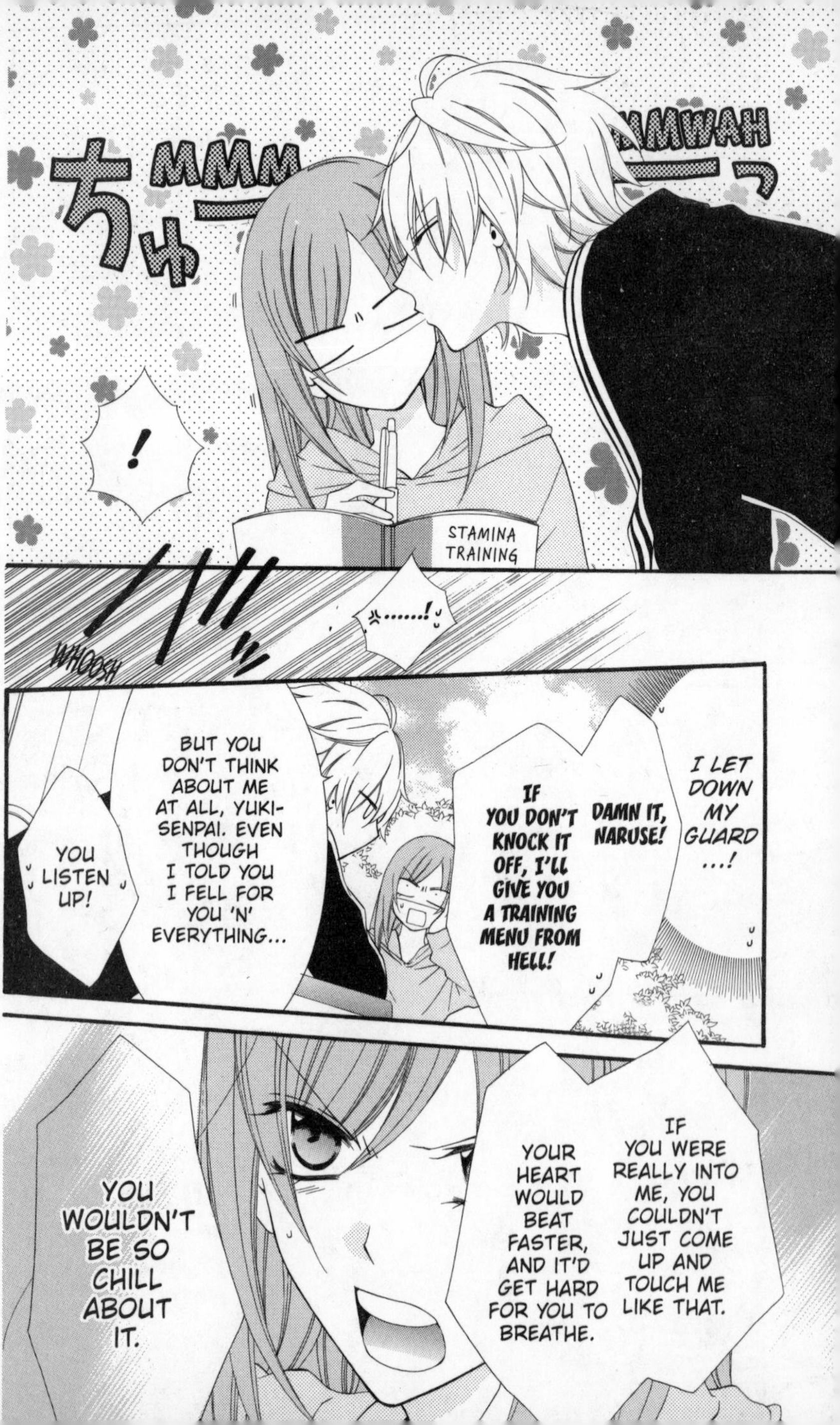
ちゅーーっ
MMM
MMWAH
!
STAMINA TRAINING
......!
WHOOSH
I LET DOWN MY GUARD ...!
DAMN IT, NARUSE!
IF YOU DON'T KNOCK IT OFF, I'LL GIVE YOU A TRAINING MENU FROM HELL!
BUT YOU DON'T THINK ABOUT ME AT ALL, YUKI-SENPAI. EVEN THOUGH I TOLD YOU I FELL FOR YOU 'N' EVERYTHING...
YOU LISTEN UP!
IF YOU WERE REALLY INTO ME, YOU COULDN'T JUST COME UP AND TOUCH ME LIKE THAT.
YOUR HEART WOULD BEAT FASTER, AND IT'D GET HARD FOR YOU TO BREATHE.
YOU WOULDN'T BE SO CHILL ABOUT IT.

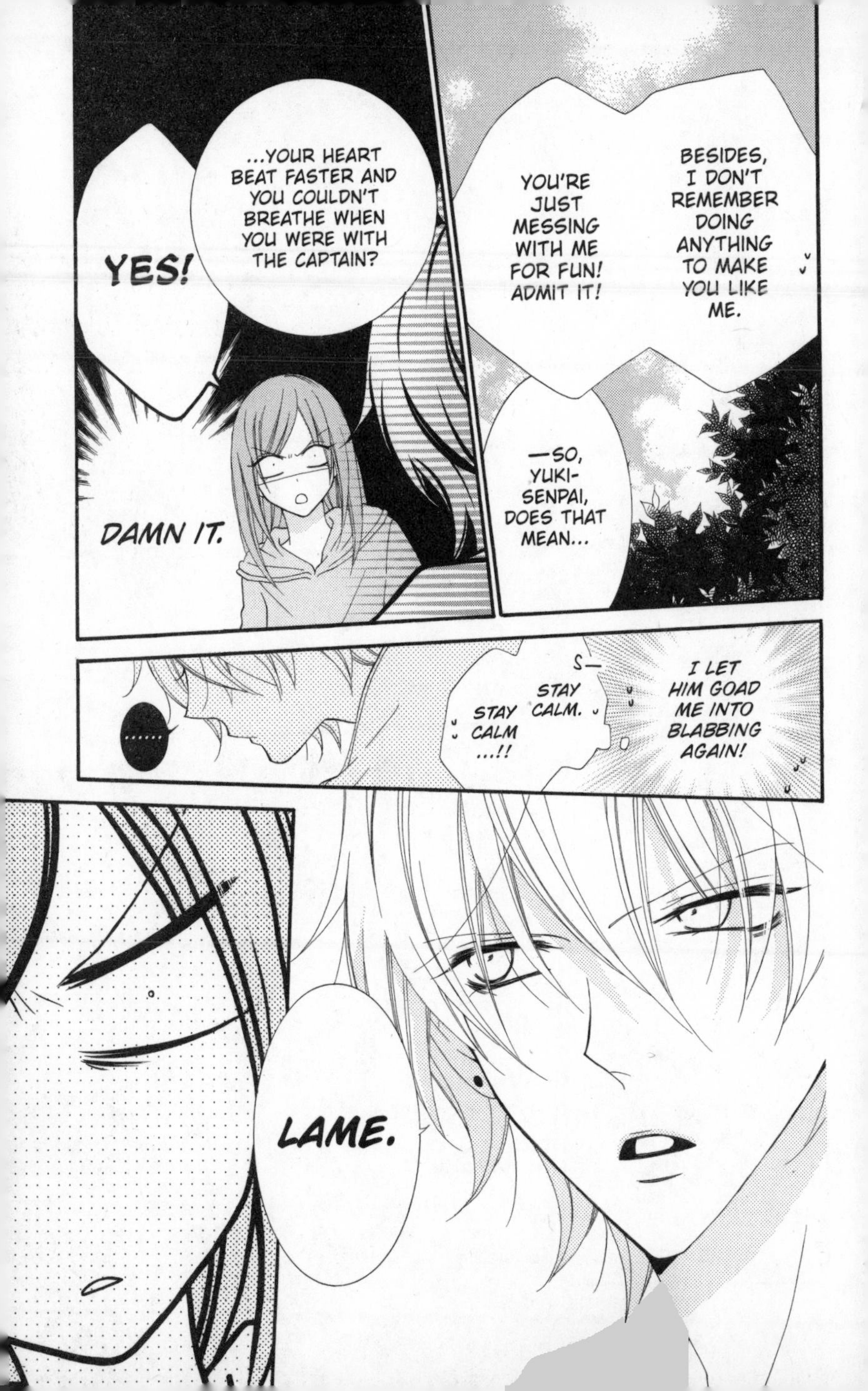
BESIDES, I DON'T REMEMBER DOING ANYTHING TO MAKE YOU LIKE ME.
YOU'RE JUST MESSING WITH ME FOR FUN! ADMIT IT!
—SO, YUKI-SENPAI, DOES THAT MEAN...
...YOUR HEART BEAT FASTER AND YOU COULDN'T BREATHE WHEN YOU WERE WITH THE CAPTAIN?
YES!
DAMN IT.
I LET HIM GOAD ME INTO BLABBING AGAIN!
S— STAY CALM.
STAY CALM ...!!
......
LAME.

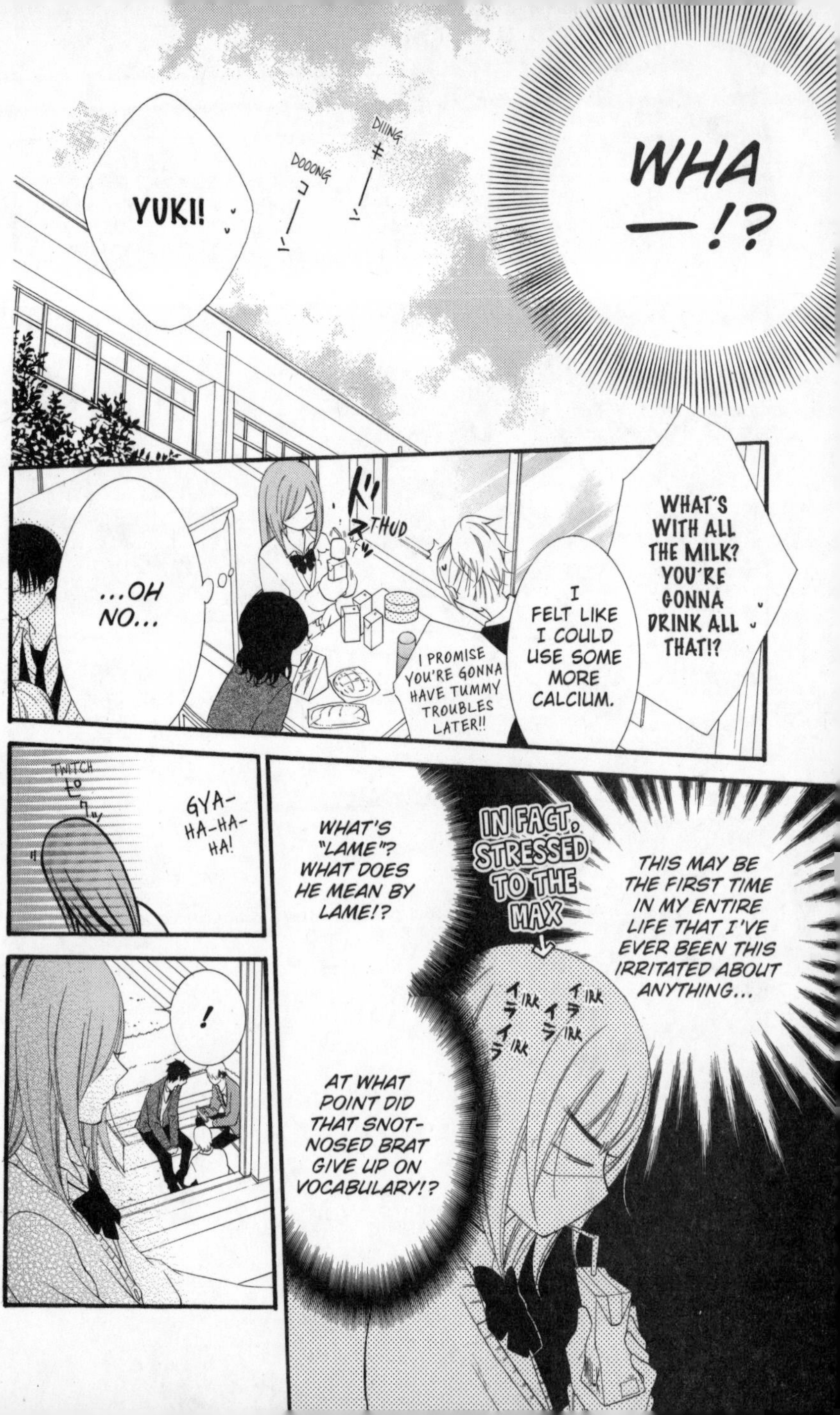
WHA—!?
DIIING
DOOONG
YUKI!
WHAT'S WITH ALL THE MILK? YOU'RE GONNA DRINK ALL THAT!?
I FELT LIKE I COULD USE SOME MORE CALCIUM.
I PROMISE YOU'RE GONNA HAVE TUMMY TROUBLES LATER!!
THUD
...OH NO...
THIS MAY BE THE FIRST TIME IN MY ENTIRE LIFE THAT I'VE EVER BEEN THIS IRRITATED ABOUT ANYTHING...
IN FACT, STRESSED TO THE MAX
WHAT'S "LAME"? WHAT DOES HE MEAN BY LAME!?
IRK IRK IRK IRK
AT WHAT POINT DID THAT SNOT-NOSED BRAT GIVE UP ON VOCABULARY!?
GYA-HA-HA-HA!
TWITCH
!

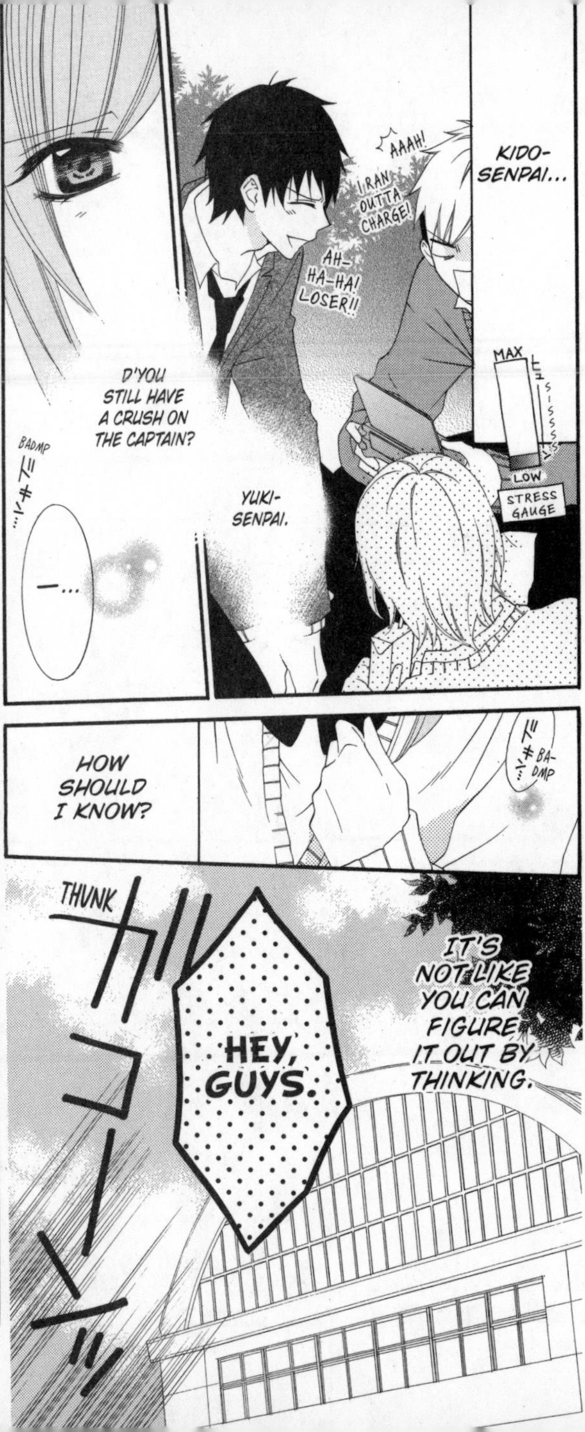
KIDO-SENPAI...
MAX
LOW
STRESS GAUGE
AAAH!
I RAN OUTTA CHARGE!
AH-HA-HA! LOSER!!
D'YOU STILL HAVE A CRUSH ON THE CAPTAIN?
YUKI-SENPAI.
BADMP
—...
BA-DMP
HOW SHOULD I KNOW?
IT'S NOT LIKE YOU CAN FIGURE IT OUT BY THINKING.
HEY, GUYS.
THUNK

02

SPORTS MANGA

The setting of this story is on the basketball team, but personally, I'm such an amateur I'm not sure I've ever held a basketball in my life. And I'm the opposite of athletic.

I bought a lot of magazines and looked up rules and stuff, but I couldn't get a feel for what being on a team was like, so I was wondering what to do when my editor called.

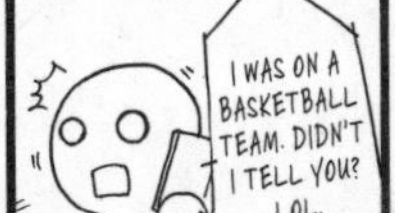
I WAS ON A BASKETBALL TEAM. DIDN'T I TELL YOU? LOL.
!!!

THAT'S ENCOURAGING...!!!

And sports manga has a lot of extras (team members), so when I'm doing the manuscript, I fall into this pit of "It wasn't supposed to be like this..." There's person after person after person.

My friend was laying the tone on the team's uniforms for the halftime scene and started shouting.

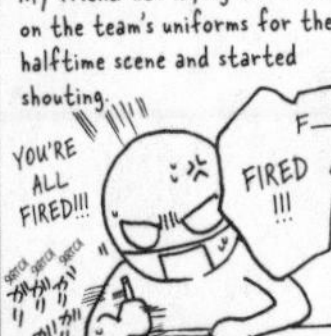
YOU'RE ALL FIRED!!!
F—
FIRED !!!

IT'S SO ENCOURAGING...!!!

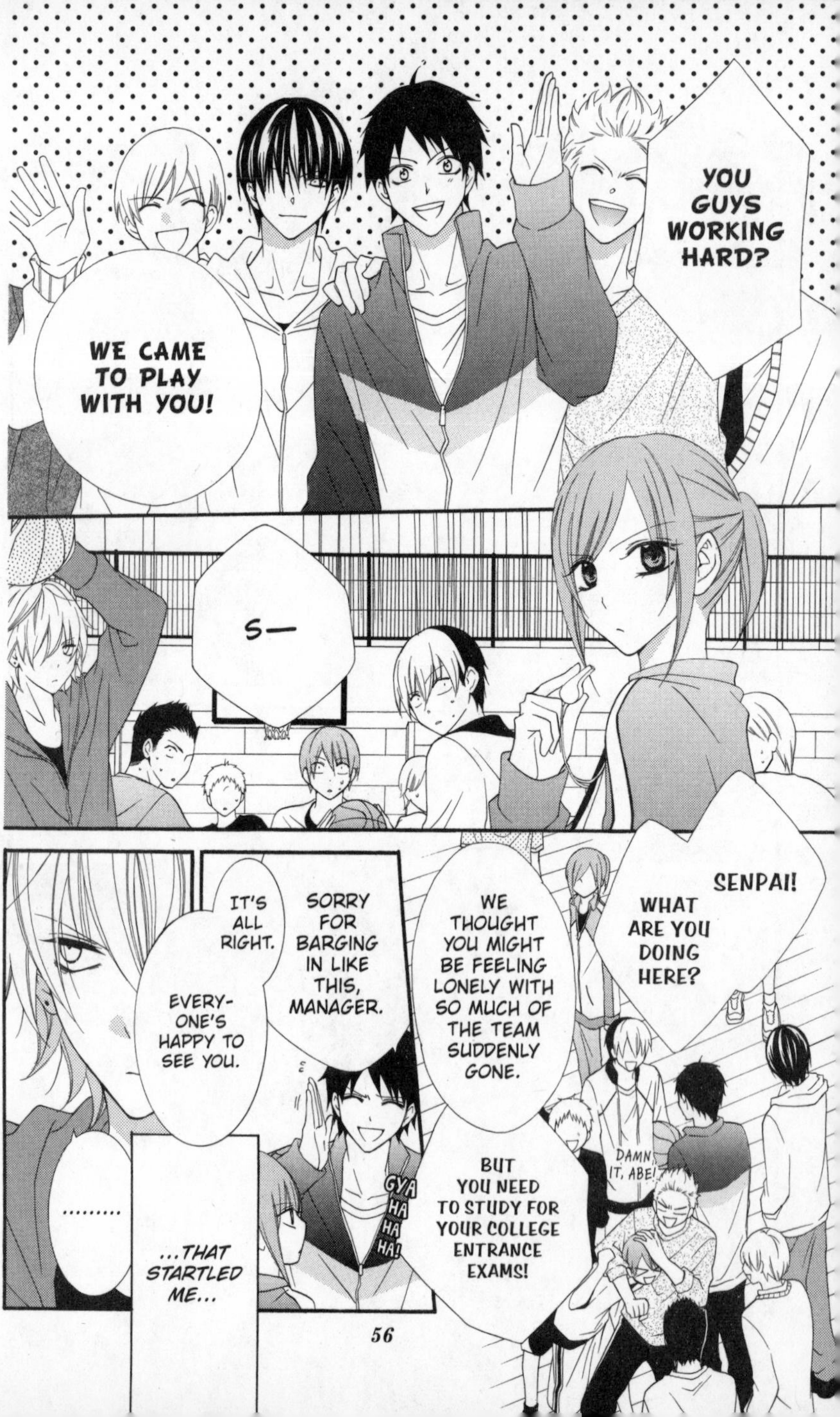
YOU GUYS WORKING HARD?
WE CAME TO PLAY WITH YOU!
S—
SENPAI!
WHAT ARE YOU DOING HERE?
WE THOUGHT YOU MIGHT BE FEELING LONELY WITH SO MUCH OF THE TEAM SUDDENLY GONE.
BUT YOU NEED TO STUDY FOR YOUR COLLEGE ENTRANCE EXAMS!
DAMN IT, ABE!
GYA HA HA HA!
SORRY FOR BARGING IN LIKE THIS, MANAGER.
IT'S ALL RIGHT.
EVERY-ONE'S HAPPY TO SEE YOU.
....
...THAT STARTLED ME...

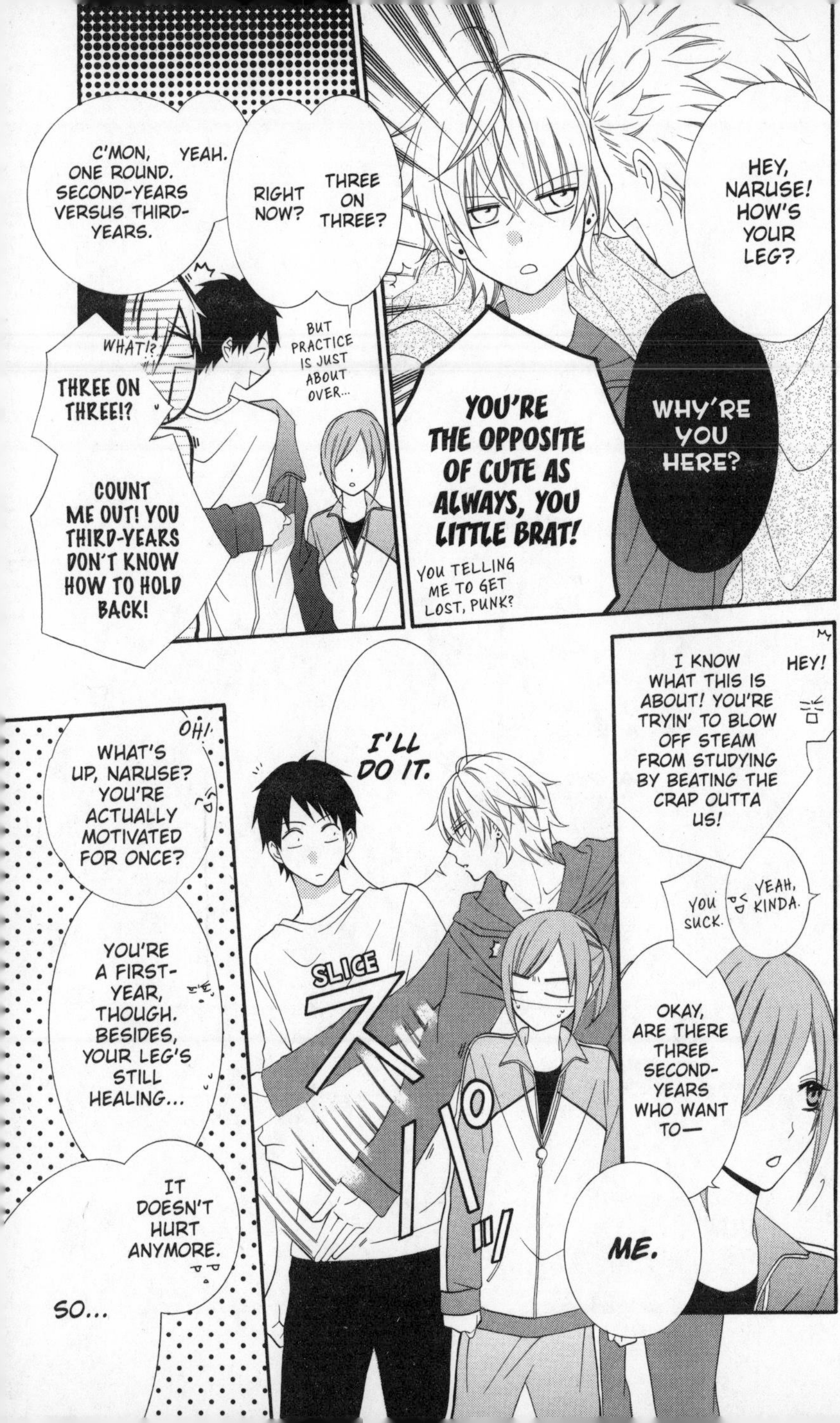
HEY, NARUSE! HOW'S YOUR LEG?
WHY'RE YOU HERE?
YOU'RE THE OPPOSITE OF CUTE AS ALWAYS, YOU LITTLE BRAT!
YOU TELLING ME TO GET LOST, PUNK?
RIGHT NOW? THREE ON THREE?
C'MON, ONE ROUND. SECOND-YEARS VERSUS THIRD-YEARS. YEAH.
BUT PRACTICE IS JUST ABOUT OVER...
WHAT!?
THREE ON THREE!?
COUNT ME OUT! YOU THIRD-YEARS DON'T KNOW HOW TO HOLD BACK!
HEY!
I KNOW WHAT THIS IS ABOUT! YOU'RE TRYIN' TO BLOW OFF STEAM FROM STUDYING BY BEATING THE CRAP OUTTA US!
YEAH, KINDA.
YOU SUCK.
OKAY, ARE THERE THREE SECOND-YEARS WHO WANT TO—
ME.
I'LL DO IT.
SLICE
OH!
WHAT'S UP, NARUSE? YOU'RE ACTUALLY MOTIVATED FOR ONCE?
YOU'RE A FIRST-YEAR, THOUGH. BESIDES, YOUR LEG'S STILL HEALING...
IT DOESN'T HURT ANYMORE.
SO...

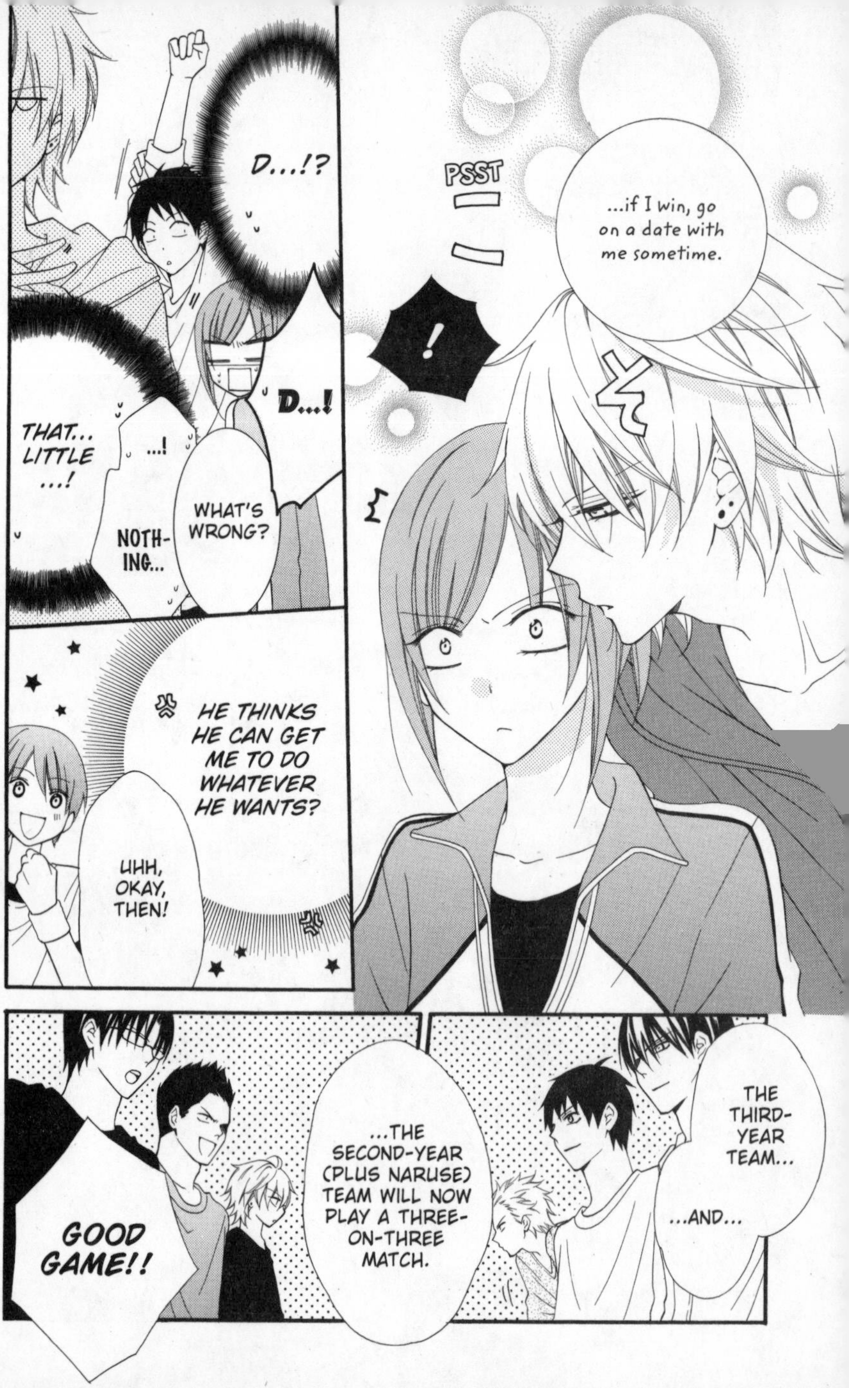
PSST
...if I win, go on a date with me sometime.
!
D...!?
D...!
WHAT'S WRONG?
...!
NOTHING...
THAT... LITTLE ...!
HE THINKS HE CAN GET ME TO DO WHATEVER HE WANTS?
UHH, OKAY, THEN!
THE THIRD-YEAR TEAM...
...AND...
...THE SECOND-YEAR (PLUS NARUSE) TEAM WILL NOW PLAY A THREE-ON-THREE MATCH.
GOOD GAME!!

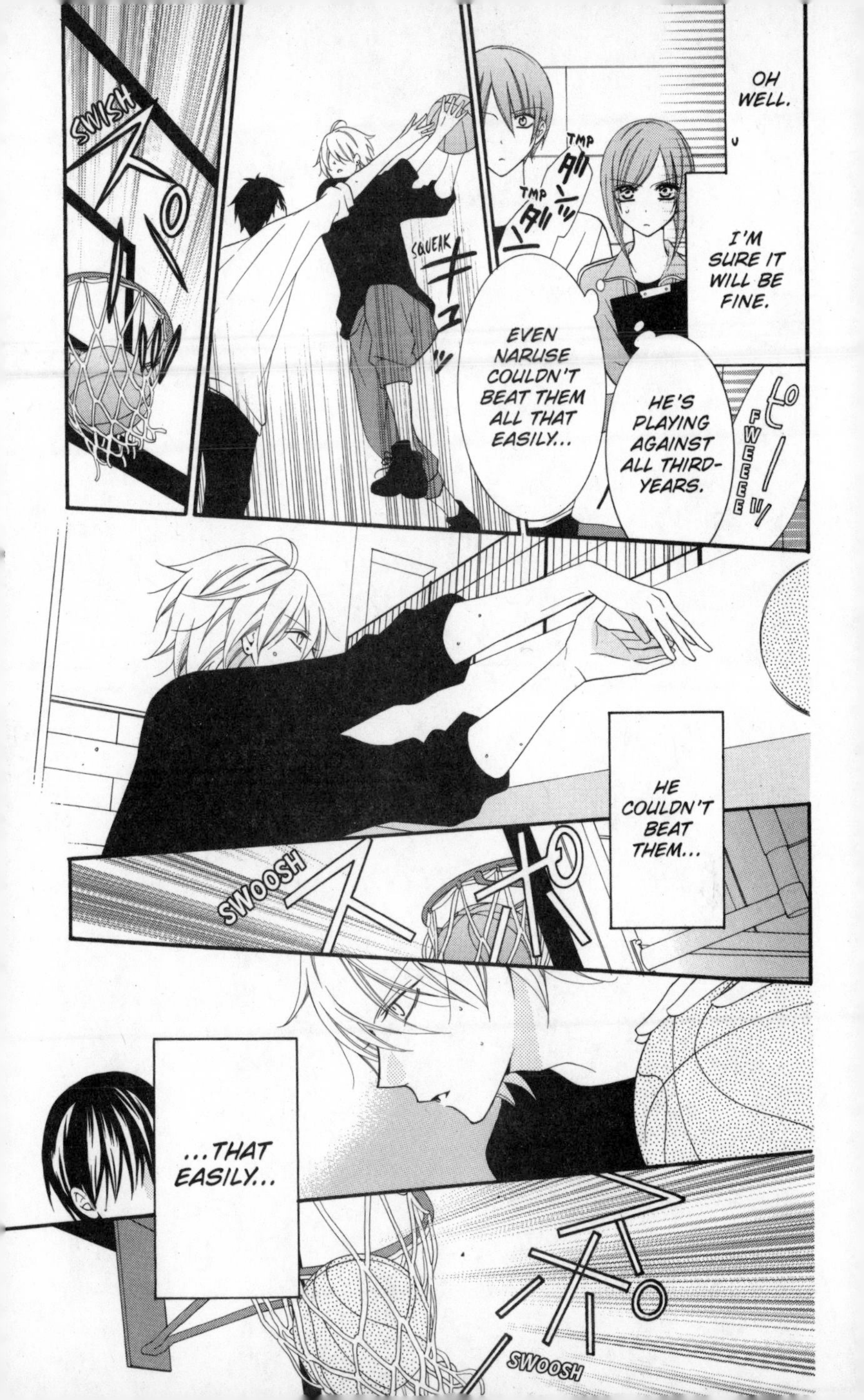
OH WELL.
I'M SURE IT WILL BE FINE.
FWEEEE
HE'S PLAYING AGAINST ALL THIRD-YEARS.
EVEN NARUSE COULDN'T BEAT THEM ALL THAT EASILY...
TMP
TMP
SQUEAK
SWISH
HE COULDN'T BEAT THEM...
SWOOSH
...THAT EASILY...
SWOOSH

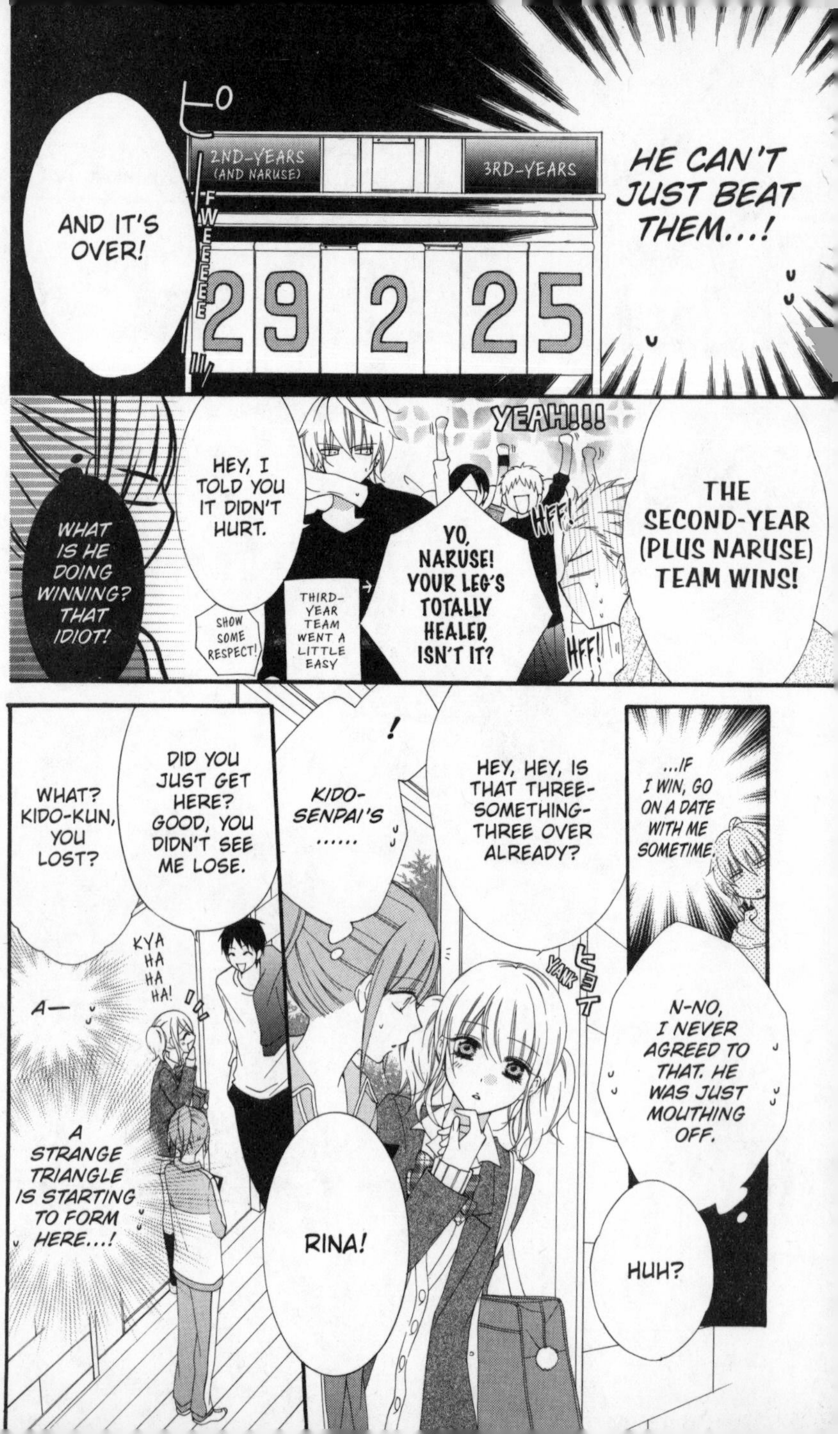
HE CAN'T JUST BEAT THEM...!
2ND-YEARS (AND NARUSE)
3RD-YEARS
29 2 25
FWEEEEE
AND IT'S OVER!
YEAH!!!
THE SECOND-YEAR (PLUS NARUSE) TEAM WINS!
HFF!
HFF!
YO, NARUSE! YOUR LEG'S TOTALLY HEALED, ISN'T IT?
HEY, I TOLD YOU IT DIDN'T HURT.
THIRD-YEAR TEAM WENT A LITTLE EASY
SHOW SOME RESPECT!
WHAT IS HE DOING WINNING? THAT IDIOT!
...IF I WIN, GO ON A DATE WITH ME SOMETIME.
N-NO, I NEVER AGREED TO THAT. HE WAS JUST MOUTHING OFF.
HUH?
HEY, HEY, IS THAT THREE-SOMETHING-THREE OVER ALREADY?
!
KIDO-SENPAI'S ......
YANK
RINA!
DID YOU JUST GET HERE? GOOD, YOU DIDN'T SEE ME LOSE.
WHAT? KIDO-KUN, YOU LOST?
KYA HA HA HA!
A—
A STRANGE TRIANGLE IS STARTING TO FORM HERE...!

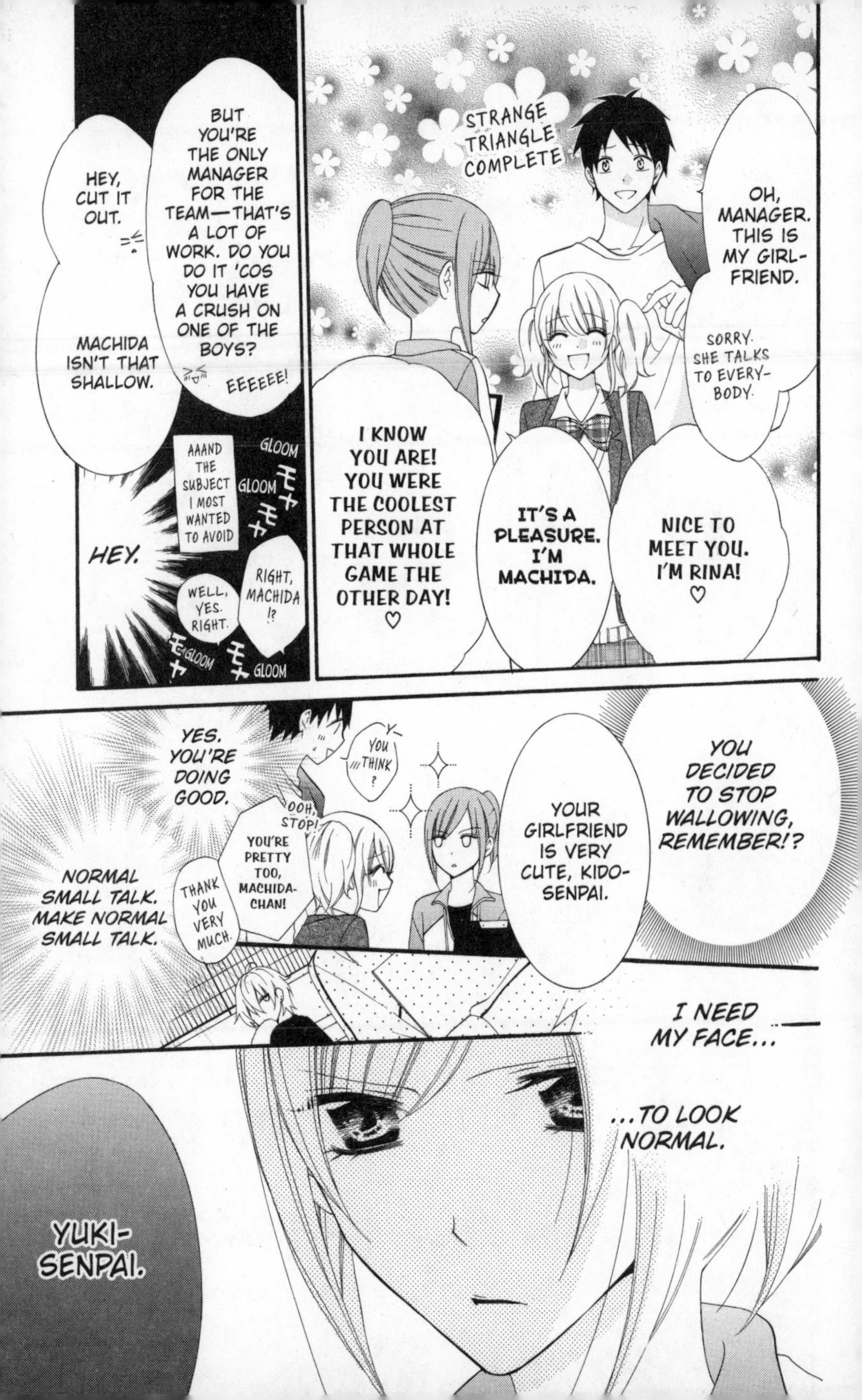
OH, MANAGER. THIS IS MY GIRLFRIEND.
SORRY. SHE TALKS TO EVERYBODY.
STRANGE TRIANGLE COMPLETE
NICE TO MEET YOU. I'M RINA! ♡
IT'S A PLEASURE. I'M MACHIDA.
I KNOW YOU ARE! YOU WERE THE COOLEST PERSON AT THAT WHOLE GAME THE OTHER DAY! ♡
BUT YOU'RE THE ONLY MANAGER FOR THE TEAM—THAT'S A LOT OF WORK. DO YOU DO IT 'COS YOU HAVE A CRUSH ON ONE OF THE BOYS?
EEEEEE!
HEY, CUT IT OUT.
MACHIDA ISN'T THAT SHALLOW.
AAAND THE SUBJECT I MOST WANTED TO AVOID
GLOOM
GLOOM
RIGHT, MACHIDA!?
WELL, YES. RIGHT.
GLOOM
GLOOM
HEY.
YOU DECIDED TO STOP WALLOWING, REMEMBER!?
YOUR GIRLFRIEND IS VERY CUTE, KIDO-SENPAI.
Y—YOU THINK?
OOH, STOP!
YOU'RE PRETTY TOO, MACHIDA-CHAN!
YES. YOU'RE DOING GOOD.
THANK YOU VERY MUCH.
NORMAL SMALL TALK. MAKE NORMAL SMALL TALK.
I NEED MY FACE...
...TO LOOK NORMAL.
YUKI-SENPAI.

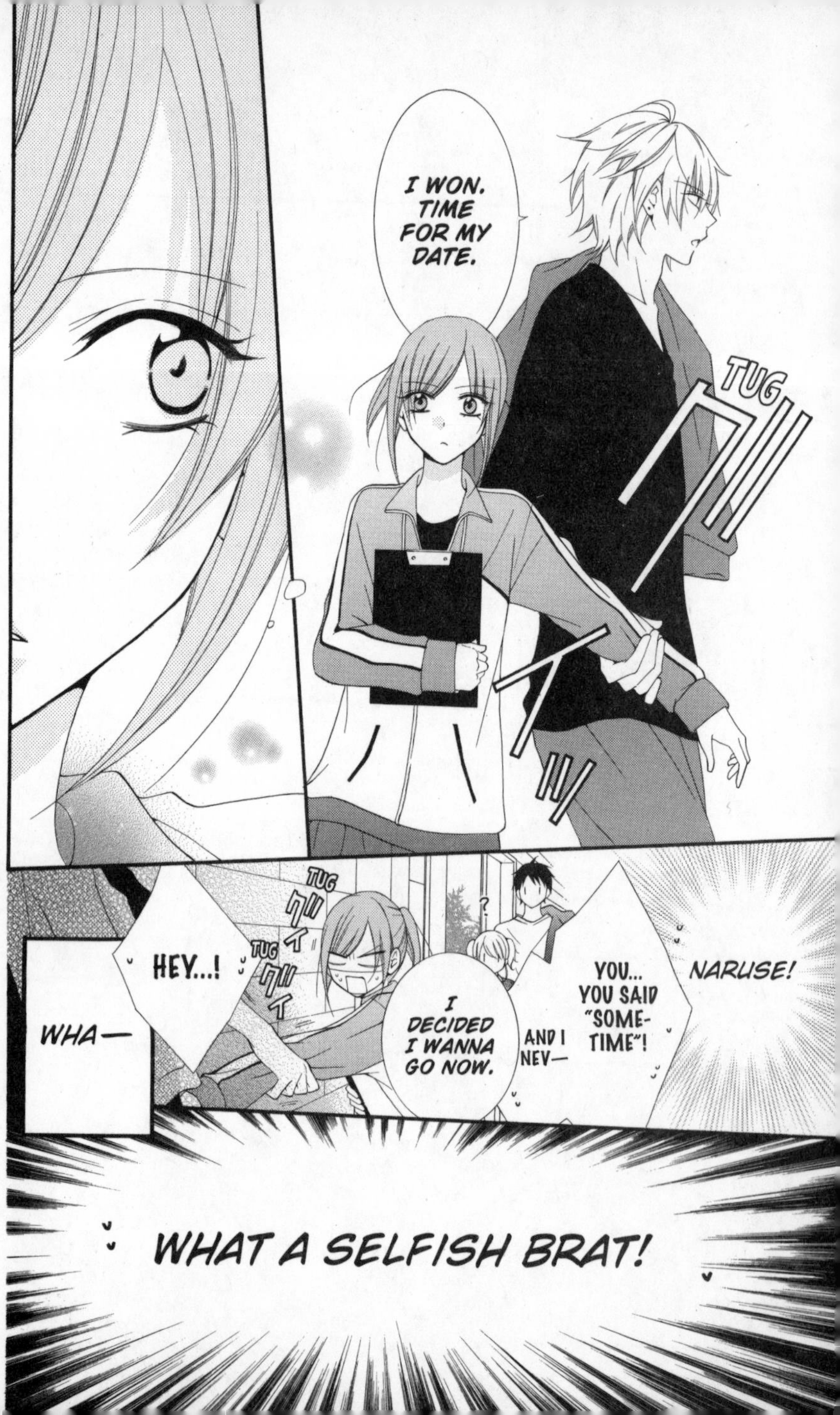

I WON. TIME FOR MY DATE.
TUG
NARUSE!
YOU... YOU SAID "SOME-TIME"!
AND I NEV—
I DECIDED I WANNA GO NOW.
TUG
TUG
HEY...!
WHA—
WHAT A SELFISH BRAT!

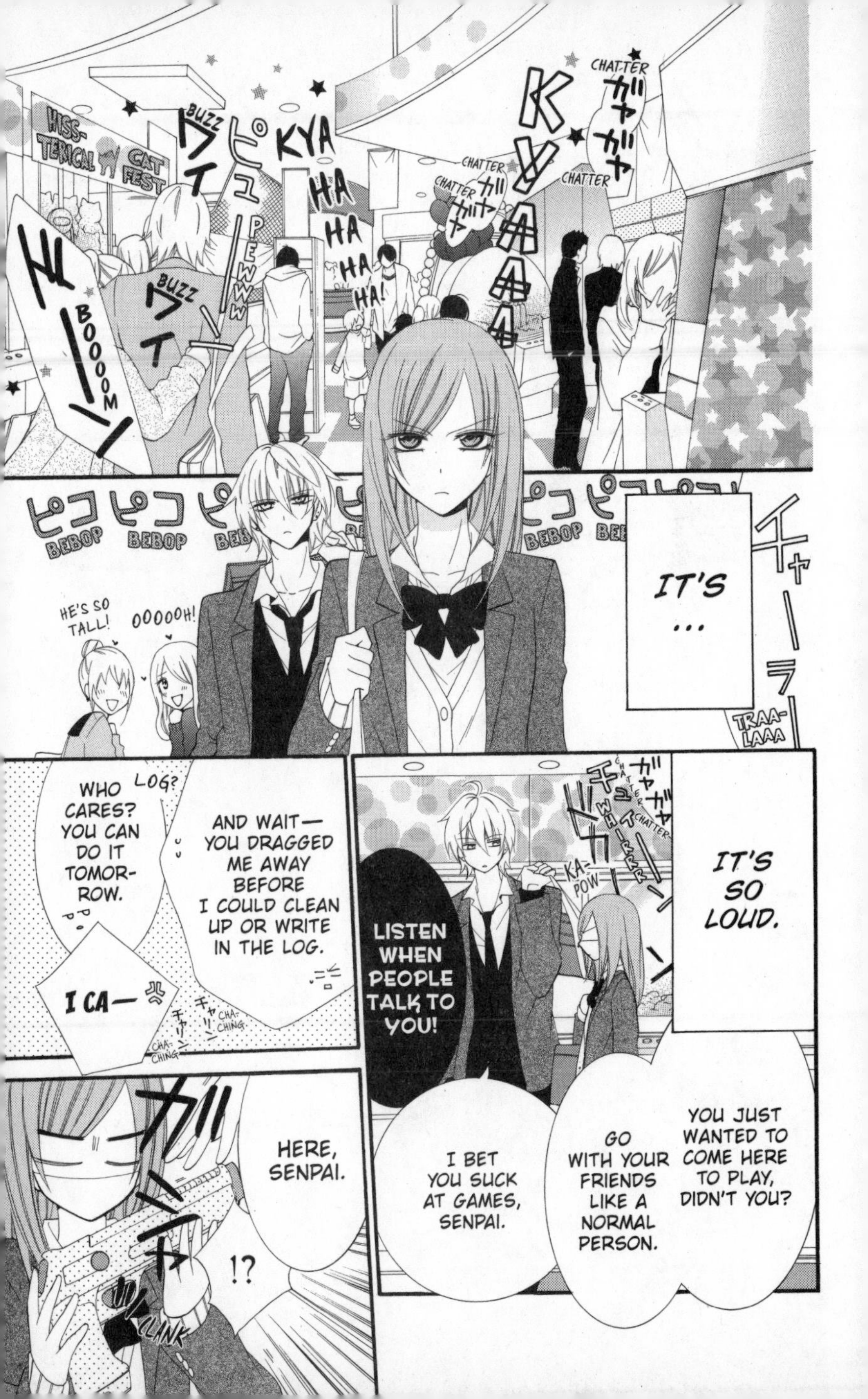
CHATTER
KYAAAA
CHATTER
CHATTER
CHATTER
HA
HA
HA
HA!
KYA
BUZZ
PEWWW
HISS-TERICAL CAT FEST
BUZZ
BOOOOOOM
IT'S ...
TRAA-LAAA
BEBOP BEBOP BEBOP
HE'S SO TALL!
OOOOOH!
IT'S SO LOUD.
CHATTER
WHIRRR
CHATTER
KA-POW
LISTEN WHEN PEOPLE TALK TO YOU!
AND WAIT— YOU DRAGGED ME AWAY BEFORE I COULD CLEAN UP OR WRITE IN THE LOG.
LOG?
WHO CARES? YOU CAN DO IT TOMORROW.
I CA—
CHA-CHING
CHA-CHING
YOU JUST WANTED TO COME HERE TO PLAY, DIDN'T YOU?
GO WITH YOUR FRIENDS LIKE A NORMAL PERSON.
I BET YOU SUCK AT GAMES, SENPAI.
HERE, SENPAI.
!?
CLANK

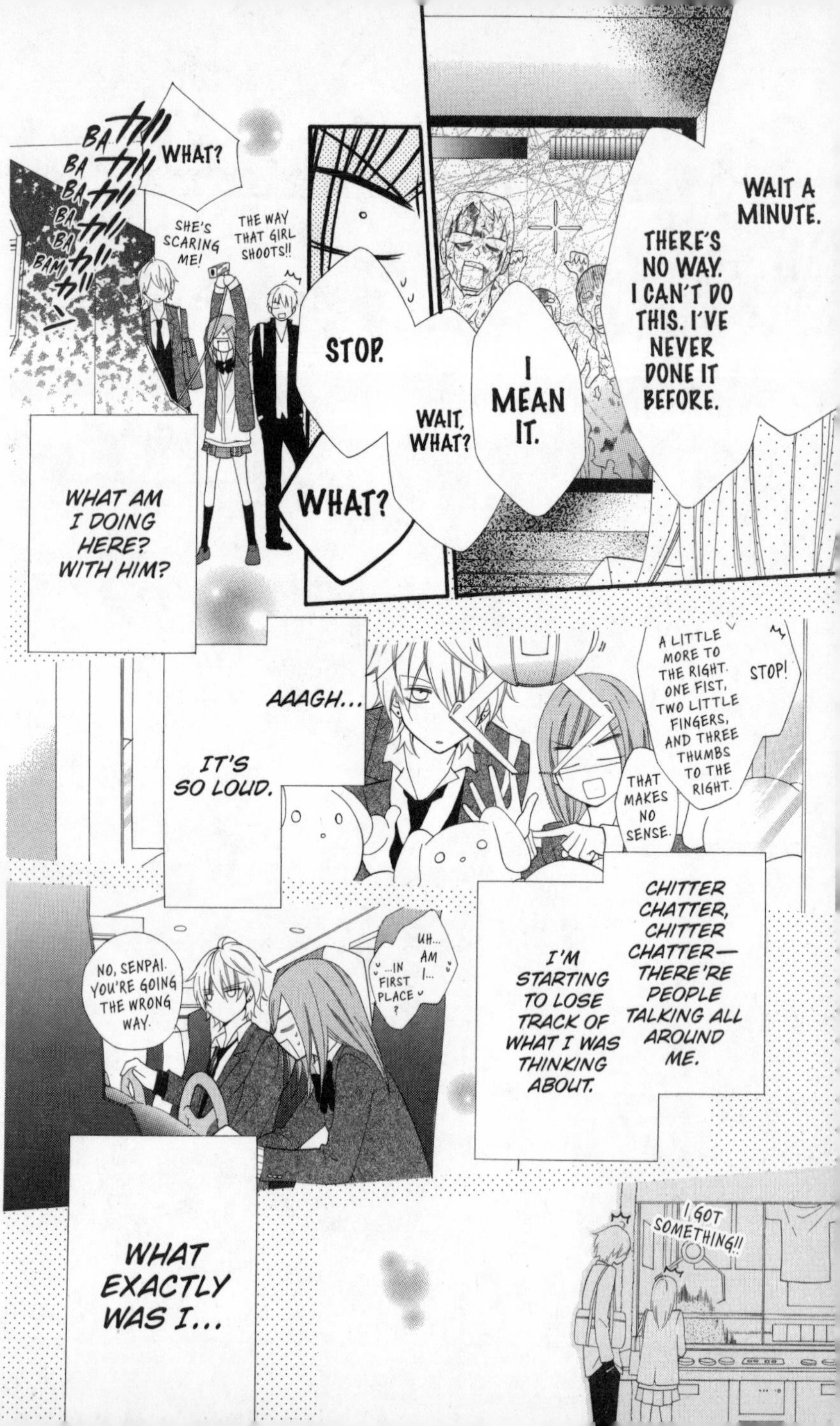
WAIT A MINUTE.
THERE'S NO WAY. I CAN'T DO THIS. I'VE NEVER DONE IT BEFORE.
I MEAN IT.
WAIT, WHAT?
STOP.
WHAT?
WHAT?
THE WAY THAT GIRL SHOOTS!!
SHE'S SCARING ME!
BA BA BA BA BA BAM
WHAT AM I DOING HERE? WITH HIM?
A LITTLE MORE TO THE RIGHT. ONE FIST, TWO LITTLE FINGERS, AND THREE THUMBS TO THE RIGHT.
STOP!
THAT MAKES NO SENSE.
AAAGH...
IT'S SO LOUD.
CHITTER CHATTER, CHITTER CHATTER—THERE'RE PEOPLE TALKING ALL AROUND ME.
I'M STARTING TO LOSE TRACK OF WHAT I WAS THINKING ABOUT.
UH... AM I...
...IN FIRST PLACE?
NO, SENPAI. YOU'RE GOING THE WRONG WAY.
I GOT SOMETHING!!
WHAT EXACTLY WAS I...

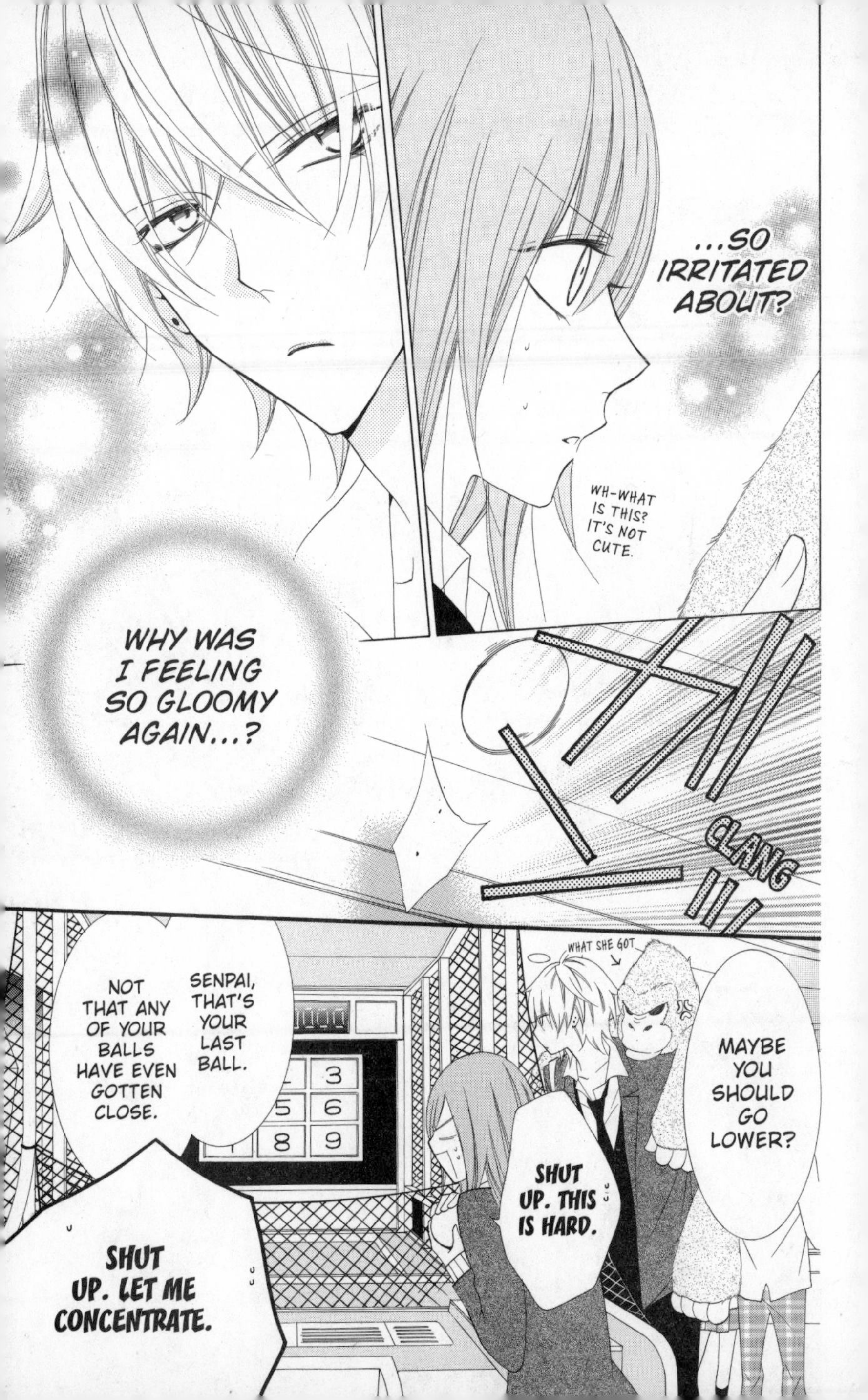
...SO IRRITATED ABOUT?
WH-WHAT IS THIS? IT'S NOT CUTE.
CLANG
WHY WAS I FEELING SO GLOOMY AGAIN...?
WHAT SHE GOT
MAYBE YOU SHOULD GO LOWER?
SHUT UP. THIS IS HARD.
SENPAI, THAT'S YOUR LAST BALL.
NOT THAT ANY OF YOUR BALLS HAVE EVEN GOTTEN CLOSE.
SHUT UP. LET ME CONCENTRATE.

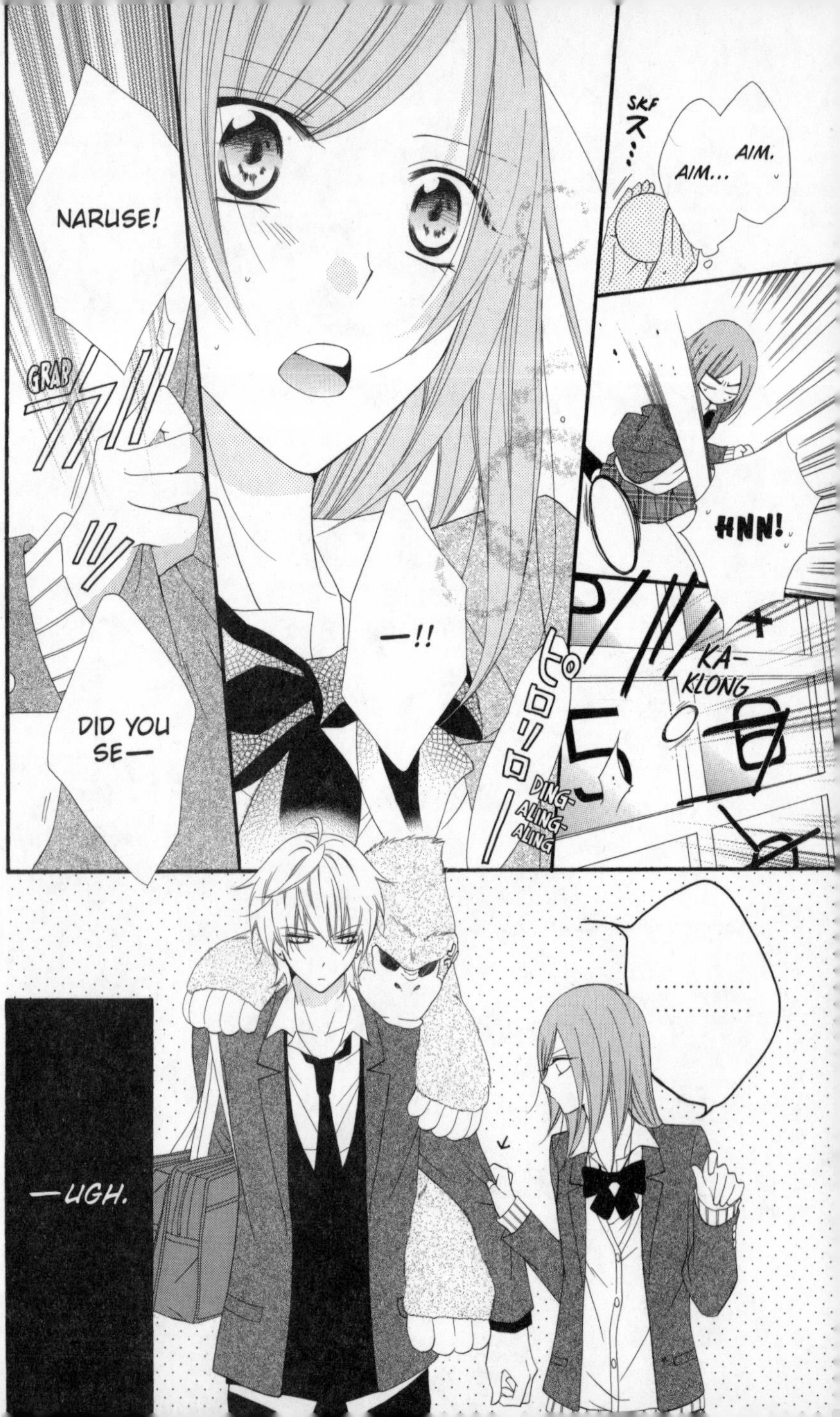

SKF
AIM. AIM...
HNN!
KA-KLONG
DING-ALING-ALING
—!!
NARUSE!
GRAB
DID YOU SE—
....
—UGH.

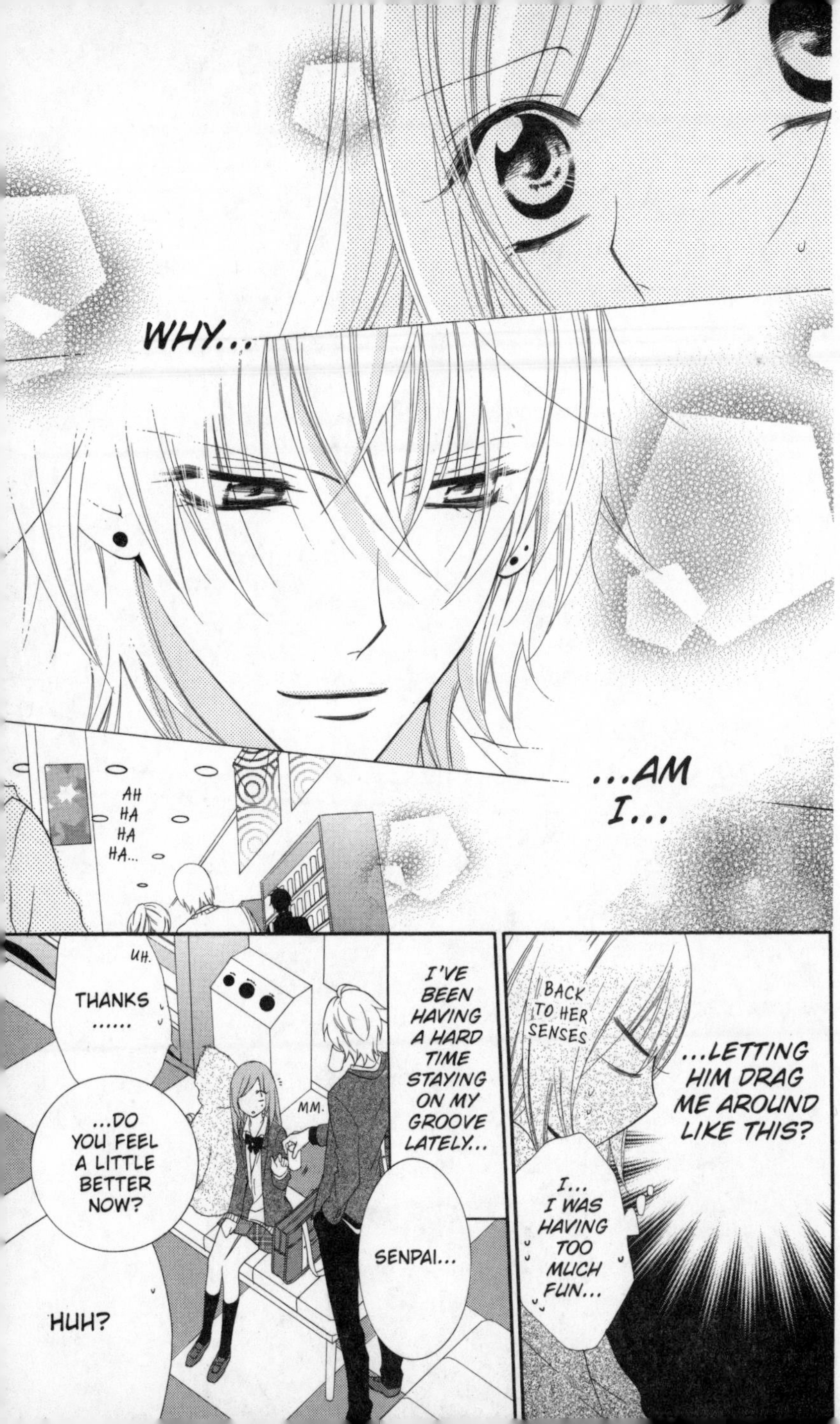
WHY...
...AM I...
AH HA HA HA...
BACK TO HER SENSES
...LETTING HIM DRAG ME AROUND LIKE THIS?
I... I WAS HAVING TOO MUCH FUN...
I'VE BEEN HAVING A HARD TIME STAYING ON MY GROOVE LATELY...
UH. THANKS......
MM.
...DO YOU FEEL A LITTLE BETTER NOW?
SENPAI...
HUH?

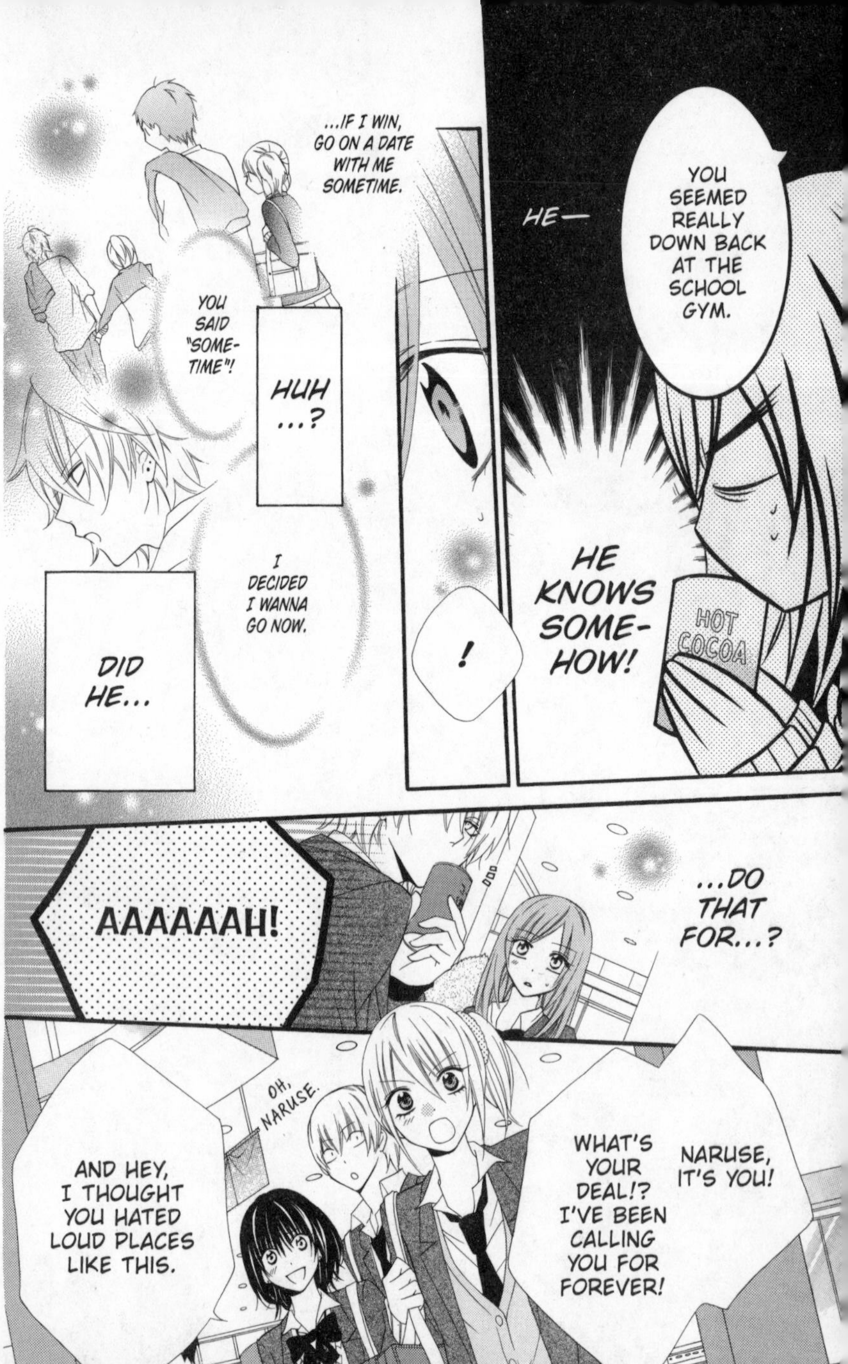
YOU SEEMED REALLY DOWN BACK AT THE SCHOOL GYM.
HE—
HE KNOWS SOME-HOW!
HOT COCOA
!
...IF I WIN, GO ON A DATE WITH ME SOMETIME.
HUH ...?
YOU SAID "SOME-TIME"!
I DECIDED I WANNA GO NOW.
DID HE...
...DO THAT FOR...?
AAAAAAH!
NARUSE, IT'S YOU!
WHAT'S YOUR DEAL!? I'VE BEEN CALLING YOU FOR FOREVER!
OH, NARUSE.
AND HEY, I THOUGHT YOU HATED LOUD PLACES LIKE THIS.

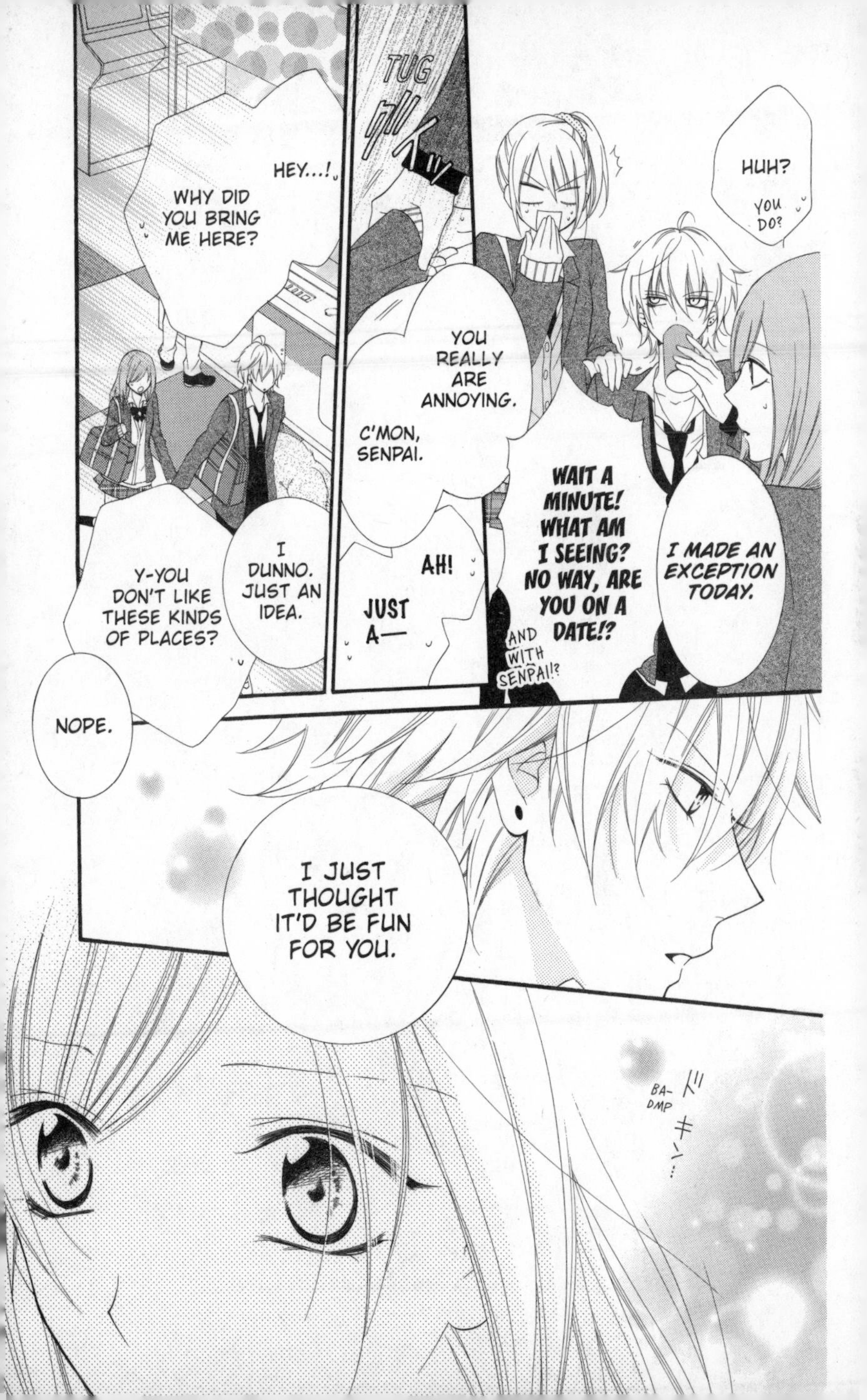
HUH?
YOU DO?
WAIT A MINUTE! WHAT AM I SEEING? NO WAY, ARE YOU ON A DATE!?
AND WITH SENPAI!?
I MADE AN EXCEPTION TODAY.
TUG
YOU REALLY ARE ANNOYING.
C'MON, SENPAI.
AH!
JUST A—
HEY...!
WHY DID YOU BRING ME HERE?
I DUNNO. JUST AN IDEA.
Y-YOU DON'T LIKE THESE KINDS OF PLACES?
NOPE.
I JUST THOUGHT IT'D BE FUN FOR YOU.
BA-DMP

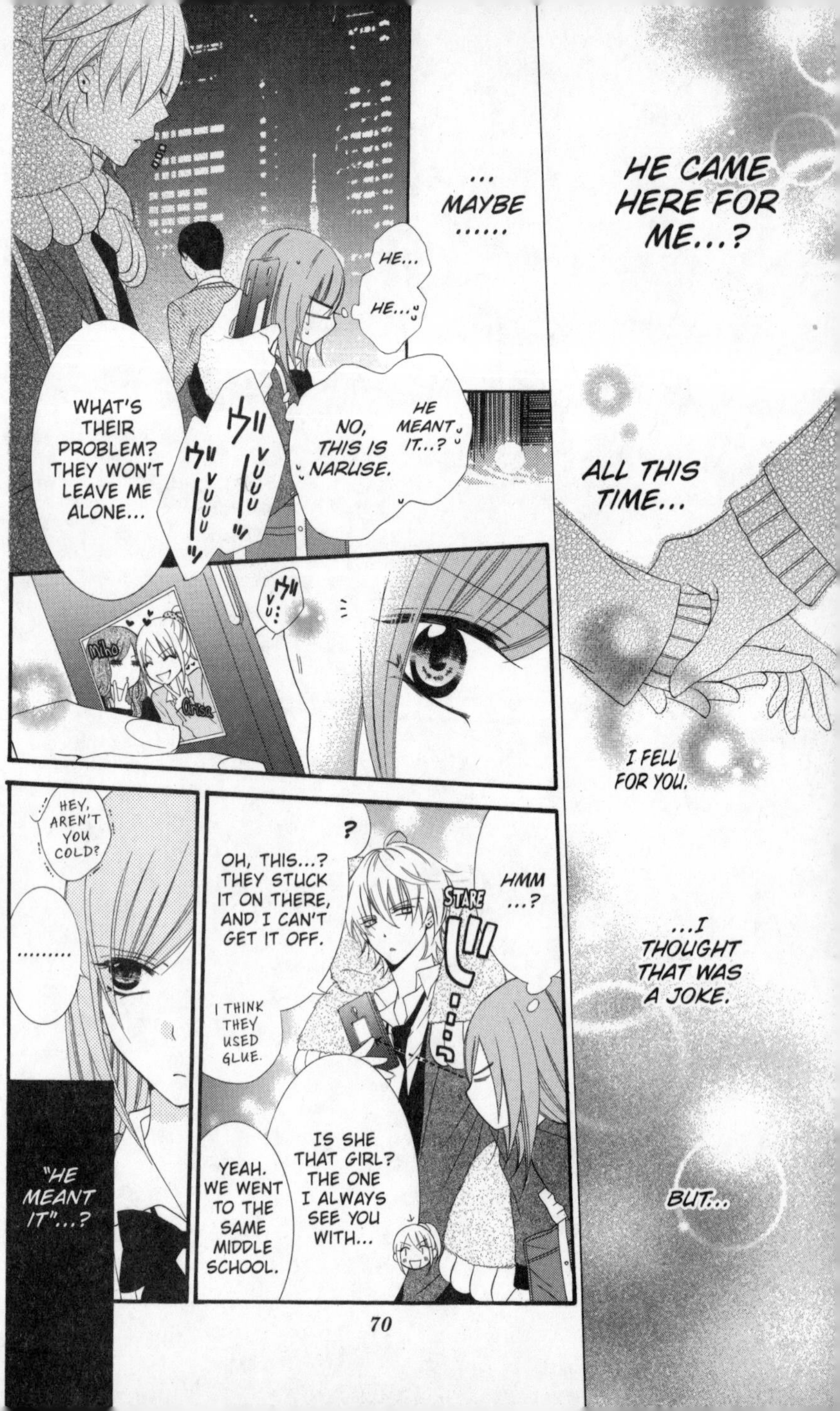
HE CAME HERE FOR ME...?
ALL THIS TIME...
I FELL FOR YOU.
...I THOUGHT THAT WAS A JOKE.
BUT...
... MAYBE ......
HE...
HE...
HE MEANT IT...?
NO, THIS IS NARUSE.
ヴーッ VUUU
ヴーッ VUUU
WHAT'S THEIR PROBLEM? THEY WON'T LEAVE ME ALONE...
ヴ VU
Miho
Arisa
HMM ...?
STARE
?
OH, THIS...? THEY STUCK IT ON THERE, AND I CAN'T GET IT OFF.
I THINK THEY USED GLUE.
IS SHE THAT GIRL? THE ONE I ALWAYS SEE YOU WITH...
YEAH. WE WENT TO THE SAME MIDDLE SCHOOL.
HEY, AREN'T YOU COLD?
....
"HE MEANT IT"...?

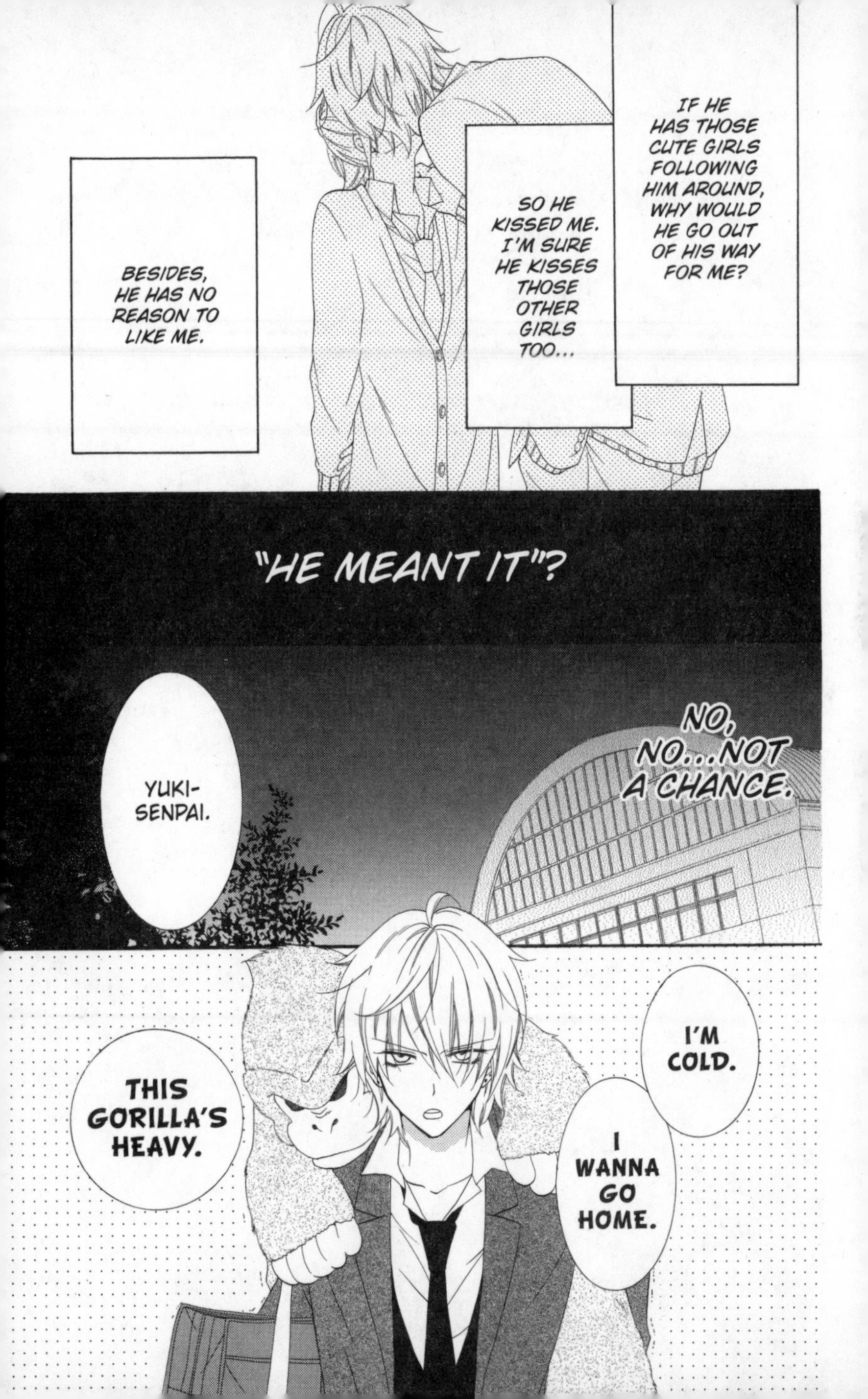
IF HE HAS THOSE CUTE GIRLS FOLLOWING HIM AROUND, WHY WOULD HE GO OUT OF HIS WAY FOR ME?
SO HE KISSED ME. I'M SURE HE KISSES THOSE OTHER GIRLS TOO...
BESIDES, HE HAS NO REASON TO LIKE ME.
"HE MEANT IT"?
NO, NO...NOT A CHANCE.
YUKI-SENPAI.
I'M COLD.
I WANNA GO HOME.
THIS GORILLA'S HEAVY.

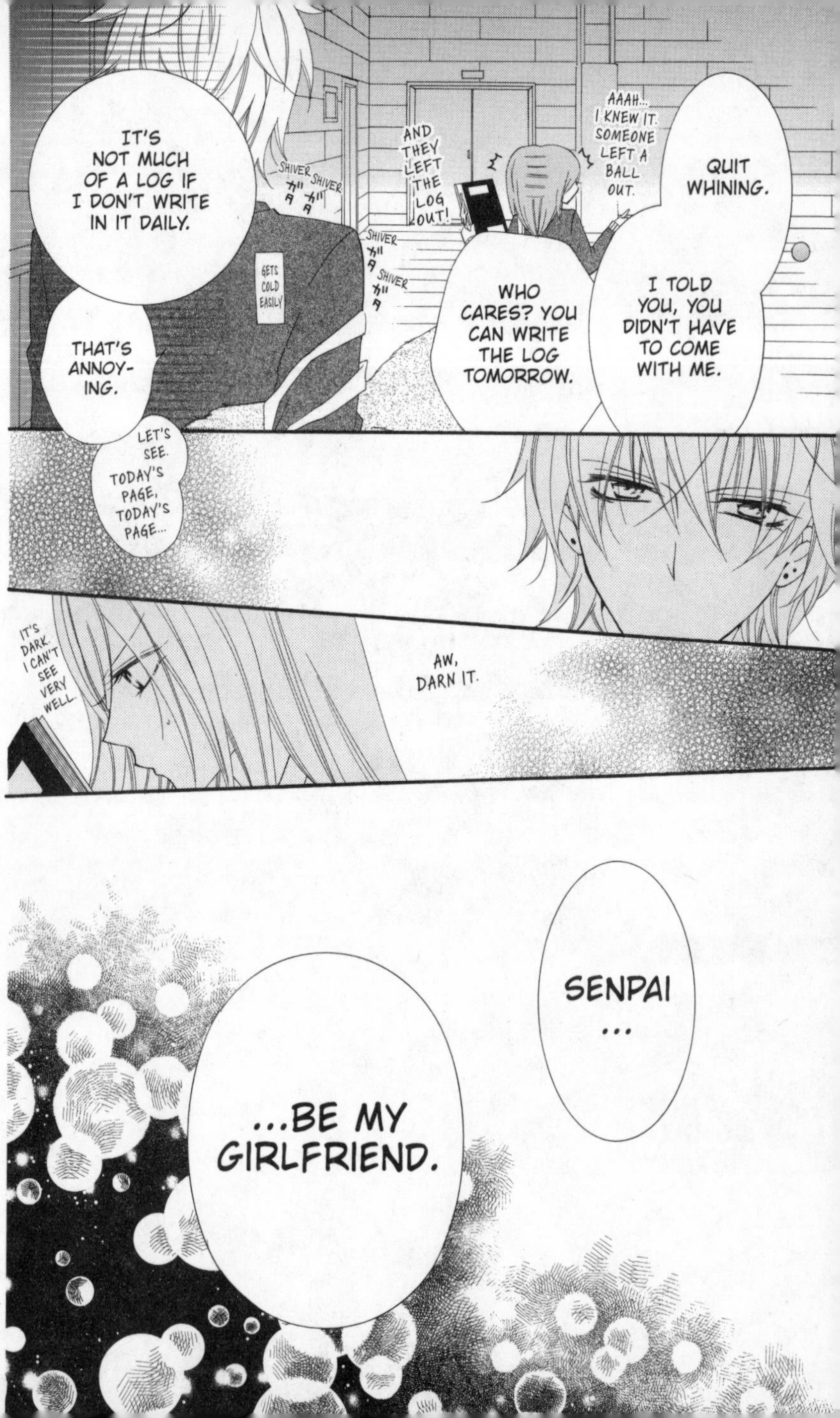
AAAH... I KNEW IT. SOMEONE LEFT A BALL OUT.
QUIT WHINING.
I TOLD YOU, YOU DIDN'T HAVE TO COME WITH ME.
AND THEY LEFT THE LOG OUT!
WHO CARES? YOU CAN WRITE THE LOG TOMORROW.
SHIVER SHIVER
SHIVER SHIVER
IT'S NOT MUCH OF A LOG IF I DON'T WRITE IN IT DAILY.
GETS COLD EASILY
THAT'S ANNOY-ING.
LET'S SEE. TODAY'S PAGE, TODAY'S PAGE...
AW, DARN IT.
IT'S DARK. I CAN'T SEE VERY WELL.
SENPAI ...
...BE MY GIRLFRIEND.

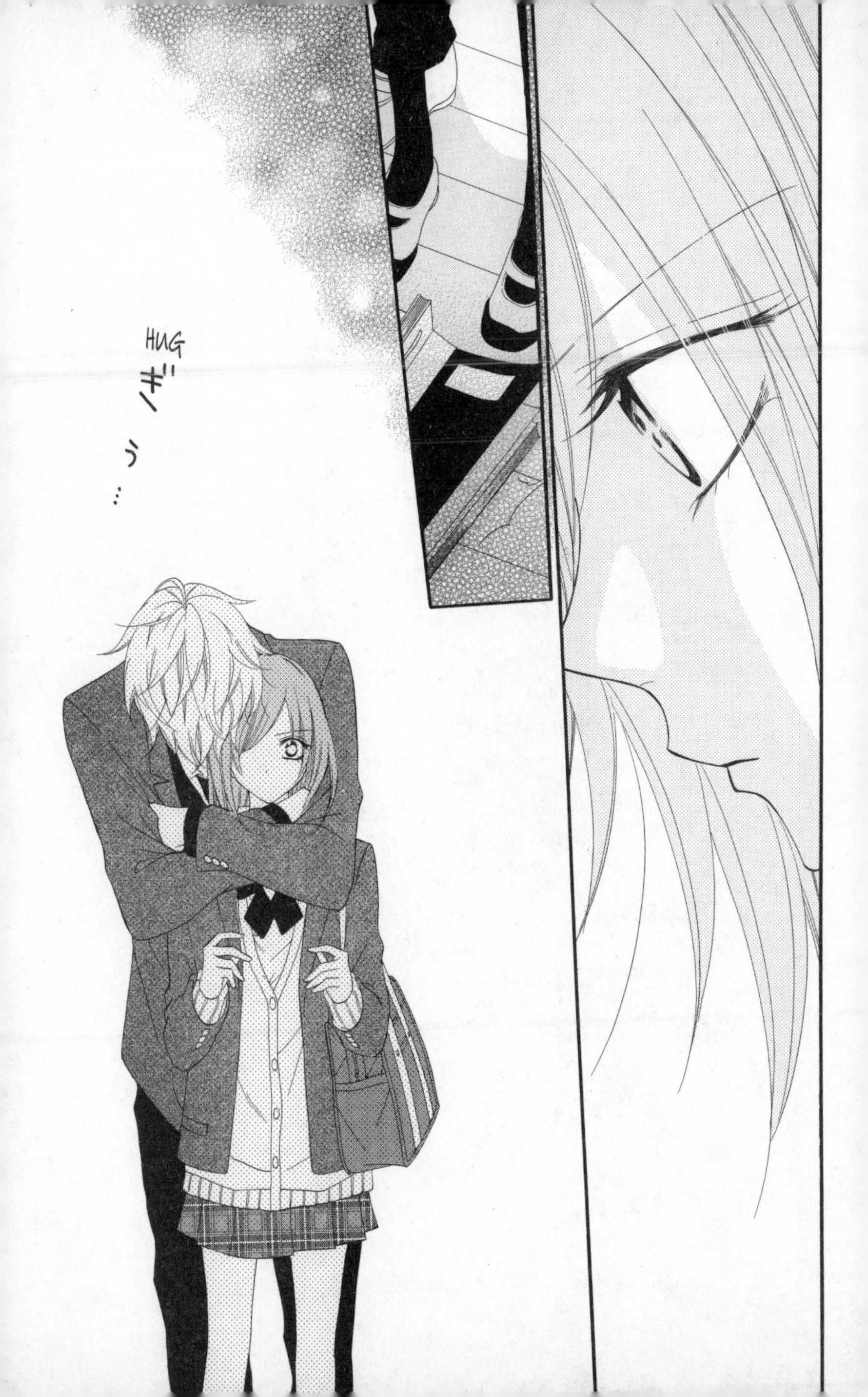
HUG
ギゥ…

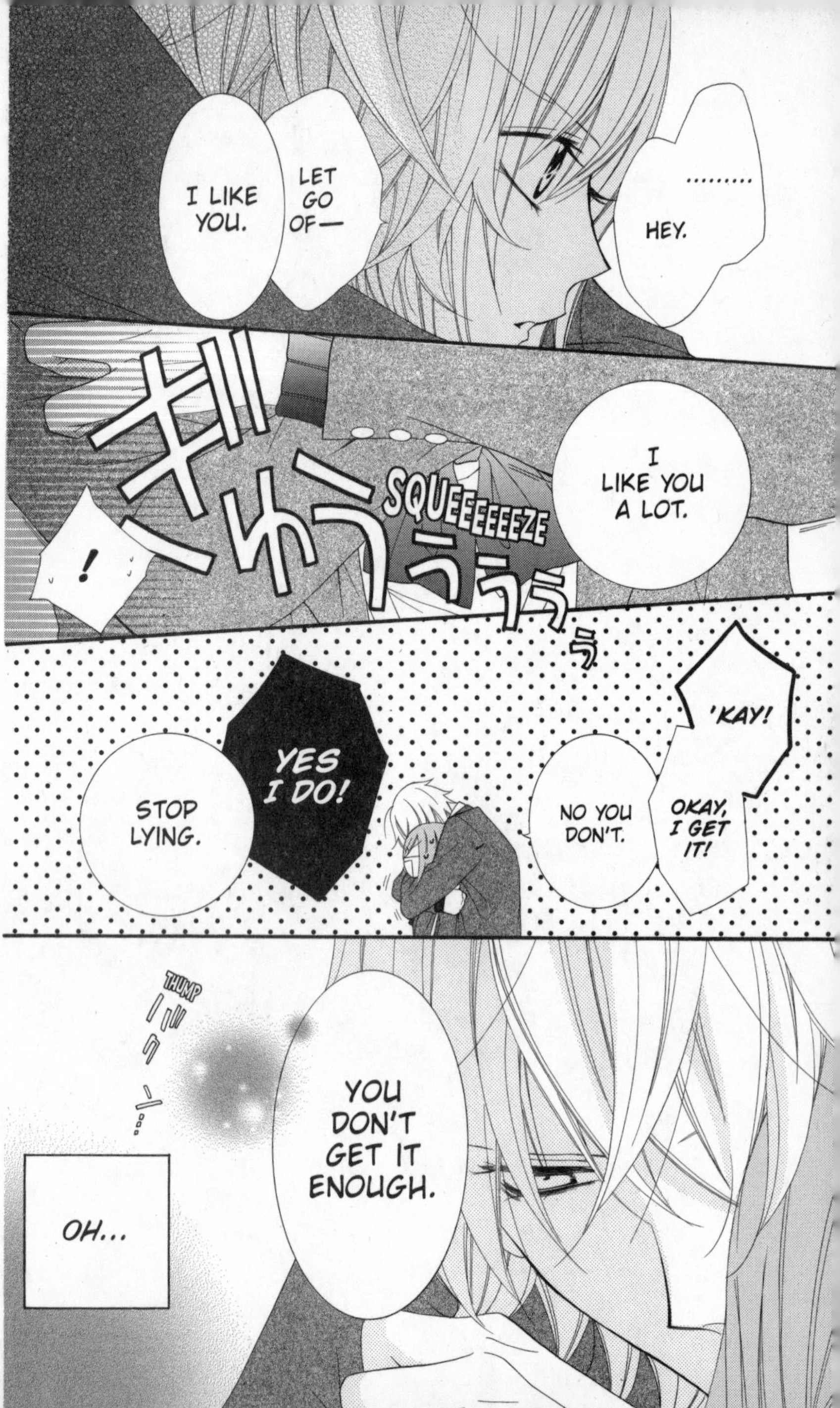
....
HEY.
LET GO OF—
I LIKE YOU.
I LIKE YOU A LOT.
SQUEEEEEEZE
!
'KAY!
OKAY, I GET IT!
NO YOU DON'T.
YES I DO!
STOP LYING.
YOU DON'T GET IT ENOUGH.
THUMP
OH...

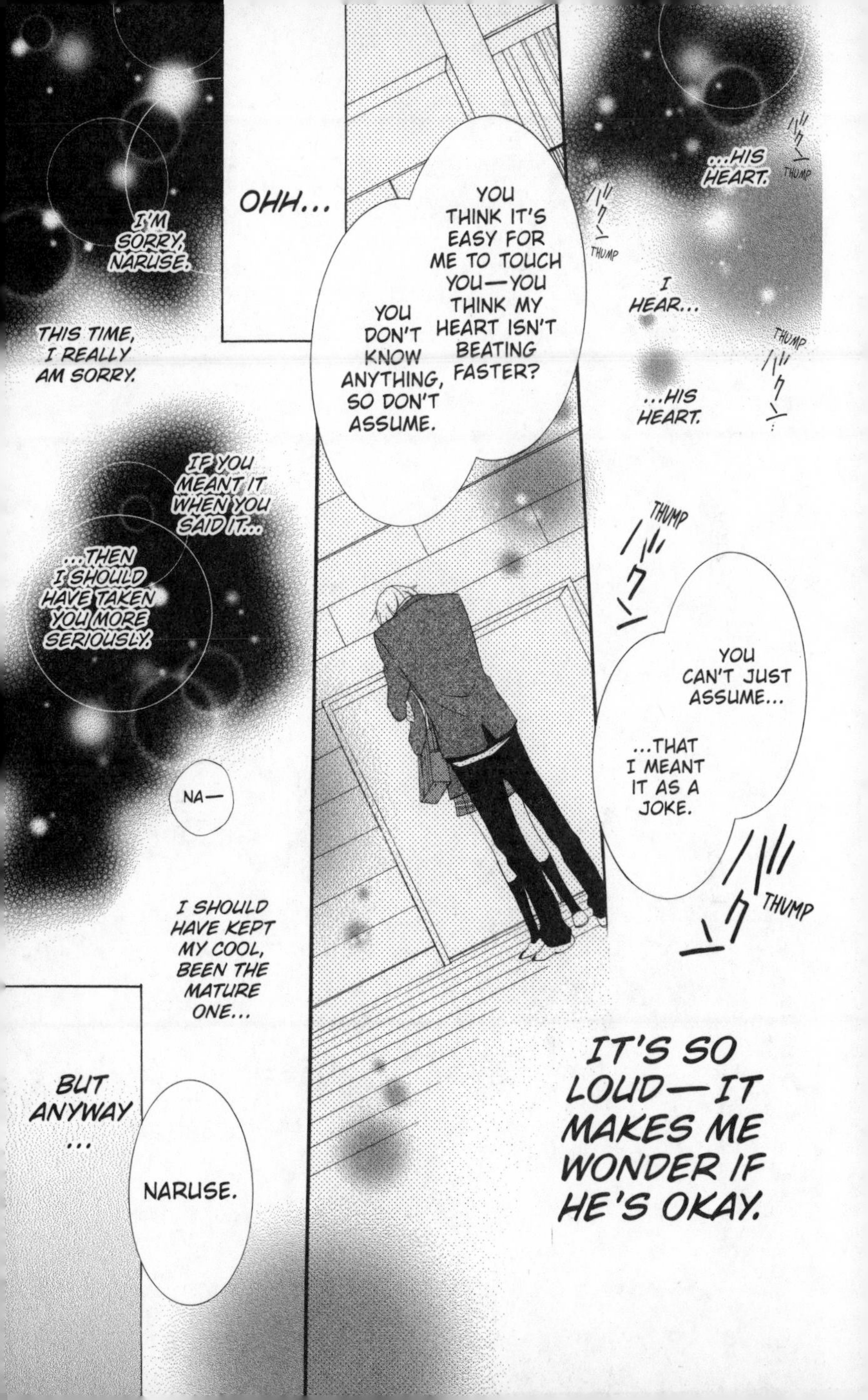

...HIS HEART.
THUMP
THUMP
I HEAR...
THUMP
...HIS HEART.
THUMP
YOU CAN'T JUST ASSUME...
...THAT I MEANT IT AS A JOKE.
THUMP
IT'S SO LOUD—IT MAKES ME WONDER IF HE'S OKAY.
YOU THINK IT'S EASY FOR ME TO TOUCH YOU—YOU THINK MY HEART ISN'T BEATING FASTER?
YOU DON'T KNOW ANYTHING, SO DON'T ASSUME.
OHH...
I'M SORRY, NARUSE.
THIS TIME, I REALLY AM SORRY.
IF YOU MEANT IT WHEN YOU SAID IT...
...THEN I SHOULD HAVE TAKEN YOU MORE SERIOUSLY.
NA—
I SHOULD HAVE KEPT MY COOL, BEEN THE MATURE ONE...
BUT ANYWAY...
NARUSE.

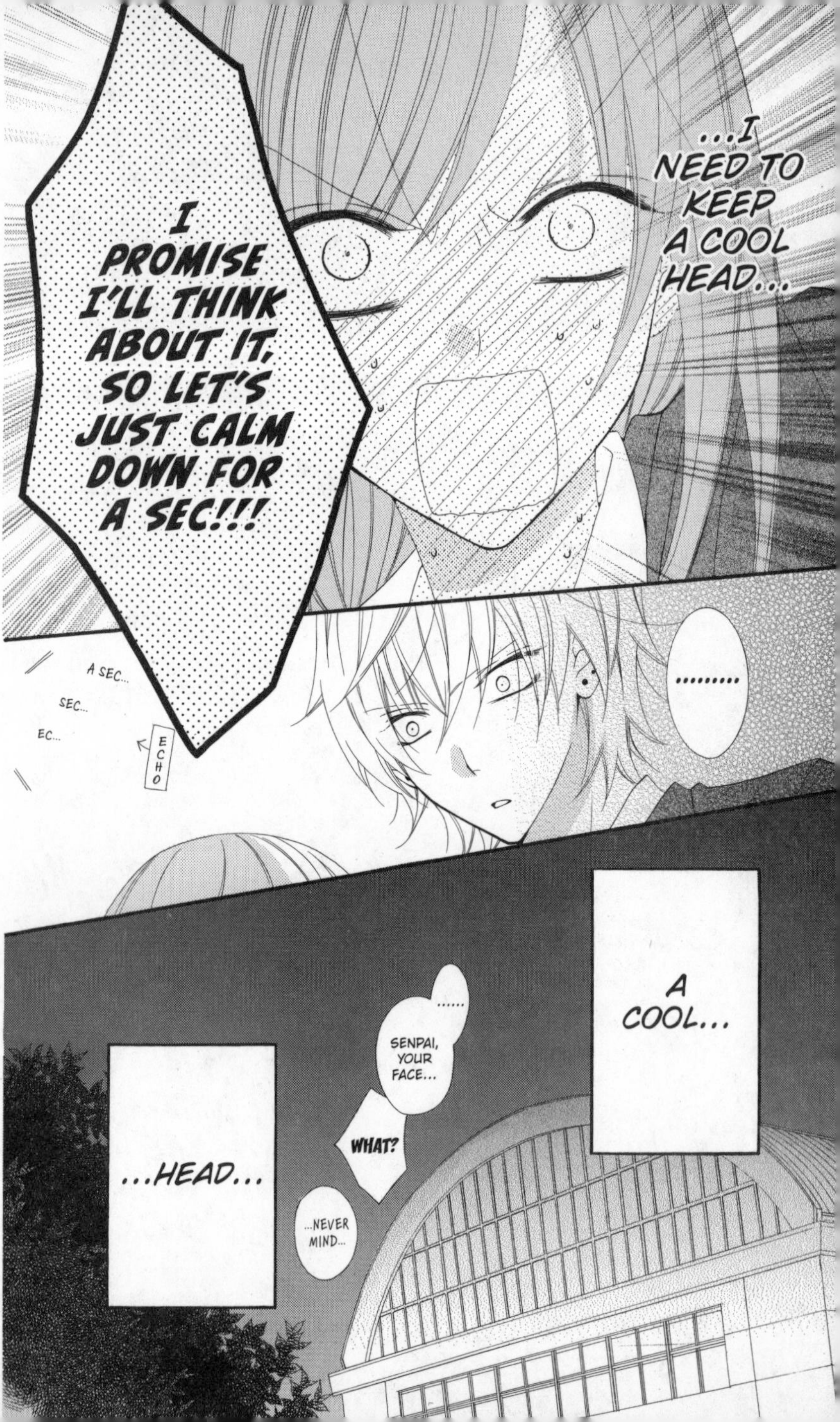
...I NEED TO KEEP A COOL HEAD...
I PROMISE I'LL THINK ABOUT IT, SO LET'S JUST CALM DOWN FOR A SEC!!!
....
A SEC...
SEC...
EC...
ECHO
A COOL...
......
SENPAI, YOUR FACE...
WHAT?
...NEVER MIND...
...HEAD...

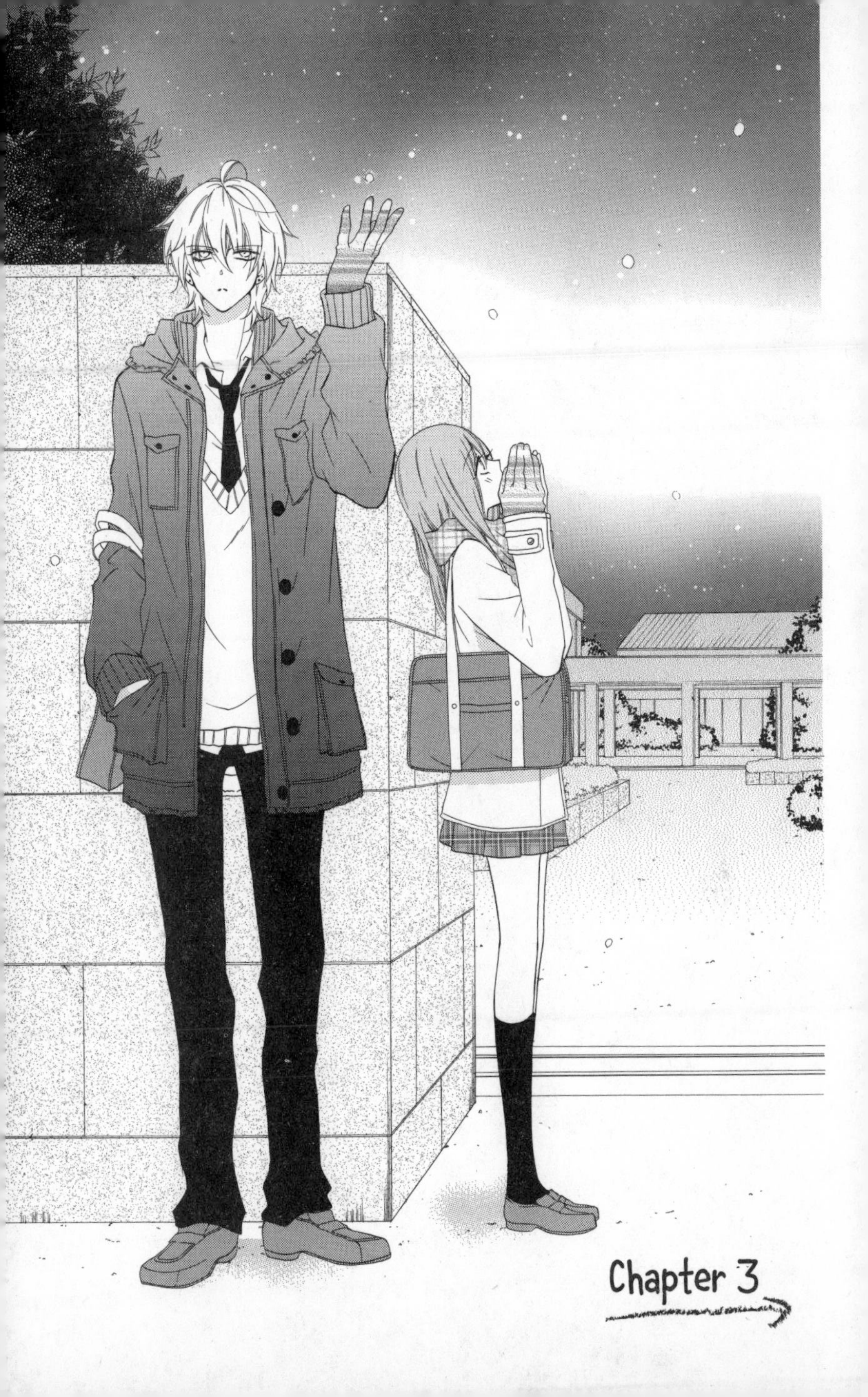
Chapter 3

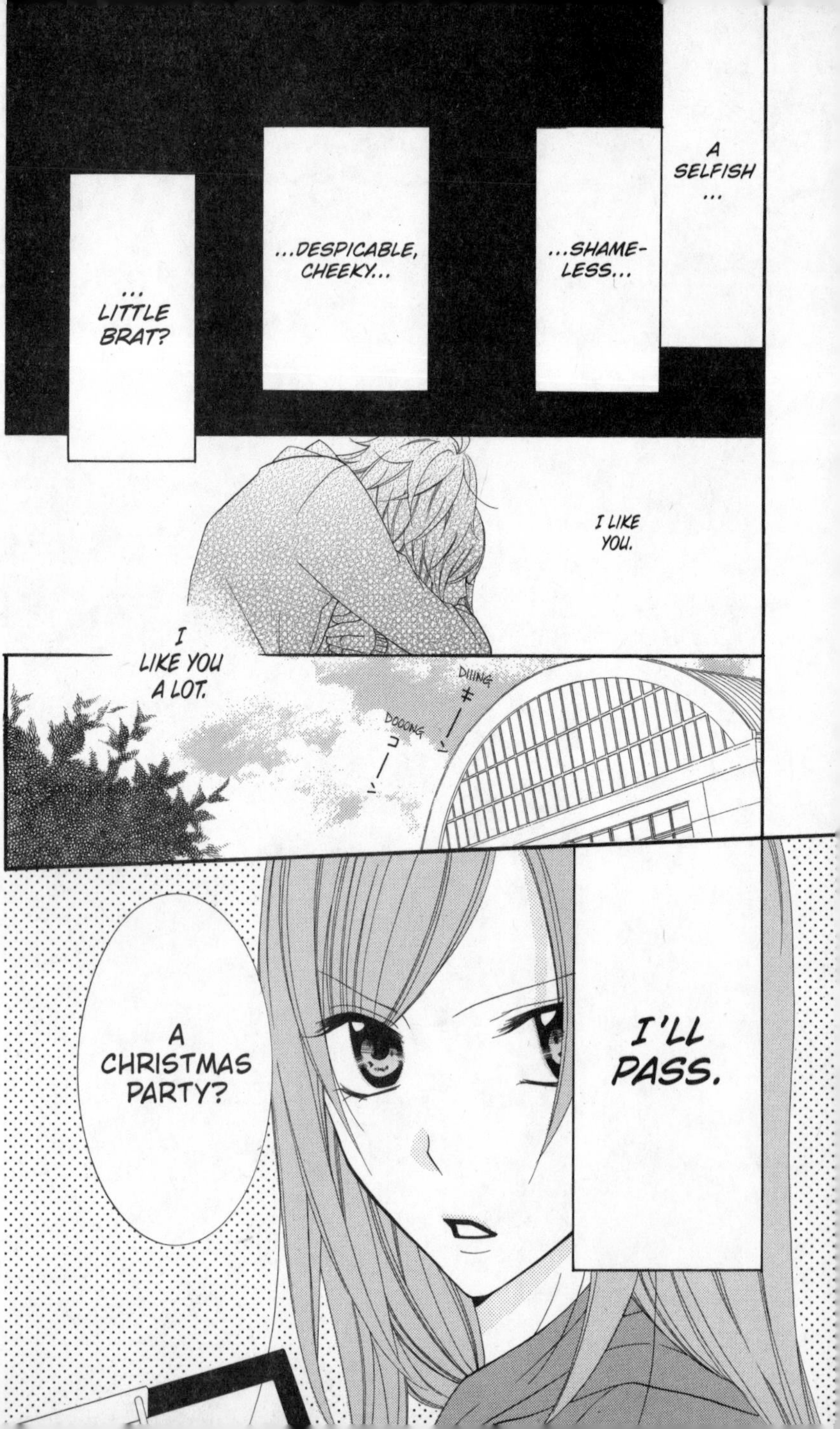
A SELFISH ...
...SHAME-LESS...
...DESPICABLE, CHEEKY...
... LITTLE BRAT?
I LIKE YOU.
I LIKE YOU A LOT.
DIIING
DOOONG
I'LL PASS.
A CHRISTMAS PARTY?

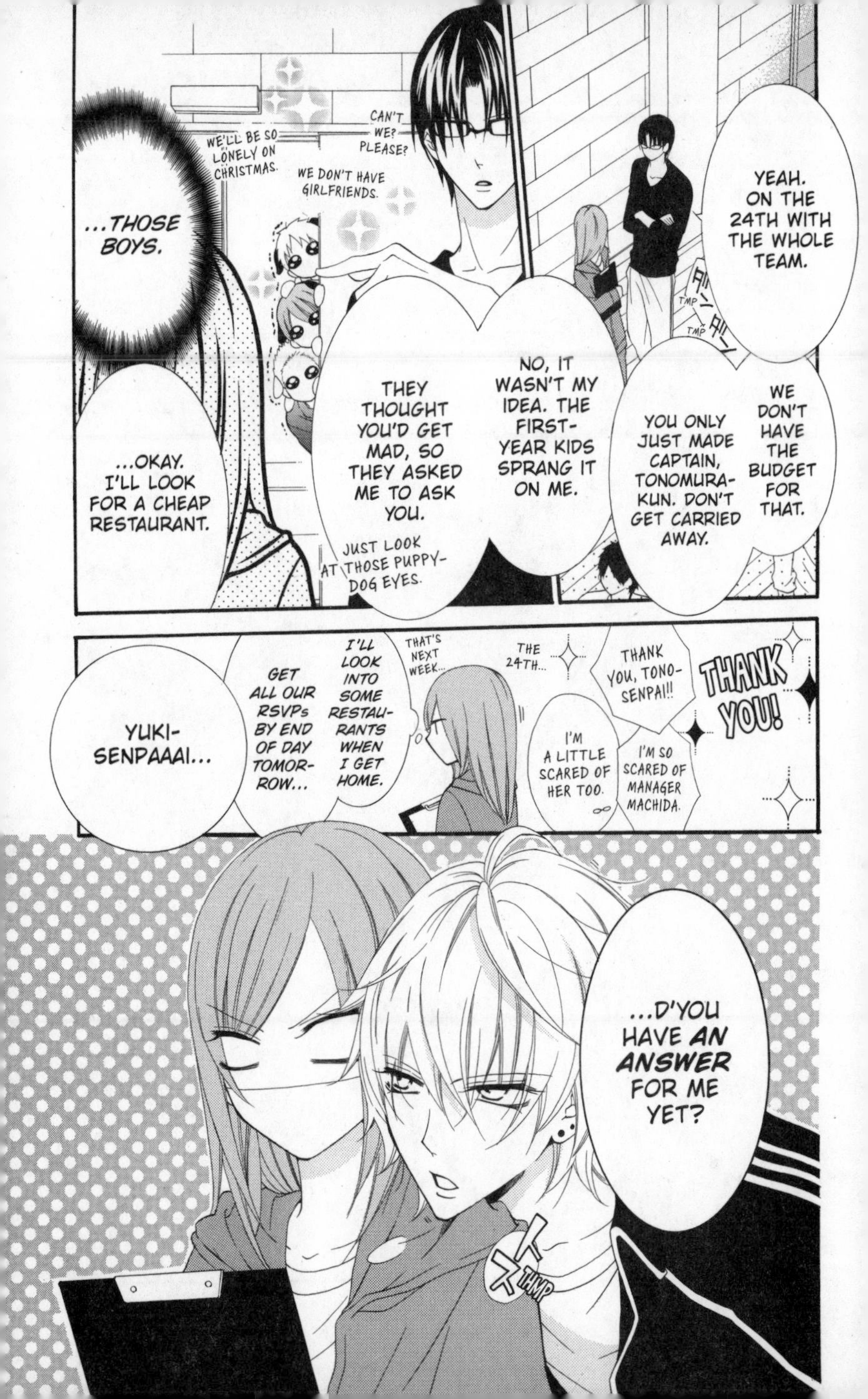
YEAH. ON THE 24TH WITH THE WHOLE TEAM.
TMP
TMP
WE DON'T HAVE THE BUDGET FOR THAT.
YOU ONLY JUST MADE CAPTAIN, TONOMURA-KUN. DON'T GET CARRIED AWAY.
NO, IT WASN'T MY IDEA. THE FIRST-YEAR KIDS SPRANG IT ON ME.
THEY THOUGHT YOU'D GET MAD, SO THEY ASKED ME TO ASK YOU.
CAN'T WE? PLEASE?
WE DON'T HAVE GIRLFRIENDS.
WE'LL BE SO LONELY ON CHRISTMAS.
JUST LOOK AT THOSE PUPPY-DOG EYES.
...THOSE BOYS.
...OKAY. I'LL LOOK FOR A CHEAP RESTAURANT.
THANK YOU!
THANK YOU, TONO-SENPAI!!
I'M SO SCARED OF MANAGER MACHIDA.
I'M A LITTLE SCARED OF HER TOO.
THE 24TH...
THAT'S NEXT WEEK...
I'LL LOOK INTO SOME RESTAURANTS WHEN I GET HOME.
GET ALL OUR RSVPs BY END OF DAY TOMORROW...
YUKI-SENPAAAI...
...D'YOU HAVE AN ANSWER FOR ME YET?
THMP

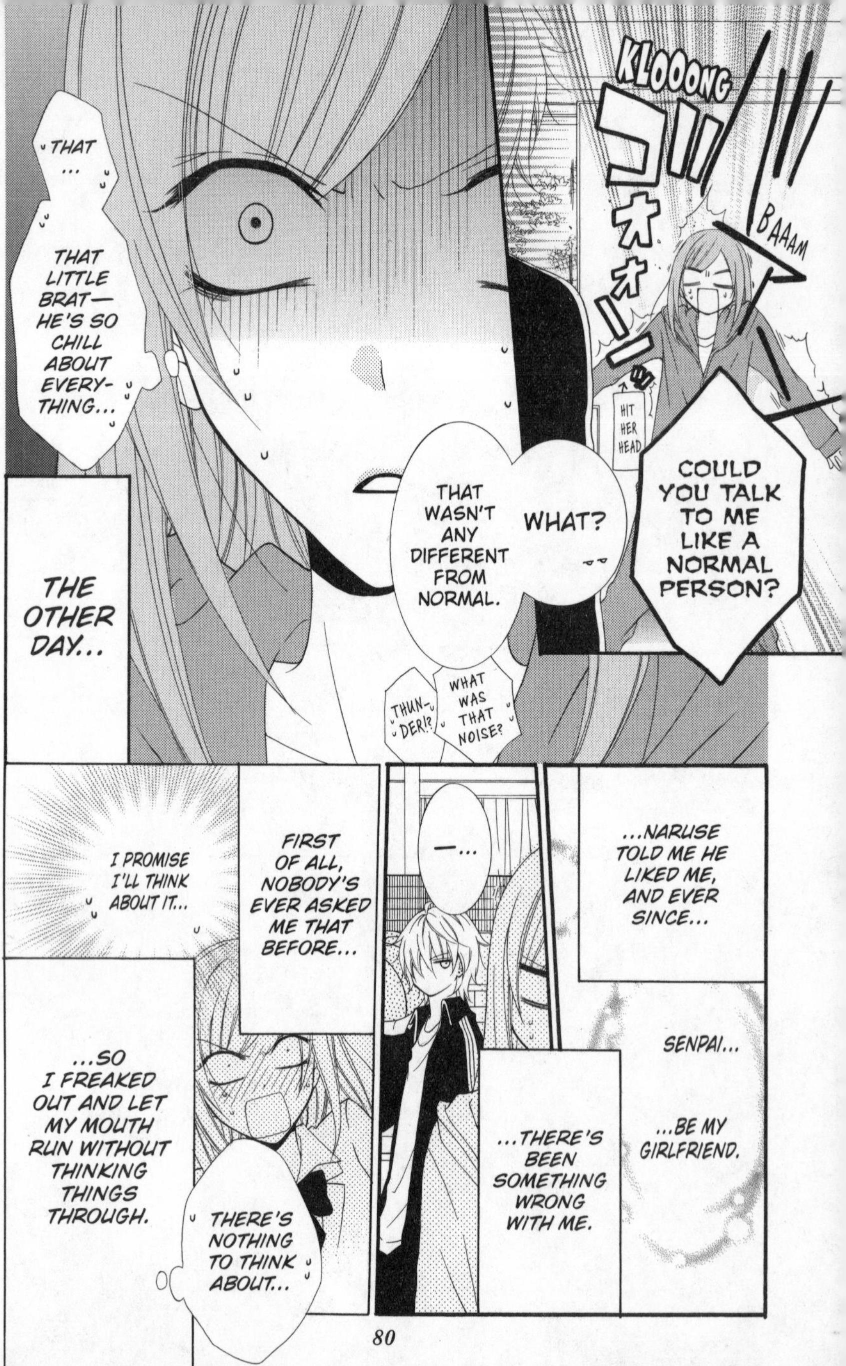
KLOOONG
BAAAM
HIT HER HEAD
COULD YOU TALK TO ME LIKE A NORMAL PERSON?
WHAT?
THAT WASN'T ANY DIFFERENT FROM NORMAL.
THAT ...
THAT LITTLE BRAT— HE'S SO CHILL ABOUT EVERY-THING...
WHAT WAS THAT NOISE?
THUN-DER!?
THE OTHER DAY...
...NARUSE TOLD ME HE LIKED ME, AND EVER SINCE...
SENPAI...
...BE MY GIRLFRIEND.
...THERE'S BEEN SOMETHING WRONG WITH ME.
—...
FIRST OF ALL, NOBODY'S EVER ASKED ME THAT BEFORE...
I PROMISE I'LL THINK ABOUT IT...
...SO I FREAKED OUT AND LET MY MOUTH RUN WITHOUT THINKING THINGS THROUGH.
THERE'S NOTHING TO THINK ABOUT...

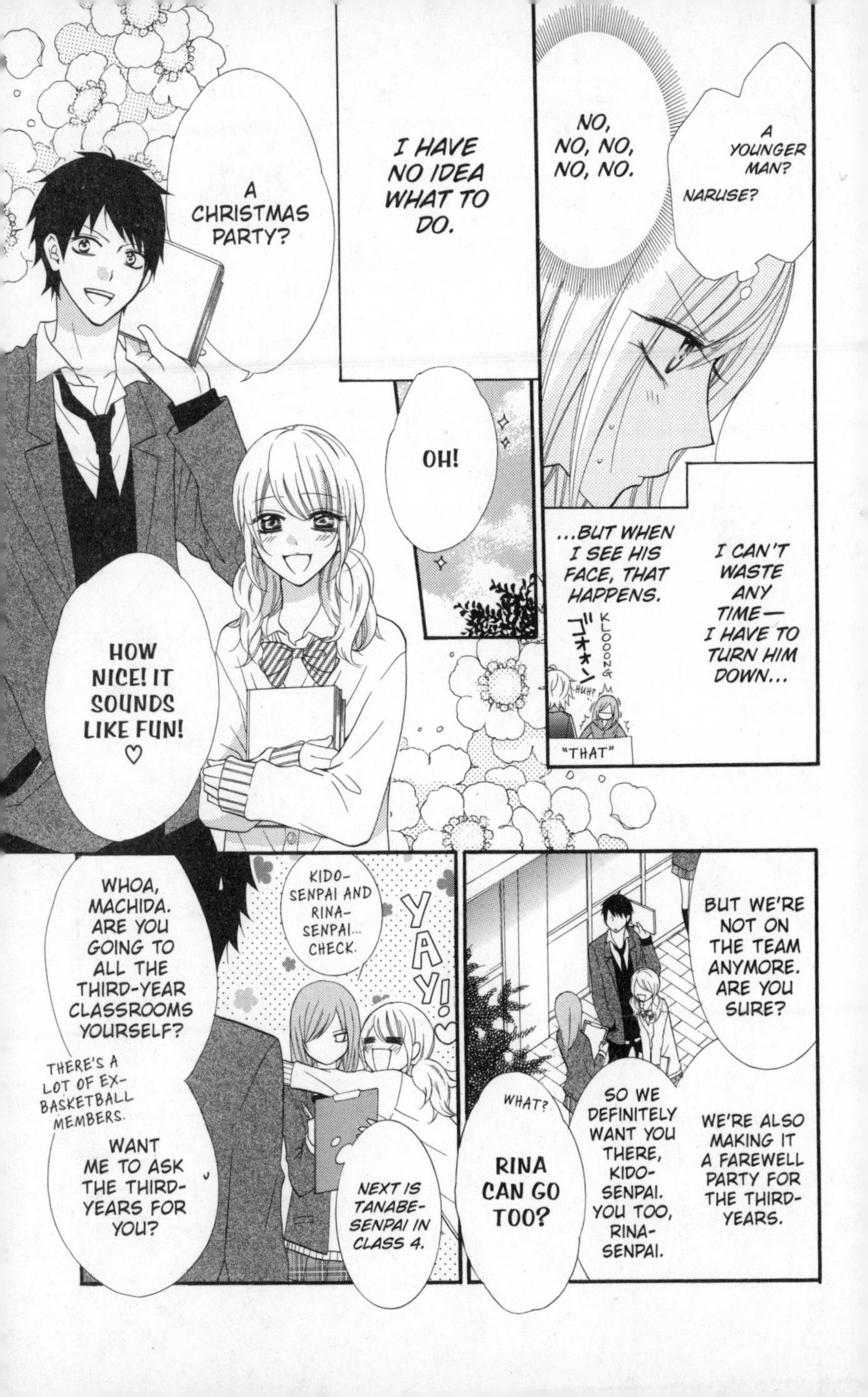
A YOUNGER MAN?
NARUSE?
NO, NO, NO, NO, NO.
I HAVE NO IDEA WHAT TO DO.
I CAN'T WASTE ANY TIME— I HAVE TO TURN HIM DOWN...
...BUT WHEN I SEE HIS FACE, THAT HAPPENS.
KLOOONG
HUH?
"THAT"
OH!
A CHRISTMAS PARTY?
HOW NICE! IT SOUNDS LIKE FUN! ♡
BUT WE'RE NOT ON THE TEAM ANYMORE. ARE YOU SURE?
WE'RE ALSO MAKING IT A FAREWELL PARTY FOR THE THIRD-YEARS.
SO WE DEFINITELY WANT YOU THERE, KIDO-SENPAI. YOU TOO, RINA-SENPAI.
WHAT?
RINA CAN GO TOO?
YAY!
KIDO-SENPAI AND RINA-SENPAI... CHECK.
NEXT IS TANABE-SENPAI IN CLASS 4.
WHOA, MACHIDA. ARE YOU GOING TO ALL THE THIRD-YEAR CLASSROOMS YOURSELF?
THERE'S A LOT OF EX-BASKETBALL MEMBERS.
WANT ME TO ASK THE THIRD-YEARS FOR YOU?

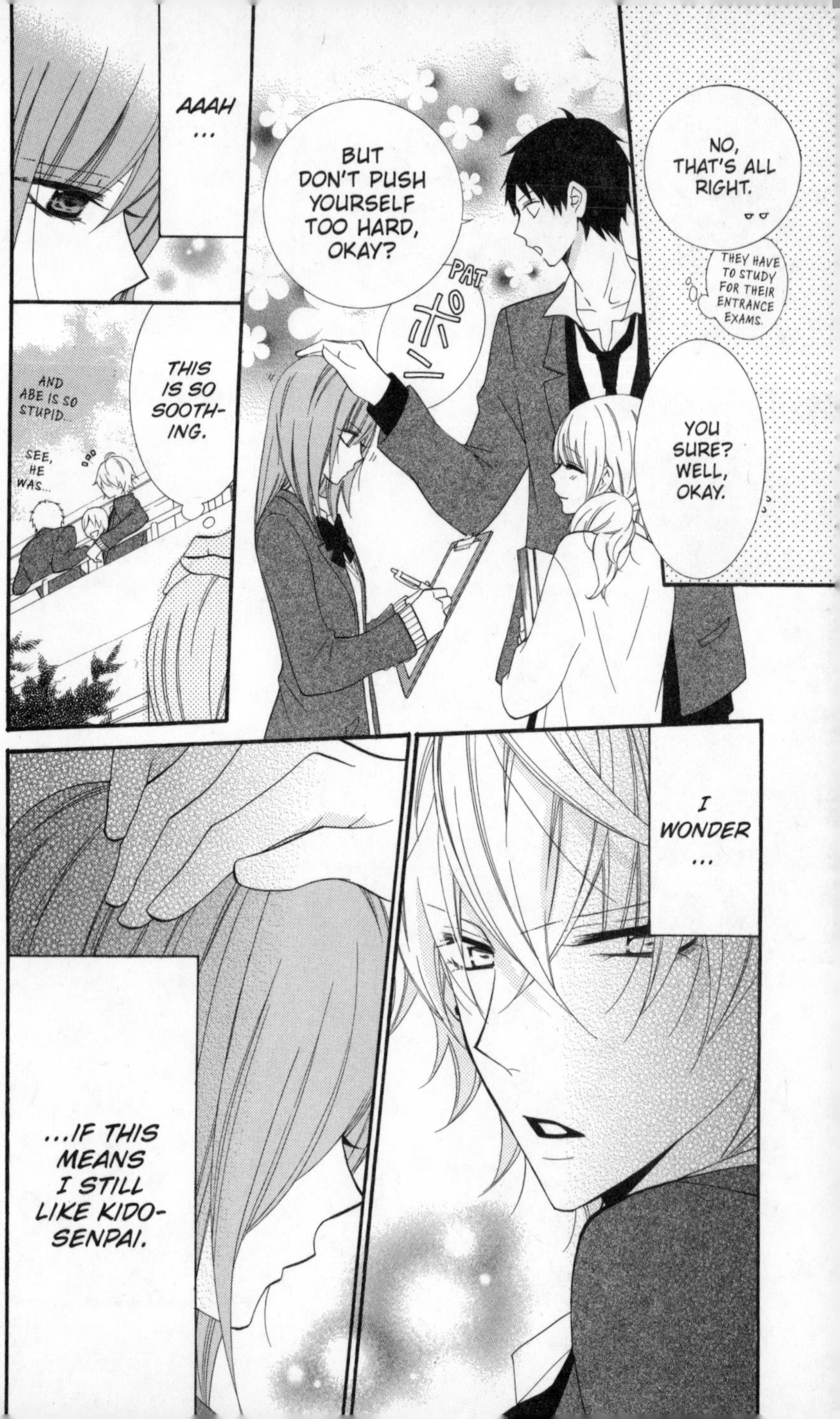
NO, THAT'S ALL RIGHT.
THEY HAVE TO STUDY FOR THEIR ENTRANCE EXAMS.
YOU SURE? WELL, OKAY.
BUT DON'T PUSH YOURSELF TOO HARD, OKAY?
PAT
ポン
AAAH ...
THIS IS SO SOOTH-ING.
AND ABE IS SO STUPID...
SEE, HE WAS...
I WONDER ...
...IF THIS MEANS I STILL LIKE KIDO-SENPAI.

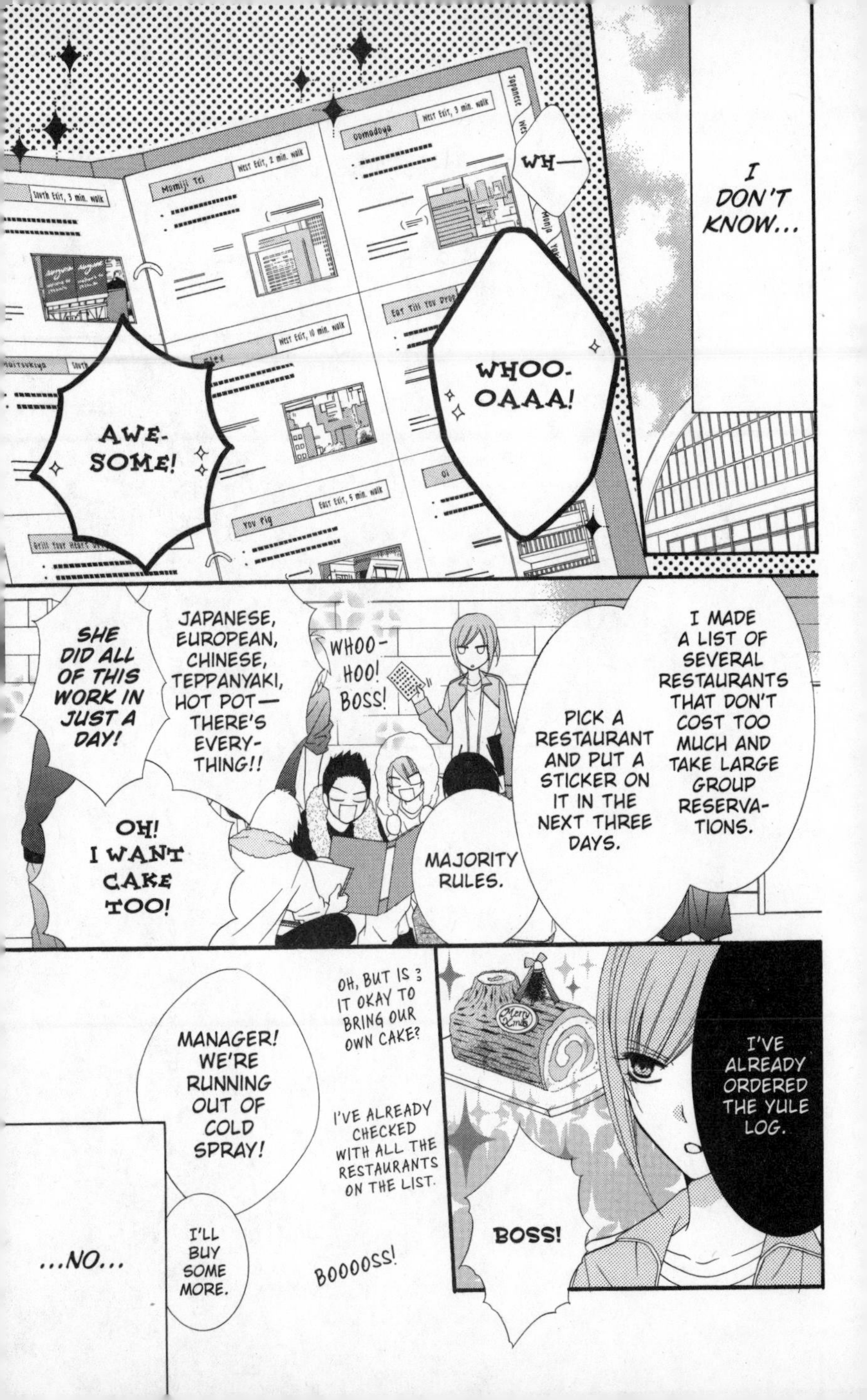
I DON'T KNOW...
WH—
WHOO-OAAA!
AWESOME!
I MADE A LIST OF SEVERAL RESTAURANTS THAT DON'T COST TOO MUCH AND TAKE LARGE GROUP RESERVATIONS.
PICK A RESTAURANT AND PUT A STICKER ON IT IN THE NEXT THREE DAYS.
MAJORITY RULES.
WHOO-HOO! BOSS!
JAPANESE, EUROPEAN, CHINESE, TEPPANYAKI, HOT POT—THERE'S EVERYTHING!!
SHE DID ALL OF THIS WORK IN JUST A DAY!
OH! I WANT CAKE TOO!
I'VE ALREADY ORDERED THE YULE LOG.
BOSS!
OH, BUT IS IT OKAY TO BRING OUR OWN CAKE?
I'VE ALREADY CHECKED WITH ALL THE RESTAURANTS ON THE LIST.
BOOOOSS!
MANAGER! WE'RE RUNNING OUT OF COLD SPRAY!
I'LL BUY SOME MORE.
...NO...

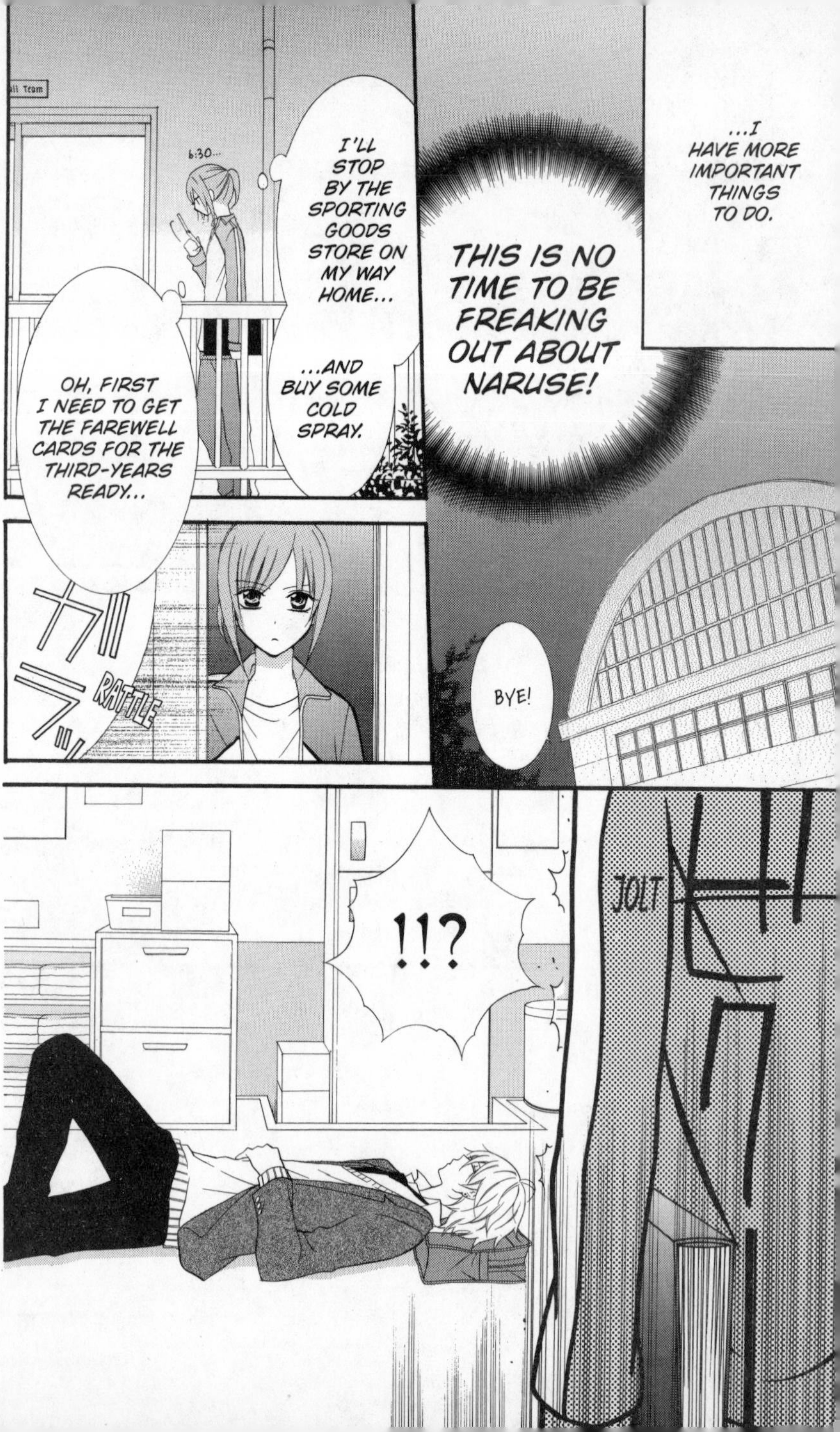
...I HAVE MORE IMPORTANT THINGS TO DO.
THIS IS NO TIME TO BE FREAKING OUT ABOUT NARUSE!
BYE!
6:30...
I'LL STOP BY THE SPORTING GOODS STORE ON MY WAY HOME...
...AND BUY SOME COLD SPRAY.
OH, FIRST I NEED TO GET THE FAREWELL CARDS FOR THE THIRD-YEARS READY...
RATTLE
JOLT
!!?

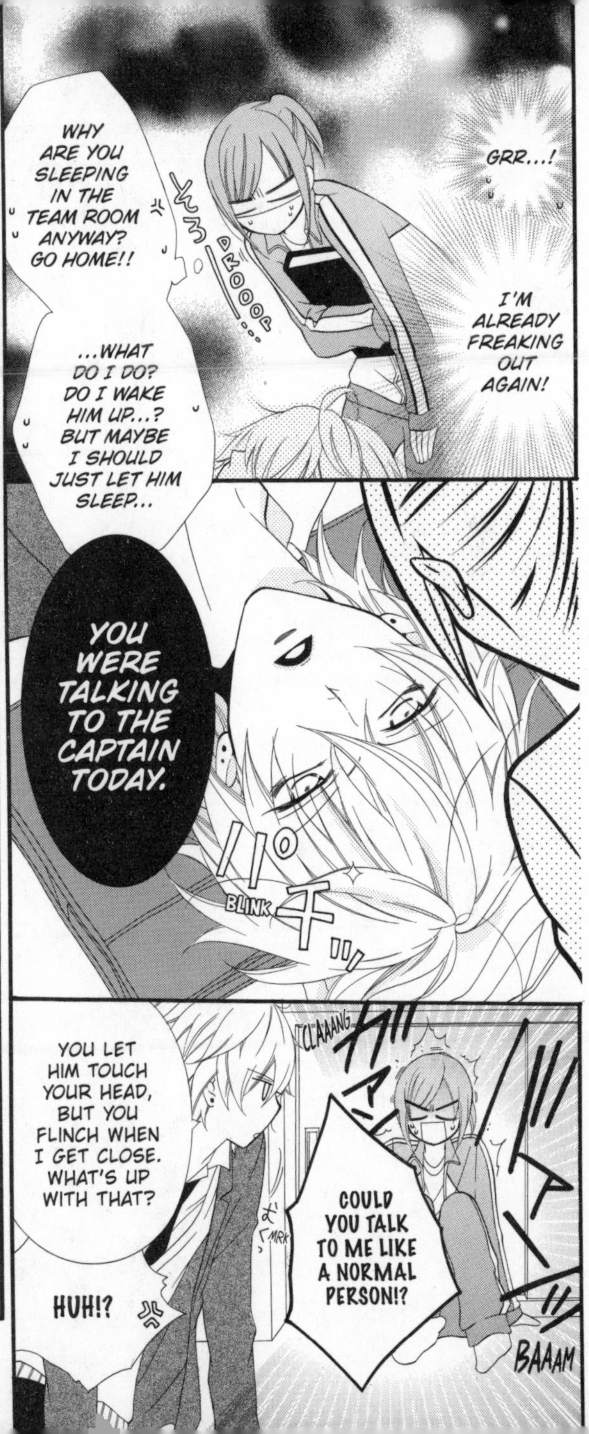
GRR...!
I'M ALREADY FREAKING OUT AGAIN!
DROOOOP...
WHY ARE YOU SLEEPING IN THE TEAM ROOM ANYWAY? GO HOME!!
...WHAT DO I DO? DO I WAKE HIM UP...? BUT MAYBE I SHOULD JUST LET HIM SLEEP...
YOU WERE TALKING TO THE CAPTAIN TODAY.
BLINK
CLAAANG
BAAAM
COULD YOU TALK TO ME LIKE A NORMAL PERSON!?
MRK
YOU LET HIM TOUCH YOUR HEAD, BUT YOU FLINCH WHEN I GET CLOSE. WHAT'S UP WITH THAT?
HUH!?

03

MYSTERIOUS NOTE

When I was moving the other day, I was packing my things, and I found tons of scribbles and notes and stuff that I must have written at some point.

I have a habit of holding a pen and writing super-low-level jokes or notes when I'm dozing off at work or when I've had a bit too much to drink.

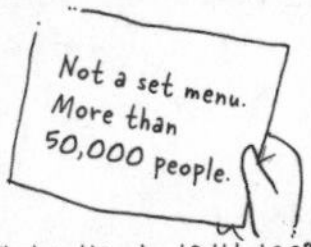
Not a set menu.
More than 50,000 people.

What is this about? It's 100% my handwriting, but why I would have written something like this is a complete and utter mystery. It's really scary.

And then, on the notepad in front of the phone at my parents' house, it says, in my mom's handwriting...

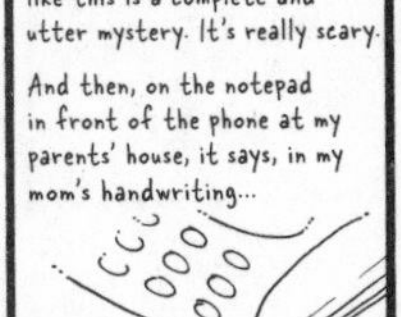
Pumpkin

In English, just like that. There aren't a whole lot of opportunities to write the word "pumpkin" in English, are there? I can't fathom what would have led to that. It's a mystery...

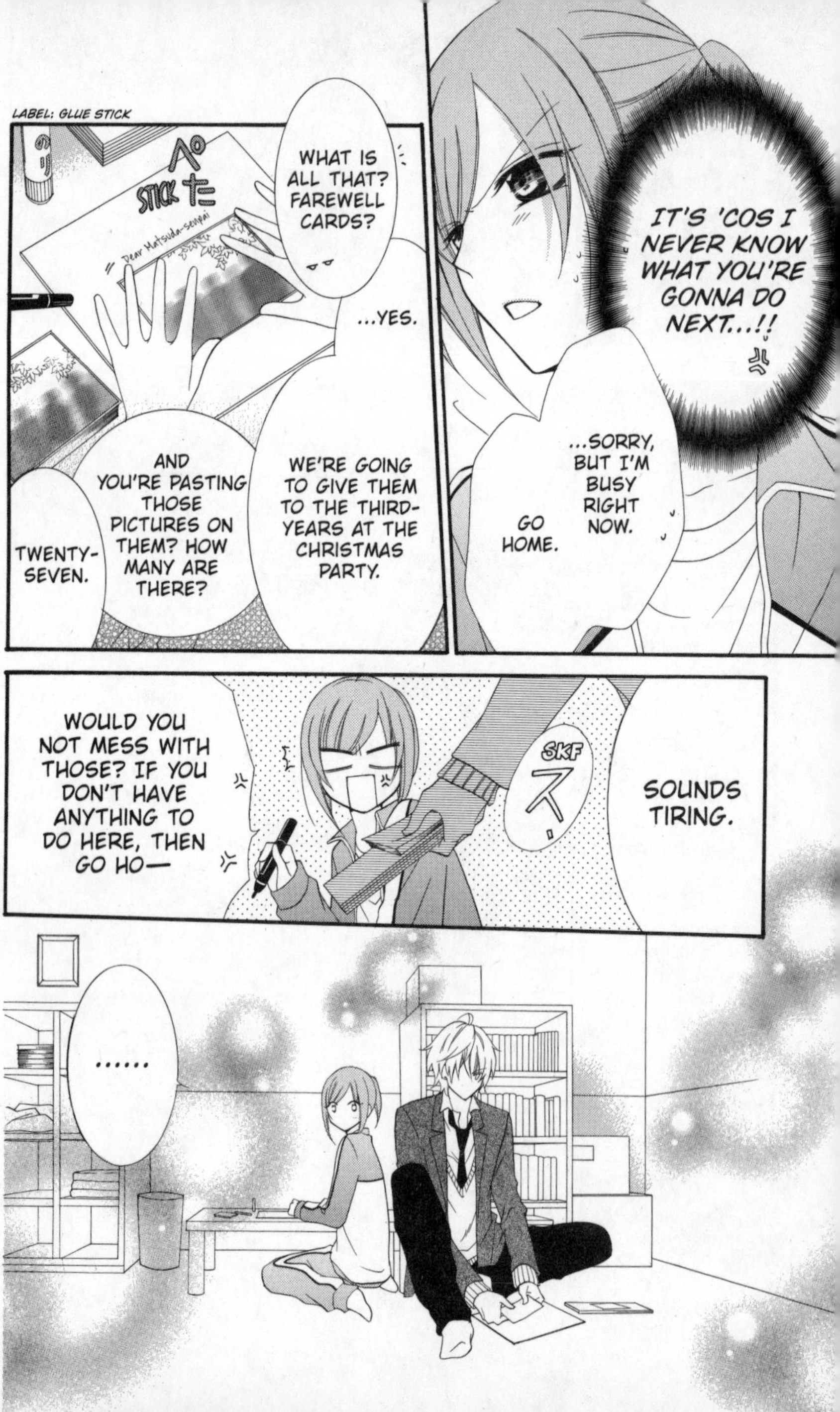
IT'S 'COS I NEVER KNOW WHAT YOU'RE GONNA DO NEXT...!!
...SORRY, BUT I'M BUSY RIGHT NOW.
GO HOME.
LABEL: GLUE STICK
STICK
Dear Matsuda-senpai
WHAT IS ALL THAT? FAREWELL CARDS?
...YES.
WE'RE GOING TO GIVE THEM TO THE THIRD-YEARS AT THE CHRISTMAS PARTY.
AND YOU'RE PASTING THOSE PICTURES ON THEM? HOW MANY ARE THERE?
TWENTY-SEVEN.
SOUNDS TIRING.
SKF
WOULD YOU NOT MESS WITH THOSE? IF YOU DON'T HAVE ANYTHING TO DO HERE, THEN GO HO—
......

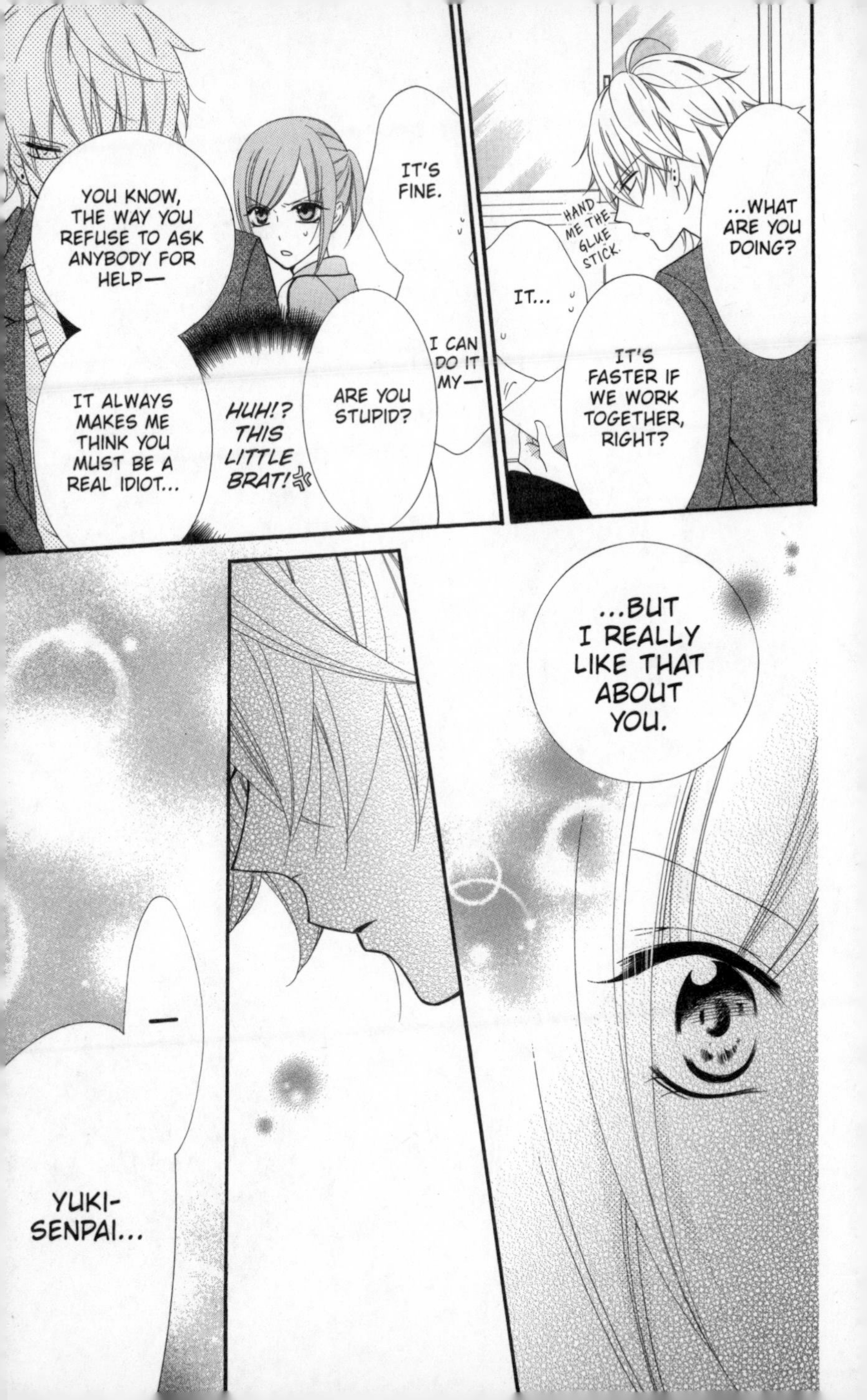
...WHAT ARE YOU DOING?
HAND ME THE GLUE STICK.
IT...
IT'S FASTER IF WE WORK TOGETHER, RIGHT?
IT'S FINE.
I CAN DO IT MY—
ARE YOU STUPID?
HUH!? THIS LITTLE BRAT!
YOU KNOW, THE WAY YOU REFUSE TO ASK ANYBODY FOR HELP—
IT ALWAYS MAKES ME THINK YOU MUST BE A REAL IDIOT...
...BUT I REALLY LIKE THAT ABOUT YOU.
—
YUKI-SENPAI...

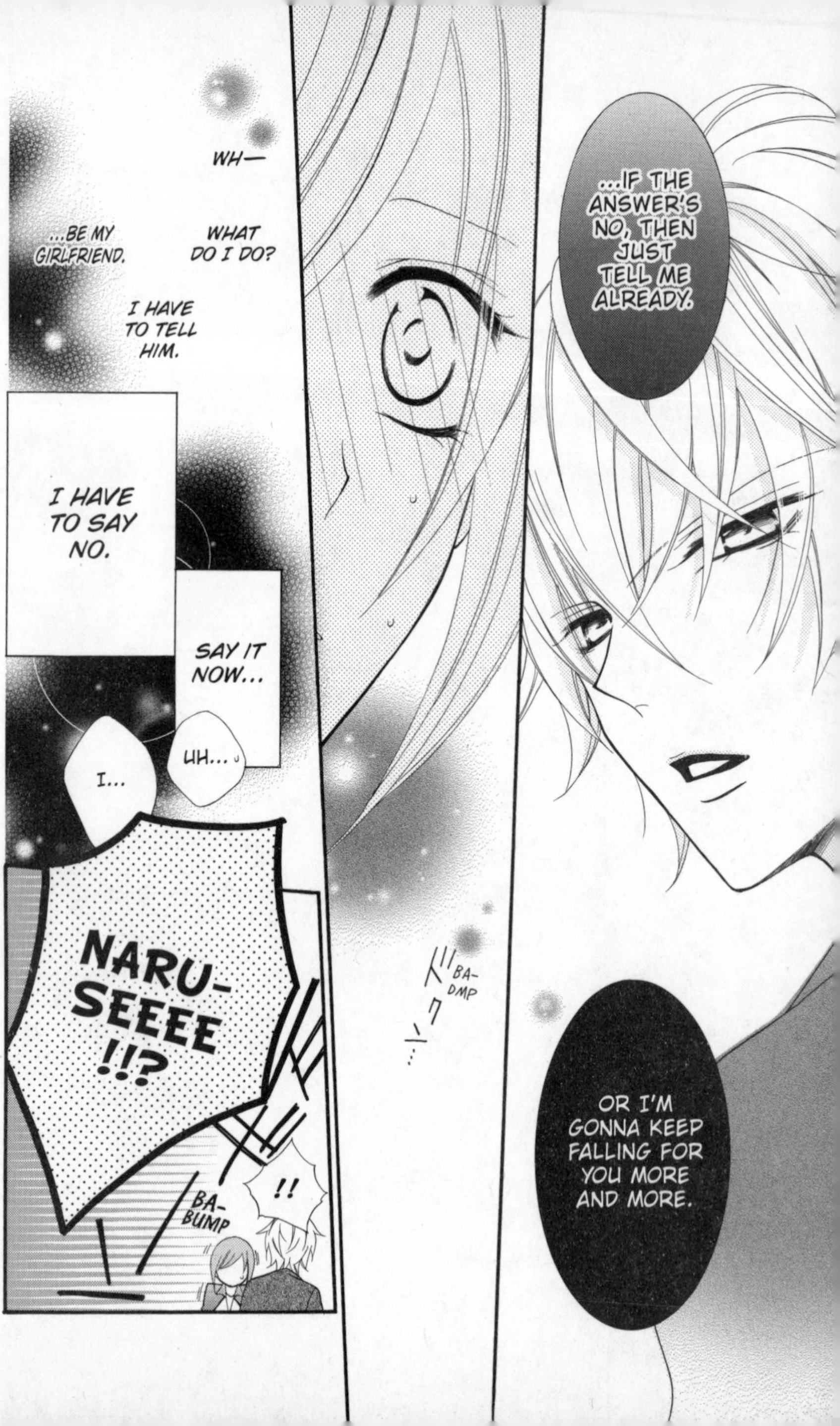
...IF THE ANSWER'S NO, THEN JUST TELL ME ALREADY.
OR I'M GONNA KEEP FALLING FOR YOU MORE AND MORE.
BA-DUMP
WH—
WHAT DO I DO?
...BE MY GIRLFRIEND.
I HAVE TO TELL HIM.
I HAVE TO SAY NO.
SAY IT NOW...
UH...
I...
NARU-SEEEEE!!?
!!
BA-BUMP

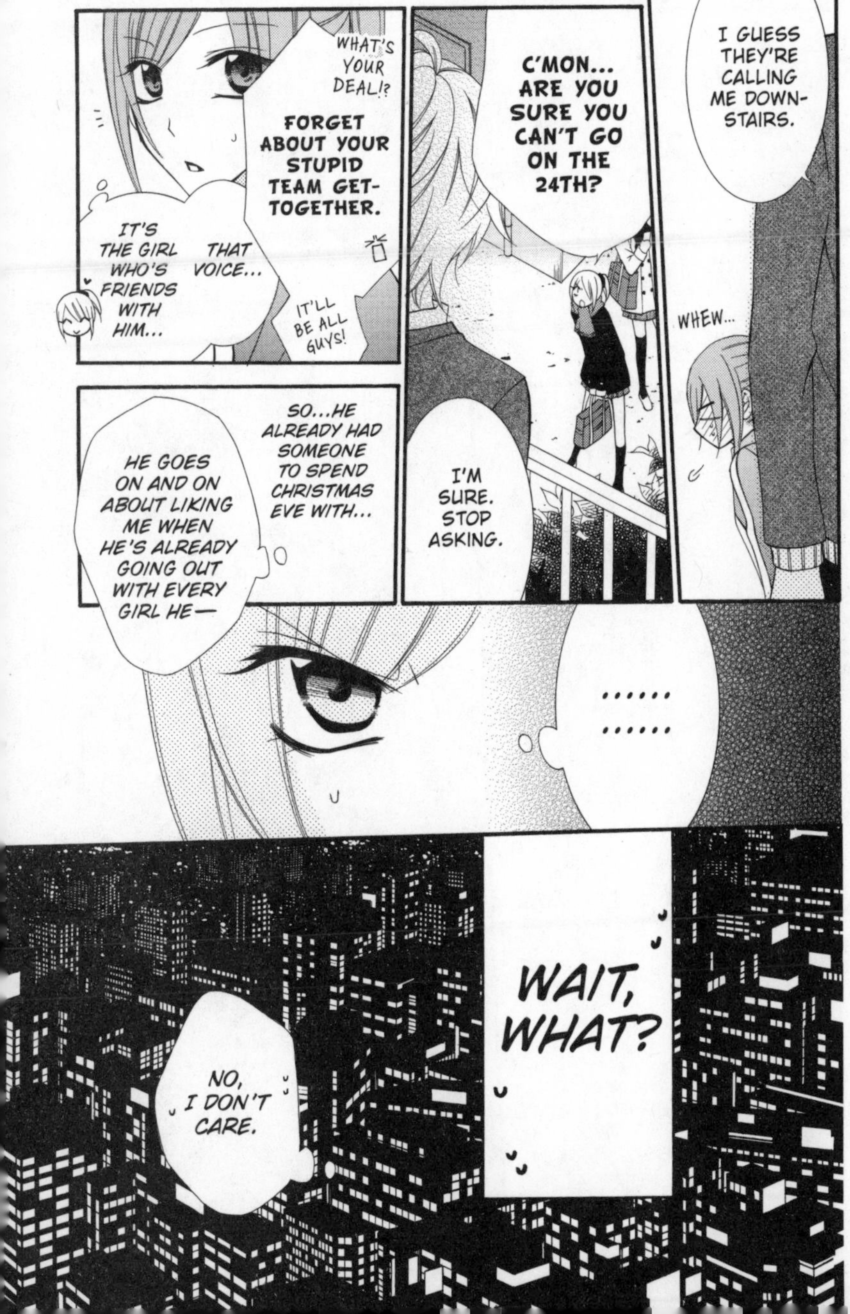
I GUESS THEY'RE CALLING ME DOWN-STAIRS.
WHEW...
C'MON... ARE YOU SURE YOU CAN'T GO ON THE 24TH?
I'M SURE. STOP ASKING.
WHAT'S YOUR DEAL!?
FORGET ABOUT YOUR STUPID TEAM GET-TOGETHER.
IT'LL BE ALL GUYS!
THAT VOICE...
IT'S THE GIRL WHO'S FRIENDS WITH HIM...
SO...HE ALREADY HAD SOMEONE TO SPEND CHRISTMAS EVE WITH...
HE GOES ON AND ON ABOUT LIKING ME WHEN HE'S ALREADY GOING OUT WITH EVERY GIRL HE—
......
......
WAIT, WHAT?
NO, I DON'T CARE.

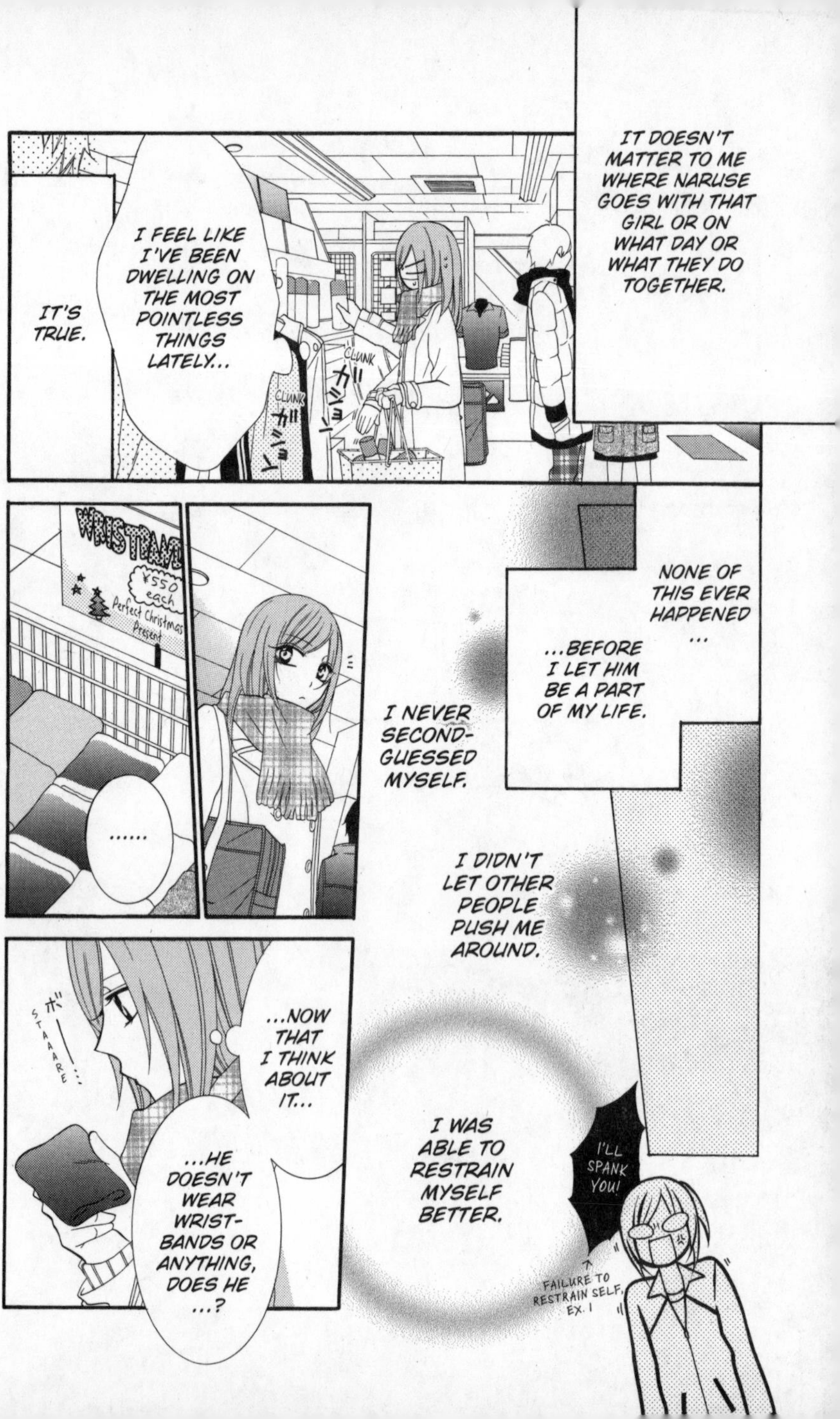
IT DOESN'T MATTER TO ME WHERE NARUSE GOES WITH THAT GIRL OR ON WHAT DAY OR WHAT THEY DO TOGETHER.
CLUNK
CLUNK
I FEEL LIKE I'VE BEEN DWELLING ON THE MOST POINTLESS THINGS LATELY...
IT'S TRUE.
NONE OF THIS EVER HAPPENED...
...BEFORE I LET HIM BE A PART OF MY LIFE.
I NEVER SECOND-GUESSED MYSELF.
¥550 each
Perfect Christmas Present
......
I DIDN'T LET OTHER PEOPLE PUSH ME AROUND.
I WAS ABLE TO RESTRAIN MYSELF BETTER.
I'LL SPANK YOU!
FAILURE TO RESTRAIN SELF, EX. 1
...NOW THAT I THINK ABOUT IT...
...HE DOESN'T WEAR WRISTBANDS OR ANYTHING, DOES HE...?
STAAARE

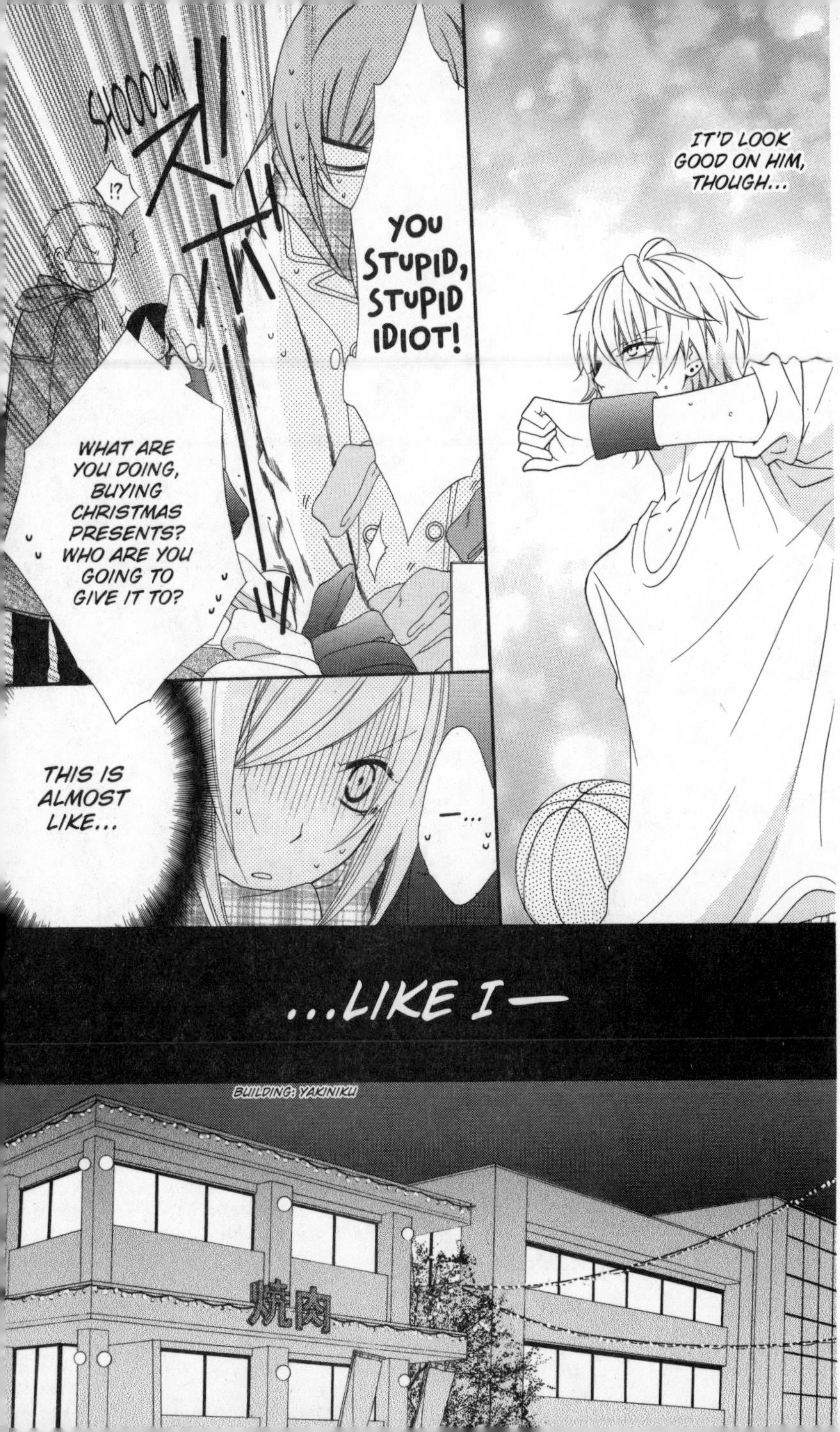
IT'D LOOK GOOD ON HIM, THOUGH...
YOU STUPID, STUPID IDIOT!
SHOOOM
!?
WHAT ARE YOU DOING, BUYING CHRISTMAS PRESENTS? WHO ARE YOU GOING TO GIVE IT TO?
—...
THIS IS ALMOST LIKE...
...LIKE I—
BUILDING: YAKINIKU
焼肉

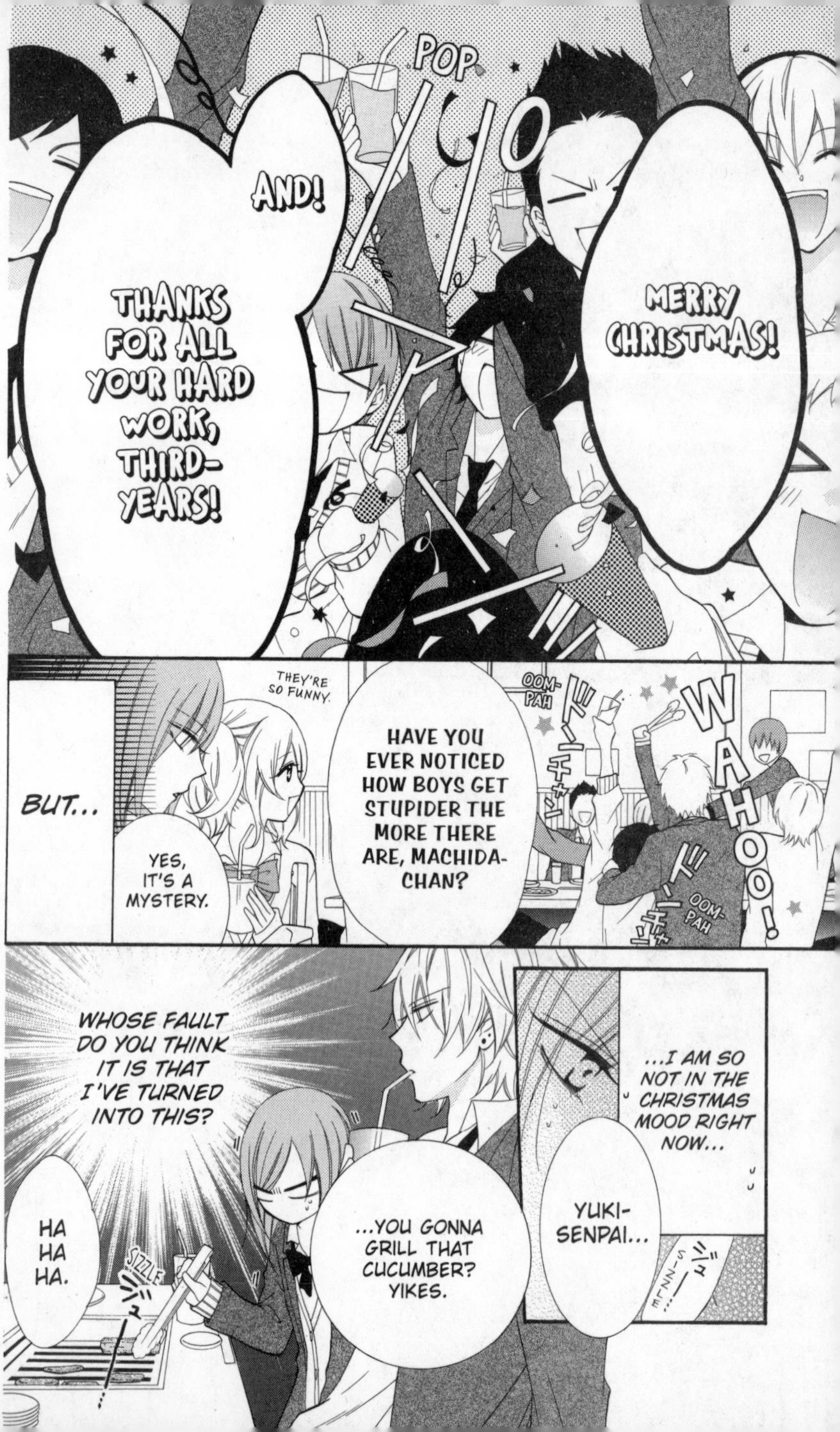
MERRY CHRISTMAS!
POP
AND!
THANKS FOR ALL YOUR HARD WORK, THIRD-YEARS!
WAHOO!
OOM-PAH
OOM-PAH
HAVE YOU EVER NOTICED HOW BOYS GET STUPIDER THE MORE THERE ARE, MACHIDA-CHAN?
THEY'RE SO FUNNY.
YES, IT'S A MYSTERY.
BUT...
...I AM SO NOT IN THE CHRISTMAS MOOD RIGHT NOW...
YUKI-SENPAI...
...YOU GONNA GRILL THAT CUCUMBER? YIKES.
WHOSE FAULT DO YOU THINK IT IS THAT I'VE TURNED INTO THIS?
HA HA HA.
SIZZLE

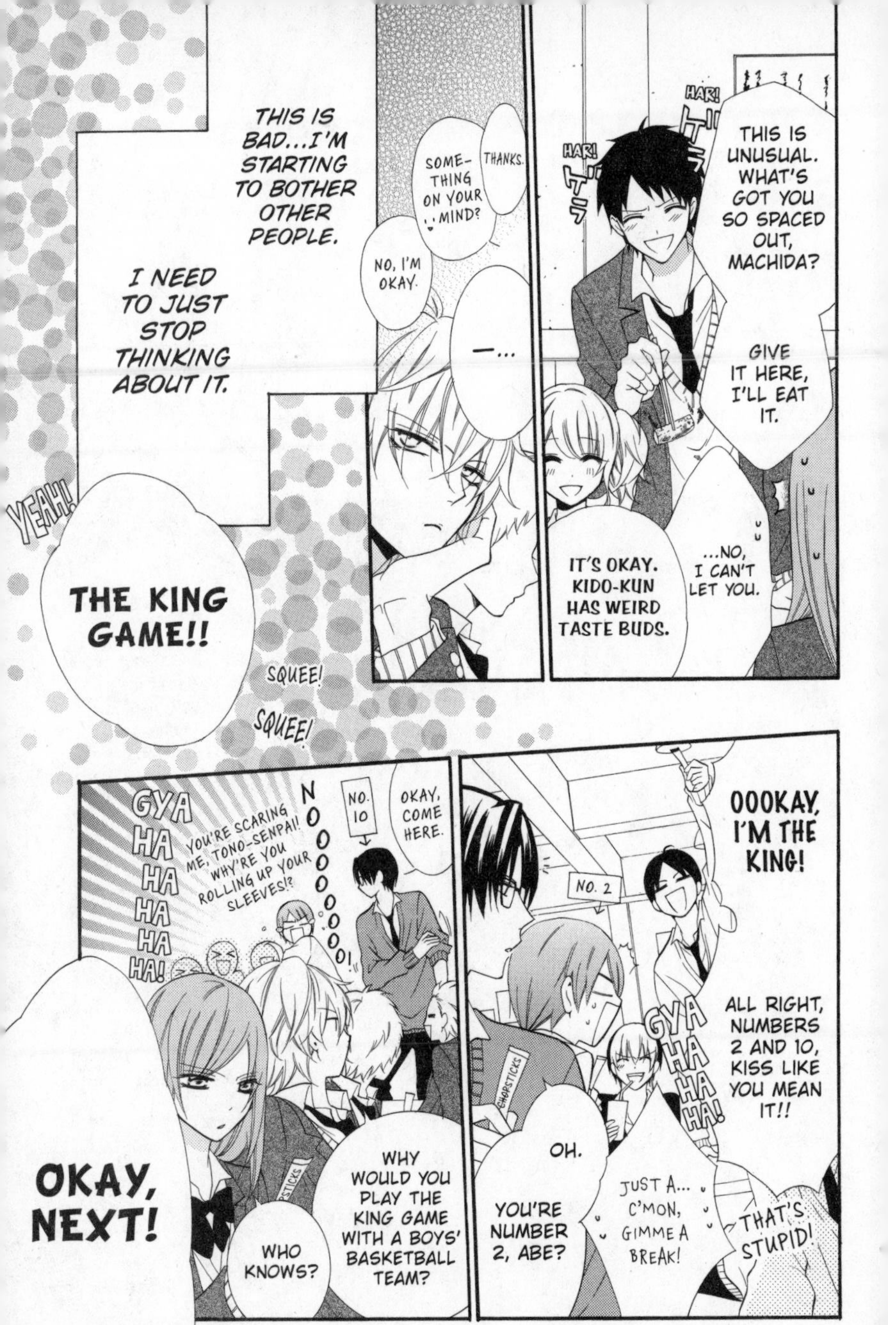
HAR! HAR!
THIS IS UNUSUAL. WHAT'S GOT YOU SO SPACED OUT, MACHIDA?
GIVE IT HERE, I'LL EAT IT.
...NO, I CAN'T LET YOU.
IT'S OKAY. KIDO-KUN HAS WEIRD TASTE BUDS.
THANKS.
SOMETHING ON YOUR MIND?
NO, I'M OKAY.
—...
THIS IS BAD...I'M STARTING TO BOTHER OTHER PEOPLE.
I NEED TO JUST STOP THINKING ABOUT IT.
YEAH!
THE KING GAME!!
SQUEE!
SQUEE!
OOOKAY, I'M THE KING!
NO. 2
ALL RIGHT, NUMBERS 2 AND 10, KISS LIKE YOU MEAN IT!!
GYA HA HA HA HA!
THAT'S STUPID!
JUST A... C'MON, GIMME A BREAK!
OH.
YOU'RE NUMBER 2, ABE?
CHOPSTICKS
OKAY, COME HERE.
NO. 10
NOOOOOOOOO!
GYA HA HA HA HA HA!
YOU'RE SCARING ME, TONO-SENPAI! WHY'RE YOU ROLLING UP YOUR SLEEVES!?
WHY WOULD YOU PLAY THE KING GAME WITH A BOYS' BASKETBALL TEAM?
WHO KNOWS?
OKAY, NEXT!

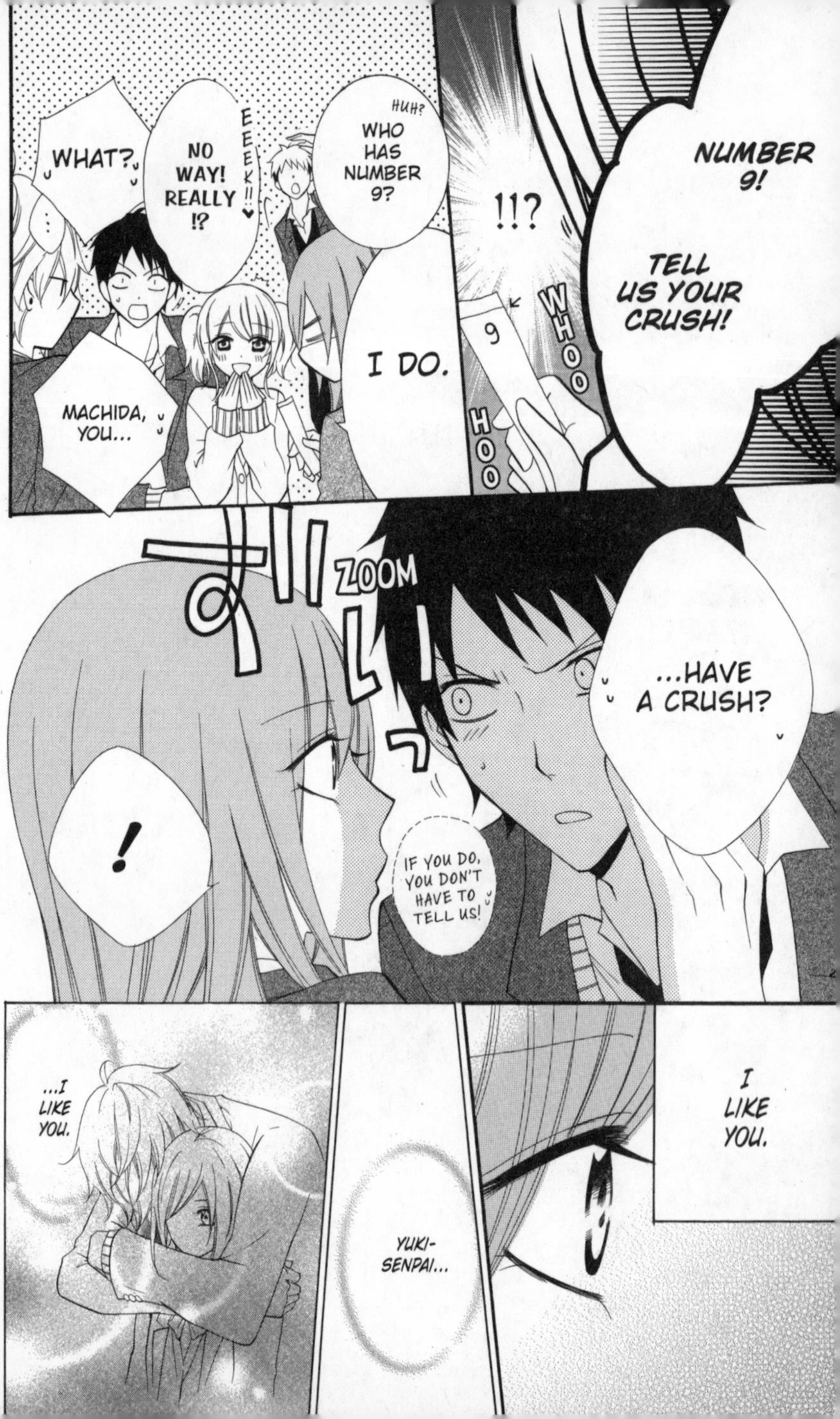
NUMBER 9!
TELL US YOUR CRUSH!
!!?
WHOO
HOO
HOO
HUH?
WHO HAS NUMBER 9?
I DO.
EEEK!!
NO WAY! REALLY!?
WHAT?
MACHIDA, YOU...
...HAVE A CRUSH?
ZOOM
!
IF YOU DO, YOU DON'T HAVE TO TELL US!
I LIKE YOU.
...I LIKE YOU.
YUKI-SENPAI...

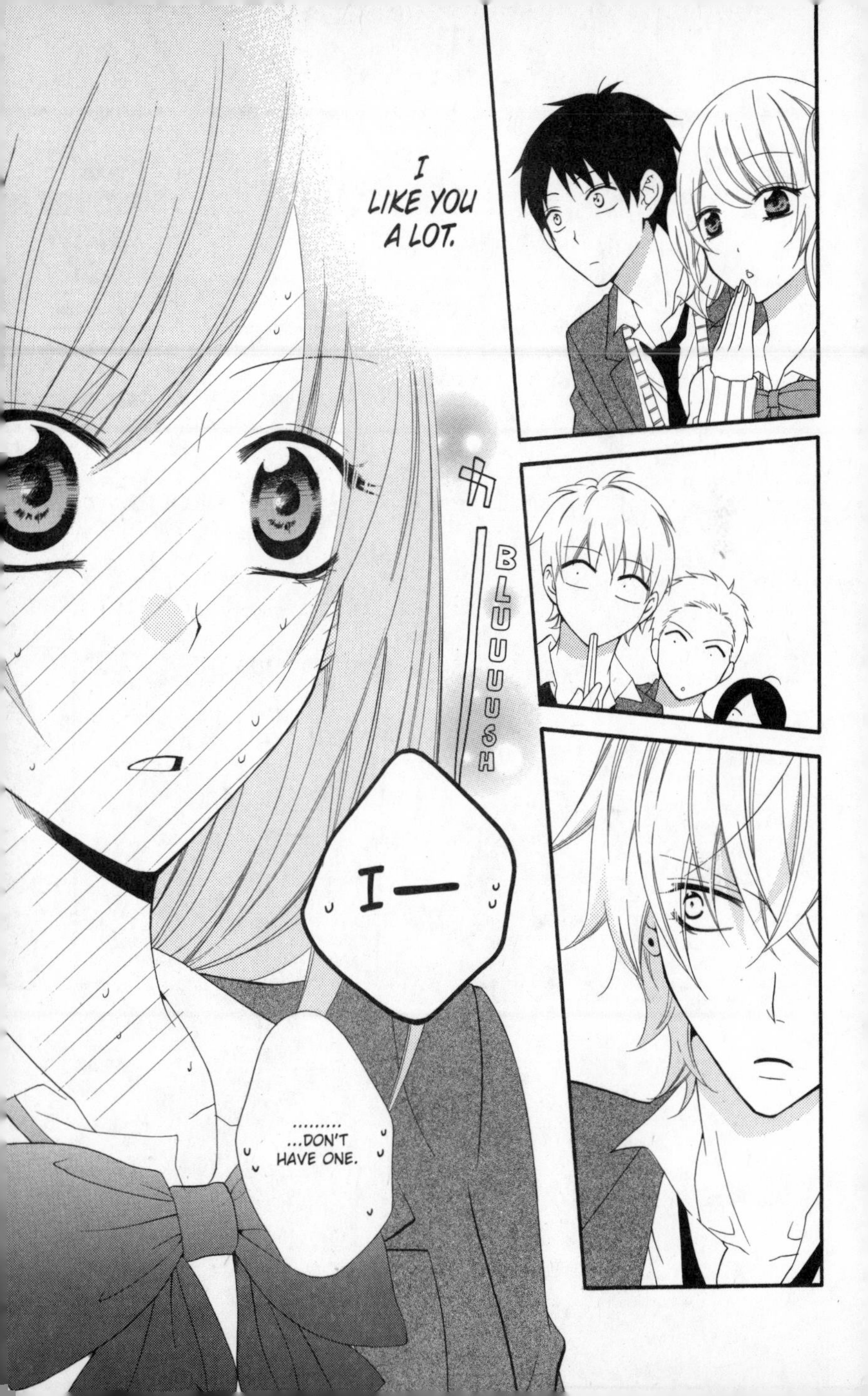
I LIKE YOU A LOT.
カ
BLUUUUUSH
I—
....
...DON'T HAVE ONE.

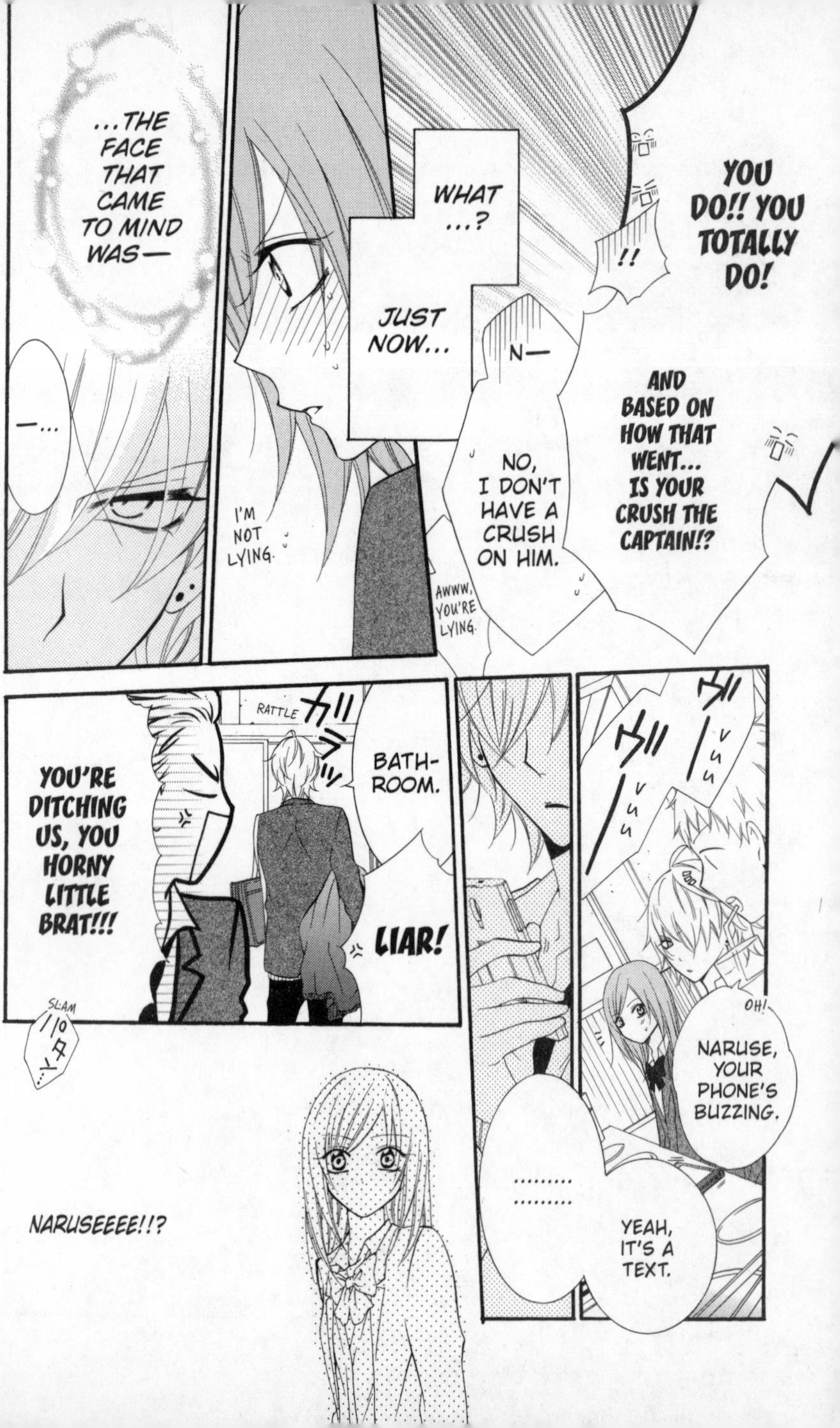
YOU DO!! YOU TOTALLY DO!
!!
AND BASED ON HOW THAT WENT... IS YOUR CRUSH THE CAPTAIN!?
N—
NO, I DON'T HAVE A CRUSH ON HIM.
AWWW, YOU'RE LYING.
WHAT ...?
JUST NOW...
I'M NOT LYING.
...THE FACE THAT CAME TO MIND WAS—
—...
VUUU
VUUU
OH!
NARUSE, YOUR PHONE'S BUZZING.
....
....
YEAH, IT'S A TEXT.
RATTLE
BATH-ROOM.
LIAR!
YOU'RE DITCHING US, YOU HORNY LITTLE BRAT!!!
SLAM
NARUSEEEE!!?

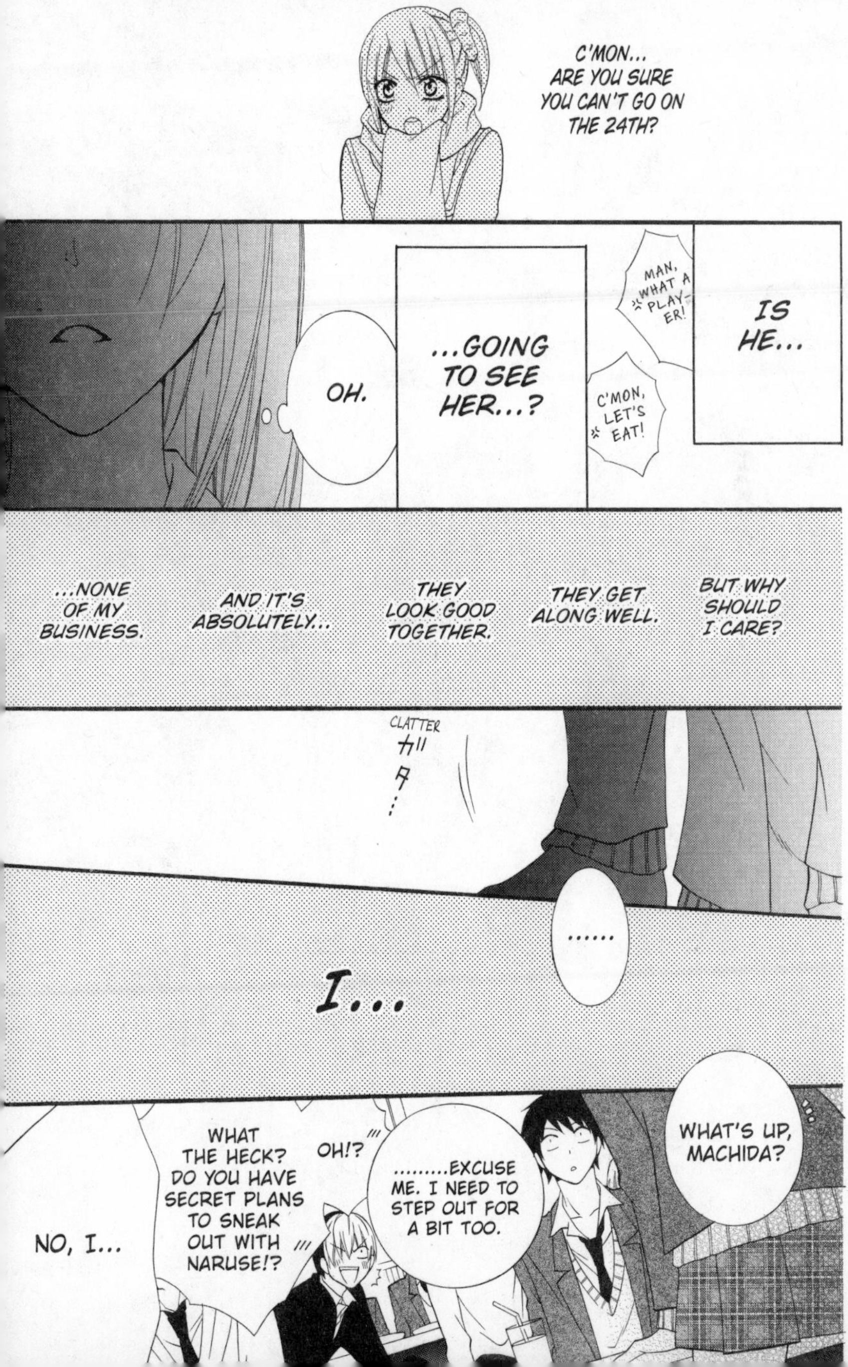

C'MON... ARE YOU SURE YOU CAN'T GO ON THE 24TH?
IS HE...
MAN, WHAT A PLAY-ER!
C'MON, LET'S EAT!
...GOING TO SEE HER...?
OH.
BUT WHY SHOULD I CARE?
THEY GET ALONG WELL.
THEY LOOK GOOD TOGETHER.
AND IT'S ABSOLUTELY...
...NONE OF MY BUSINESS.
CLATTER
カタ...
......
I...
WHAT'S UP, MACHIDA?
.........EXCUSE ME. I NEED TO STEP OUT FOR A BIT TOO.
OH!?
WHAT THE HECK? DO YOU HAVE SECRET PLANS TO SNEAK OUT WITH NARUSE!?
NO, I...

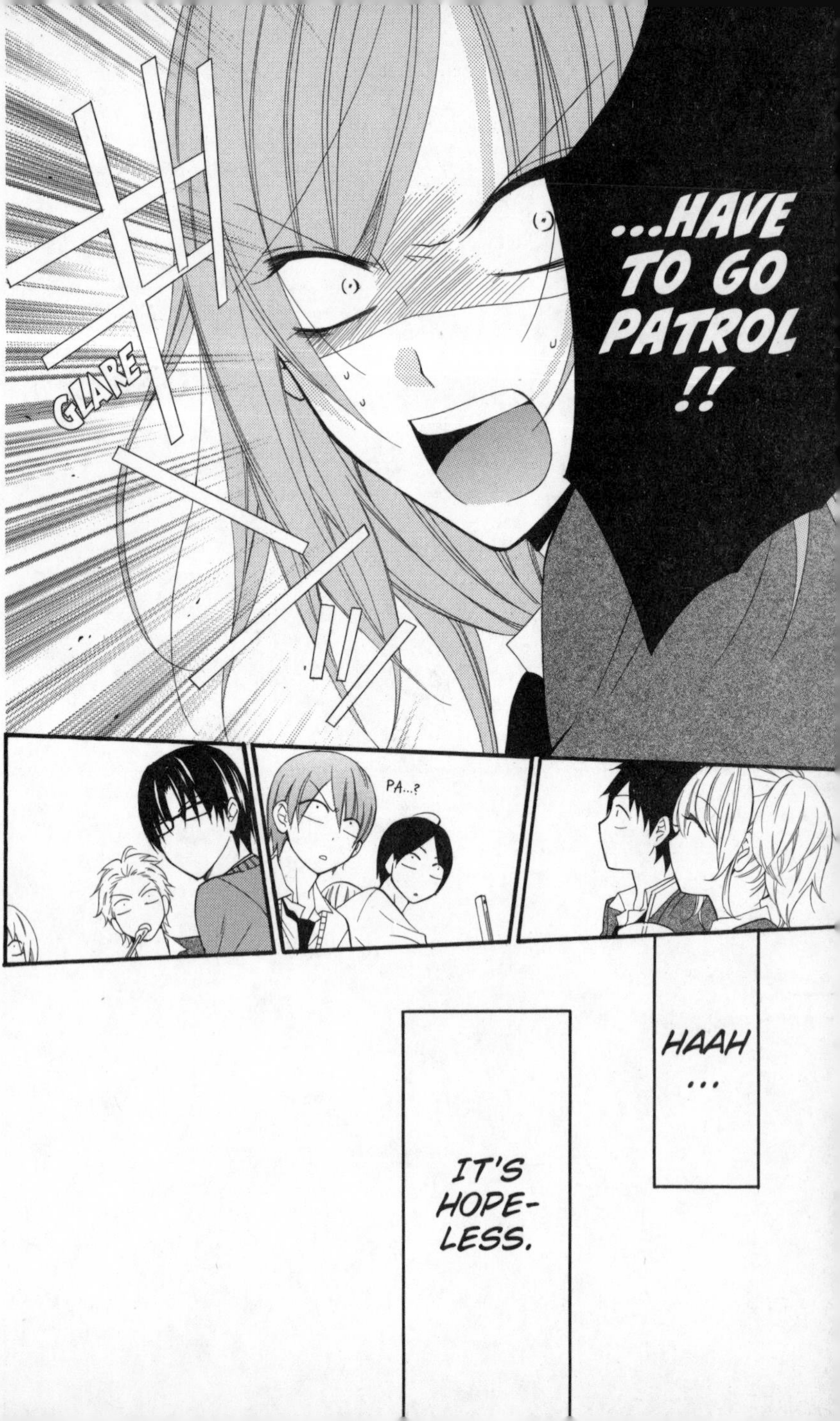
...HAVE TO GO PATROL!!
GLARE
PA...?
HAAH...
IT'S HOPE-LESS.

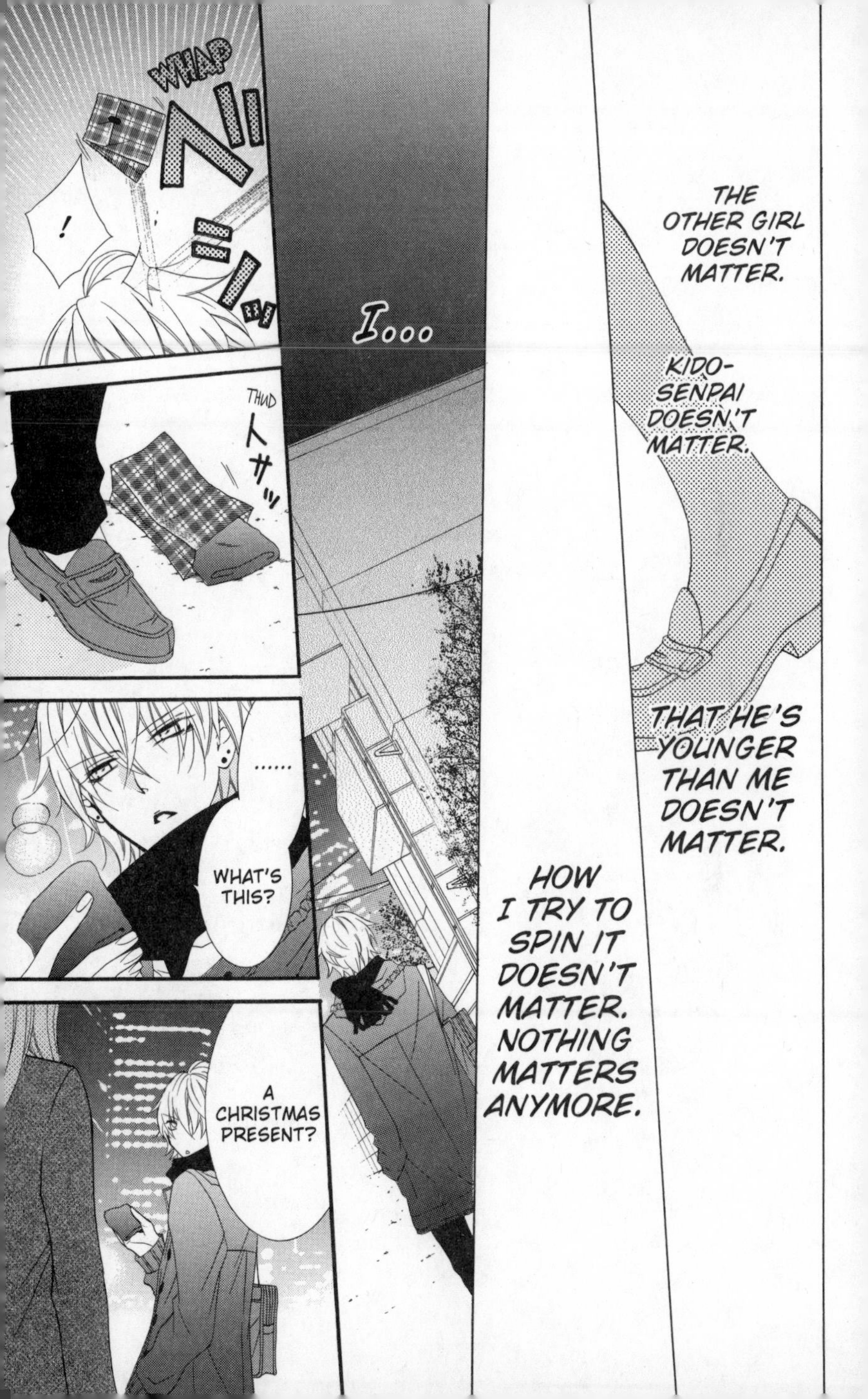
THE OTHER GIRL DOESN'T MATTER.
KIDO-SENPAI DOESN'T MATTER.
THAT HE'S YOUNGER THAN ME DOESN'T MATTER.
HOW I TRY TO SPIN IT DOESN'T MATTER. NOTHING MATTERS ANYMORE.
I...
WHAP
!
THUD
トサッ
......
WHAT'S THIS?
A CHRISTMAS PRESENT?

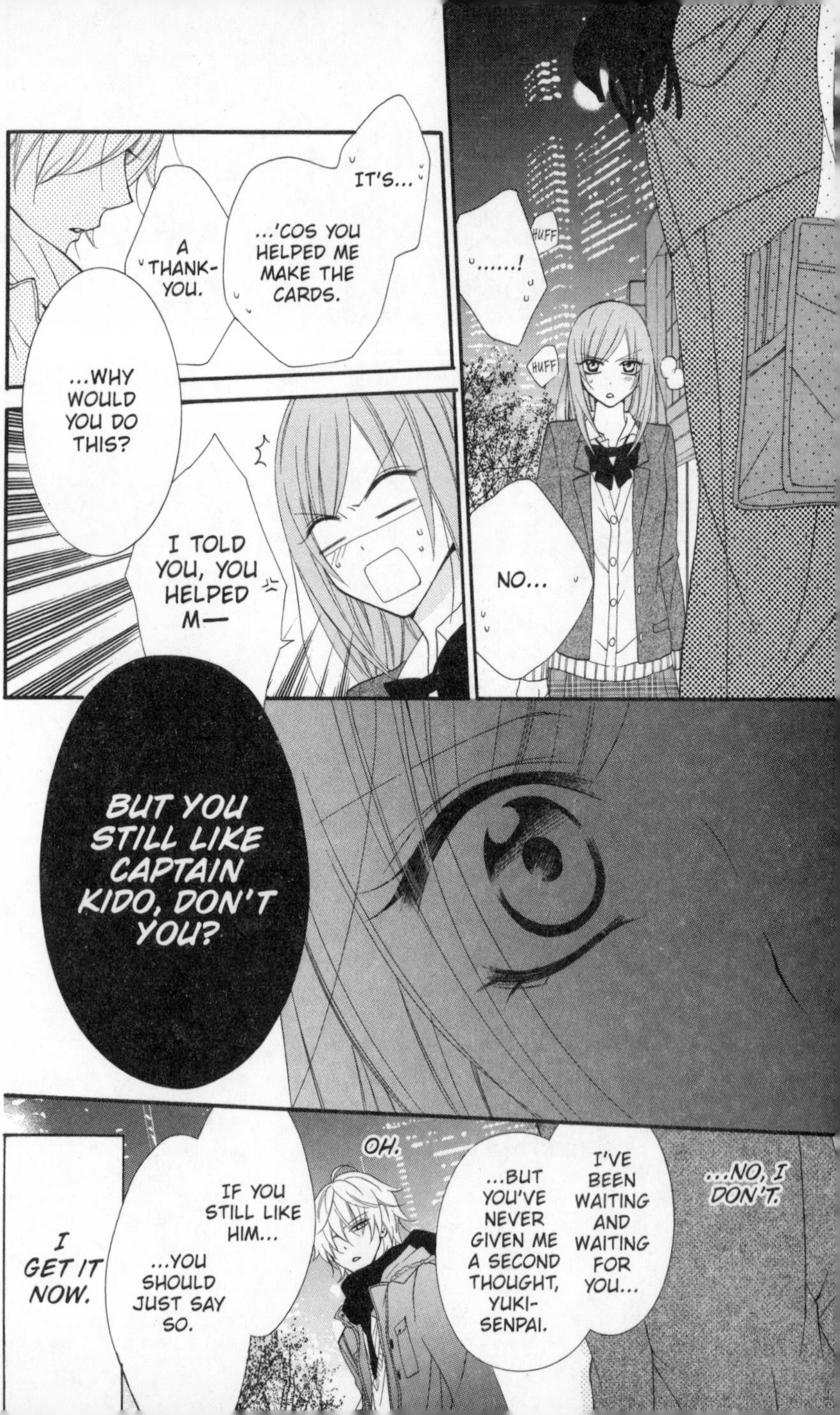
HUFF
......!
HUFF
NO...
IT'S...
...'COS YOU HELPED ME MAKE THE CARDS.
A THANK-YOU.
...WHY WOULD YOU DO THIS?
I TOLD YOU, YOU HELPED M—
BUT YOU STILL LIKE CAPTAIN KIDO, DON'T YOU?
...NO, I DON'T.
OH.
I'VE BEEN WAITING AND WAITING FOR YOU...
...BUT YOU'VE NEVER GIVEN ME A SECOND THOUGHT, YUKI-SENPAI.
IF YOU STILL LIKE HIM...
...YOU SHOULD JUST SAY SO.
I GET IT NOW.

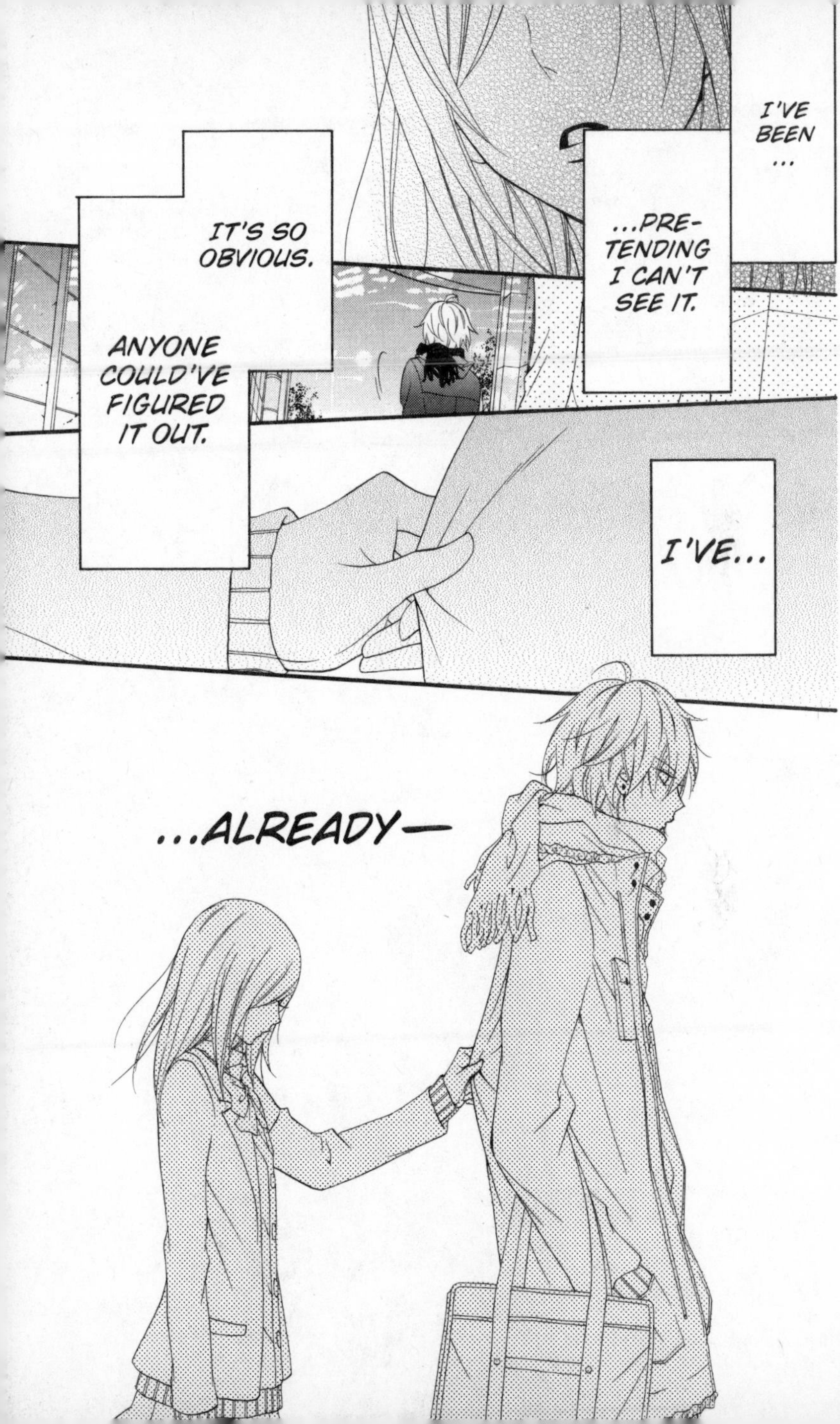
I'VE BEEN...
...PRE-TENDING I CAN'T SEE IT.
IT'S SO OBVIOUS.
ANYONE COULD'VE FIGURED IT OUT.
I'VE...
...ALREADY—

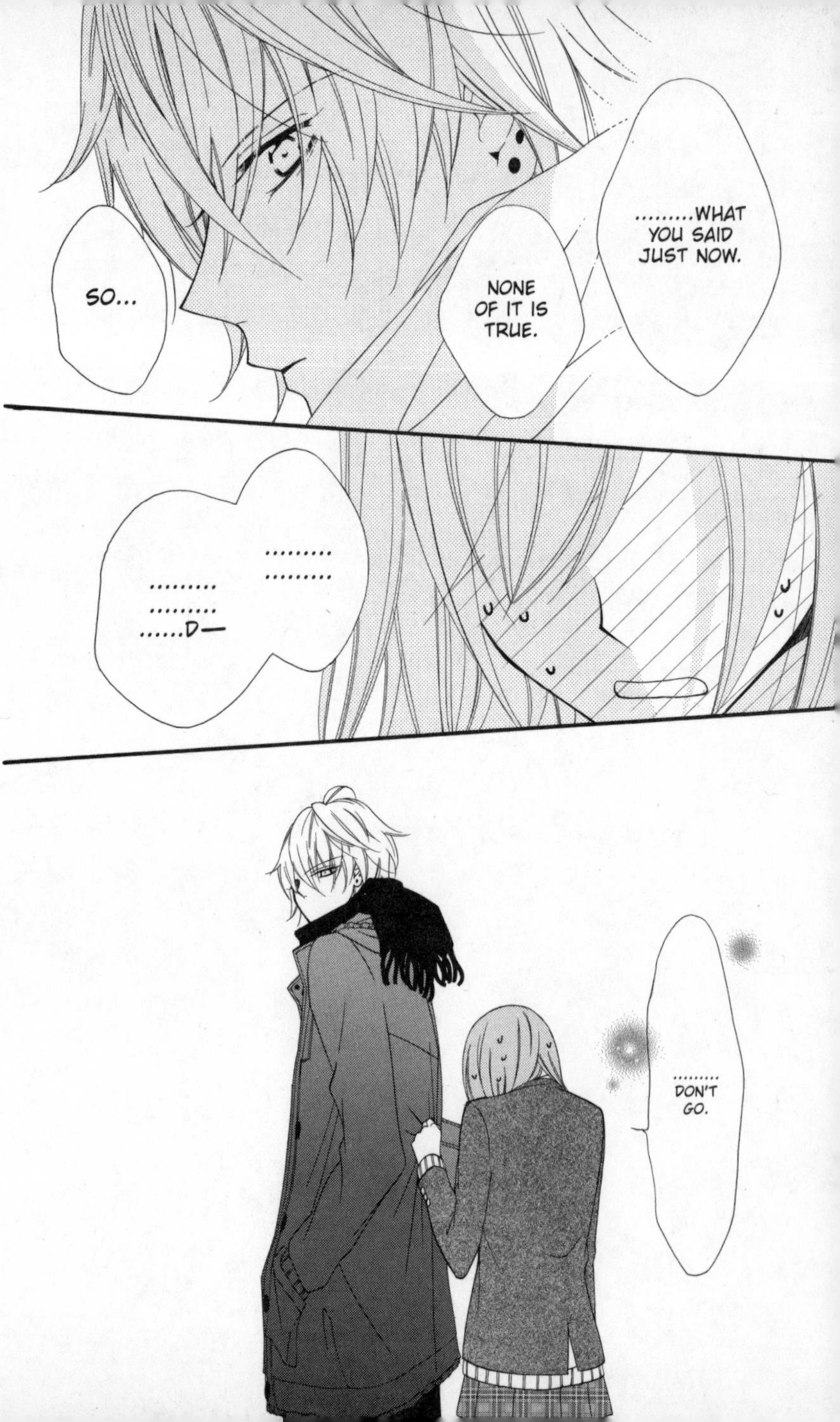
.........WHAT YOU SAID JUST NOW.
NONE OF IT IS TRUE.
SO...
....D—
.... DON'T GO.

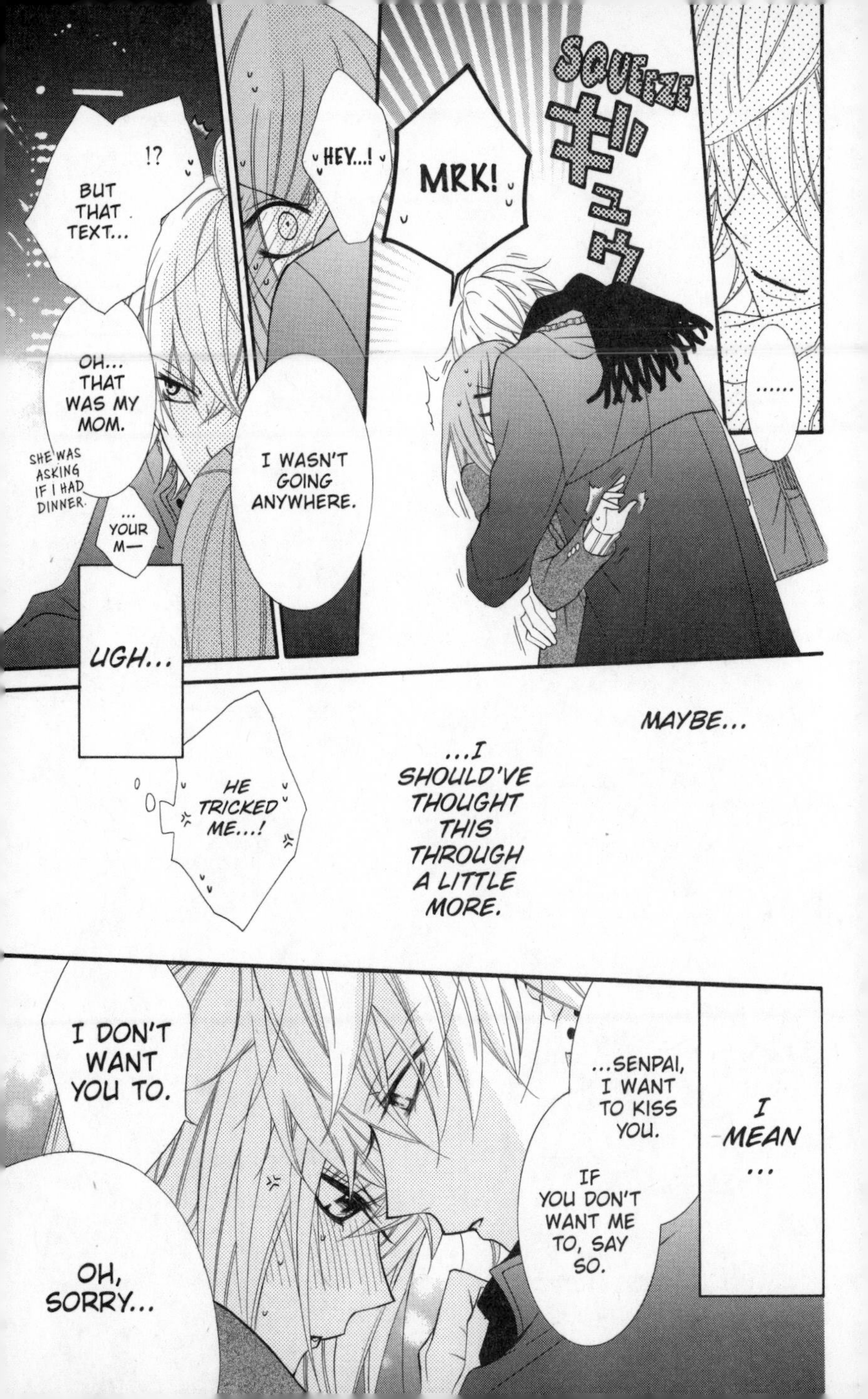
......
SQUEEZE
MRK!
HEY...!
I WASN'T GOING ANYWHERE.
!?
BUT THAT TEXT...
OH... THAT WAS MY MOM.
SHE WAS ASKING IF I HAD DINNER.
...YOUR M—
UGH...
MAYBE...
...I SHOULD'VE THOUGHT THIS THROUGH A LITTLE MORE.
HE TRICKED ME...!
I MEAN...
...SENPAI, I WANT TO KISS YOU.
IF YOU DON'T WANT ME TO, SAY SO.
I DON'T WANT YOU TO.
OH, SORRY...

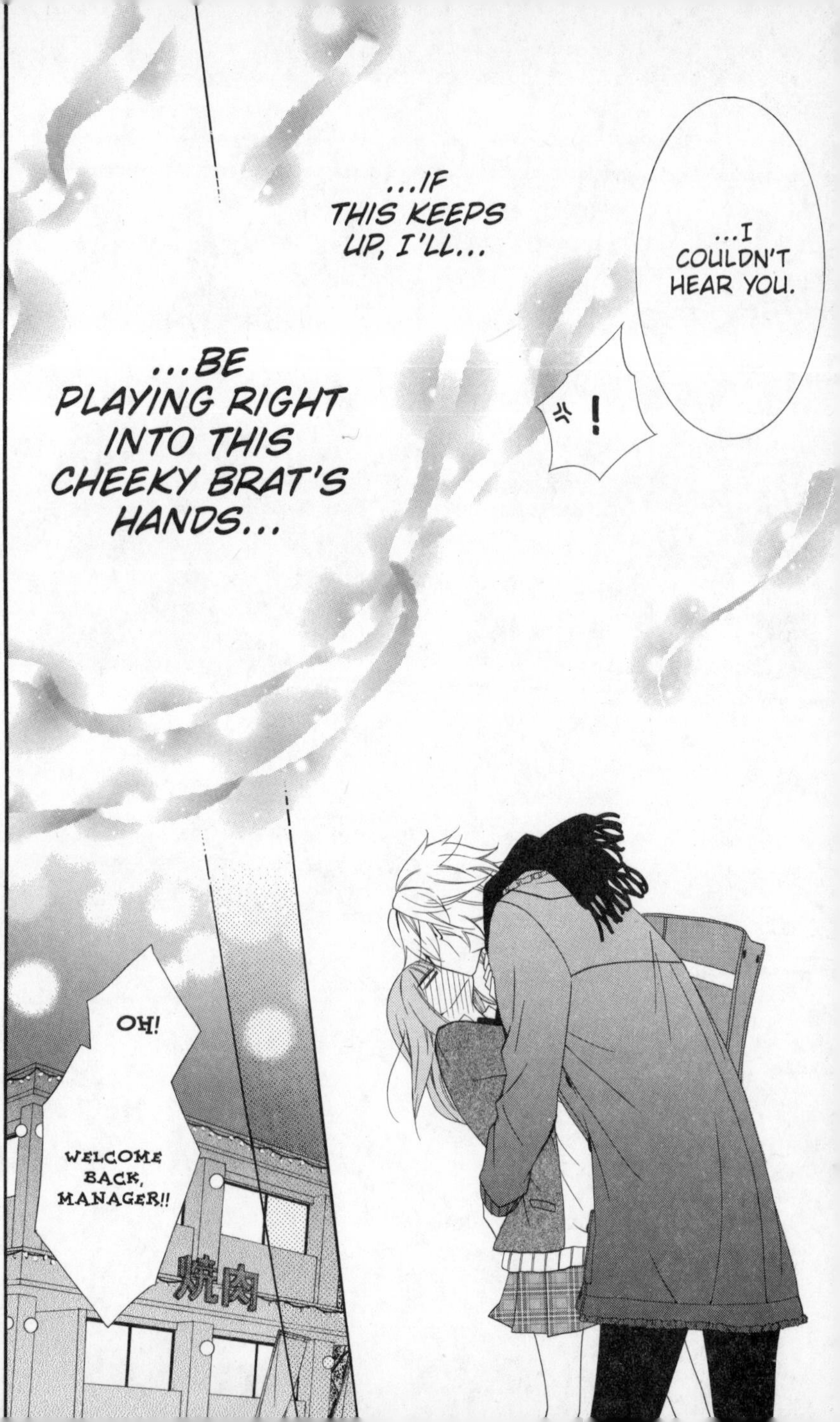
...I COULDN'T HEAR YOU.
!
...IF THIS KEEPS UP, I'LL...
...BE PLAYING RIGHT INTO THIS CHEEKY BRAT'S HANDS...
OH!
WELCOME BACK, MANAGER!!
焼肉

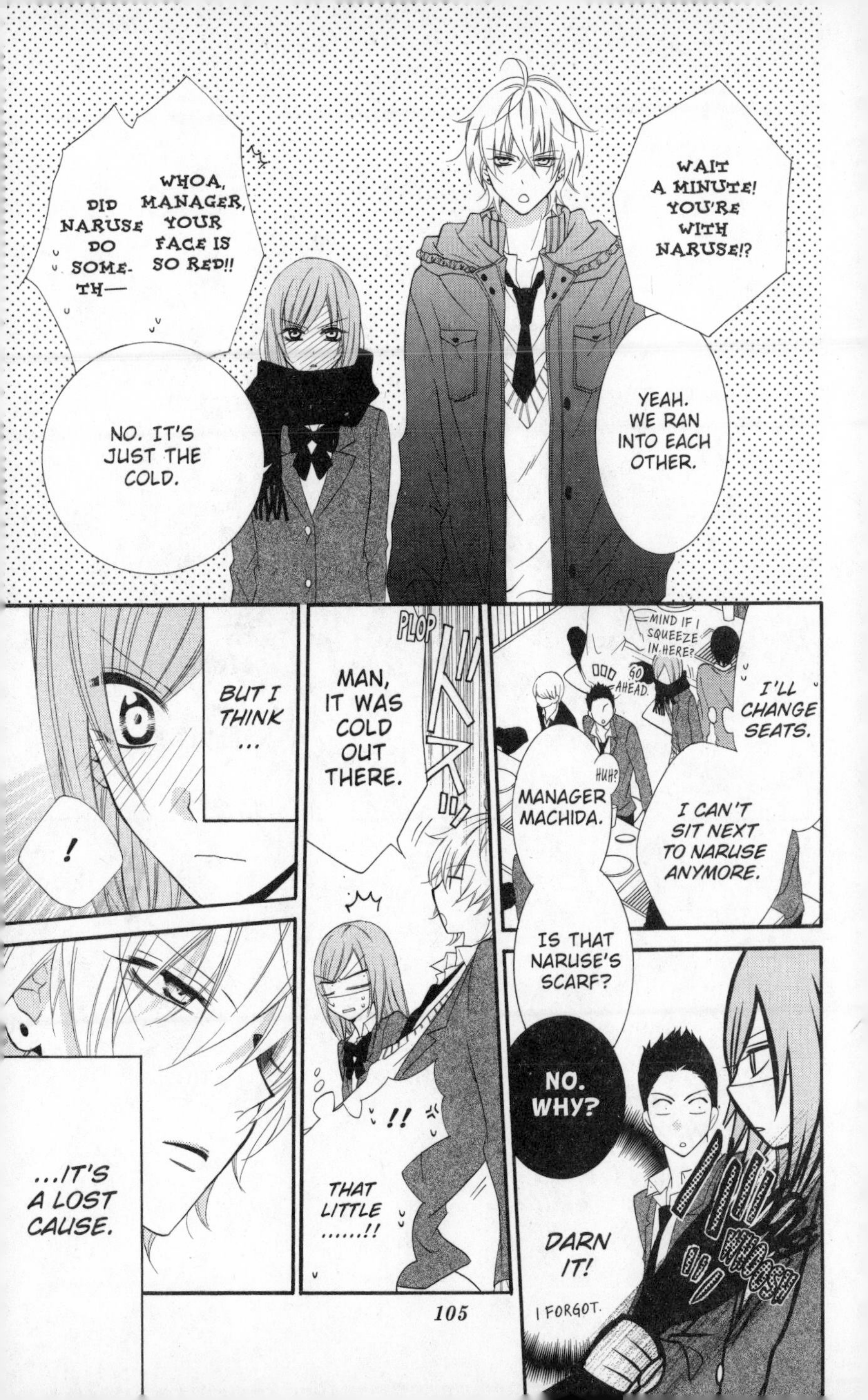
WAIT A MINUTE! YOU'RE WITH NARUSE!?
YEAH. WE RAN INTO EACH OTHER.
WHOA, MANAGER, YOUR FACE IS SO RED!!
DID NARUSE DO SOME-TH—
NO. IT'S JUST THE COLD.
MIND IF I SQUEEZE IN HERE?
GO AHEAD.
I'LL CHANGE SEATS.
HUH?
MANAGER MACHIDA.
I CAN'T SIT NEXT TO NARUSE ANYMORE.
IS THAT NARUSE'S SCARF?
NO. WHY?
DARN IT!
I FORGOT.
PLOP
MAN, IT WAS COLD OUT THERE.
!!
THAT LITTLE ......!!
BUT I THINK ...
!
...IT'S A LOST CAUSE.

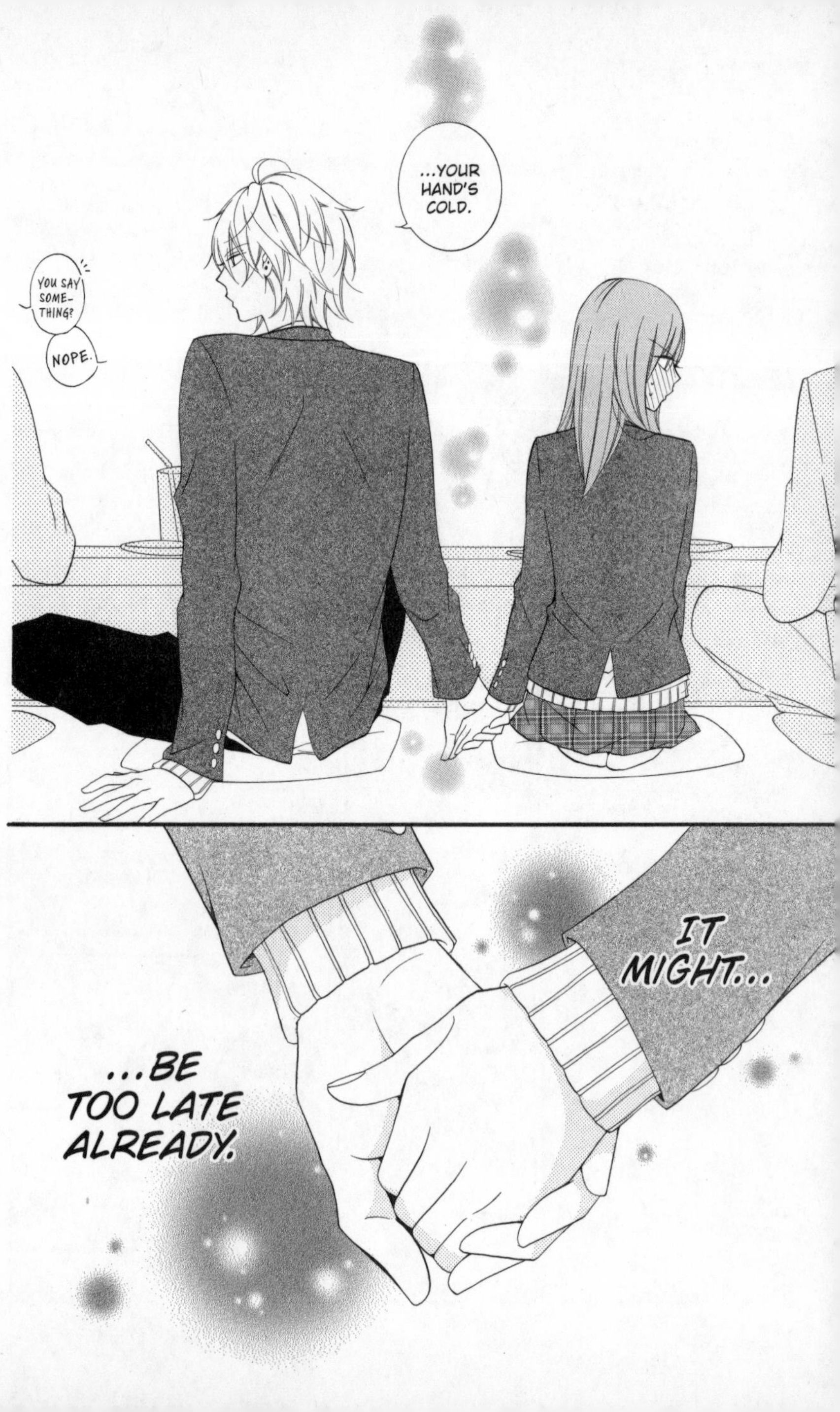
...YOUR HAND'S COLD.
YOU SAY SOME-THING?
NOPE.
IT MIGHT...
...BE TOO LATE ALREADY.

THE FAREWELL CARDS THEY GAVE TO THE SENPAIS
AT THE CHRISTMAS PARTY
Dear Tanabe-senpai
TAKE CARE!
WHOA!!
THANKS, GUYS!
IS THIS PICTURE FROM OUR SUMMER TRAINING CAMP?
BUZZ
WHOA! I'M SUPER TAN!
BUZZ
!?
HEY!!
WHO GAVE ME A UNI-BROW!?

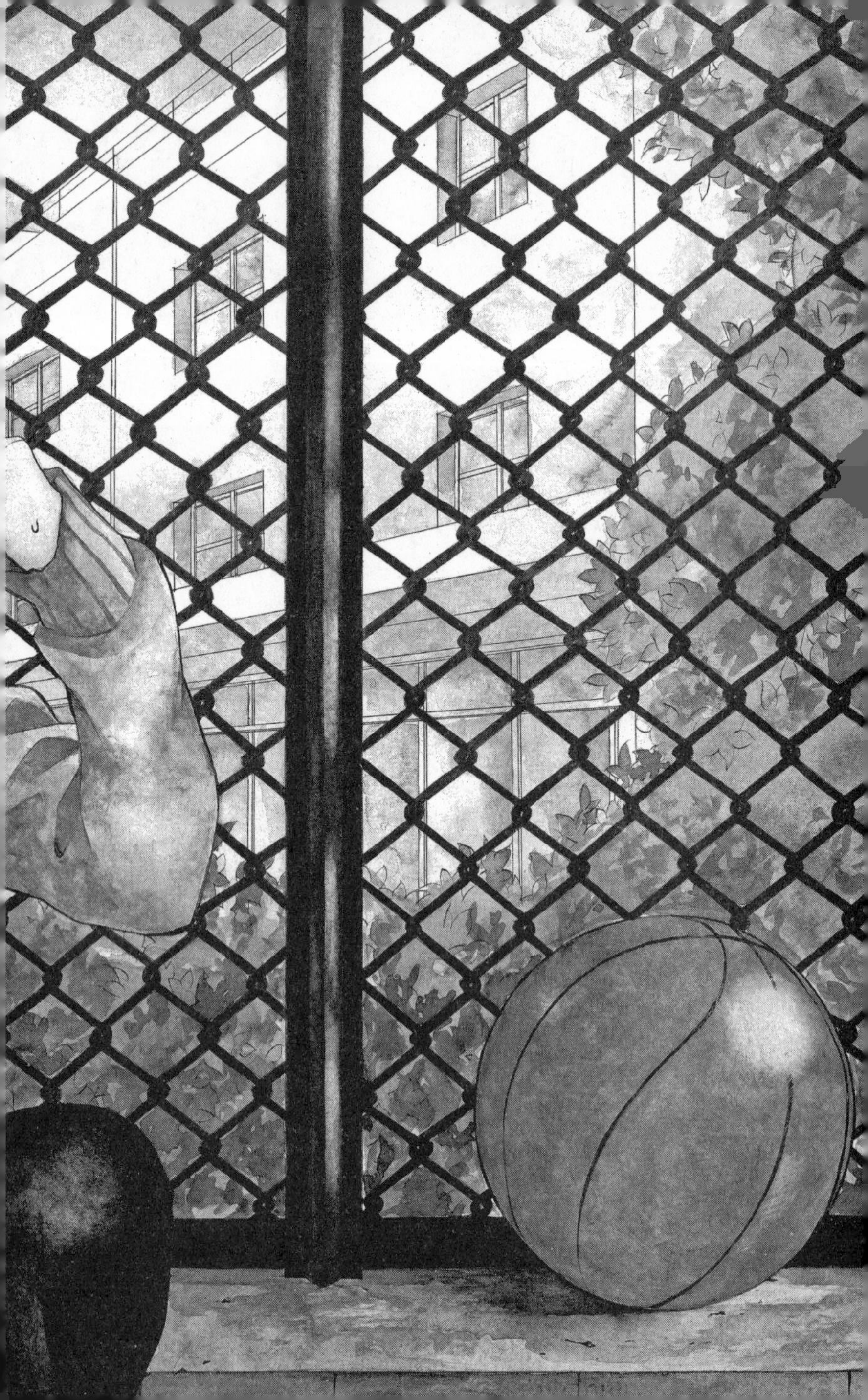

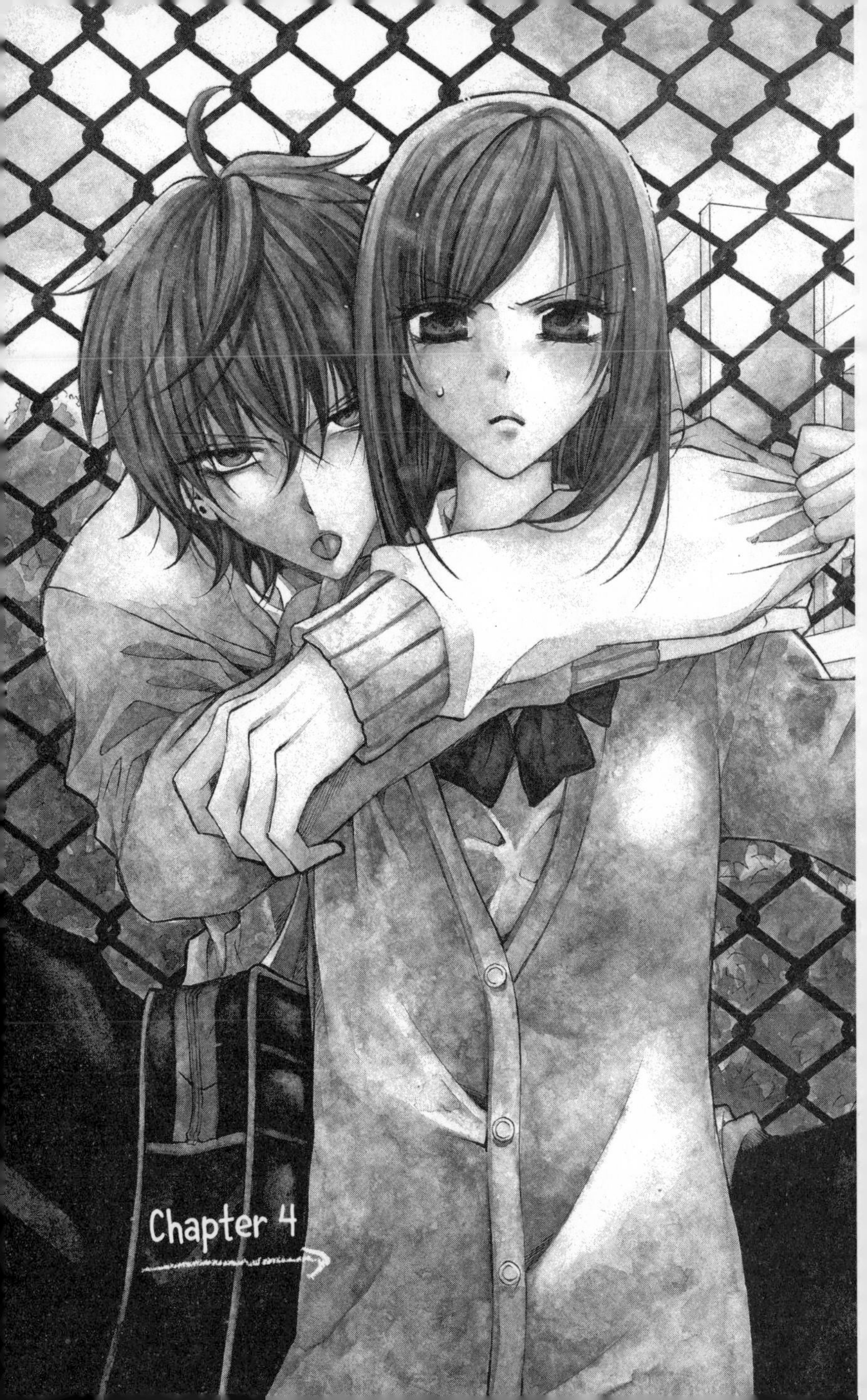
Chapter 4

CHEEKY BRAT

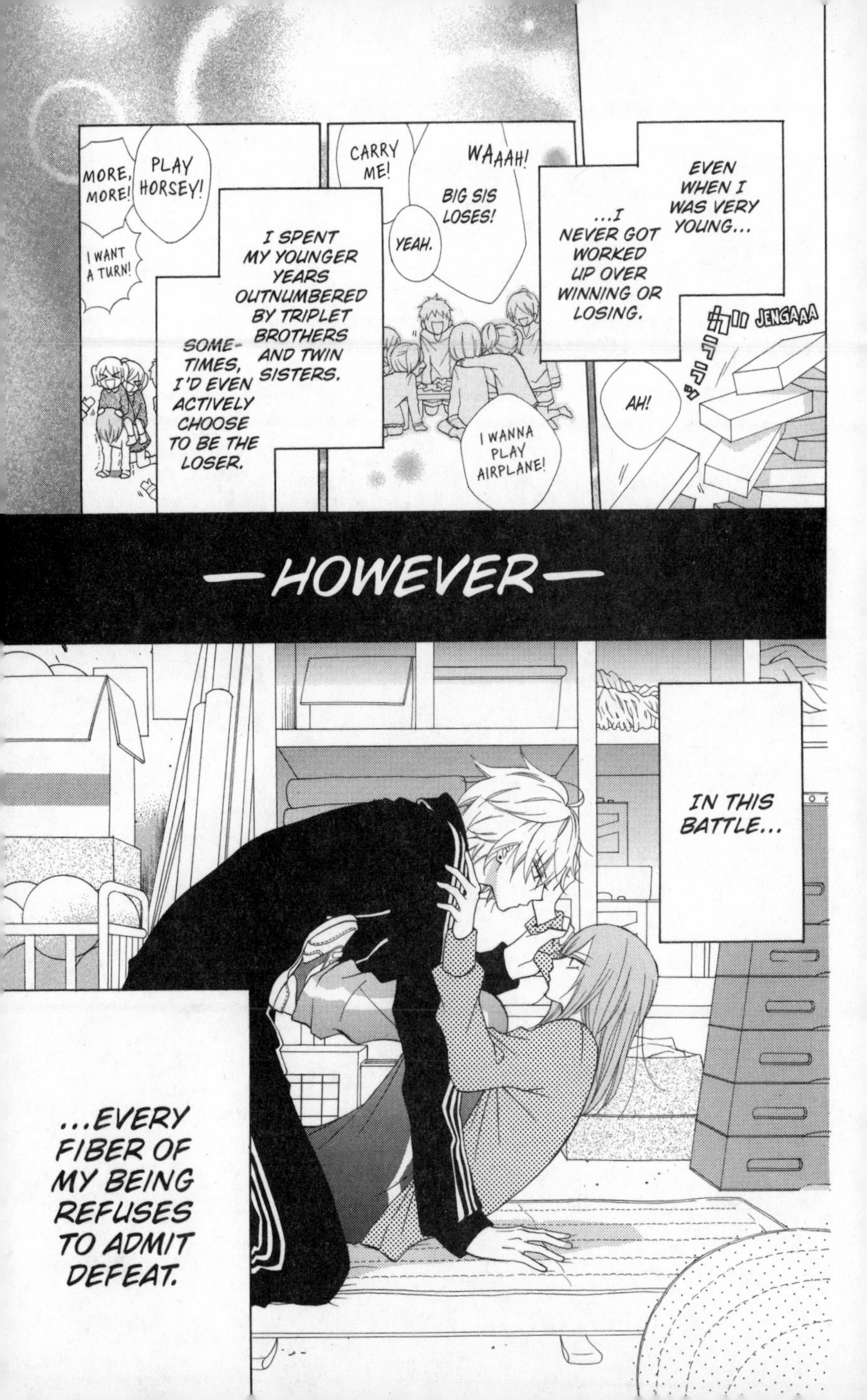
EVEN WHEN I WAS VERY YOUNG...
...I NEVER GOT WORKED UP OVER WINNING OR LOSING.
JENGAAA
AH!
WAAAH!
CARRY ME!
BIG SIS LOSES!
YEAH.
I WANNA PLAY AIRPLANE!
I SPENT MY YOUNGER YEARS OUTNUMBERED BY TRIPLET BROTHERS AND TWIN SISTERS.
PLAY HORSEY!
MORE, MORE!
I WANT A TURN!
SOMETIMES, I'D EVEN ACTIVELY CHOOSE TO BE THE LOSER.
—HOWEVER—
IN THIS BATTLE...
...EVERY FIBER OF MY BEING REFUSES TO ADMIT DEFEAT.

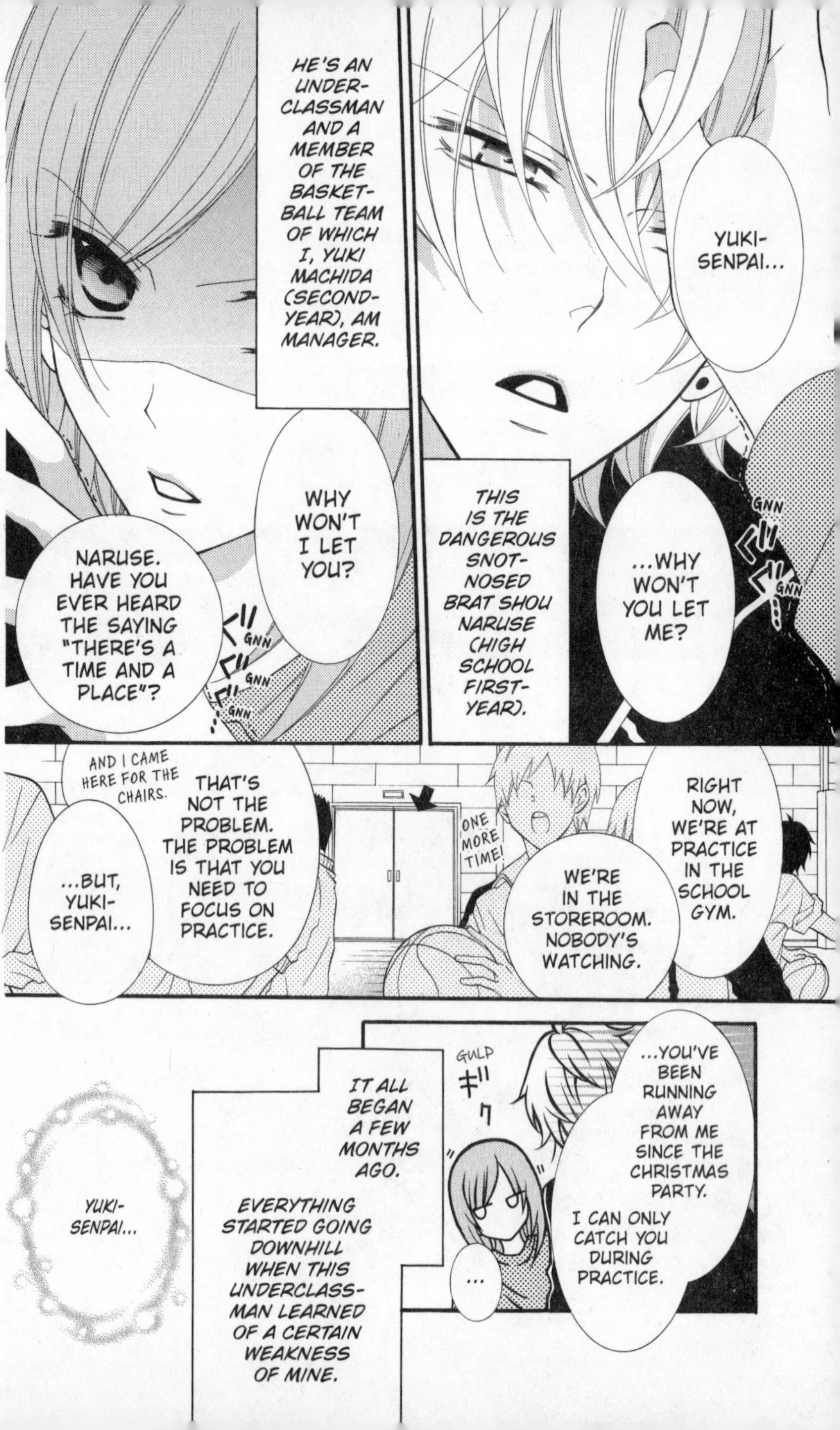
YUKI-SENPAI...
THIS IS THE DANGEROUS SNOT-NOSED BRAT SHOU NARUSE (HIGH SCHOOL FIRST-YEAR).
GNN
GNN
...WHY WON'T YOU LET ME?
HE'S AN UNDER-CLASSMAN AND A MEMBER OF THE BASKET-BALL TEAM OF WHICH I, YUKI MACHIDA (SECOND-YEAR), AM MANAGER.
WHY WON'T I LET YOU?
GNN
GNN
GNN
NARUSE. HAVE YOU EVER HEARD THE SAYING "THERE'S A TIME AND A PLACE"?
RIGHT NOW, WE'RE AT PRACTICE IN THE SCHOOL GYM.
WE'RE IN THE STOREROOM. NOBODY'S WATCHING.
ONE MORE TIME!
THAT'S NOT THE PROBLEM. THE PROBLEM IS THAT YOU NEED TO FOCUS ON PRACTICE.
AND I CAME HERE FOR THE CHAIRS.
...BUT, YUKI-SENPAI...
...YOU'VE BEEN RUNNING AWAY FROM ME SINCE THE CHRISTMAS PARTY.
I CAN ONLY CATCH YOU DURING PRACTICE.
GULP
...
IT ALL BEGAN A FEW MONTHS AGO.
EVERYTHING STARTED GOING DOWNHILL WHEN THIS UNDERCLASS-MAN LEARNED OF A CERTAIN WEAKNESS OF MINE.
YUKI-SENPAI...

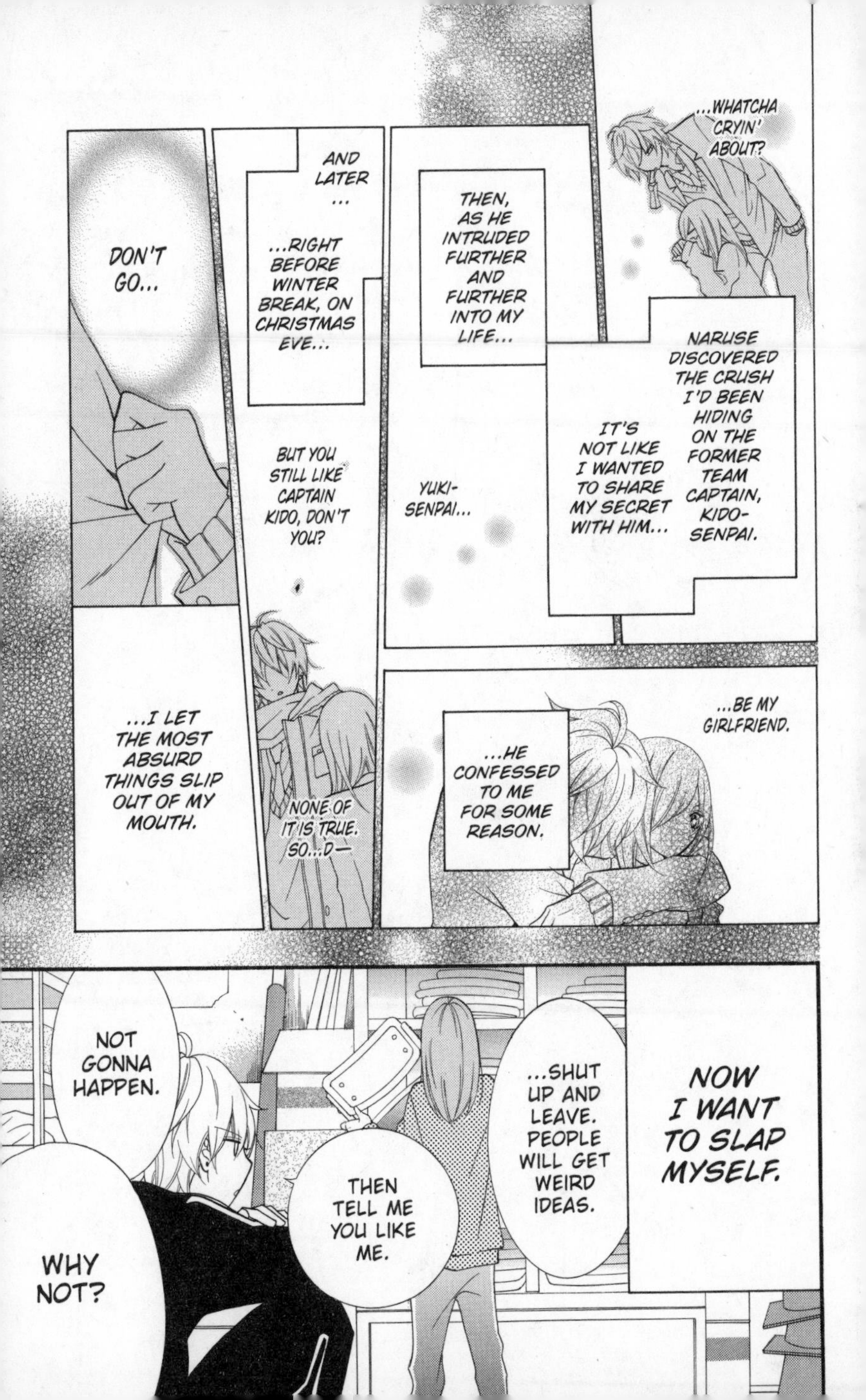
...WHATCHA CRYIN' ABOUT?
NARUSE DISCOVERED THE CRUSH I'D BEEN HIDING ON THE FORMER TEAM CAPTAIN, KIDO-SENPAI.
IT'S NOT LIKE I WANTED TO SHARE MY SECRET WITH HIM...
THEN, AS HE INTRUDED FURTHER AND FURTHER INTO MY LIFE...
YUKI-SENPAI...
...BE MY GIRLFRIEND.
...HE CONFESSED TO ME FOR SOME REASON.
AND LATER ...
...RIGHT BEFORE WINTER BREAK, ON CHRISTMAS EVE...
BUT YOU STILL LIKE CAPTAIN KIDO, DON'T YOU?
NONE OF IT IS TRUE. SO...D—
DON'T GO...
...I LET THE MOST ABSURD THINGS SLIP OUT OF MY MOUTH.
NOW I WANT TO SLAP MYSELF.
...SHUT UP AND LEAVE. PEOPLE WILL GET WEIRD IDEAS.
THEN TELL ME YOU LIKE ME.
NOT GONNA HAPPEN.
WHY NOT?

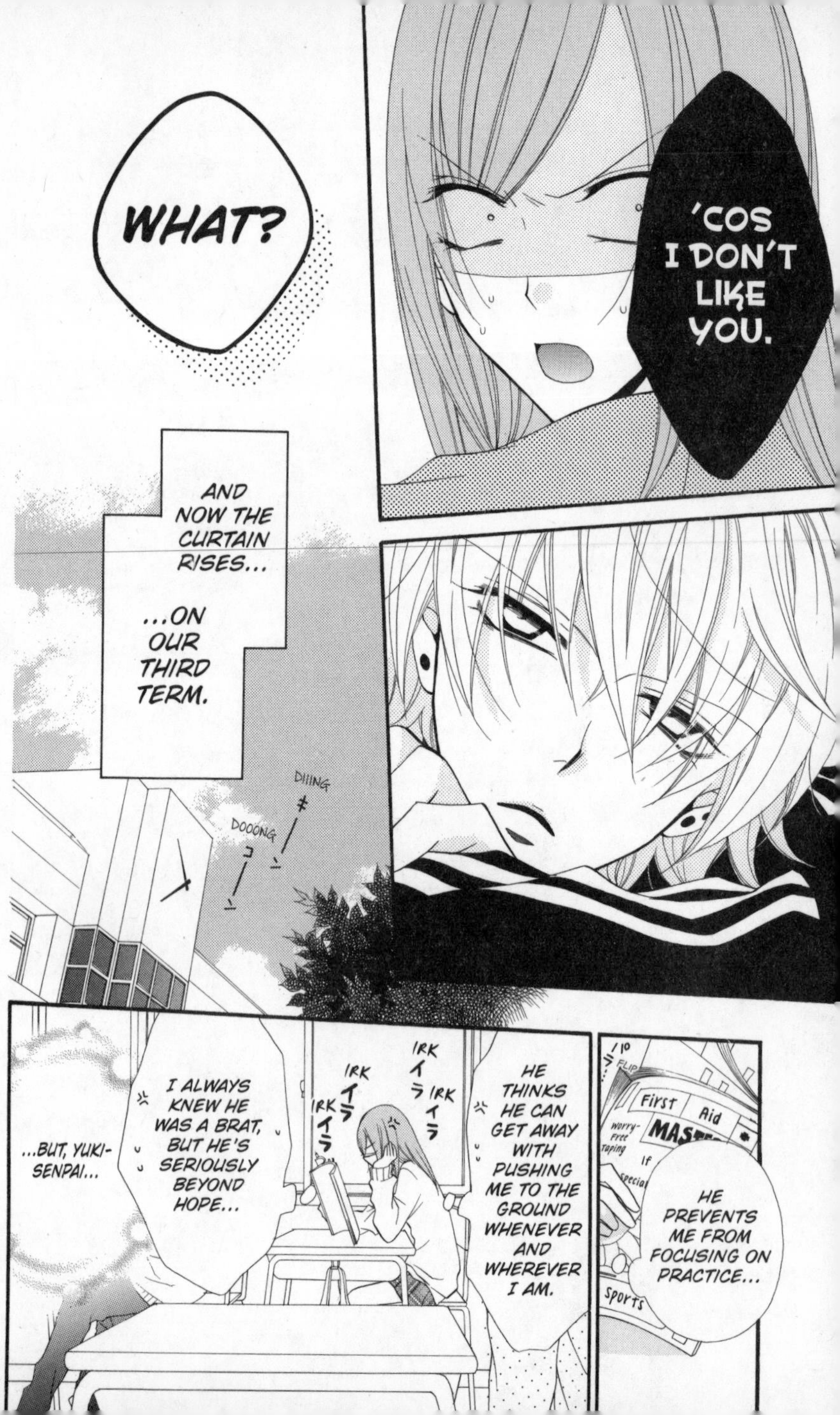
'COS I DON'T LIKE YOU.
WHAT?
AND NOW THE CURTAIN RISES...
...ON OUR THIRD TERM.
DIIING
DOOONG
FLIP
First Aid
Worry-Free Taping
Sports
HE PREVENTS ME FROM FOCUSING ON PRACTICE...
HE THINKS HE CAN GET AWAY WITH PUSHING ME TO THE GROUND WHENEVER AND WHEREVER I AM.
IRK
IRK
IRK
IRK
I ALWAYS KNEW HE WAS A BRAT, BUT HE'S SERIOUSLY BEYOND HOPE...
...BUT, YUKI-SENPAI...

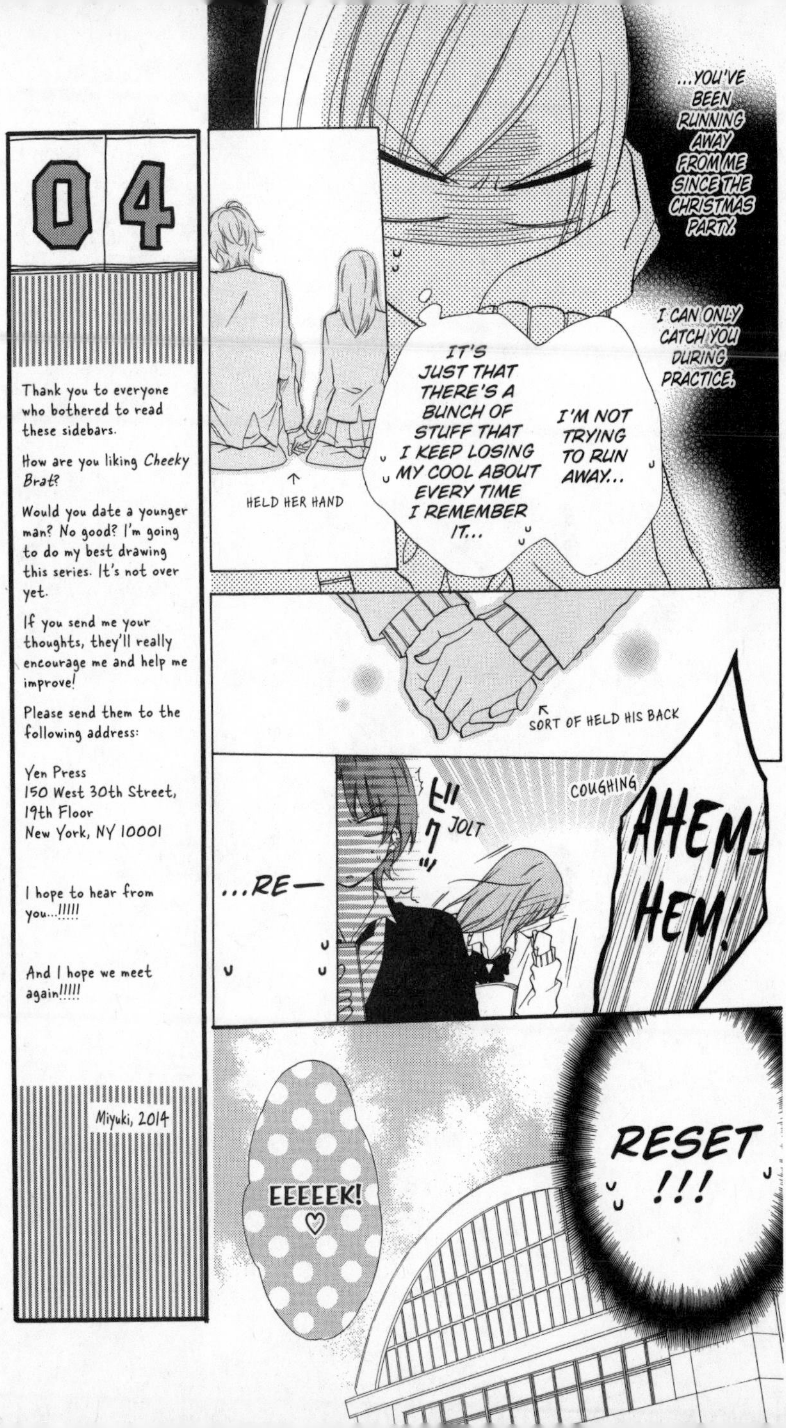
...YOU'VE BEEN RUNNING AWAY FROM ME SINCE THE CHRISTMAS PARTY.
I CAN ONLY CATCH YOU DURING PRACTICE.
I'M NOT TRYING TO RUN AWAY...
IT'S JUST THAT THERE'S A BUNCH OF STUFF THAT I KEEP LOSING MY COOL ABOUT EVERY TIME I REMEMBER IT...
HELD HER HAND
SORT OF HELD HIS BACK
COUGHING
AHEM-HEM!
JOLT
...RE—
RESET!!!
EEEEEK! ♡

04

Thank you to everyone who bothered to read these sidebars.

How are you liking *Cheeky Brat*?

Would you date a younger man? No good? I'm going to do my best drawing this series. It's not over yet.

If you send me your thoughts, they'll really encourage me and help me improve!

Please send them to the following address:

Yen Press
150 West 30th Street,
19th Floor
New York, NY 10001

I hope to hear from you...!!!!!

And I hope we meet again!!!!!

Miyuki, 2014

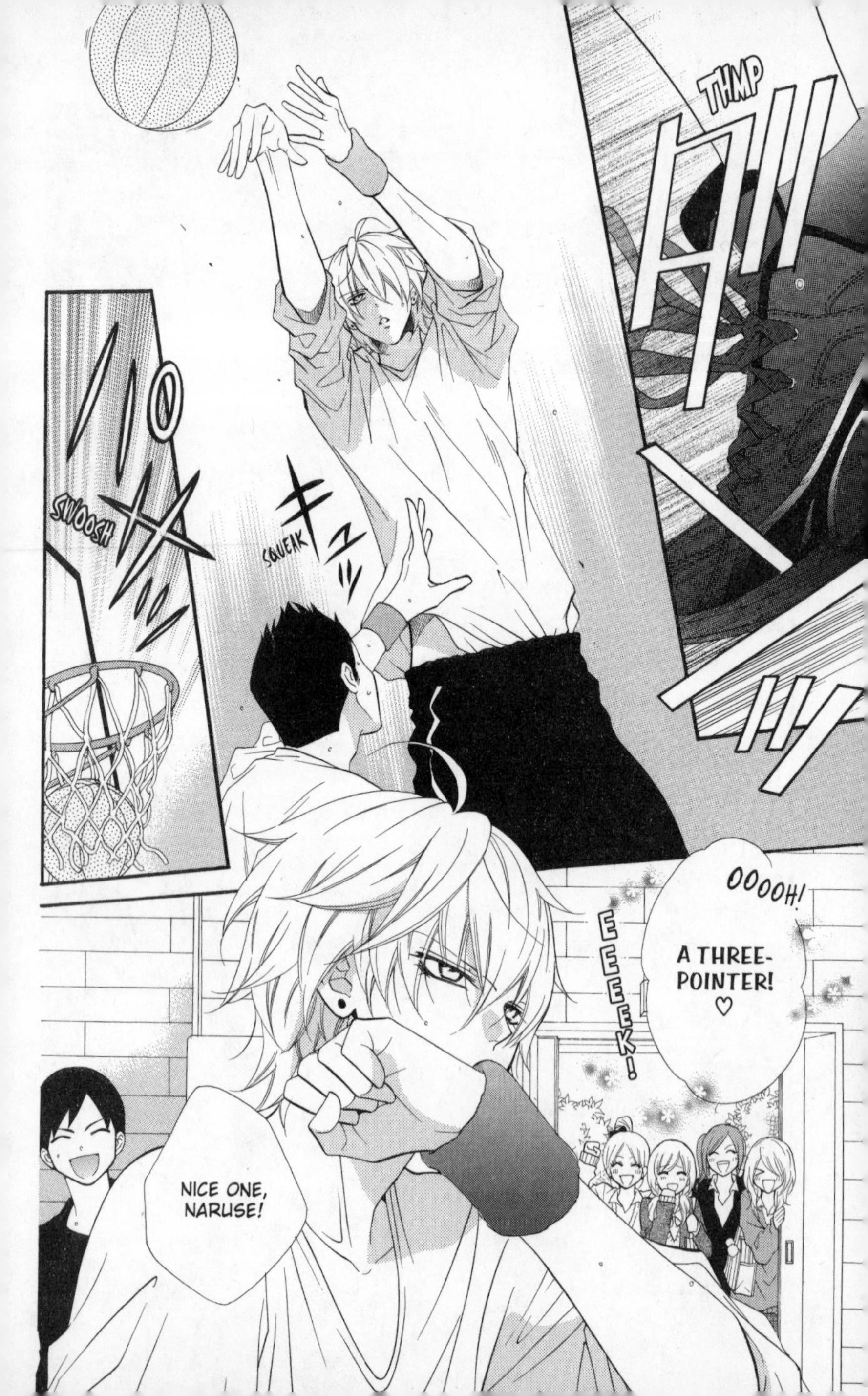
THMP
SQUEAK
SWOOSH
OOOOH!
A THREE-POINTER! ♡
EEEEK!
NICE ONE, NARUSE!

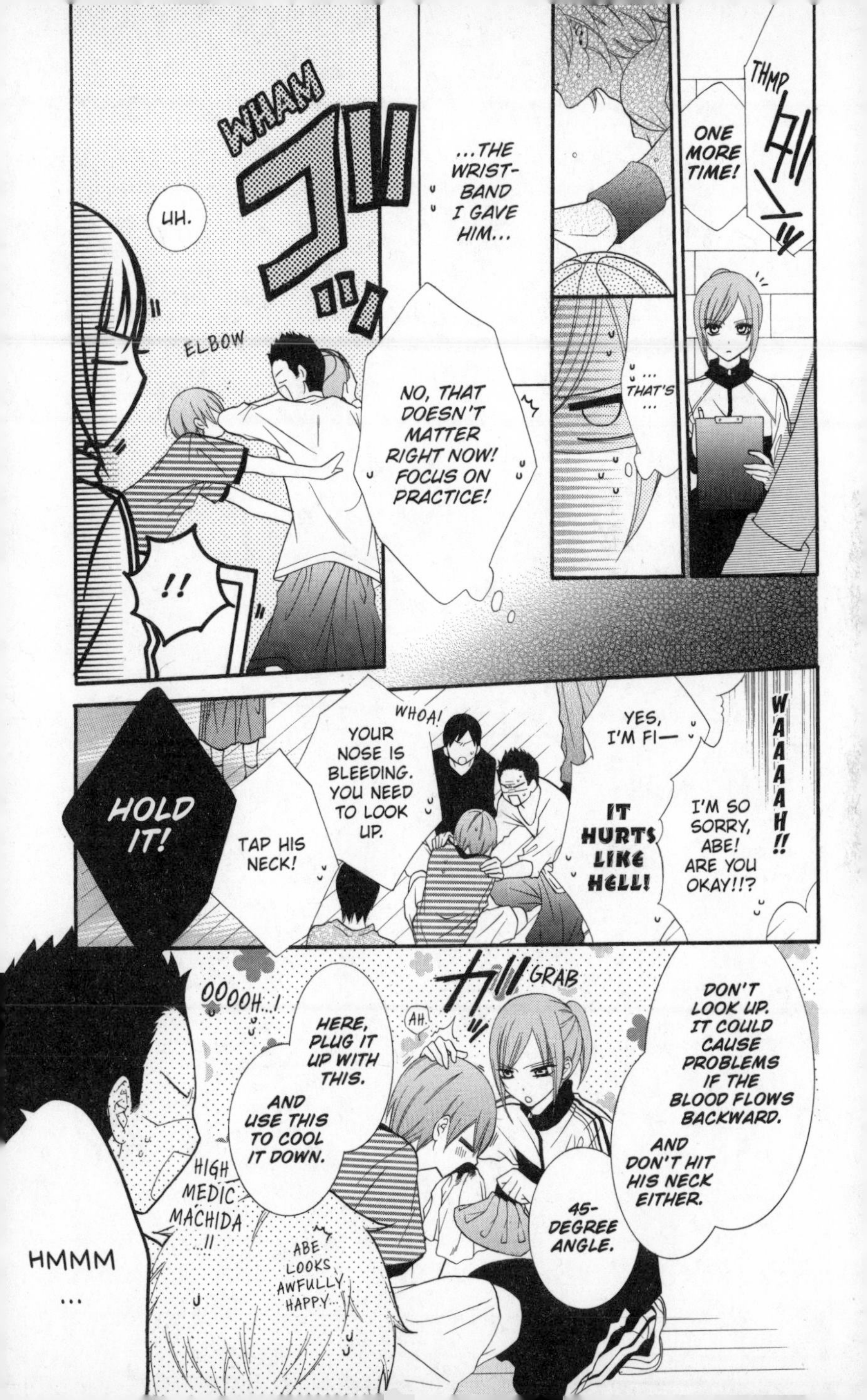
THMP
ONE MORE TIME!
...THAT'S...
...THE WRIST-BAND I GAVE HIM...
NO, THAT DOESN'T MATTER RIGHT NOW! FOCUS ON PRACTICE!
WHAM
UH.
ELBOW
!!
WAAAAAH!!
YES, I'M FI—
I'M SO SORRY, ABE! ARE YOU OKAY!!?
IT HURTS LIKE HELL!
WHOA!
YOUR NOSE IS BLEEDING. YOU NEED TO LOOK UP.
TAP HIS NECK!
HOLD IT!
GRAB
DON'T LOOK UP. IT COULD CAUSE PROBLEMS IF THE BLOOD FLOWS BACKWARD.
AND DON'T HIT HIS NECK EITHER.
45-DEGREE ANGLE.
AH.
HERE, PLUG IT UP WITH THIS.
AND USE THIS TO COOL IT DOWN.
OOOOH...!
HIGH MEDIC MACHIDA...!!
ABE LOOKS AWFULLY HAPPY...
HMMM...

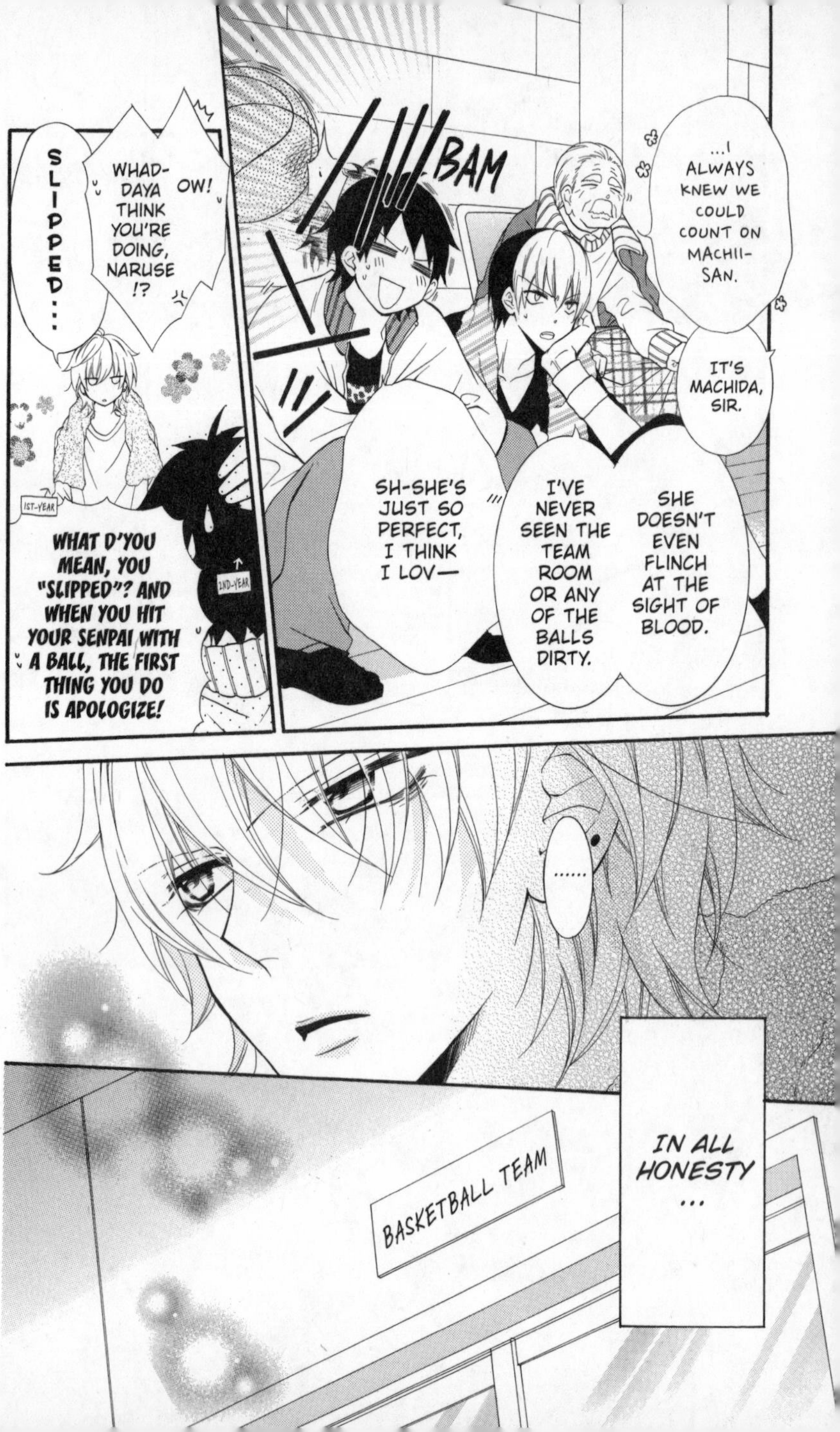
...I ALWAYS KNEW WE COULD COUNT ON MACHII-SAN.
IT'S MACHIDA, SIR.
BAM
SHE DOESN'T EVEN FLINCH AT THE SIGHT OF BLOOD.
I'VE NEVER SEEN THE TEAM ROOM OR ANY OF THE BALLS DIRTY.
SH-SHE'S JUST SO PERFECT, I THINK I LOV—
OW!
WHAD-DAYA THINK YOU'RE DOING, NARUSE!?
SLIPPED...
1ST-YEAR
2ND-YEAR
WHAT D'YOU MEAN, YOU "SLIPPED"? AND WHEN YOU HIT YOUR SENPAI WITH A BALL, THE FIRST THING YOU DO IS APOLOGIZE!
......
IN ALL HONESTY...
BASKETBALL TEAM

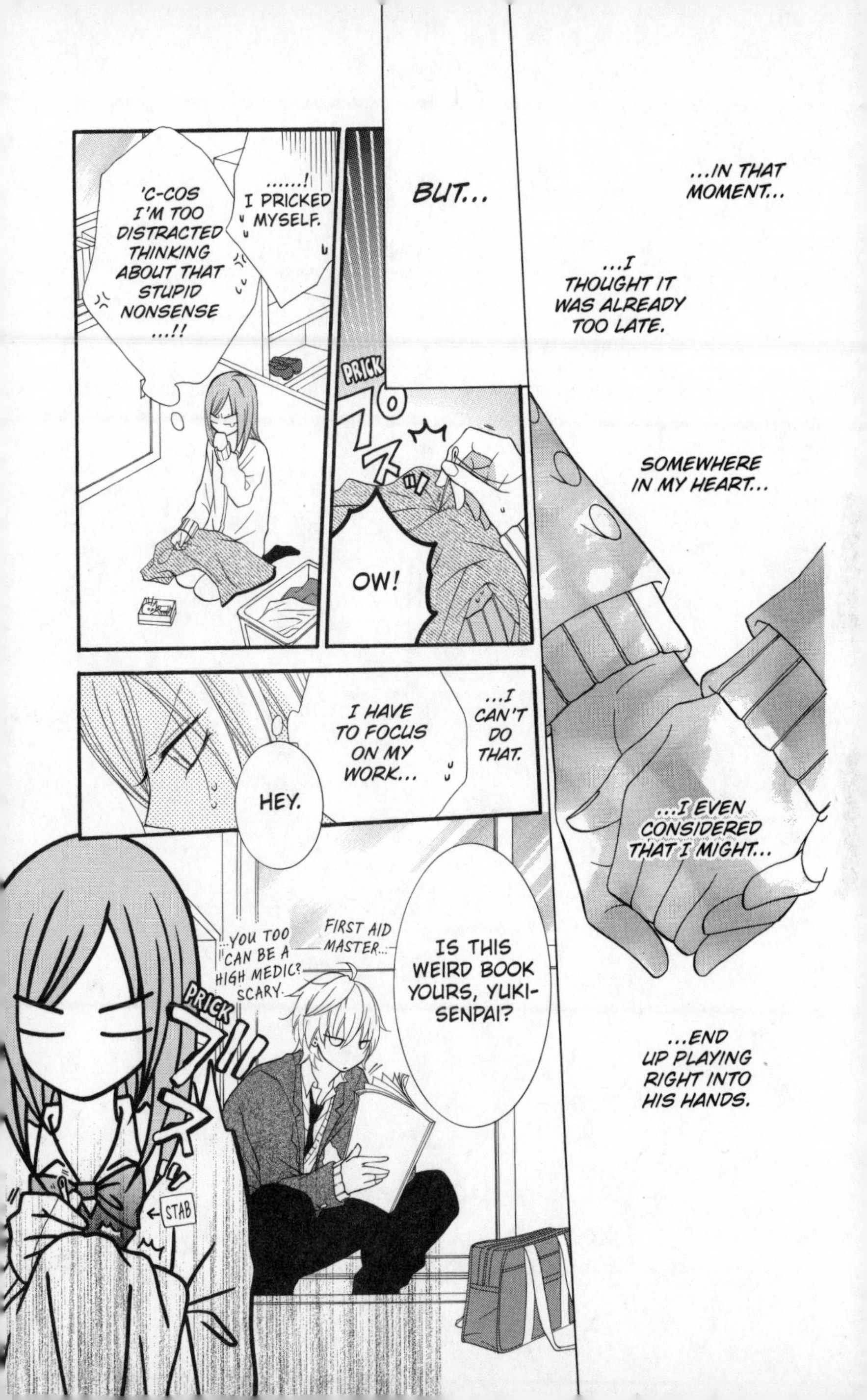
...IN THAT MOMENT...
...I THOUGHT IT WAS ALREADY TOO LATE.
SOMEWHERE IN MY HEART...
...I EVEN CONSIDERED THAT I MIGHT...
...END UP PLAYING RIGHT INTO HIS HANDS.
BUT...
PRICK
OW!
......! I PRICKED MYSELF.
'C-COS I'M TOO DISTRACTED THINKING ABOUT THAT STUPID NONSENSE ...!!
...I CAN'T DO THAT.
I HAVE TO FOCUS ON MY WORK...
HEY.
IS THIS WEIRD BOOK YOURS, YUKI-SENPAI?
FIRST AID MASTER...
...YOU TOO CAN BE A HIGH MEDIC? SCARY.
PRICK
STAB

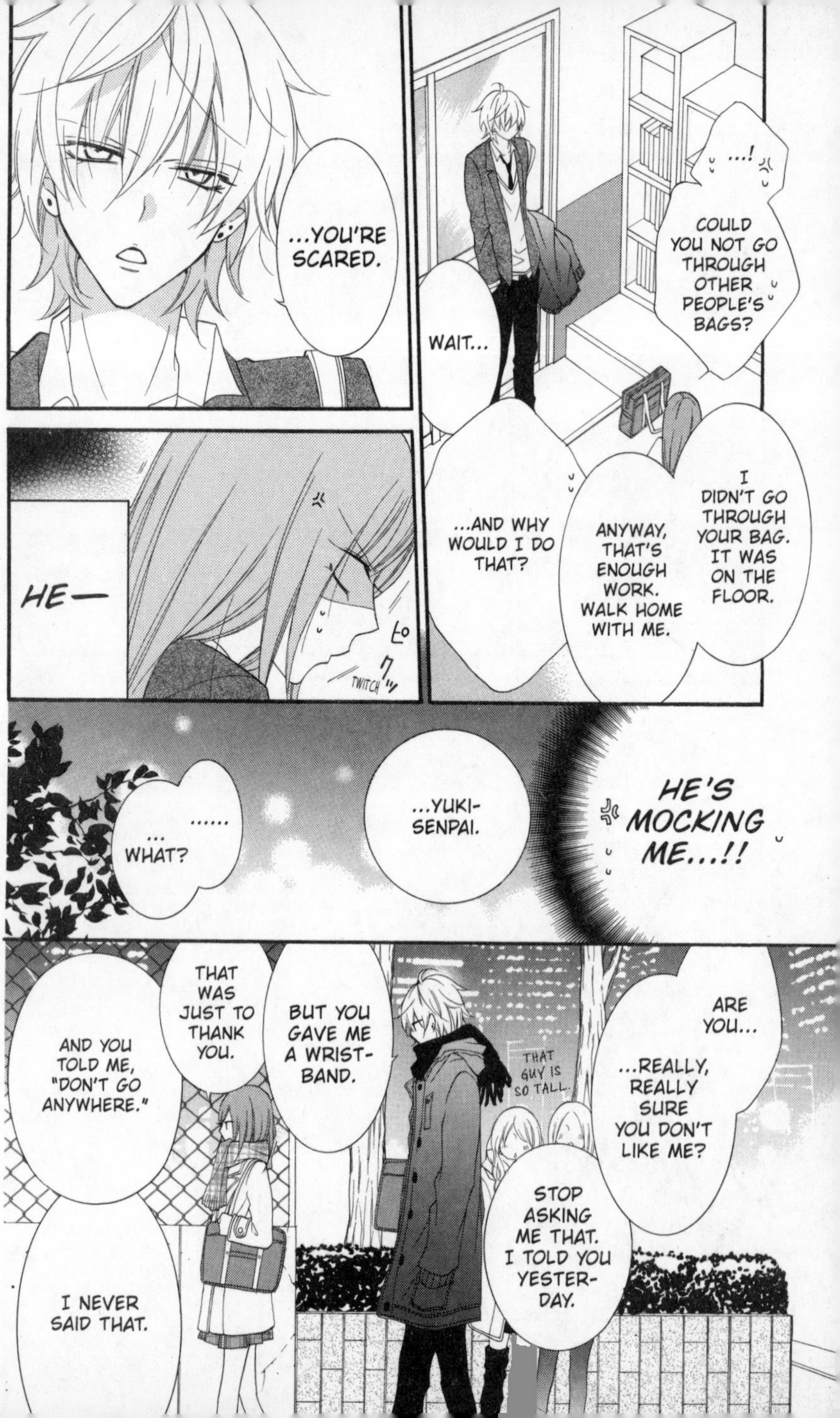
...!
COULD YOU NOT GO THROUGH OTHER PEOPLE'S BAGS?
WAIT...
I DIDN'T GO THROUGH YOUR BAG. IT WAS ON THE FLOOR.
ANYWAY, THAT'S ENOUGH WORK. WALK HOME WITH ME.
...AND WHY WOULD I DO THAT?
...YOU'RE SCARED.
HE—
TWITCH
HE'S MOCKING ME...!!
...YUKI-SENPAI.
......
... WHAT?
ARE YOU...
...REALLY, REALLY SURE YOU DON'T LIKE ME?
STOP ASKING ME THAT. I TOLD YOU YESTER-DAY.
THAT GUY IS SO TALL.
BUT YOU GAVE ME A WRIST-BAND.
THAT WAS JUST TO THANK YOU.
AND YOU TOLD ME, "DON'T GO ANYWHERE."
I NEVER SAID THAT.

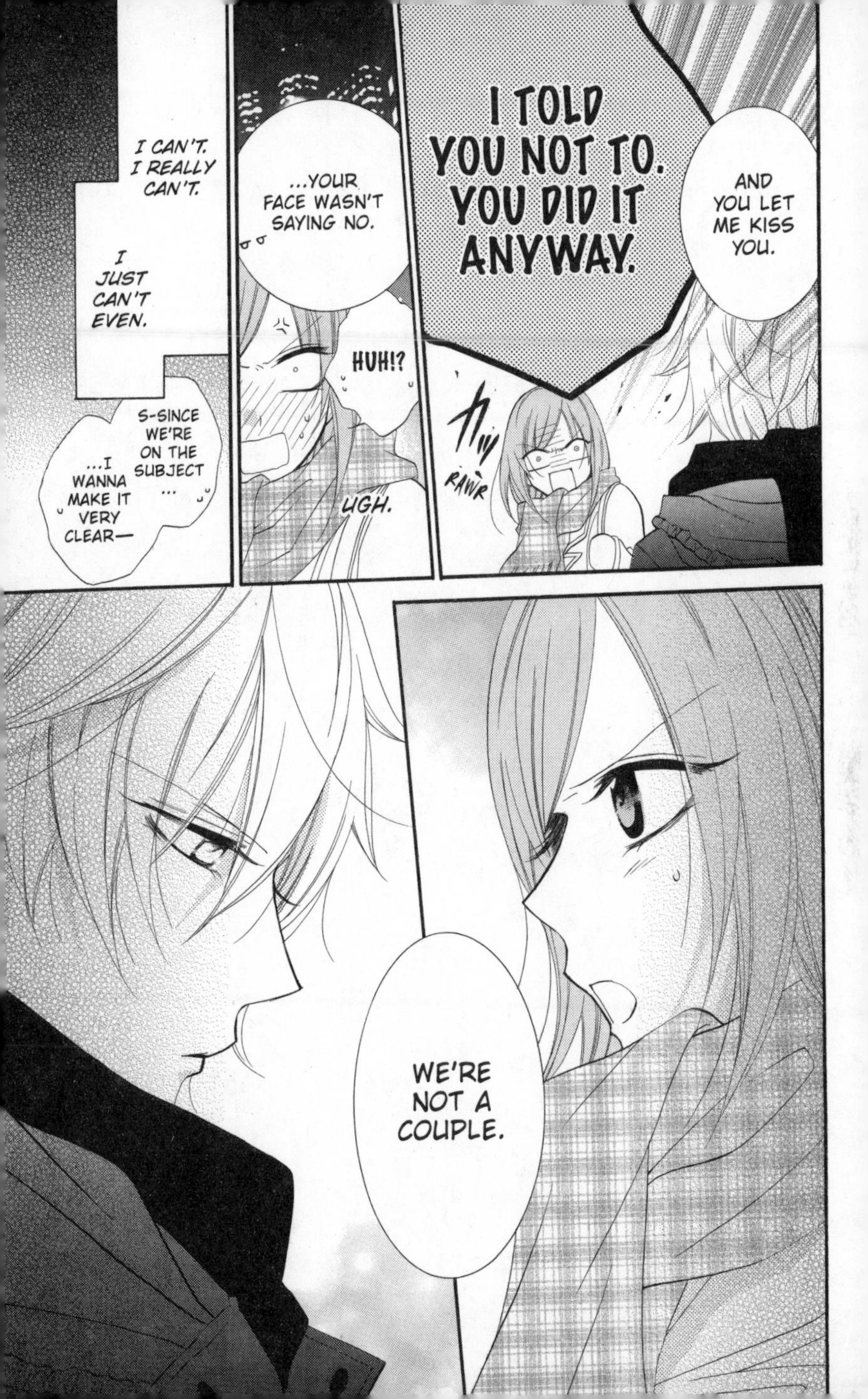
AND YOU LET ME KISS YOU.
I TOLD YOU NOT TO. YOU DID IT ANYWAY.
RAWR
...YOUR FACE WASN'T SAYING NO.
HUH!?
UGH.
I CAN'T. I REALLY CAN'T.
I JUST CAN'T EVEN.
S-SINCE WE'RE ON THE SUBJECT...
...I WANNA MAKE IT VERY CLEAR—
WE'RE NOT A COUPLE.

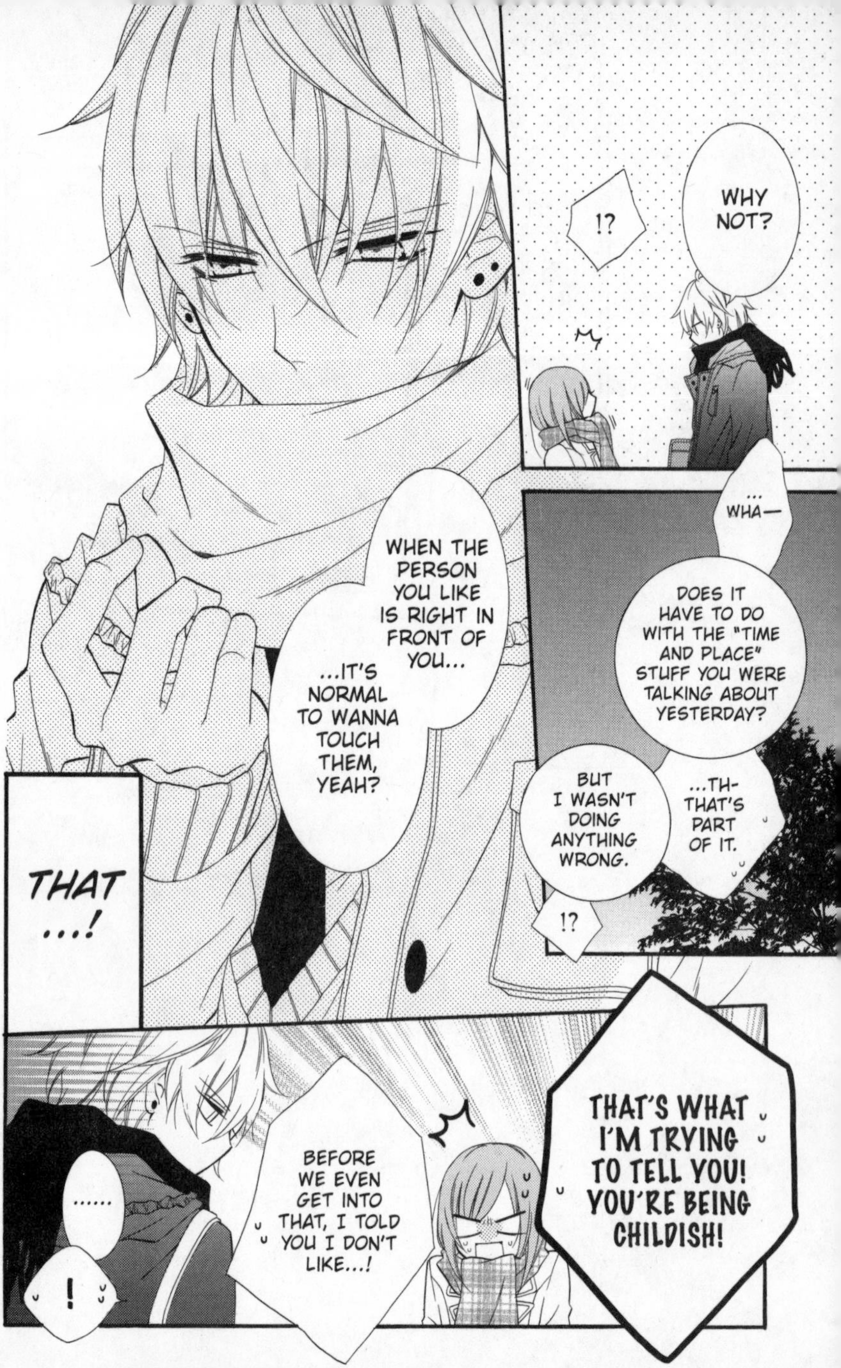
WHY NOT?
!?
...WHA—
DOES IT HAVE TO DO WITH THE "TIME AND PLACE" STUFF YOU WERE TALKING ABOUT YESTERDAY?
...TH-THAT'S PART OF IT.
BUT I WASN'T DOING ANYTHING WRONG.
!?
WHEN THE PERSON YOU LIKE IS RIGHT IN FRONT OF YOU...
...IT'S NORMAL TO WANNA TOUCH THEM, YEAH?
THAT...!
THAT'S WHAT I'M TRYING TO TELL YOU! YOU'RE BEING CHILDISH!
BEFORE WE EVEN GET INTO THAT, I TOLD YOU I DON'T LIKE...!
......
!

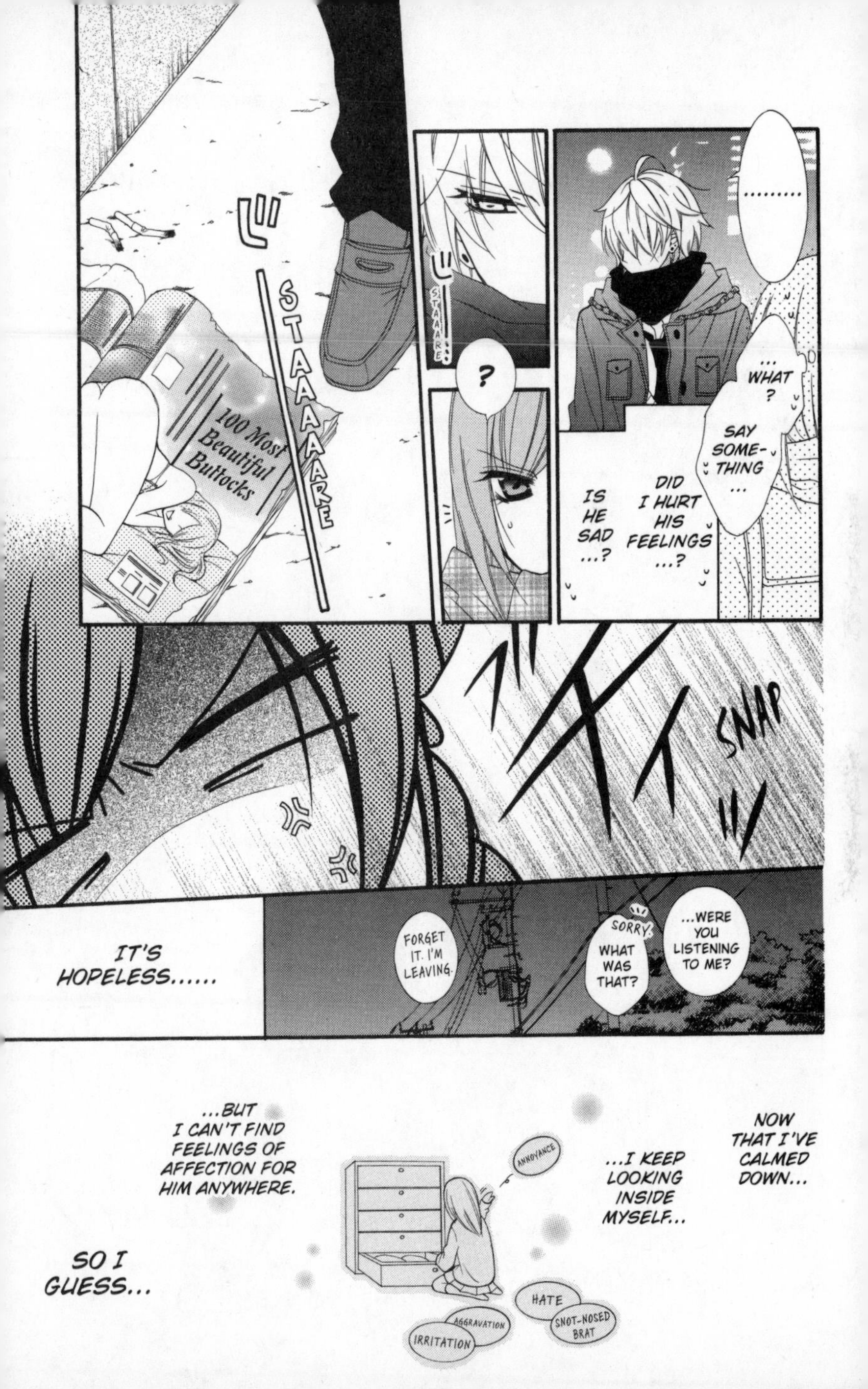

....
...WHAT?
SAY SOME-THING...
DID I HURT HIS FEELINGS...?
IS HE SAD...?
じ
STAAAARE
?
じ
STAAAAAAARE
100 Most Beautiful Buttocks
SNAP
...WERE YOU LISTENING TO ME?
SORRY. WHAT WAS THAT?
FORGET IT. I'M LEAVING.
IT'S HOPELESS......
NOW THAT I'VE CALMED DOWN...
...I KEEP LOOKING INSIDE MYSELF...
...BUT I CAN'T FIND FEELINGS OF AFFECTION FOR HIM ANYWHERE.
ANNOYANCE
HATE
SNOT-NOSED BRAT
AGGRAVATION
IRRITATION
SO I GUESS...

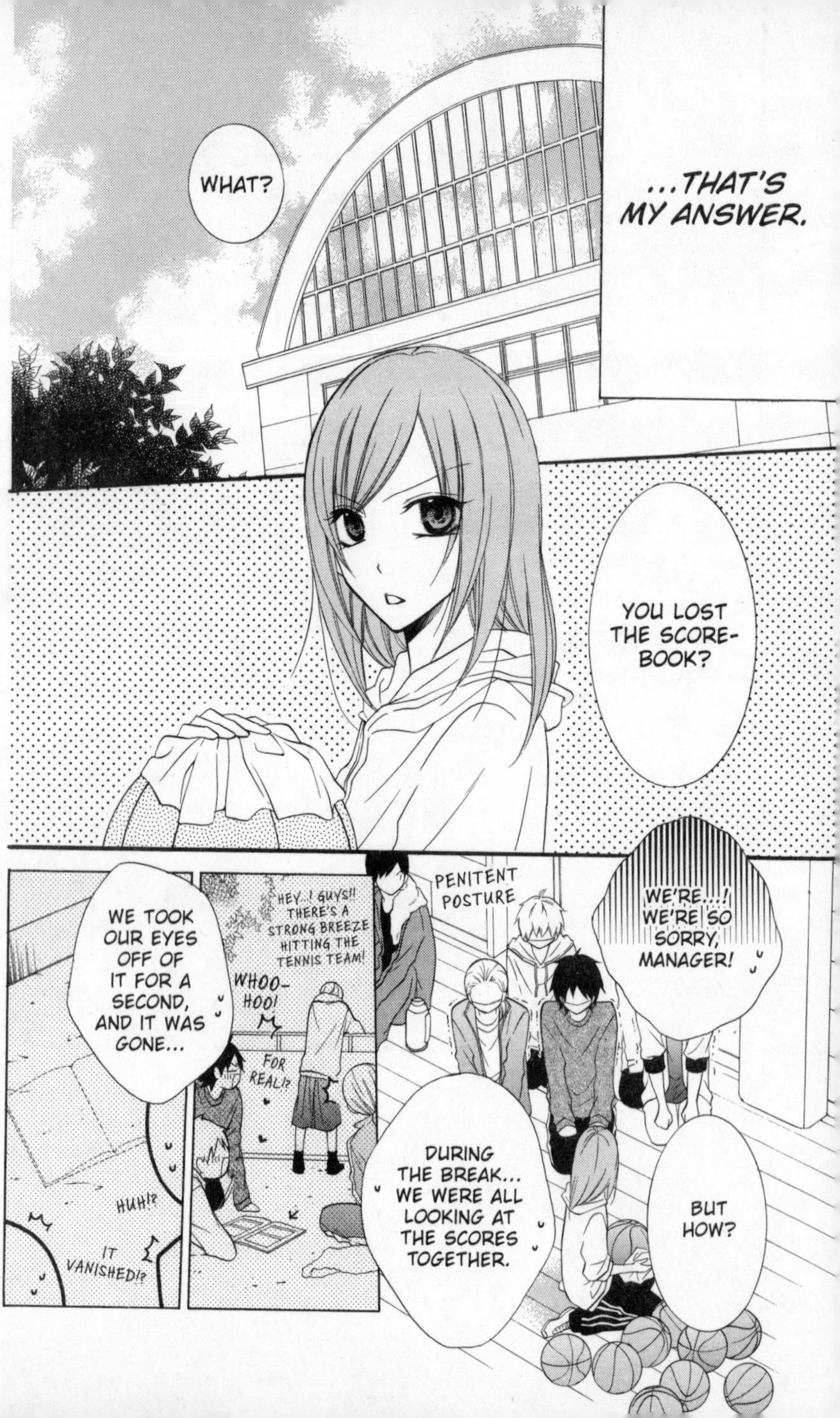
...THAT'S MY ANSWER.
WHAT?
YOU LOST THE SCORE-BOOK?
WE'RE...! WE'RE SO SORRY, MANAGER!
PENITENT POSTURE
BUT HOW?
DURING THE BREAK... WE WERE ALL LOOKING AT THE SCORES TOGETHER.
WE TOOK OUR EYES OFF OF IT FOR A SECOND, AND IT WAS GONE...
HEY...! GUYS!! THERE'S A STRONG BREEZE HITTING THE TENNIS TEAM!
WHOO-HOO!
FOR REAL!?
HUH!?
IT VANISHED!?

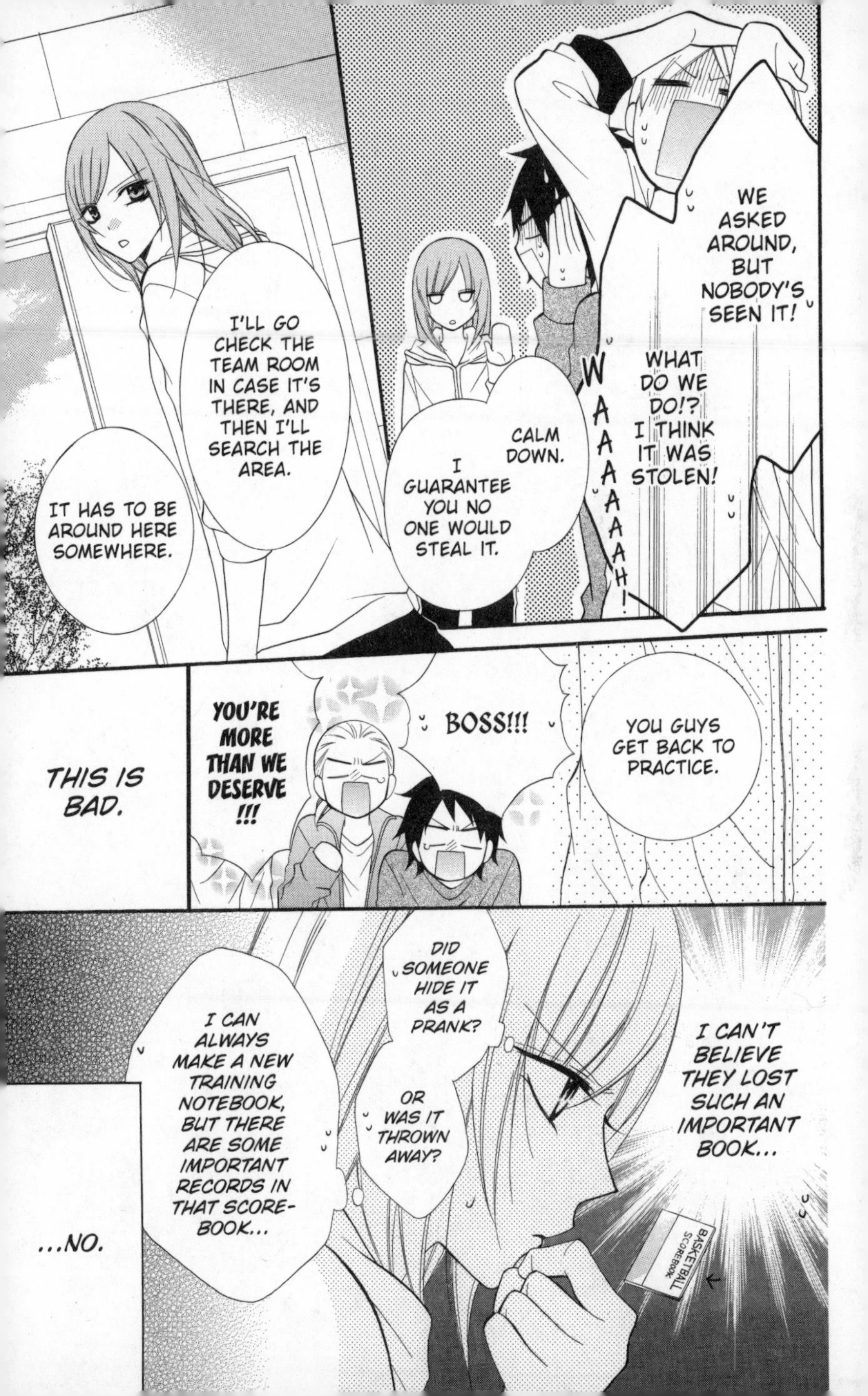
WE ASKED AROUND, BUT NOBODY'S SEEN IT!
WHAT DO WE DO!? I THINK IT WAS STOLEN!
WAAAAAAAH!
CALM DOWN.
I GUARANTEE YOU NO ONE WOULD STEAL IT.
I'LL GO CHECK THE TEAM ROOM IN CASE IT'S THERE, AND THEN I'LL SEARCH THE AREA.
IT HAS TO BE AROUND HERE SOMEWHERE.
YOU GUYS GET BACK TO PRACTICE.
BOSS!!!
YOU'RE MORE THAN WE DESERVE!!!
THIS IS BAD.
I CAN'T BELIEVE THEY LOST SUCH AN IMPORTANT BOOK...
BASKETBALL SCOREBOOK
DID SOMEONE HIDE IT AS A PRANK?
OR WAS IT THROWN AWAY?
I CAN ALWAYS MAKE A NEW TRAINING NOTEBOOK, BUT THERE ARE SOME IMPORTANT RECORDS IN THAT SCORE-BOOK...
...NO.

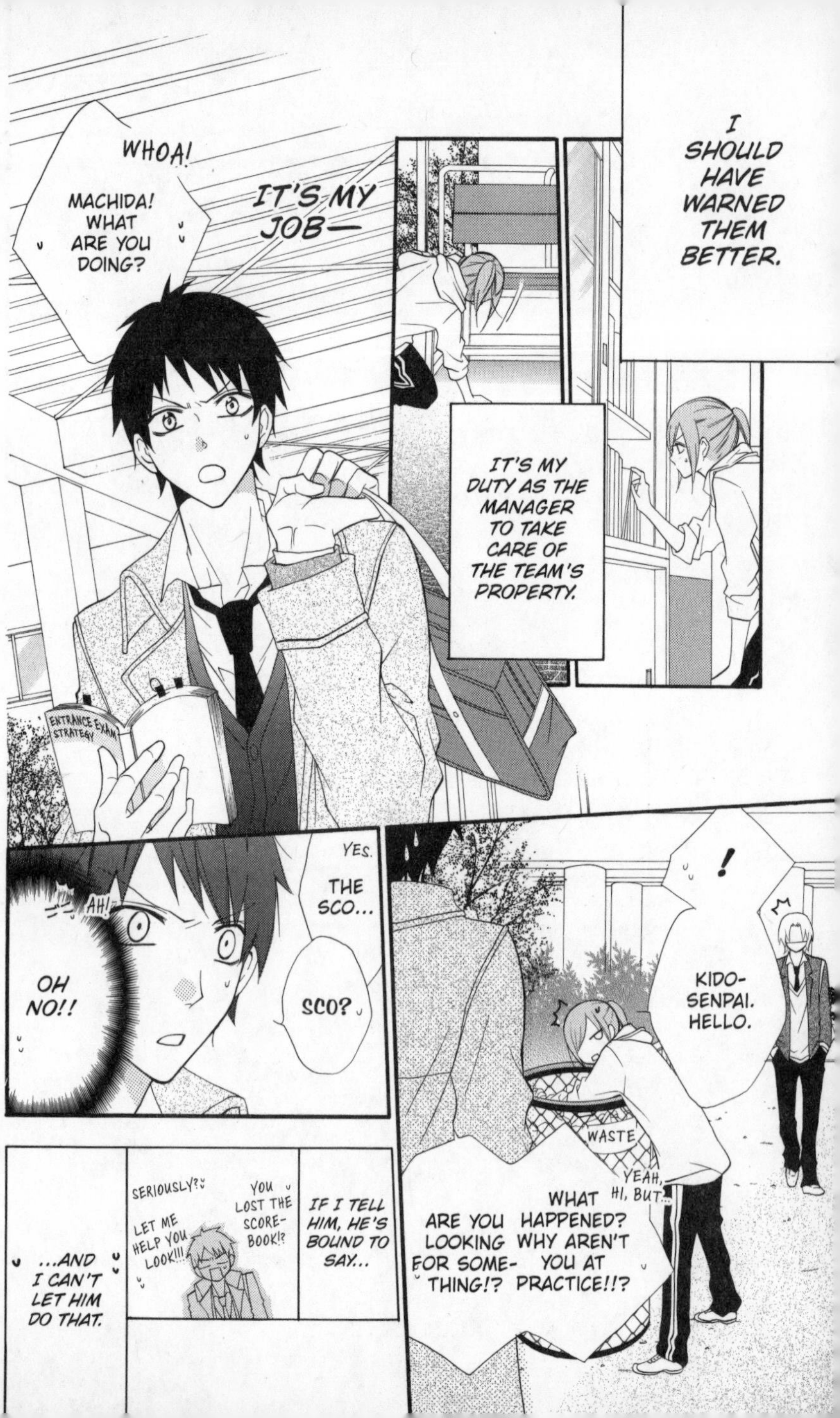

I SHOULD HAVE WARNED THEM BETTER.
IT'S MY DUTY AS THE MANAGER TO TAKE CARE OF THE TEAM'S PROPERTY.
IT'S MY JOB—
WHOA!
MACHIDA! WHAT ARE YOU DOING?
ENTRANCE EXAM STRATEGY
!
KIDO-SENPAI. HELLO.
YEAH, HI, BUT...
WHAT HAPPENED? WHY AREN'T YOU AT PRACTICE!!?
ARE YOU LOOKING FOR SOME-THING!?
WASTE
YES.
THE SCO...
SCO?
AH!
OH NO!!
IF I TELL HIM, HE'S BOUND TO SAY...
YOU LOST THE SCORE-BOOK!?
SERIOUSLY?
LET ME HELP YOU LOOK!!!
...AND I CAN'T LET HIM DO THAT.

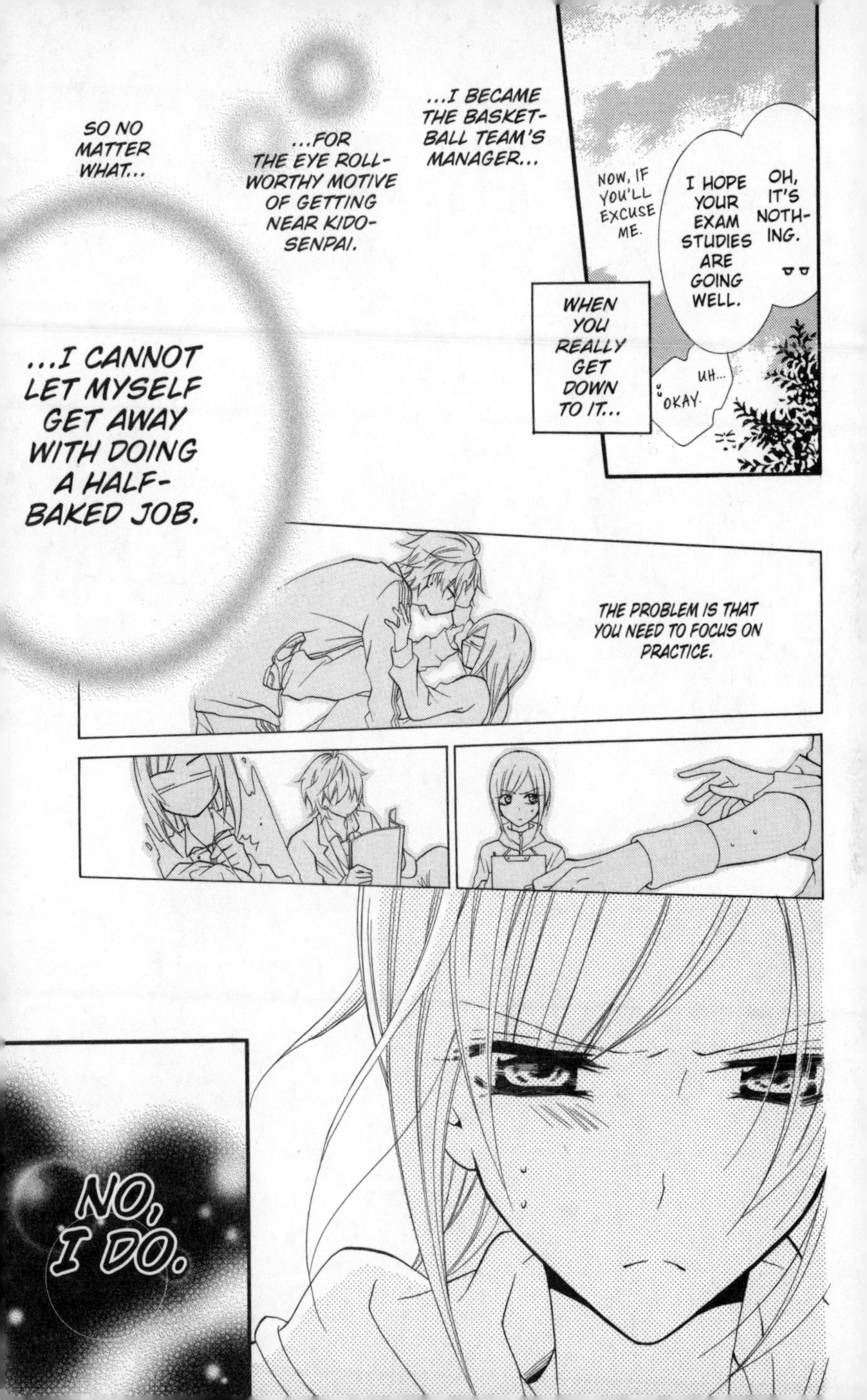

OH, IT'S NOTHING.
I HOPE YOUR EXAM STUDIES ARE GOING WELL.
NOW, IF YOU'LL EXCUSE ME.
UH... OKAY.
WHEN YOU REALLY GET DOWN TO IT...
...I BECAME THE BASKETBALL TEAM'S MANAGER...
...FOR THE EYE ROLL-WORTHY MOTIVE OF GETTING NEAR KIDO-SENPAI.
SO NO MATTER WHAT...
...I CANNOT LET MYSELF GET AWAY WITH DOING A HALF-BAKED JOB.
THE PROBLEM IS THAT YOU NEED TO FOCUS ON PRACTICE.
NO, I DO.

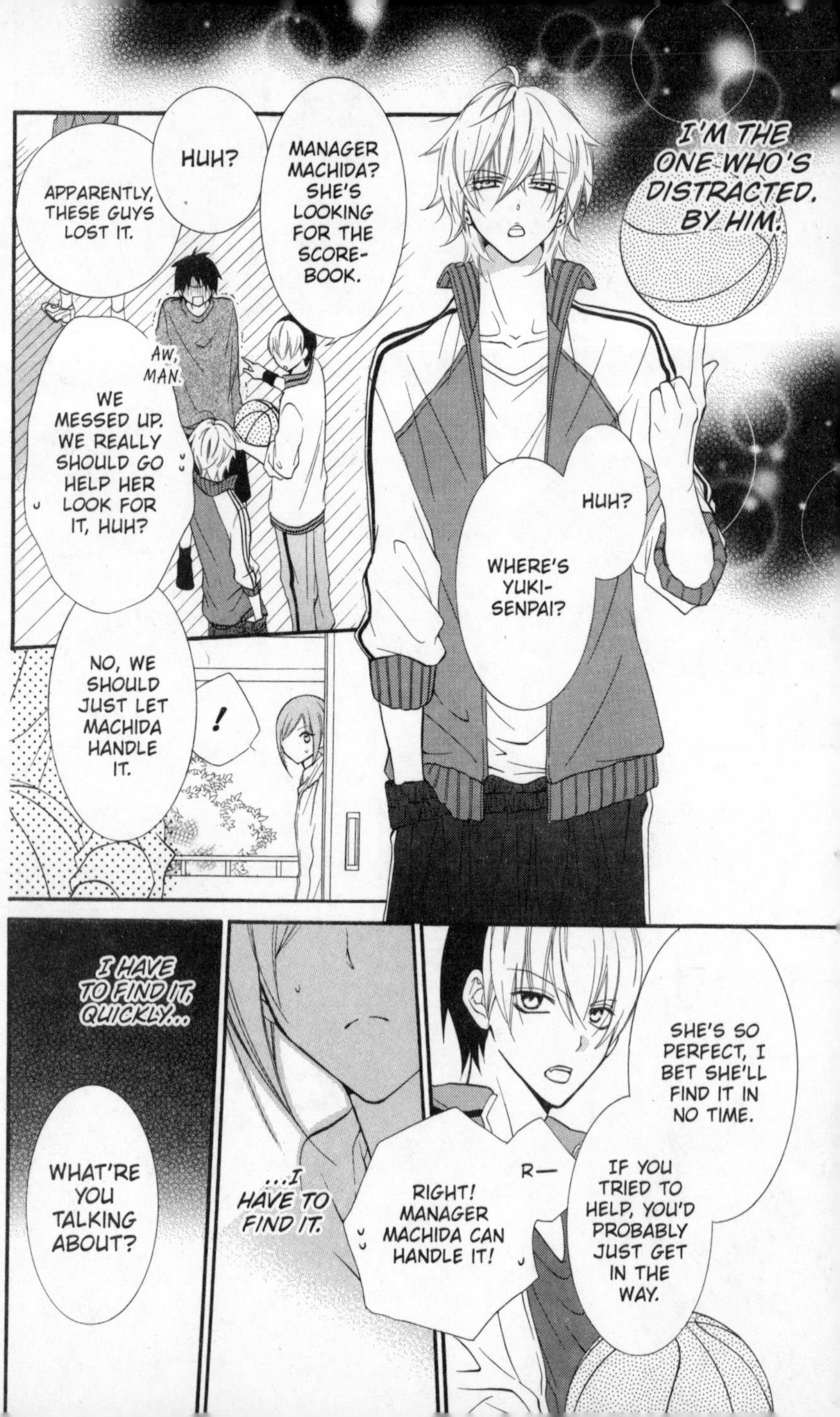
I'M THE ONE WHO'S DISTRACTED. BY HIM.
HUH?
WHERE'S YUKI-SENPAI?
MANAGER MACHIDA? SHE'S LOOKING FOR THE SCORE-BOOK.
HUH?
APPARENTLY, THESE GUYS LOST IT.
AW, MAN.
WE MESSED UP. WE REALLY SHOULD GO HELP HER LOOK FOR IT, HUH?
!
NO, WE SHOULD JUST LET MACHIDA HANDLE IT.
SHE'S SO PERFECT, I BET SHE'LL FIND IT IN NO TIME.
IF YOU TRIED TO HELP, YOU'D PROBABLY JUST GET IN THE WAY.
R—
RIGHT! MANAGER MACHIDA CAN HANDLE IT!
...I HAVE TO FIND IT.
I HAVE TO FIND IT, QUICKLY...
WHAT'RE YOU TALKING ABOUT?

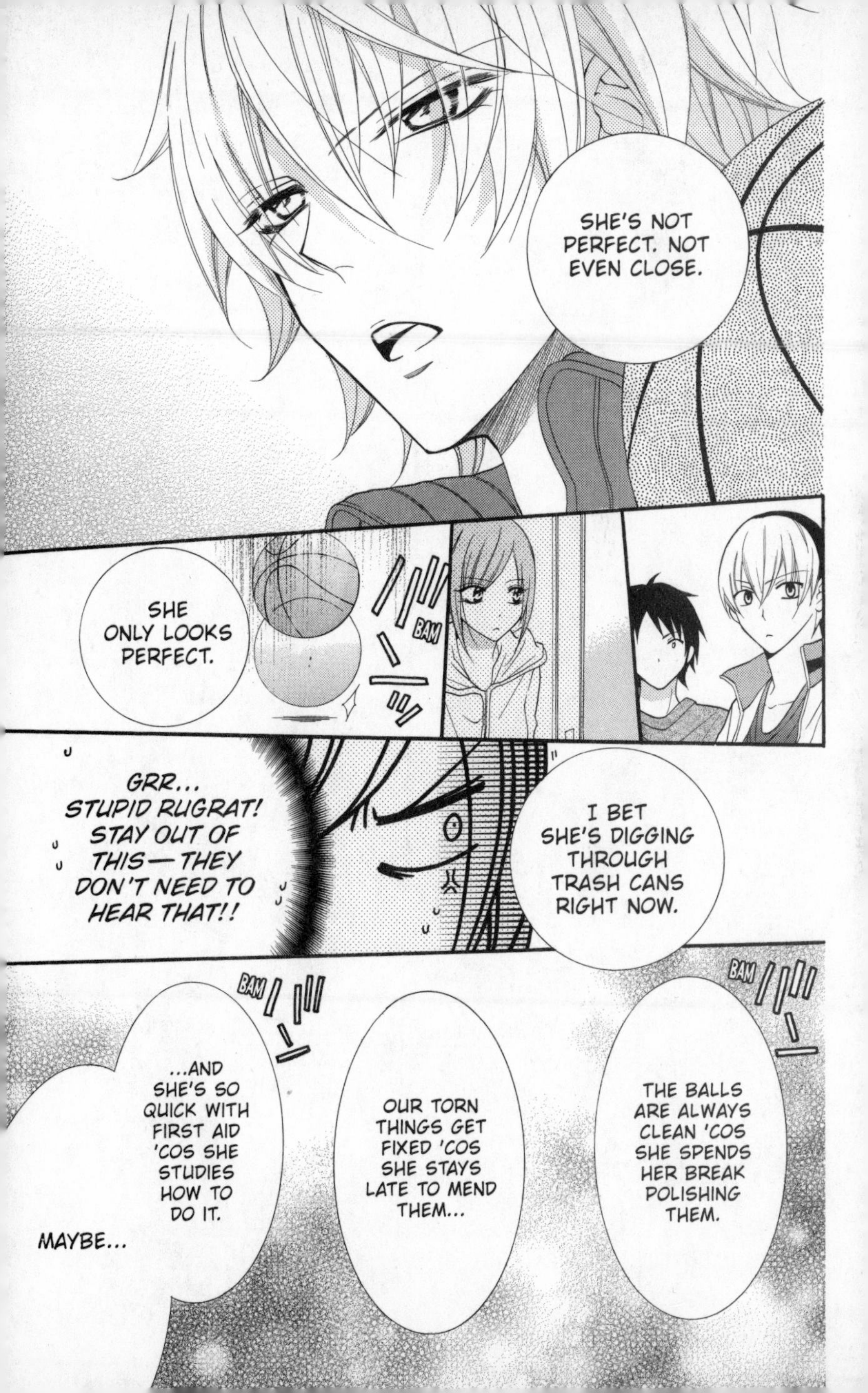
SHE'S NOT PERFECT. NOT EVEN CLOSE.
BAM
SHE ONLY LOOKS PERFECT.
I BET SHE'S DIGGING THROUGH TRASH CANS RIGHT NOW.
GRR... STUPID RUGRAT! STAY OUT OF THIS—THEY DON'T NEED TO HEAR THAT!!
BAM
THE BALLS ARE ALWAYS CLEAN 'COS SHE SPENDS HER BREAK POLISHING THEM.
OUR TORN THINGS GET FIXED 'COS SHE STAYS LATE TO MEND THEM...
BAM
...AND SHE'S SO QUICK WITH FIRST AID 'COS SHE STUDIES HOW TO DO IT.
MAYBE...

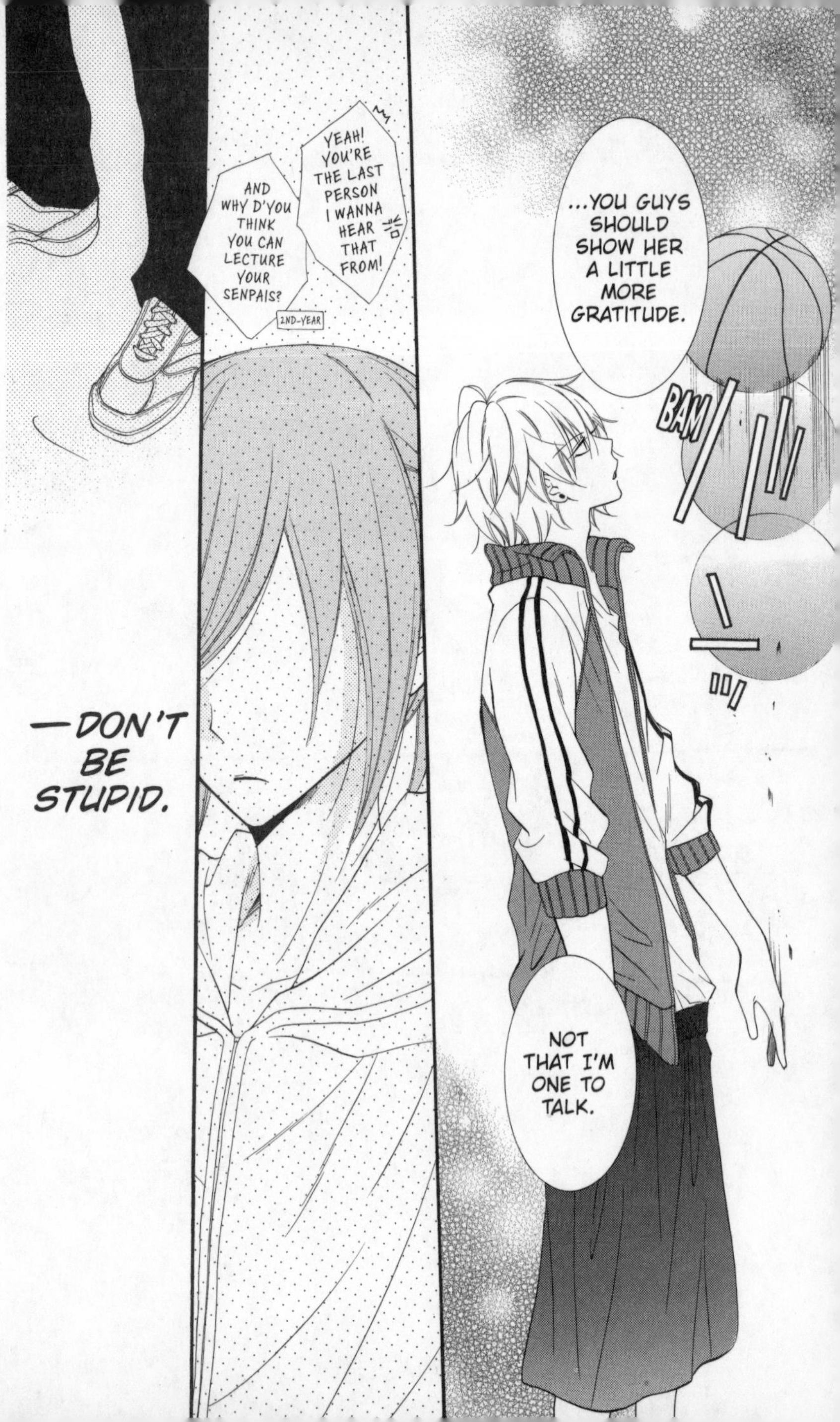
...YOU GUYS SHOULD SHOW HER A LITTLE MORE GRATITUDE.
BAM
NOT THAT I'M ONE TO TALK.
YEAH! YOU'RE THE LAST PERSON I WANNA HEAR THAT FROM!
AND WHY D'YOU THINK YOU CAN LECTURE YOUR SENPAIS?
2ND-YEAR
—DON'T BE STUPID.

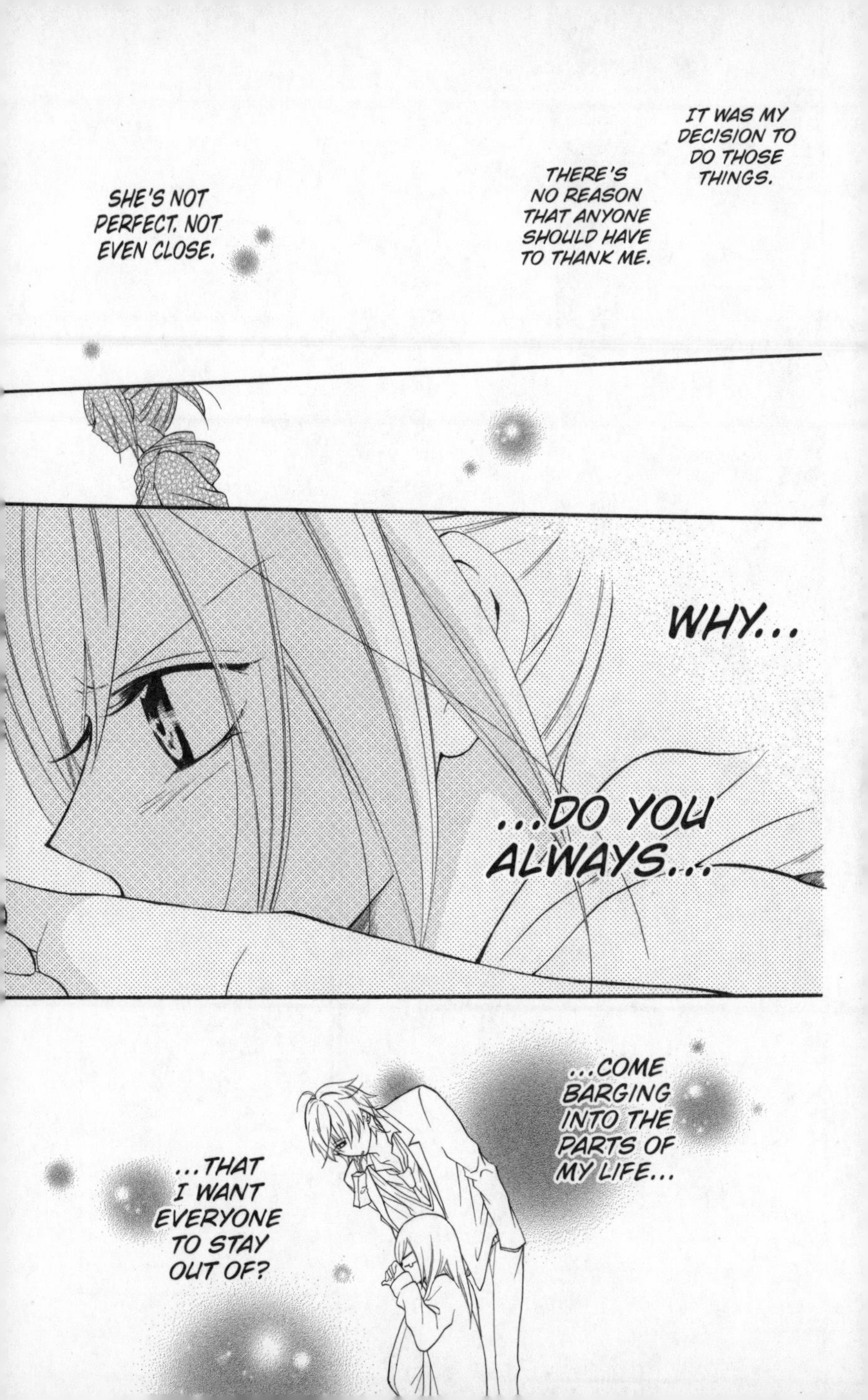
IT WAS MY DECISION TO DO THOSE THINGS.
THERE'S NO REASON THAT ANYONE SHOULD HAVE TO THANK ME.
SHE'S NOT PERFECT. NOT EVEN CLOSE.
WHY...
...DO YOU ALWAYS...
...COME BARGING INTO THE PARTS OF MY LIFE...
...THAT I WANT EVERYONE TO STAY OUT OF?

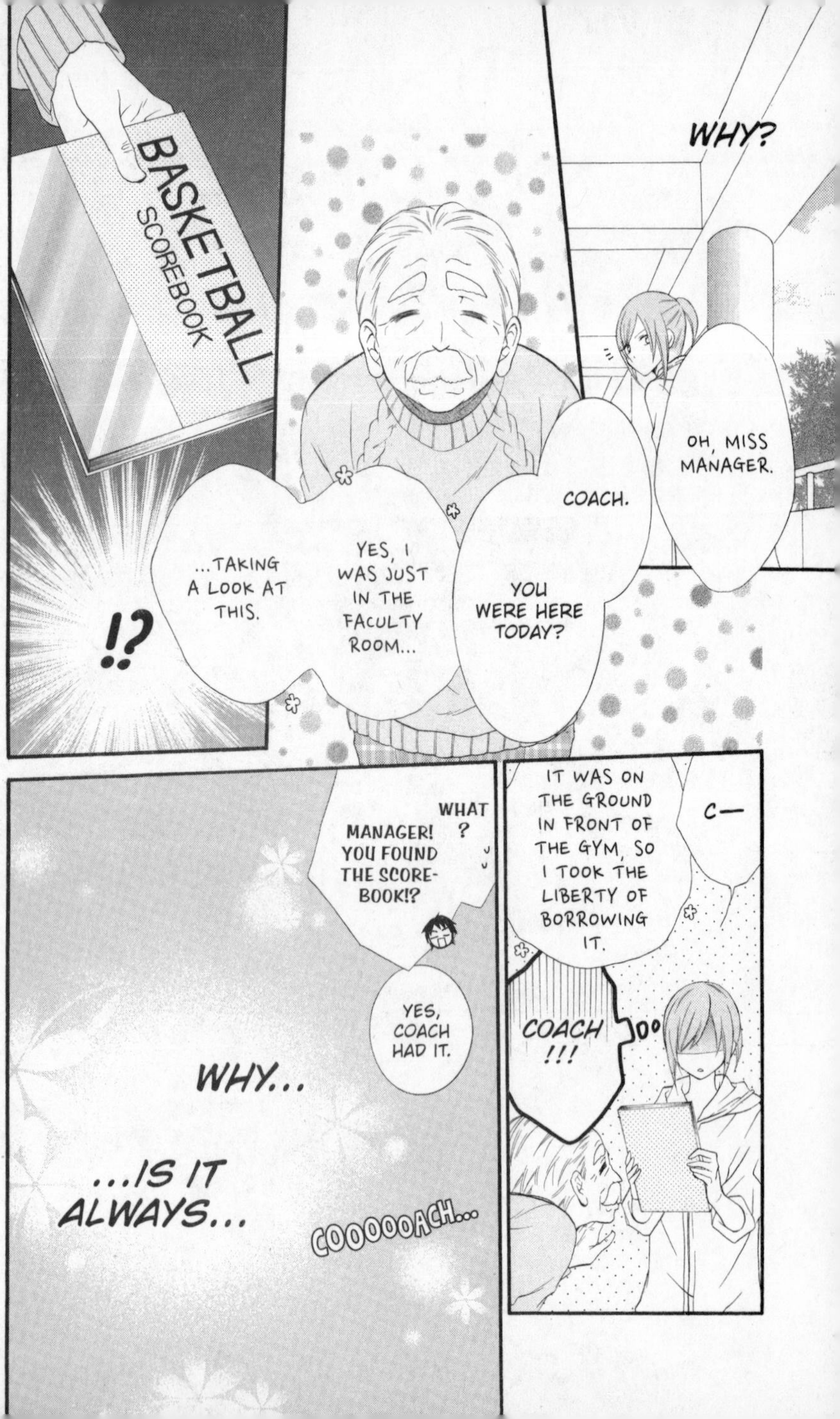
WHY?
OH, MISS MANAGER.
COACH.
YOU WERE HERE TODAY?
YES, I WAS JUST IN THE FACULTY ROOM...
...TAKING A LOOK AT THIS.
BASKETBALL SCOREBOOK
!?
C—
IT WAS ON THE GROUND IN FRONT OF THE GYM, SO I TOOK THE LIBERTY OF BORROWING IT.
COACH!!!
WHAT?
MANAGER! YOU FOUND THE SCORE-BOOK!?
YES, COACH HAD IT.
WHY...
...IS IT ALWAYS...
COOOOOACH...

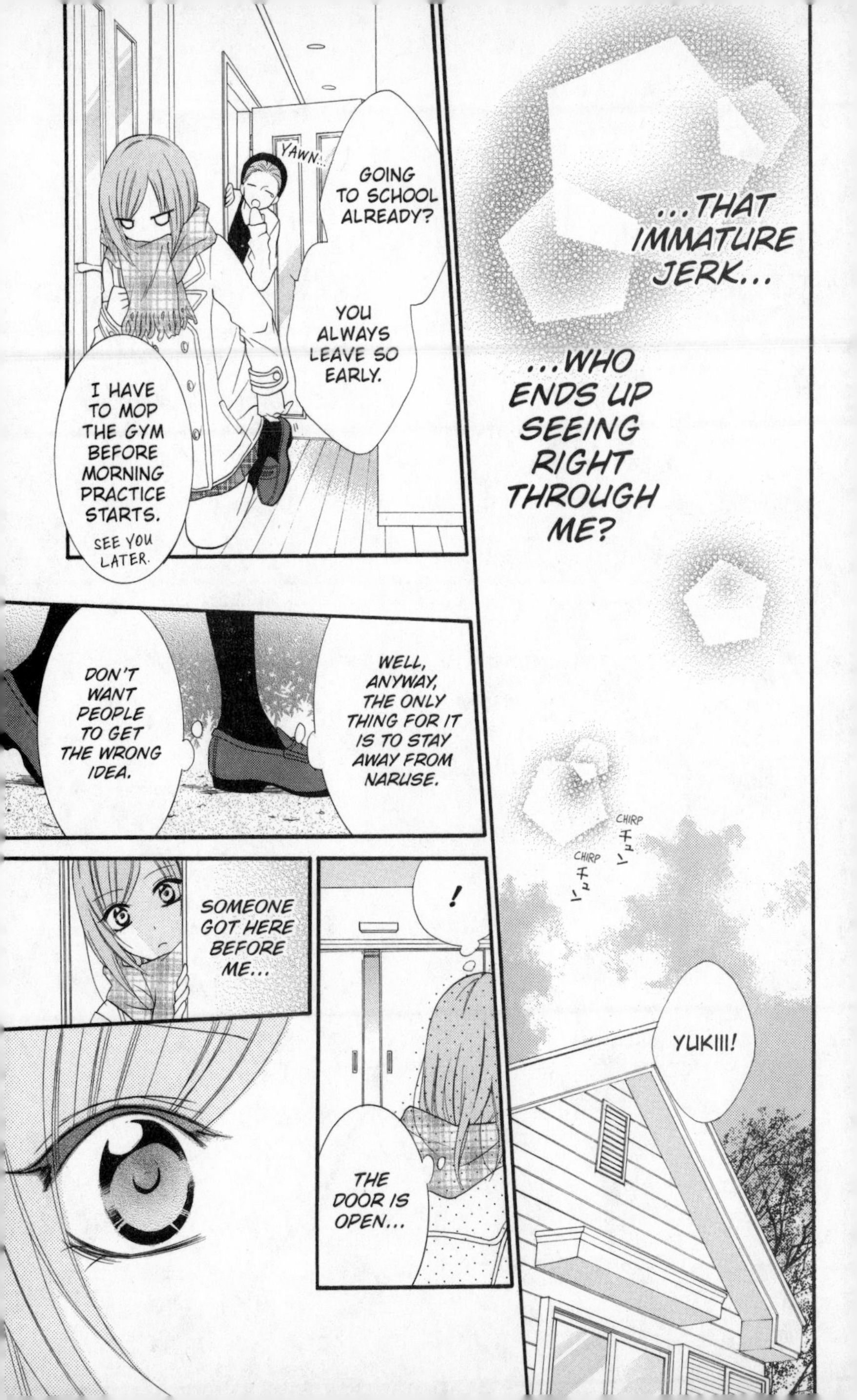

...THAT IMMATURE JERK...
...WHO ENDS UP SEEING RIGHT THROUGH ME?
CHIRP
チュン
CHIRP
チュン
YUKIII!
YAWN...
GOING TO SCHOOL ALREADY?
YOU ALWAYS LEAVE SO EARLY.
I HAVE TO MOP THE GYM BEFORE MORNING PRACTICE STARTS.
SEE YOU LATER.
WELL, ANYWAY, THE ONLY THING FOR IT IS TO STAY AWAY FROM NARUSE.
DON'T WANT PEOPLE TO GET THE WRONG IDEA.
!
THE DOOR IS OPEN...
SOMEONE GOT HERE BEFORE ME...

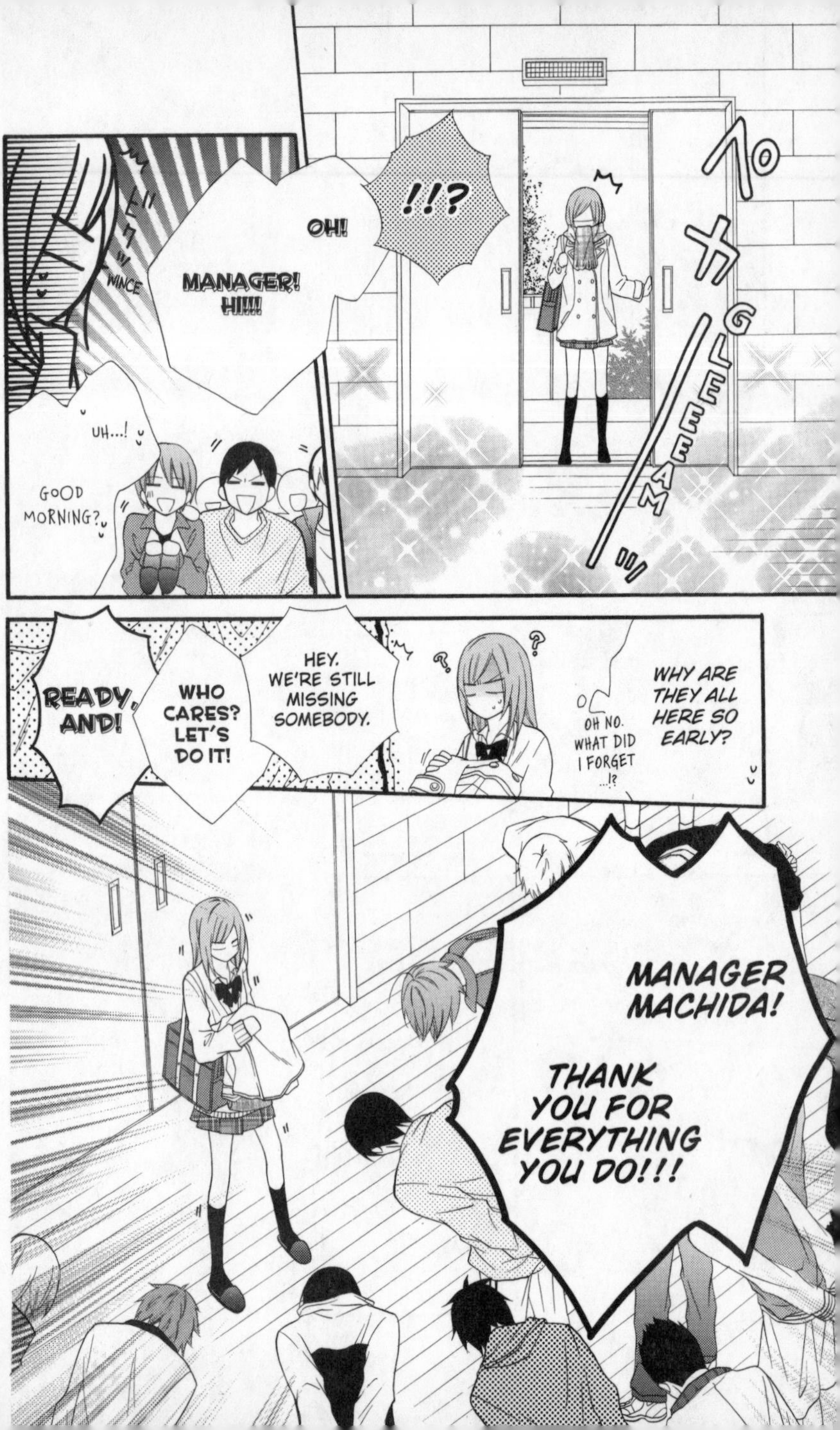
GLEEEAM
!!?
OH!
MANAGER! HI!!!!
WINCE
UH...!
GOOD MORNING?
WHY ARE THEY ALL HERE SO EARLY?
OH NO. WHAT DID I FORGET ...!?
HEY. WE'RE STILL MISSING SOMEBODY.
WHO CARES? LET'S DO IT!
READY, AND!
MANAGER MACHIDA!
THANK YOU FOR EVERYTHING YOU DO!!!

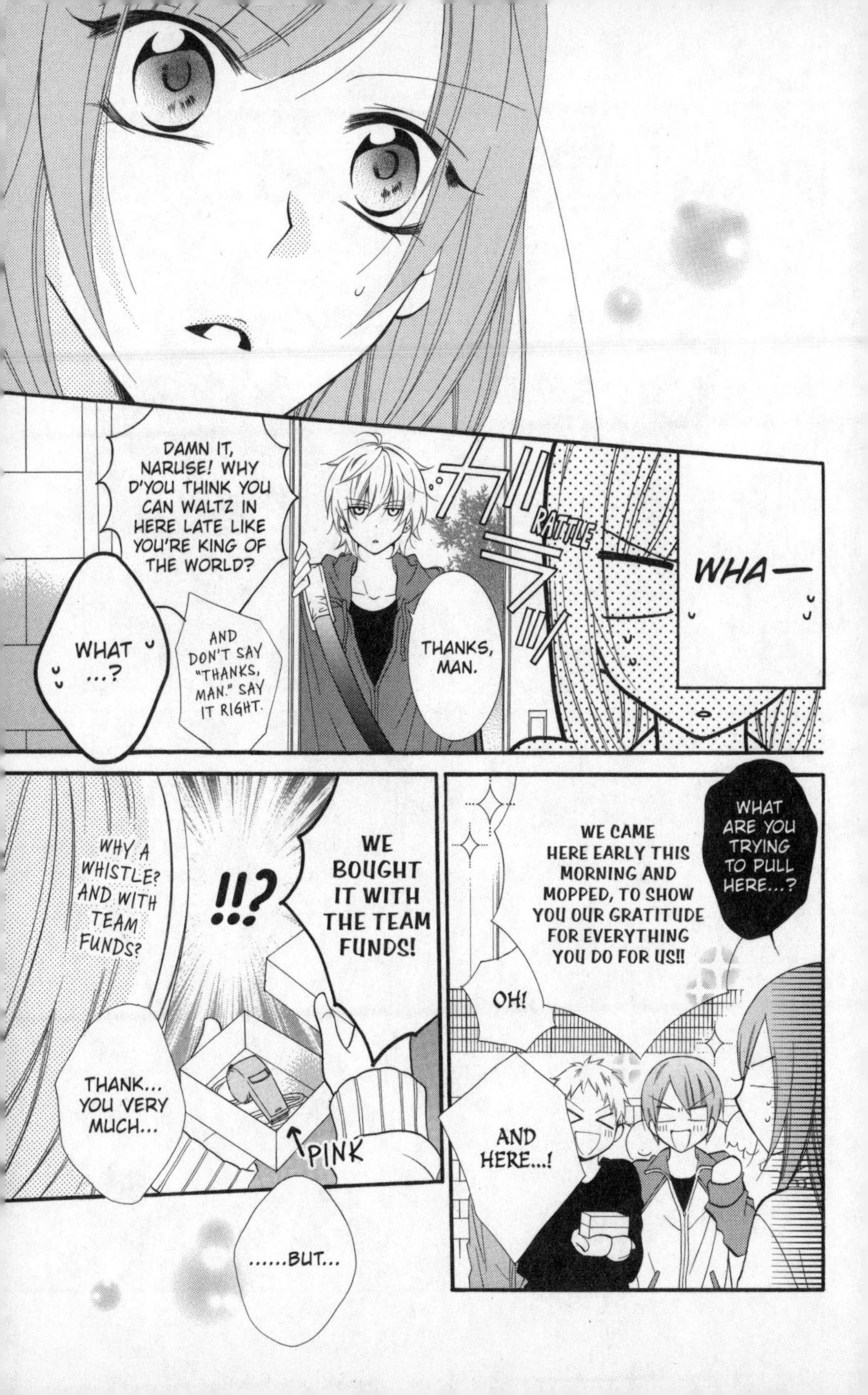
WHA—
RATTLE
THANKS, MAN.
DAMN IT, NARUSE! WHY D'YOU THINK YOU CAN WALTZ IN HERE LATE LIKE YOU'RE KING OF THE WORLD?
AND DON'T SAY "THANKS, MAN." SAY IT RIGHT.
WHAT ...?
WHAT ARE YOU TRYING TO PULL HERE...?
WE CAME HERE EARLY THIS MORNING AND MOPPED, TO SHOW YOU OUR GRATITUDE FOR EVERYTHING YOU DO FOR US!!
OH!
AND HERE...!
WE BOUGHT IT WITH THE TEAM FUNDS!
!!?
WHY A WHISTLE? AND WITH TEAM FUNDS?
THANK... YOU VERY MUCH...
PINK
......BUT...

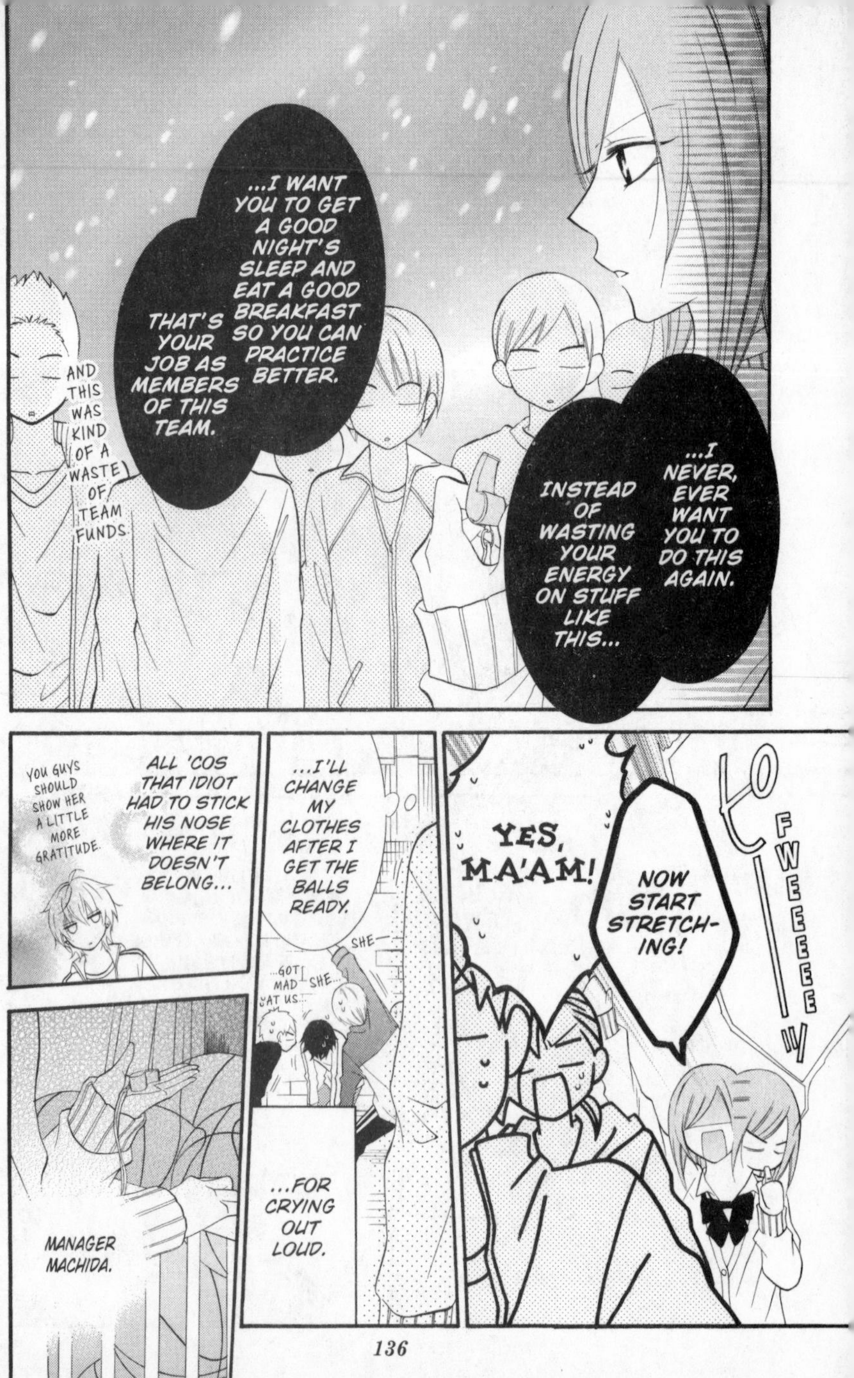
...I NEVER, EVER WANT YOU TO DO THIS AGAIN.
INSTEAD OF WASTING YOUR ENERGY ON STUFF LIKE THIS...
...I WANT YOU TO GET A GOOD NIGHT'S SLEEP AND EAT A GOOD BREAKFAST SO YOU CAN PRACTICE BETTER.
THAT'S YOUR JOB AS MEMBERS OF THIS TEAM.
AND THIS WAS KIND OF A WASTE OF TEAM FUNDS.
FWEEEEE
NOW START STRETCHING!
YES, MA'AM!
...I'LL CHANGE MY CLOTHES AFTER I GET THE BALLS READY.
SHE—
SHE...
...GOT MAD AT US...
...FOR CRYING OUT LOUD.
ALL 'COS THAT IDIOT HAD TO STICK HIS NOSE WHERE IT DOESN'T BELONG...
YOU GUYS SHOULD SHOW HER A LITTLE MORE GRATITUDE.
MANAGER MACHIDA.

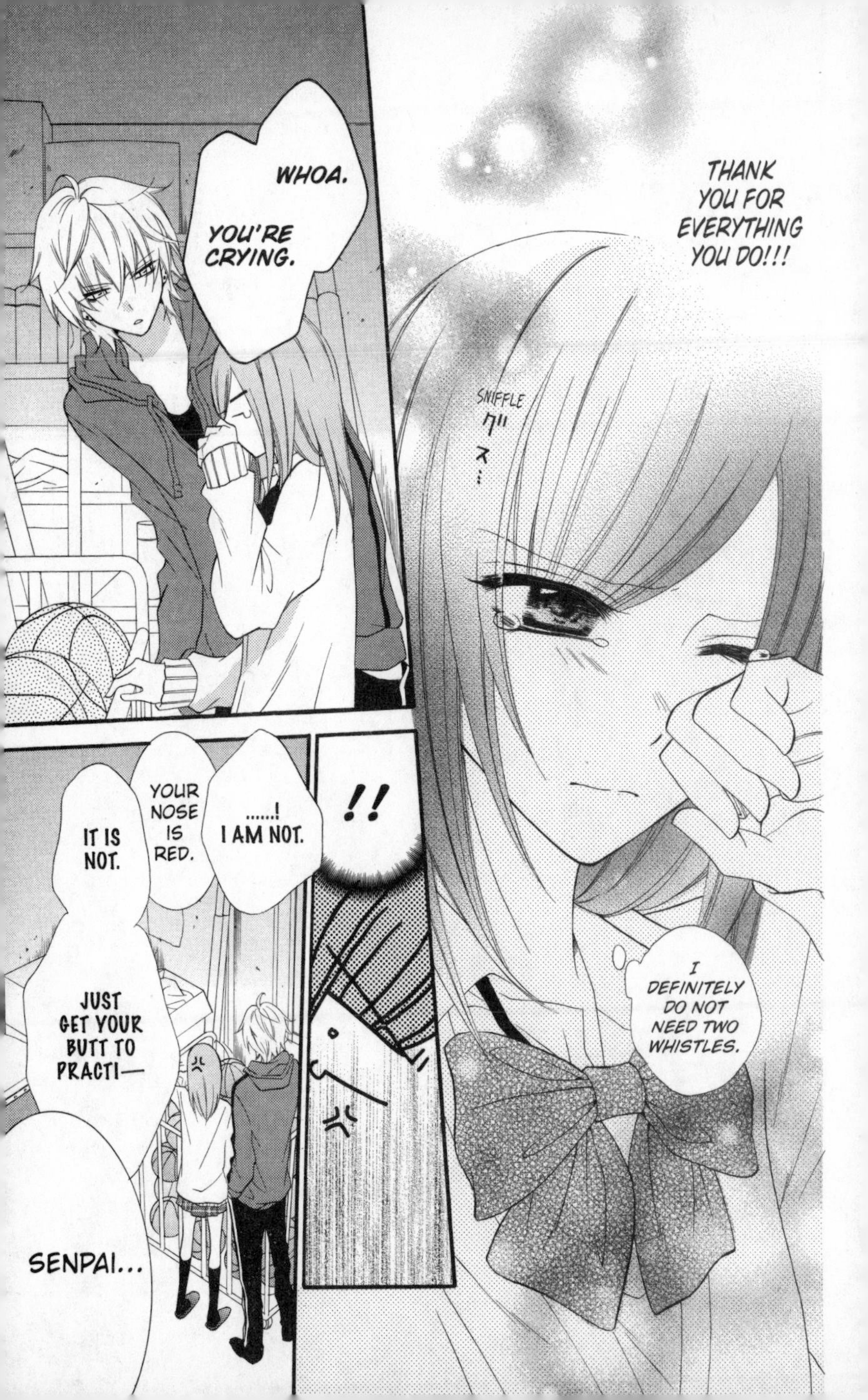
THANK YOU FOR EVERYTHING YOU DO!!!
SNIFFLE
グス…
I DEFINITELY DO NOT NEED TWO WHISTLES.
WHOA.
YOU'RE CRYING.
!!
......! I AM NOT.
YOUR NOSE IS RED.
IT IS NOT.
JUST GET YOUR BUTT TO PRACTI—
SENPAI...

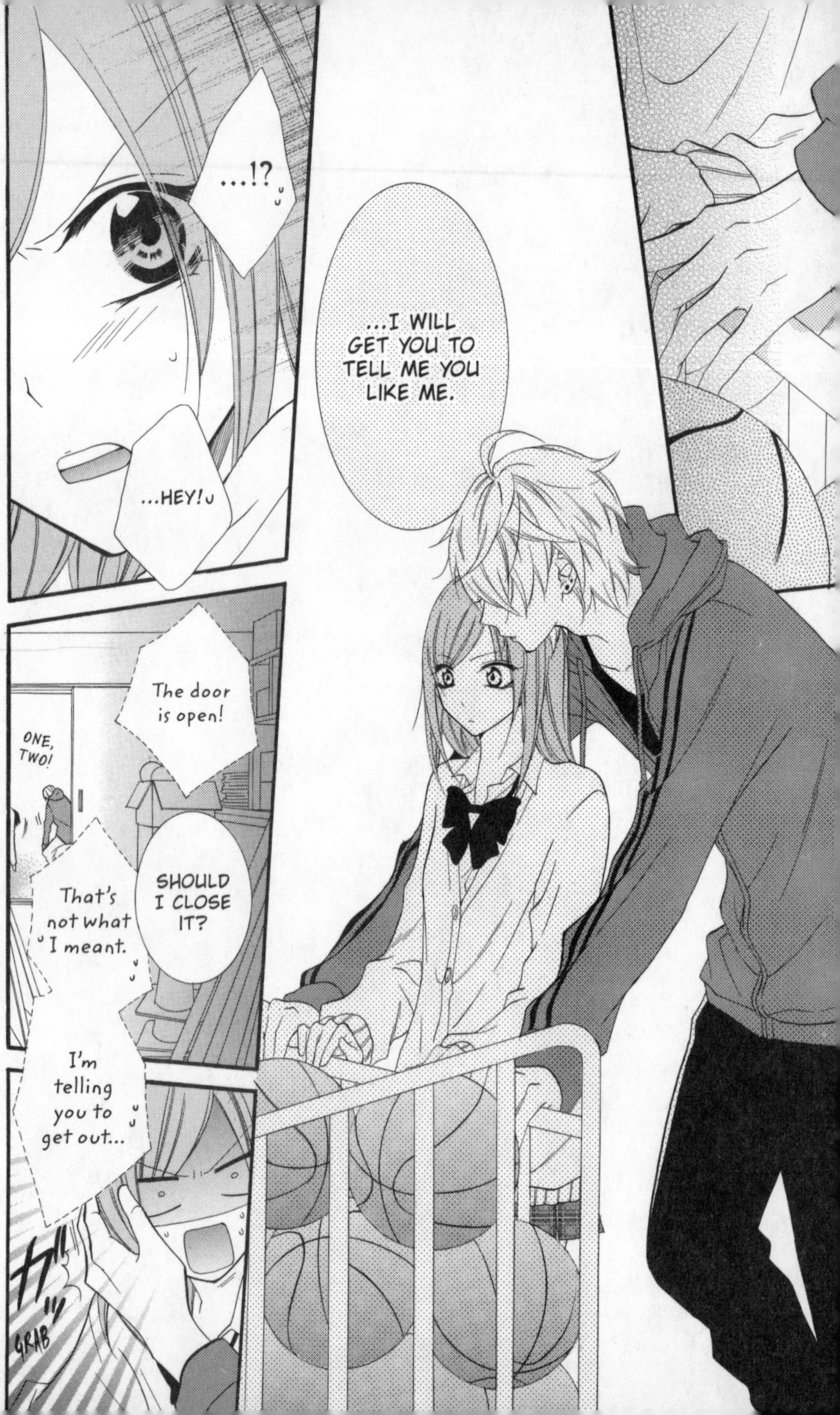
...I WILL GET YOU TO TELL ME YOU LIKE ME.
...!?
...HEY!
The door is open!
ONE, TWO!
SHOULD I CLOSE IT?
That's not what I meant.
I'm telling you to get out...
GRAB

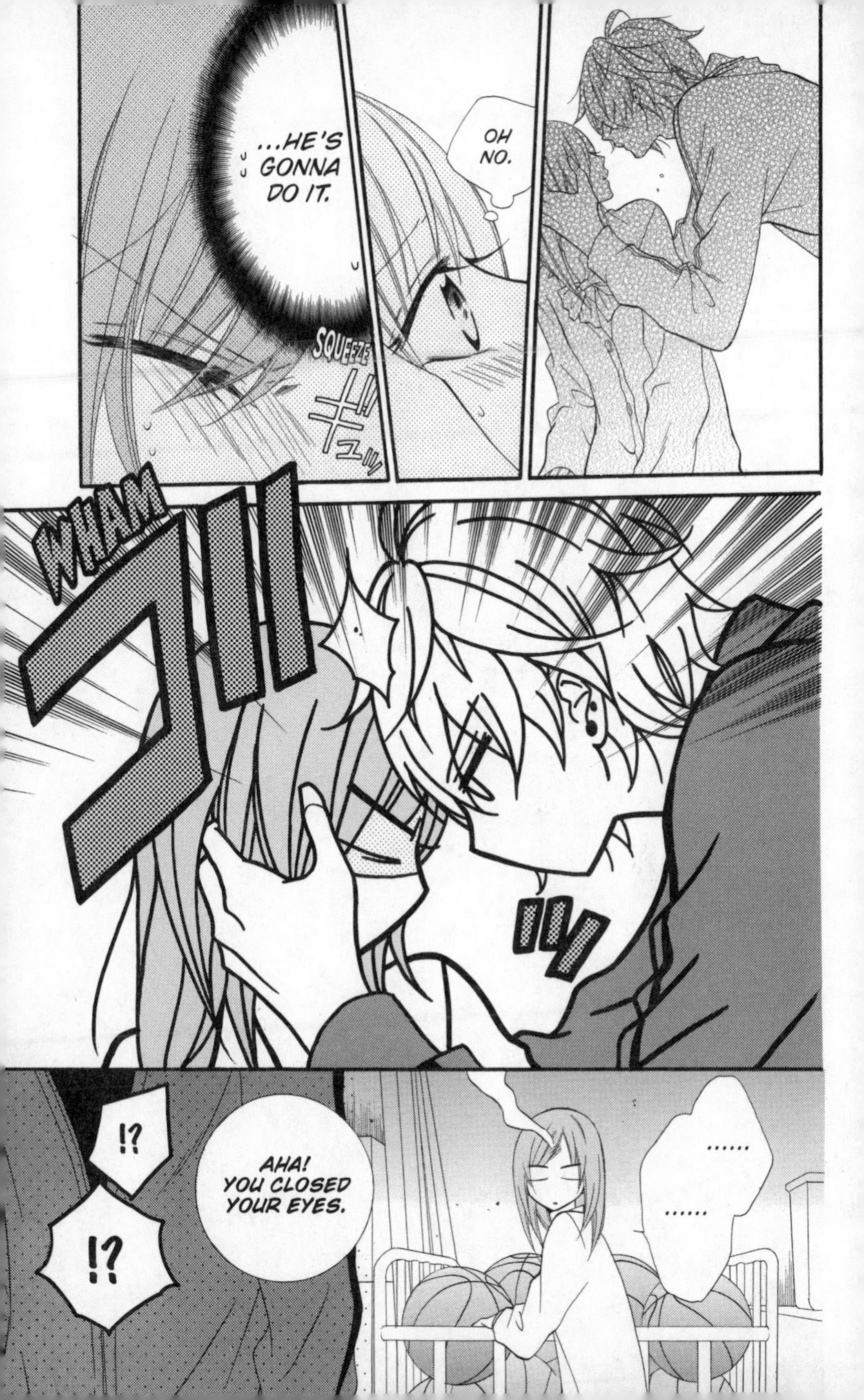
OH NO.
...HE'S GONNA DO IT.
SQUEEZE
ギュッ
WHAM
......
......
AHA! YOU CLOSED YOUR EYES.
!?
!?

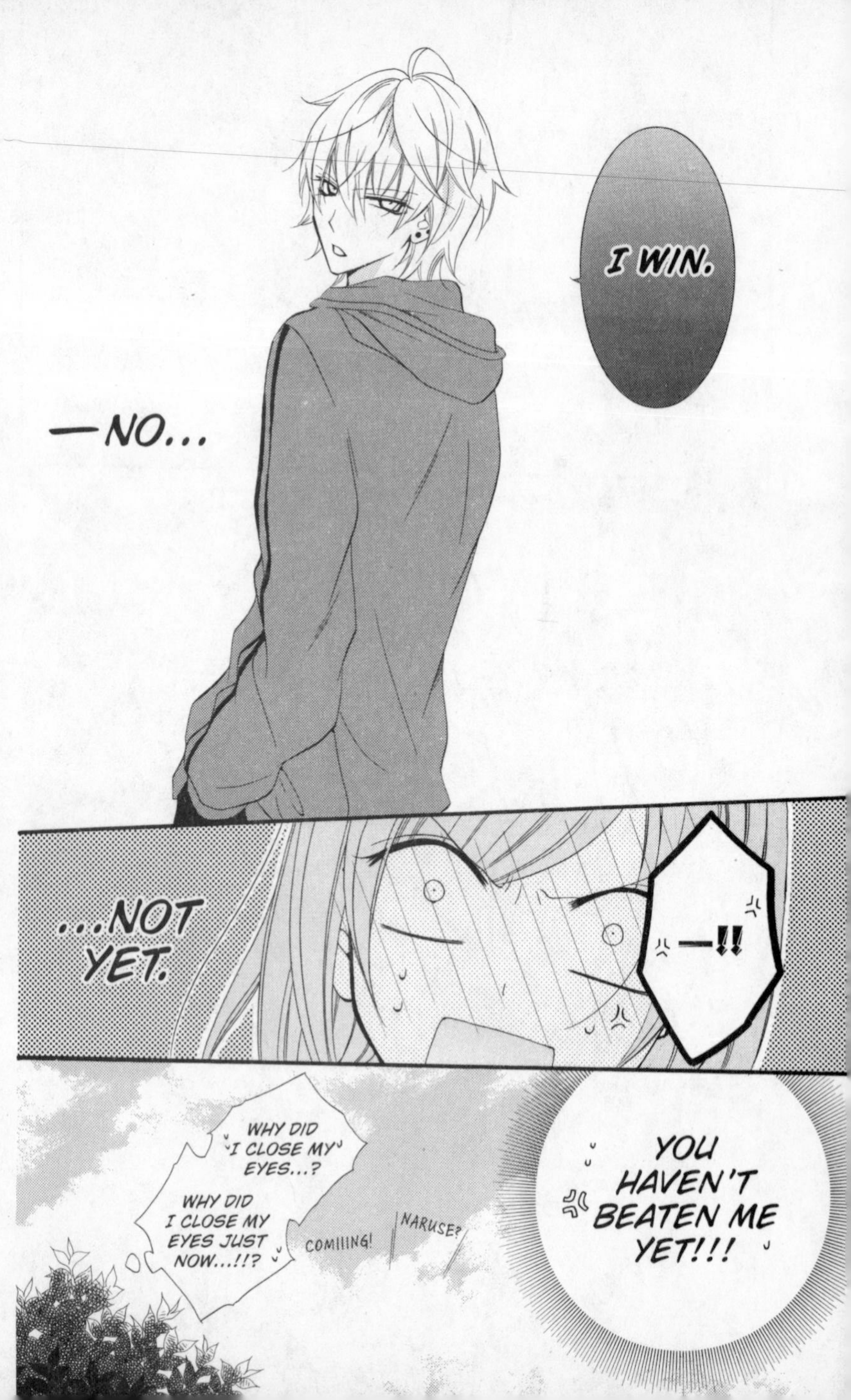
I WIN.
—NO...
—!!
...NOT YET.
YOU HAVEN'T BEATEN ME YET!!!
NARUSE?
COMIIING!
WHY DID I CLOSE MY EYES...?
WHY DID I CLOSE MY EYES JUST NOW...!!?

Chapter 5

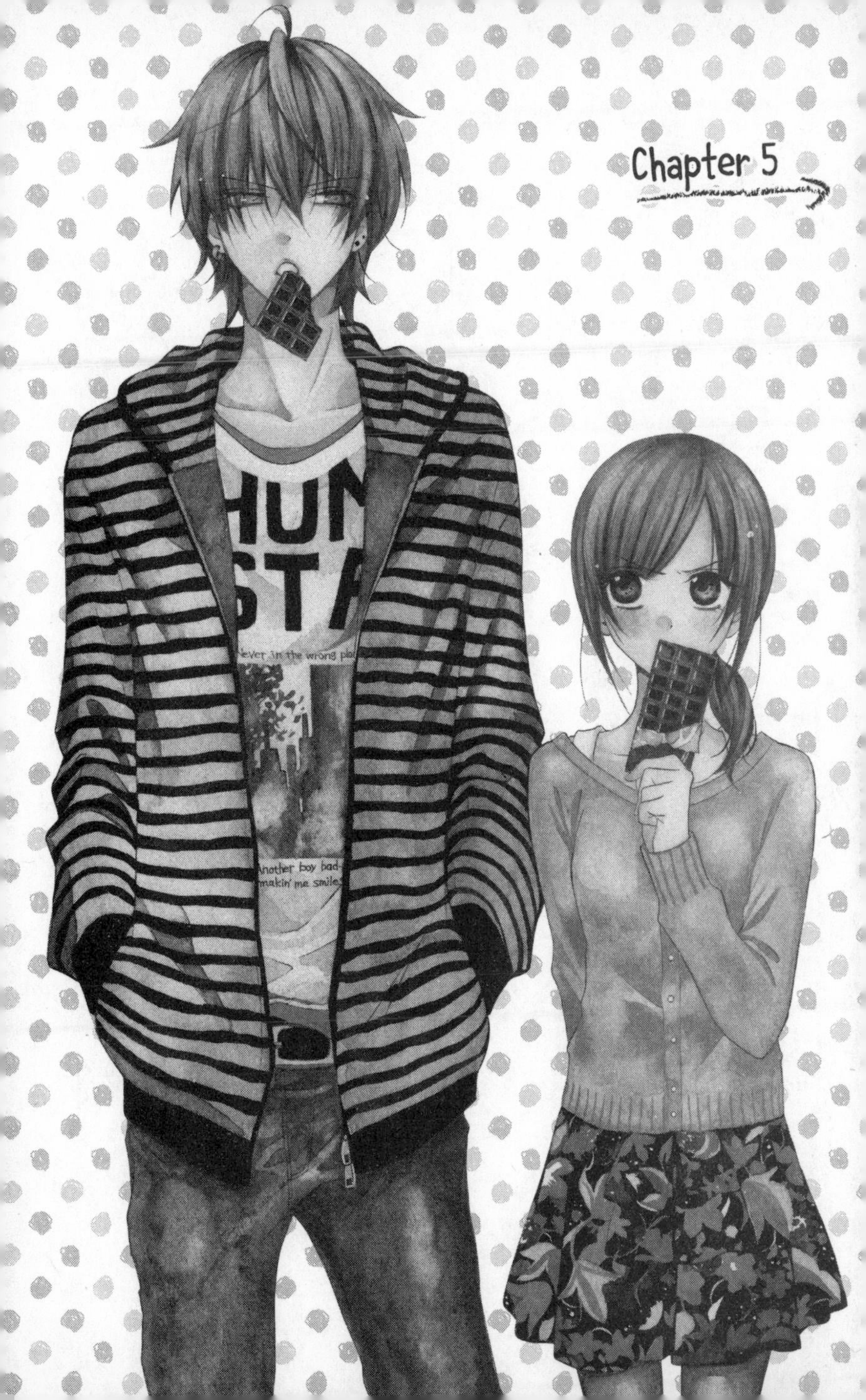

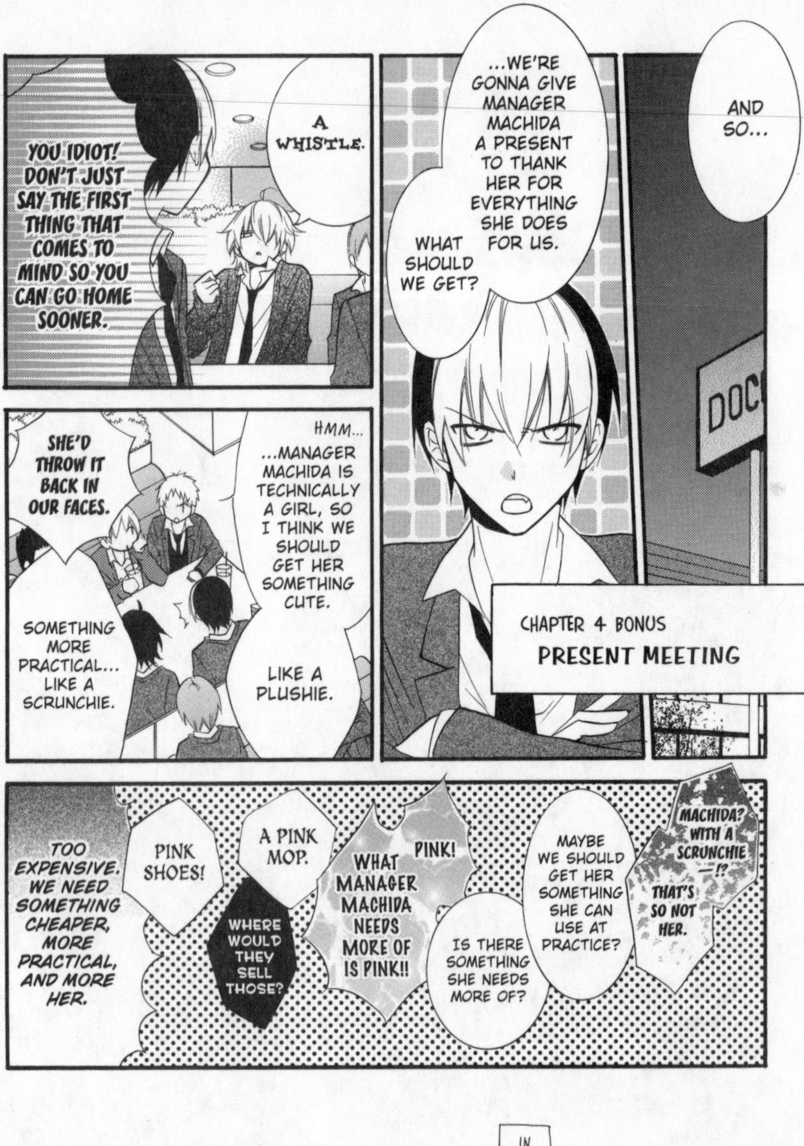
AND SO...
CHAPTER 4 BONUS
PRESENT MEETING
...WE'RE GONNA GIVE MANAGER MACHIDA A PRESENT TO THANK HER FOR EVERYTHING SHE DOES FOR US.
WHAT SHOULD WE GET?
A WHISTLE.
YOU IDIOT! DON'T JUST SAY THE FIRST THING THAT COMES TO MIND SO YOU CAN GO HOME SOONER.
HMM...
...MANAGER MACHIDA IS TECHNICALLY A GIRL, SO I THINK WE SHOULD GET HER SOMETHING CUTE.
LIKE A PLUSHIE.
SHE'D THROW IT BACK IN OUR FACES.
SOMETHING MORE PRACTICAL... LIKE A SCRUNCHIE.
MACHIDA? WITH A SCRUNCHIE—!?
THAT'S SO NOT HER.
MAYBE WE SHOULD GET HER SOMETHING SHE CAN USE AT PRACTICE?
IS THERE SOMETHING SHE NEEDS MORE OF?
PINK!
WHAT MANAGER MACHIDA NEEDS MORE OF IS PINK!!
A PINK MOP.
WHERE WOULD THEY SELL THOSE?
PINK SHOES!
TOO EXPENSIVE. WE NEED SOMETHING CHEAPER, MORE PRACTICAL, AND MORE HER.
IN THE END...

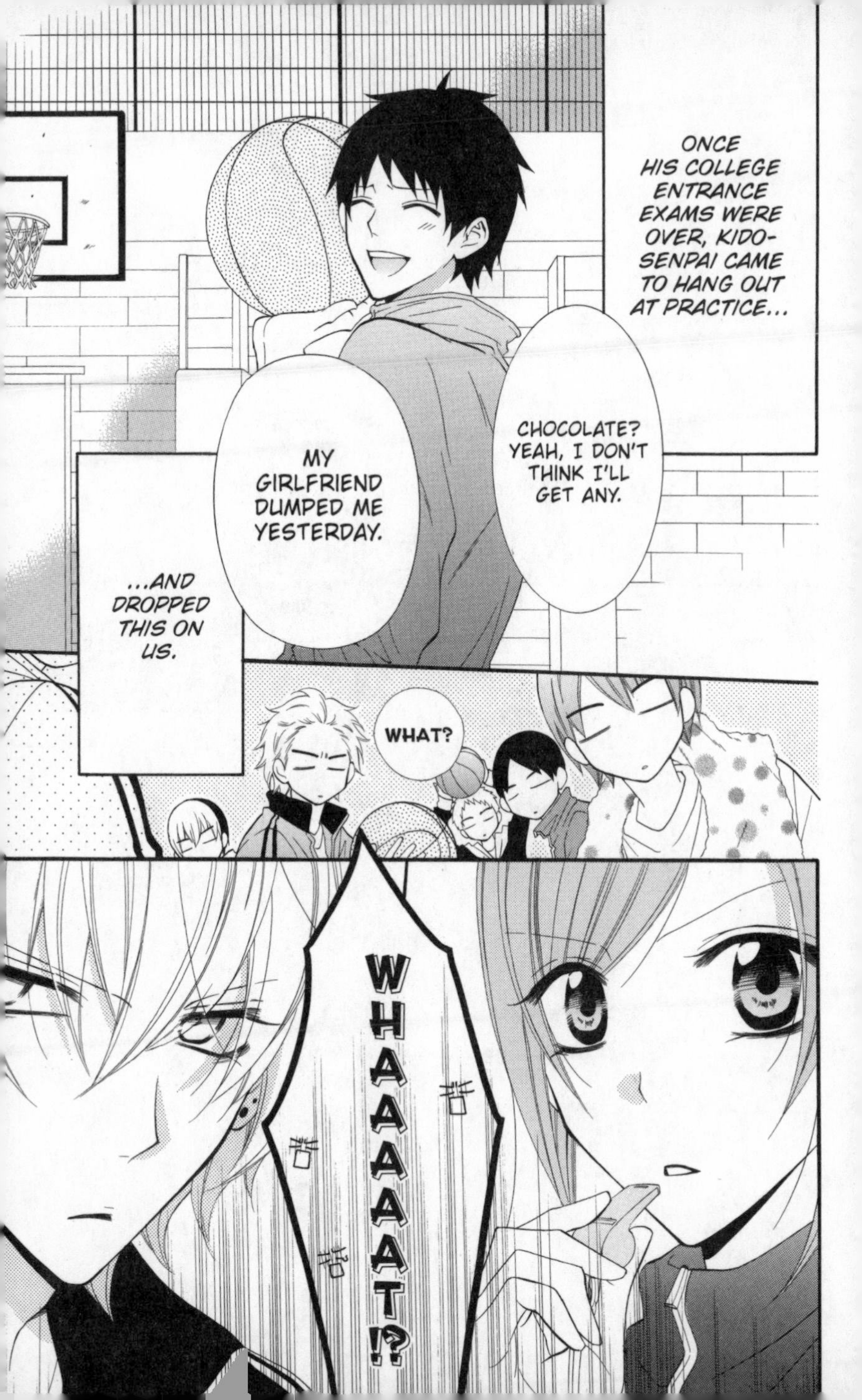
ONCE HIS COLLEGE ENTRANCE EXAMS WERE OVER, KIDO-SENPAI CAME TO HANG OUT AT PRACTICE...
CHOCOLATE? YEAH, I DON'T THINK I'LL GET ANY.
MY GIRLFRIEND DUMPED ME YESTERDAY.
...AND DROPPED THIS ON US.
WHAT?
WHAAAAAAT!?

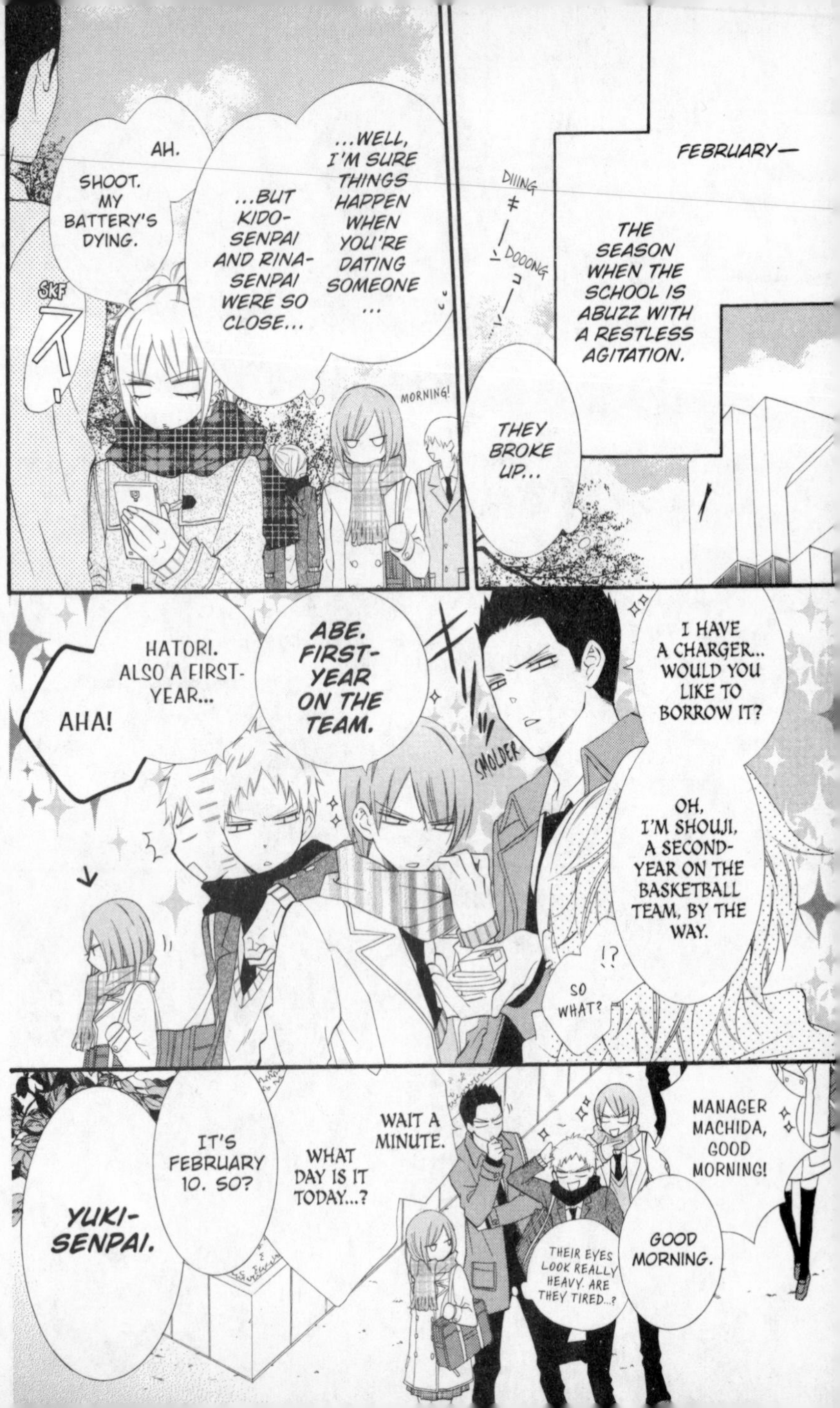
FEBRUARY—
THE SEASON WHEN THE SCHOOL IS ABUZZ WITH A RESTLESS AGITATION.
DIIING
DOOONG
THEY BROKE UP...
...WELL, I'M SURE THINGS HAPPEN WHEN YOU'RE DATING SOMEONE ...
...BUT KIDO-SENPAI AND RINA-SENPAI WERE SO CLOSE...
MORNING!
AH.
SHOOT. MY BATTERY'S DYING.
SKF
I HAVE A CHARGER... WOULD YOU LIKE TO BORROW IT?
OH, I'M SHOUJI, A SECOND-YEAR ON THE BASKETBALL TEAM, BY THE WAY.
!?
SO WHAT?
SMOLDER
ABE. FIRST-YEAR ON THE TEAM.
HATORI. ALSO A FIRST-YEAR...
AHA!
MANAGER MACHIDA, GOOD MORNING!
GOOD MORNING.
THEIR EYES LOOK REALLY HEAVY. ARE THEY TIRED...?
WAIT A MINUTE.
WHAT DAY IS IT TODAY...?
IT'S FEBRUARY 10. SO?
YUKI-SENPAI.

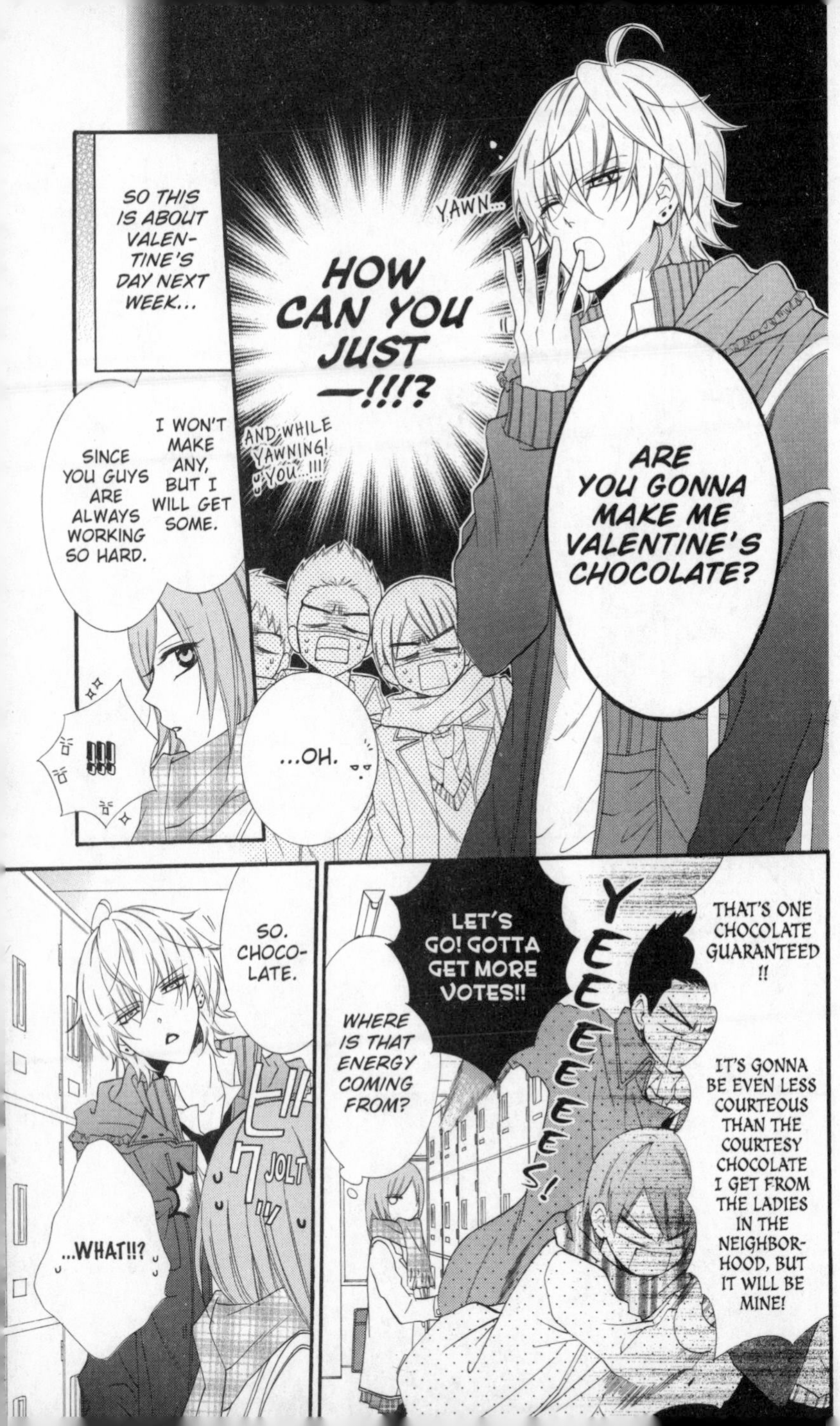
YAWN...
ARE YOU GONNA MAKE ME VALENTINE'S CHOCOLATE?
HOW CAN YOU JUST—!!!?
AND WHILE YAWNING! YOU...!!!
SO THIS IS ABOUT VALENTINE'S DAY NEXT WEEK...
I WON'T MAKE ANY, BUT I WILL GET SOME. SINCE YOU GUYS ARE ALWAYS WORKING SO HARD.
...OH.
!!!!
YEEEEEEES!
THAT'S ONE CHOCOLATE GUARANTEED!!
LET'S GO! GOTTA GET MORE VOTES!!
IT'S GONNA BE EVEN LESS COURTEOUS THAN THE COURTESY CHOCOLATE I GET FROM THE LADIES IN THE NEIGHBORHOOD, BUT IT WILL BE MINE!
WHERE IS THAT ENERGY COMING FROM?
SO. CHOCOLATE.
JOLT
...WHAT!!?

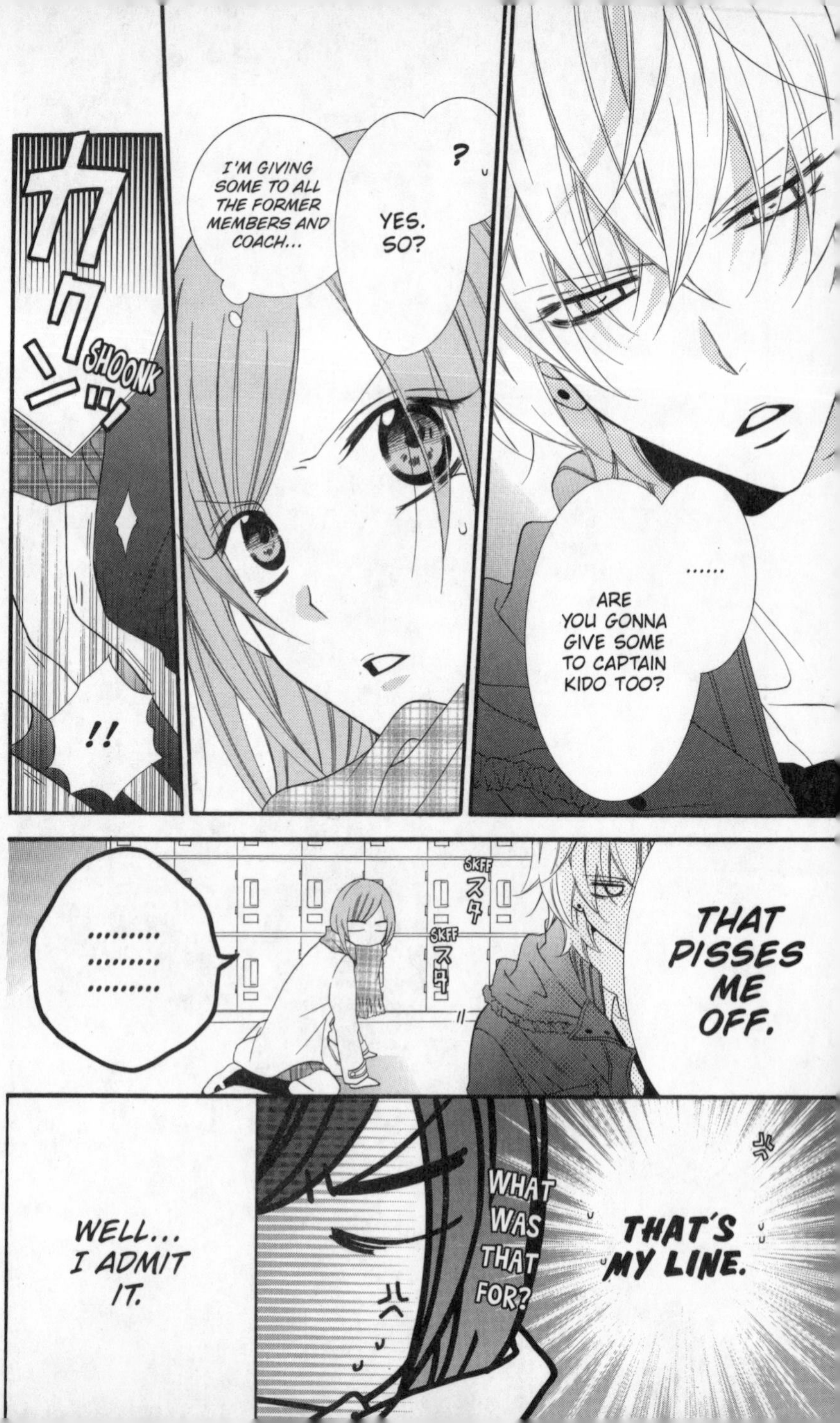
......
ARE YOU GONNA GIVE SOME TO CAPTAIN KIDO TOO?
? YES. SO?
I'M GIVING SOME TO ALL THE FORMER MEMBERS AND COACH...
SHOONK
!!
THAT PISSES ME OFF.
SKFF
SKFF
....
....
....
THAT'S MY LINE.
WHAT WAS THAT FOR?
WELL... I ADMIT IT.

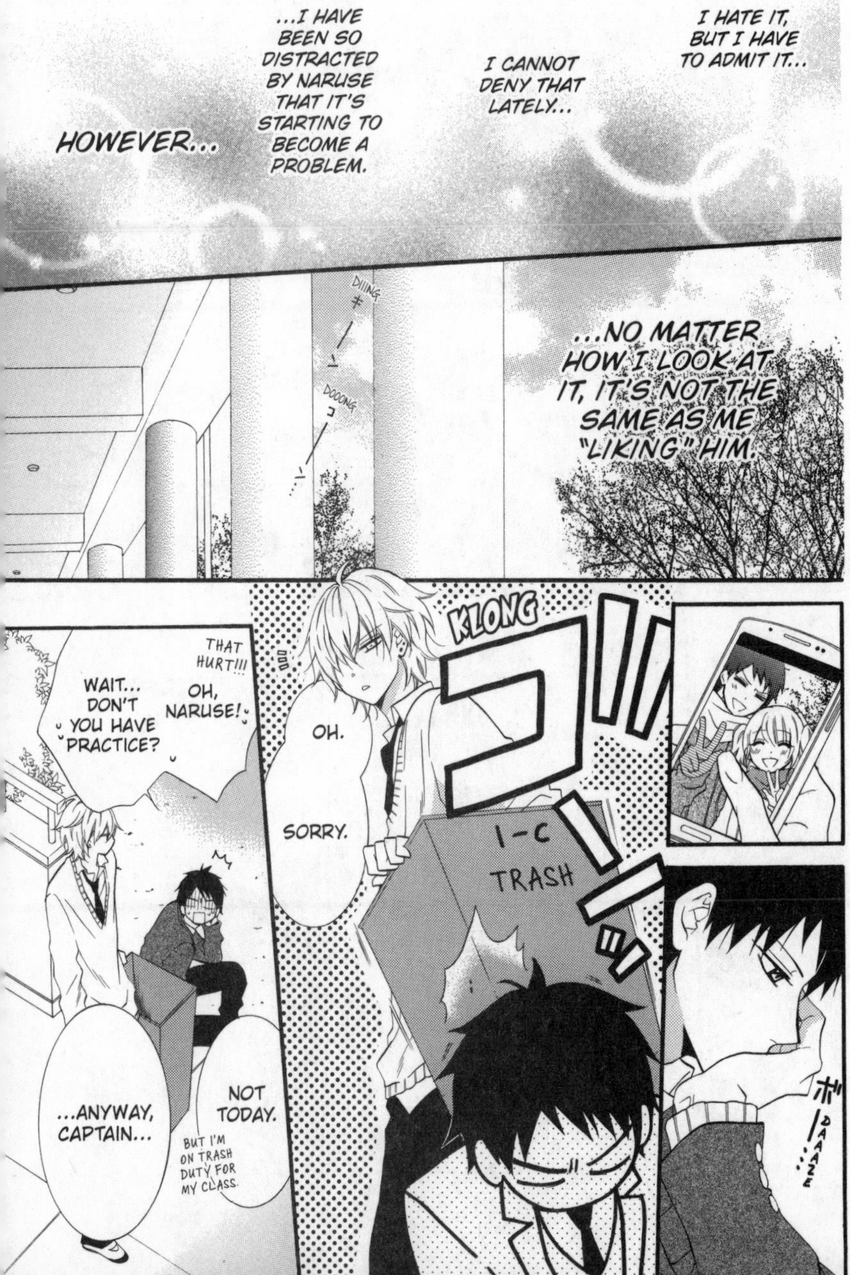
I HATE IT, BUT I HAVE TO ADMIT IT...
I CANNOT DENY THAT LATELY...
...I HAVE BEEN SO DISTRACTED BY NARUSE THAT IT'S STARTING TO BECOME A PROBLEM.
HOWEVER...
...NO MATTER HOW I LOOK AT IT, IT'S NOT THE SAME AS ME "LIKING" HIM.
DIIING
DOOONG
DAAAZE
KLONG
OH.
SORRY.
I-C TRASH
THAT HURT!!!
OH, NARUSE!
WAIT... DON'T YOU HAVE PRACTICE?
NOT TODAY.
BUT I'M ON TRASH DUTY FOR MY CLASS.
...ANYWAY, CAPTAIN...

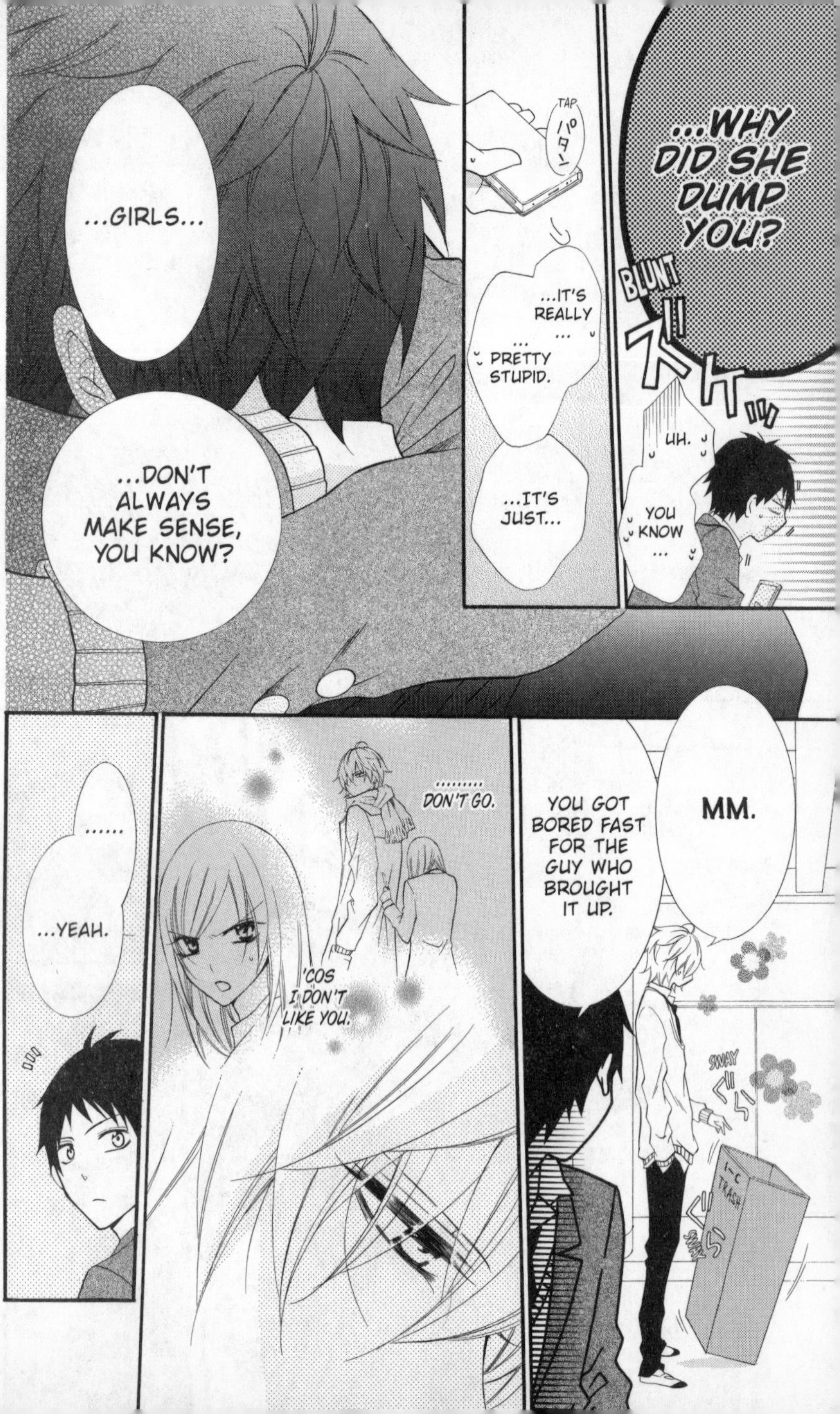
...WHY DID SHE DUMP YOU?
BLUNT
UH.
YOU KNOW ...
TAP
...IT'S REALLY ... ... PRETTY STUPID.
...IT'S JUST...
...GIRLS...
...DON'T ALWAYS MAKE SENSE, YOU KNOW?
MM.
YOU GOT BORED FAST FOR THE GUY WHO BROUGHT IT UP.
SWAY
I-C TRASH
SWAY
.... DON'T GO.
'COS I DON'T LIKE YOU.
......
...YEAH.

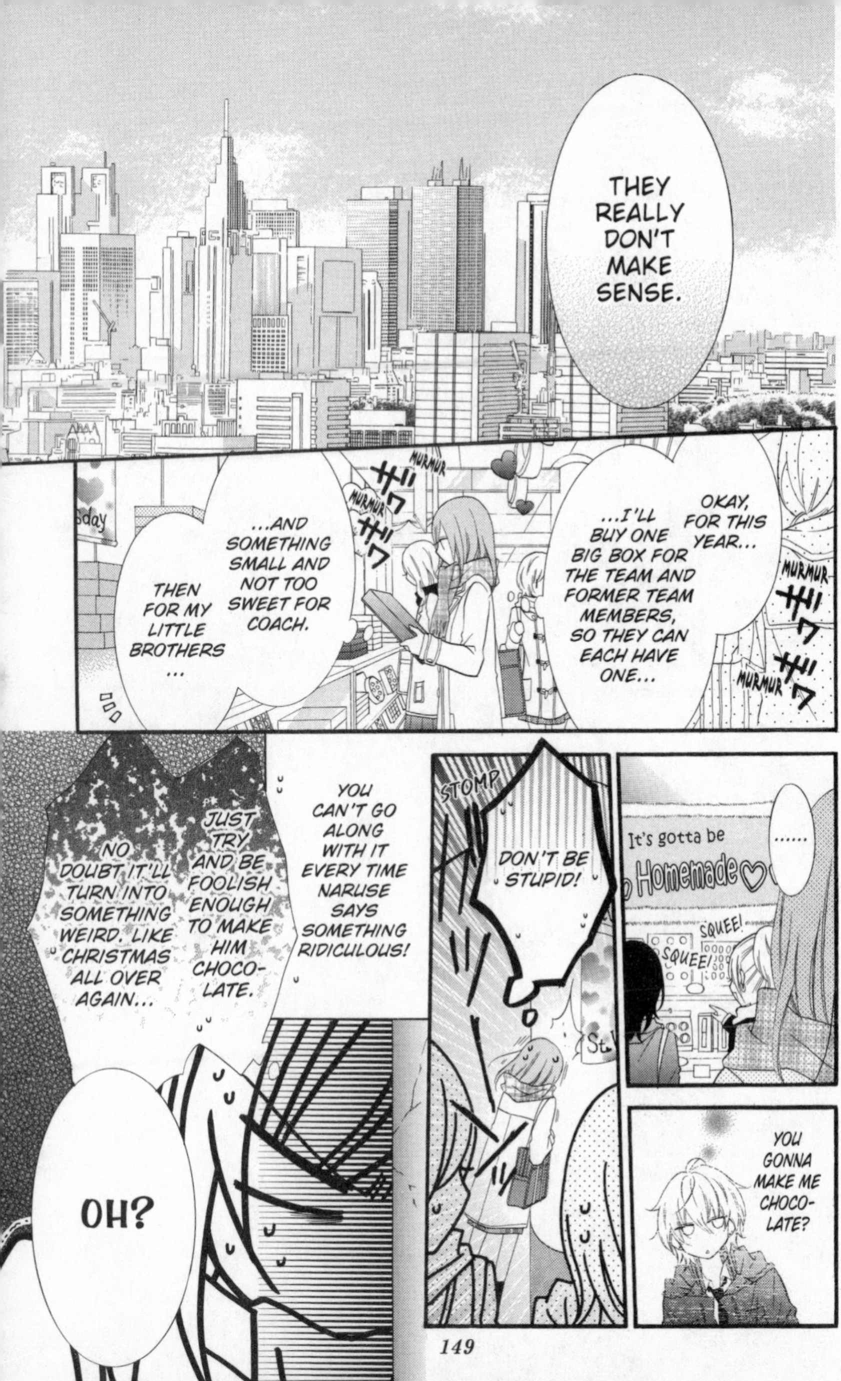
THEY REALLY DON'T MAKE SENSE.
OKAY, FOR THIS YEAR...
...I'LL BUY ONE BIG BOX FOR THE TEAM AND FORMER TEAM MEMBERS, SO THEY CAN EACH HAVE ONE...
MURMUR
MURMUR
MURMUR
MURMUR
...AND SOMETHING SMALL AND NOT TOO SWEET FOR COACH.
THEN FOR MY LITTLE BROTHERS...
......
It's gotta be
Homemade♡
SQUEE!
SQUEE!
YOU GONNA MAKE ME CHOCO-LATE?
STOMP
DON'T BE STUPID!
YOU CAN'T GO ALONG WITH IT EVERY TIME NARUSE SAYS SOMETHING RIDICULOUS!
JUST TRY AND BE FOOLISH ENOUGH TO MAKE HIM CHOCO-LATE.
NO DOUBT IT'LL TURN INTO SOMETHING WEIRD. LIKE CHRISTMAS ALL OVER AGAIN...
OH?

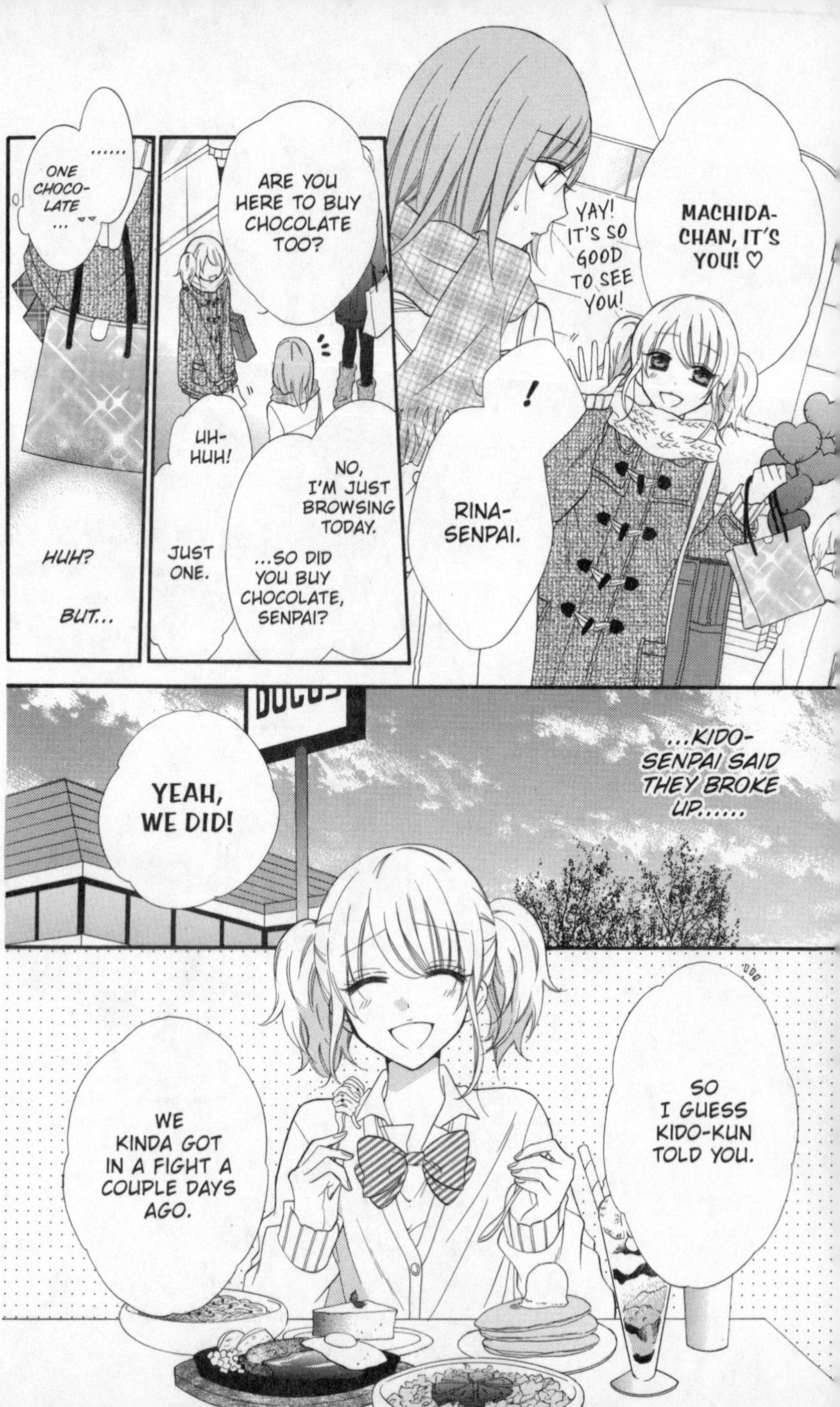
MACHIDA-CHAN, IT'S YOU! ♡
YAY! IT'S SO GOOD TO SEE YOU!
!
RINA-SENPAI.
ARE YOU HERE TO BUY CHOCOLATE TOO?
NO, I'M JUST BROWSING TODAY.
UH-HUH!
...SO DID YOU BUY CHOCOLATE, SENPAI?
JUST ONE.
......
ONE CHOCOLATE ...
HUH?
BUT...
...KIDO-SENPAI SAID THEY BROKE UP......
YEAH, WE DID!
SO I GUESS KIDO-KUN TOLD YOU.
WE KINDA GOT IN A FIGHT A COUPLE DAYS AGO.

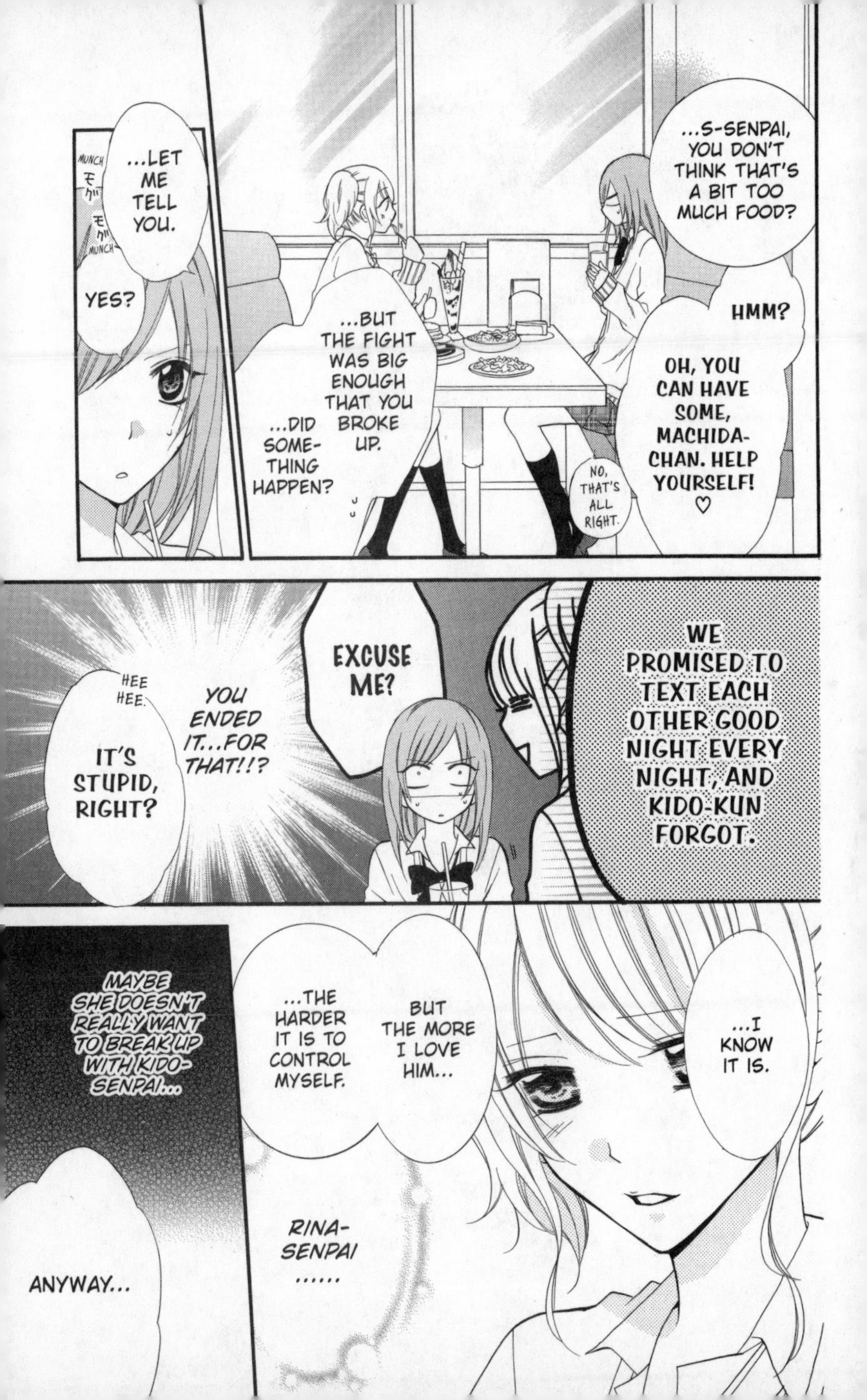
...S-SENPAI, YOU DON'T THINK THAT'S A BIT TOO MUCH FOOD?
HMM?
OH, YOU CAN HAVE SOME, MACHIDA-CHAN. HELP YOURSELF! ♡
NO, THAT'S ALL RIGHT.
...BUT THE FIGHT WAS BIG ENOUGH THAT YOU BROKE UP.
...DID SOMETHING HAPPEN?
...LET ME TELL YOU.
MUNCH
MUNCH
YES?
WE PROMISED TO TEXT EACH OTHER GOOD NIGHT EVERY NIGHT, AND KIDO-KUN FORGOT.
EXCUSE ME?
YOU ENDED IT...FOR THAT!!?
HEE HEE.
IT'S STUPID, RIGHT?
...I KNOW IT IS.
BUT THE MORE I LOVE HIM...
...THE HARDER IT IS TO CONTROL MYSELF.
RINA-SENPAI ......
MAYBE SHE DOESN'T REALLY WANT TO BREAK UP WITH KIDO-SENPAI...
ANYWAY...

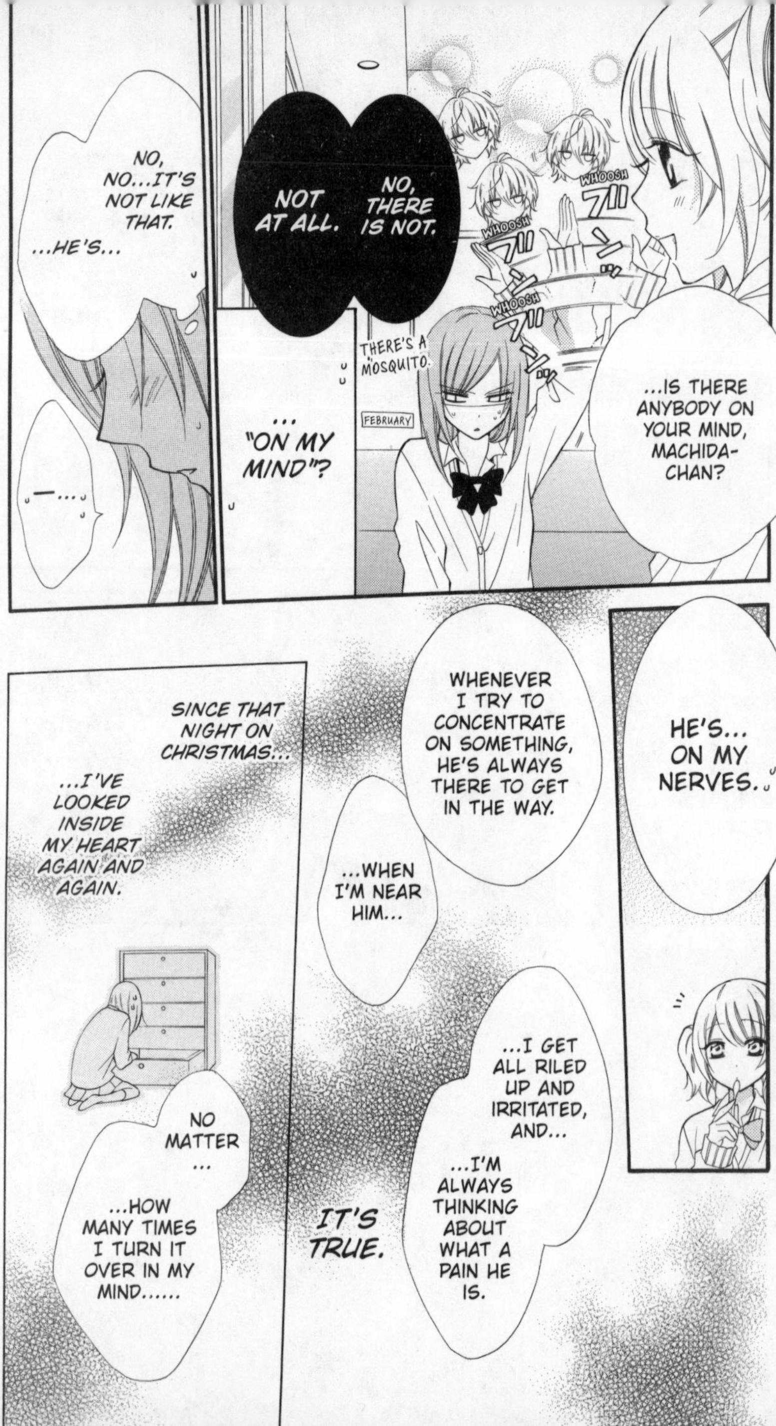
...IS THERE ANYBODY ON YOUR MIND, MACHIDA-CHAN?
WHOOSH
WHOOSH
WHOOSH
NO, THERE IS NOT.
NOT AT ALL.
THERE'S A MOSQUITO.
FEBRUARY
... "ON MY MIND"?
NO, NO...IT'S NOT LIKE THAT. ...HE'S...
—...
HE'S... ON MY NERVES.
WHENEVER I TRY TO CONCENTRATE ON SOMETHING, HE'S ALWAYS THERE TO GET IN THE WAY.
...WHEN I'M NEAR HIM...
...I GET ALL RILED UP AND IRRITATED, AND...
...I'M ALWAYS THINKING ABOUT WHAT A PAIN HE IS.
IT'S TRUE.
SINCE THAT NIGHT ON CHRISTMAS...
...I'VE LOOKED INSIDE MY HEART AGAIN AND AGAIN.
NO MATTER ...
...HOW MANY TIMES I TURN IT OVER IN MY MIND......

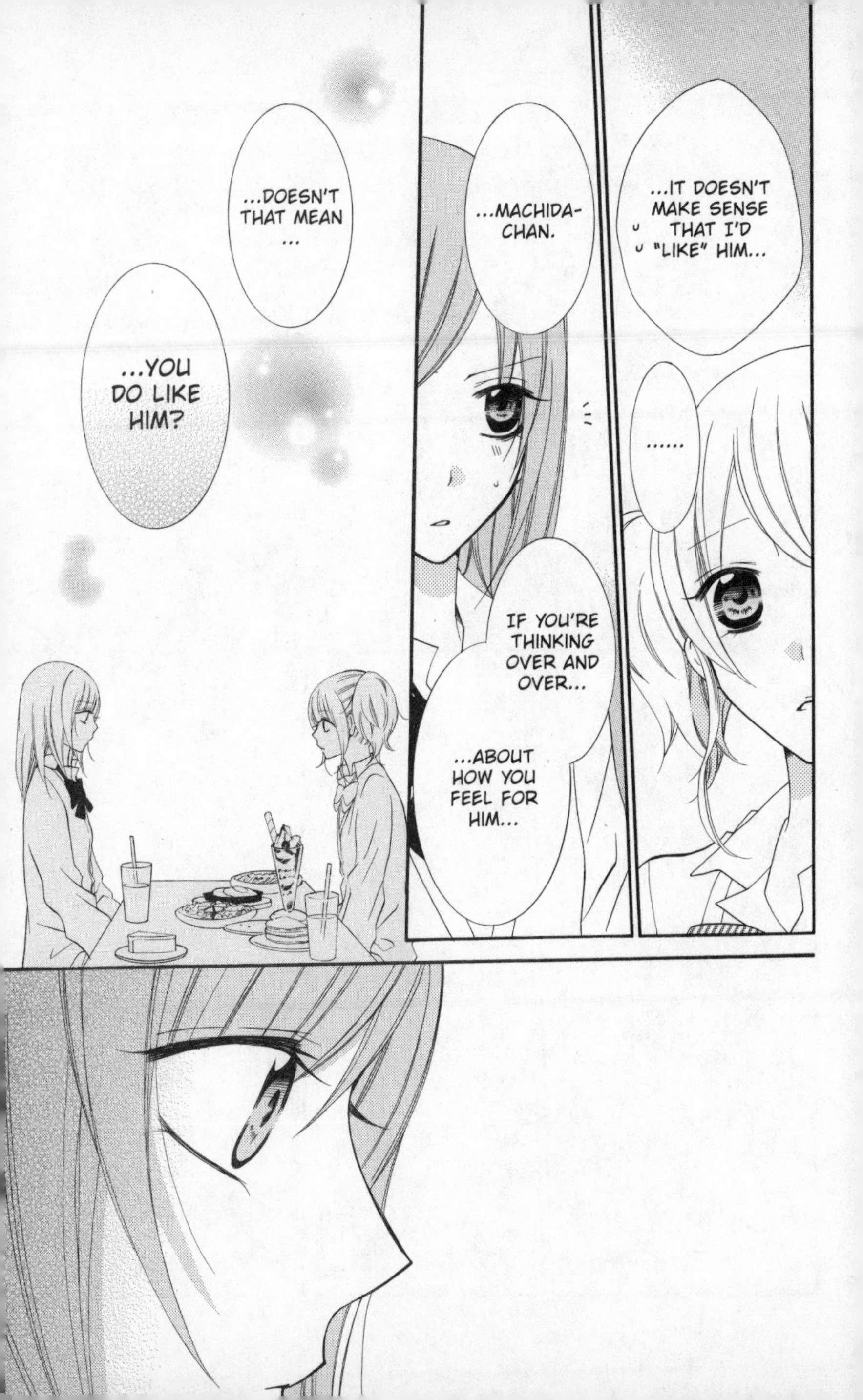
...IT DOESN'T MAKE SENSE THAT I'D "LIKE" HIM...
......
...MACHIDA-CHAN.
IF YOU'RE THINKING OVER AND OVER...
...ABOUT HOW YOU FEEL FOR HIM...
...DOESN'T THAT MEAN ...
...YOU DO LIKE HIM?

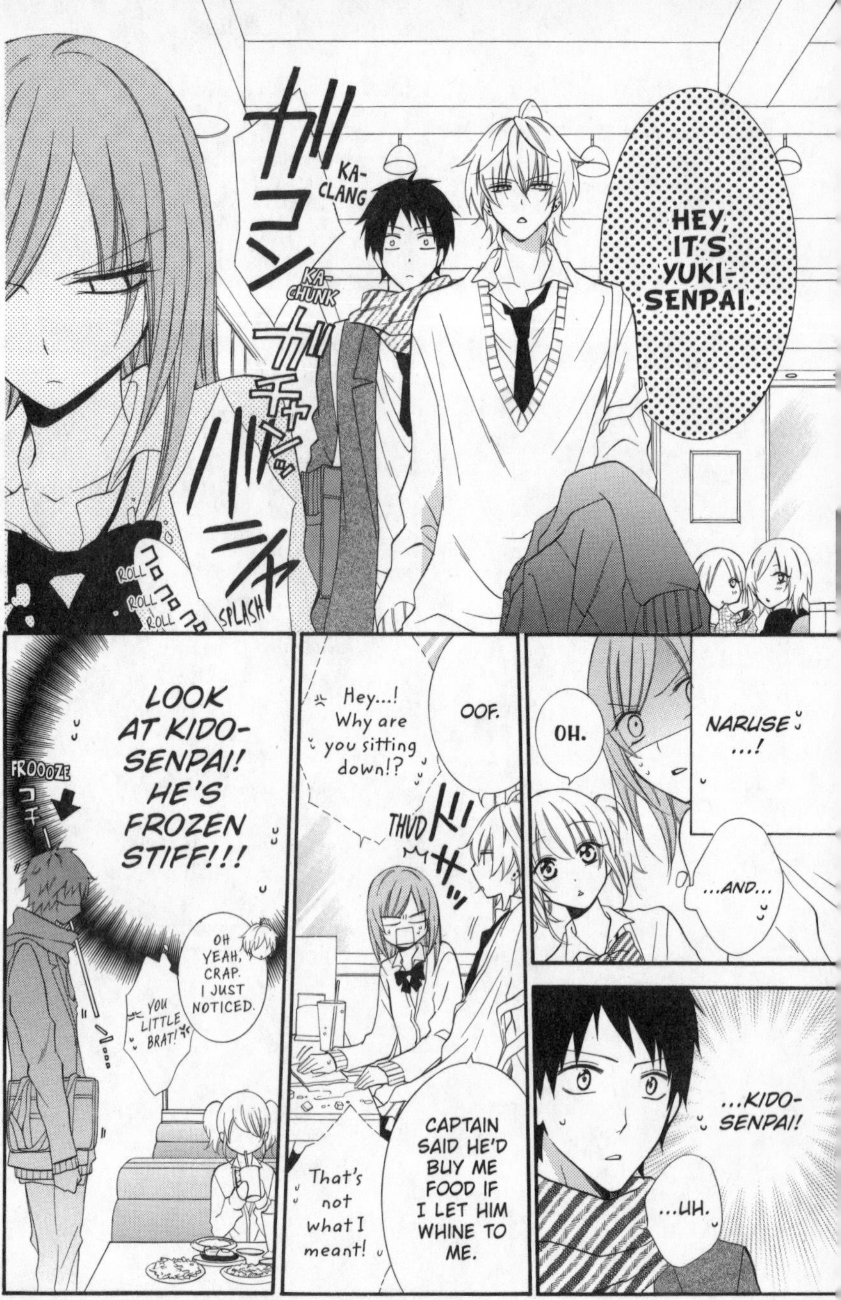
HEY, IT'S YUKI-SENPAI.
KA-CLANG
KA-CHUNK
SPLASH
ROLL ROLL ROLL
NARUSE ...!
OH.
...AND...
...KIDO-SENPAI!
...UH.
OOF.
Hey...! Why are you sitting down!?
THUD
CAPTAIN SAID HE'D BUY ME FOOD IF I LET HIM WHINE TO ME.
That's not what I meant!
LOOK AT KIDO-SENPAI! HE'S FROZEN STIFF!!!
FROOOZE
OH YEAH, CRAP. I JUST NOTICED.
YOU LITTLE BRAT!

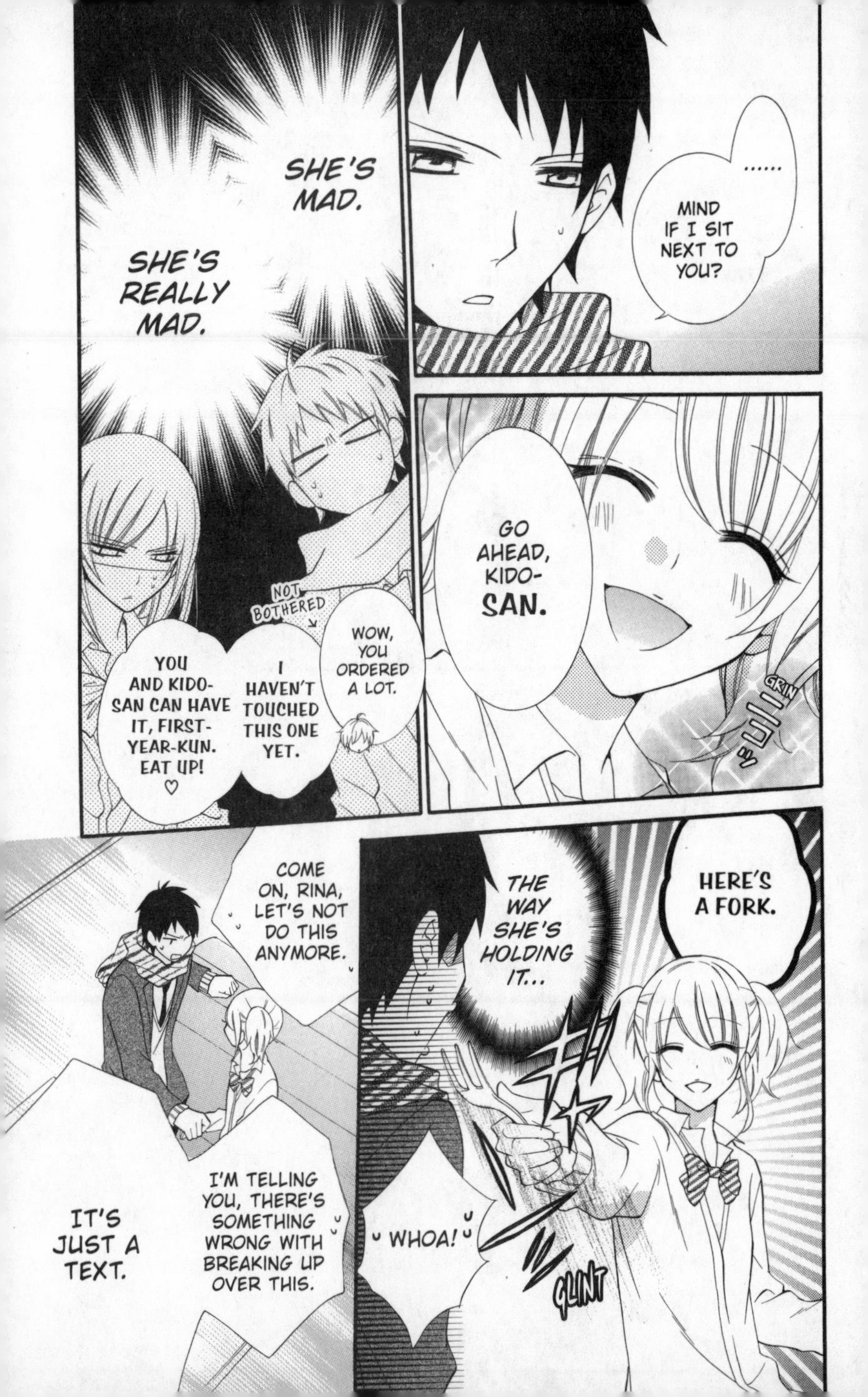
......
MIND IF I SIT NEXT TO YOU?
GO AHEAD, KIDO-SAN.
GRIN
SHE'S MAD.
SHE'S REALLY MAD.
NOT BOTHERED
WOW, YOU ORDERED A LOT.
I HAVEN'T TOUCHED THIS ONE YET.
YOU AND KIDO-SAN CAN HAVE IT, FIRST-YEAR-KUN. EAT UP! ♡
HERE'S A FORK.
THE WAY SHE'S HOLDING IT...
WHOA!
GLINT
COME ON, RINA, LET'S NOT DO THIS ANYMORE.
I'M TELLING YOU, THERE'S SOMETHING WRONG WITH BREAKING UP OVER THIS.
IT'S JUST A TEXT.

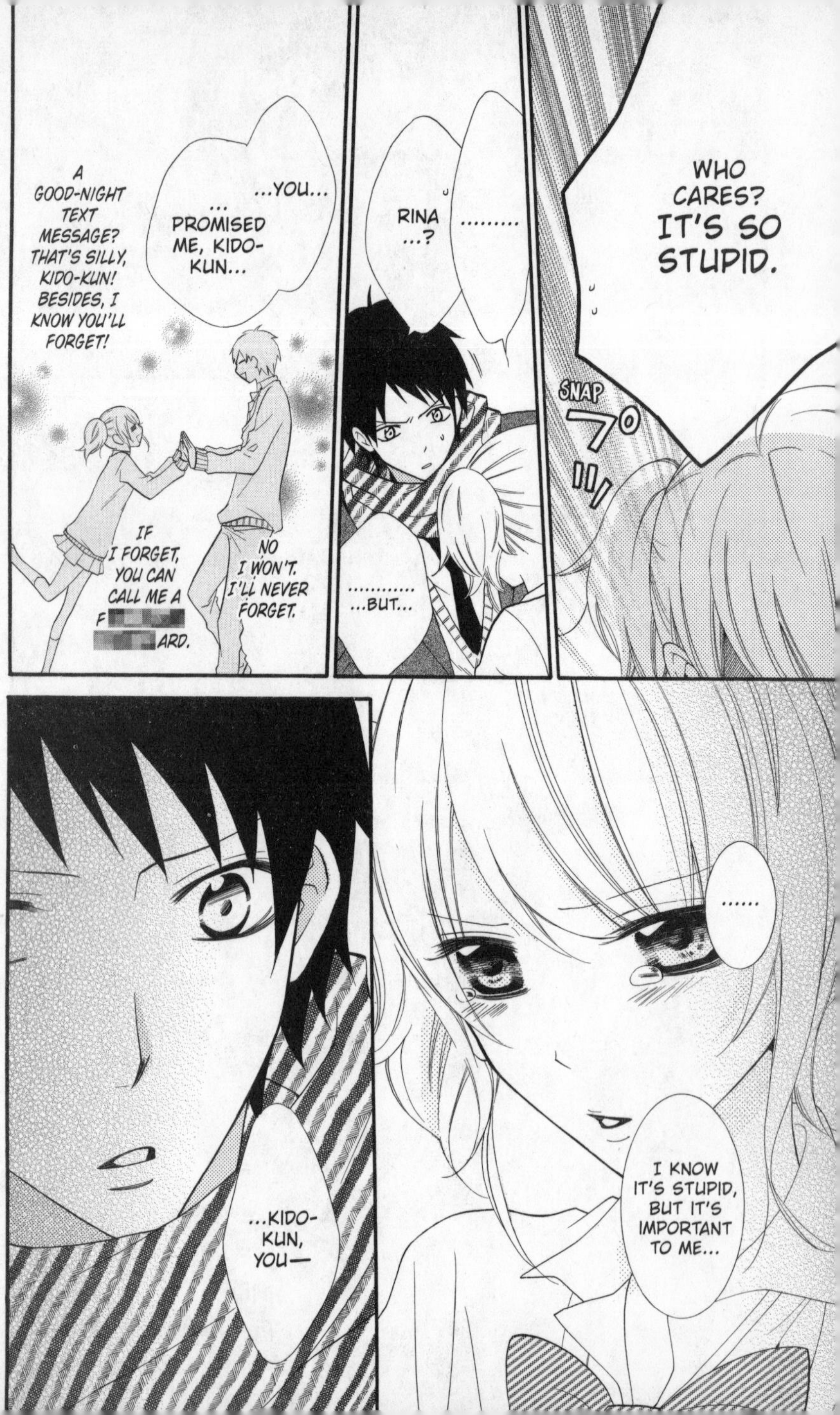
WHO CARES? IT'S SO STUPID.
SNAP
....
RINA ...?
....BUT...
...YOU... ... PROMISED ME, KIDO-KUN...
A GOOD-NIGHT TEXT MESSAGE? THAT'S SILLY, KIDO-KUN! BESIDES, I KNOW YOU'LL FORGET!
NO I WON'T. I'LL NEVER FORGET.
IF I FORGET, YOU CAN CALL ME A F[redacted]ARD.
......
I KNOW IT'S STUPID, BUT IT'S IMPORTANT TO ME...
...KIDO-KUN, YOU—

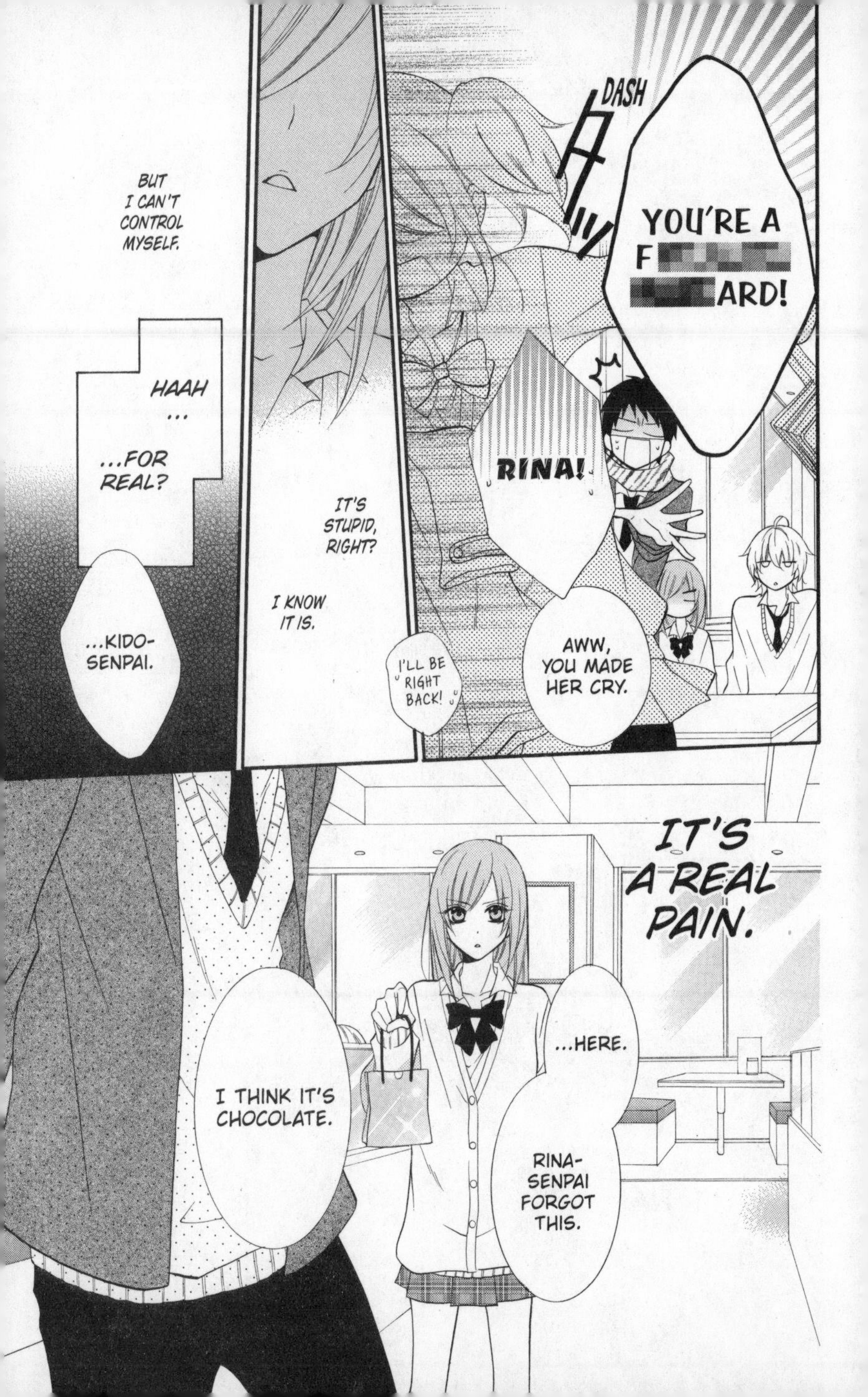
YOU'RE A F[redacted]ARD!
DASH
RINA!
AWW, YOU MADE HER CRY.
I'LL BE RIGHT BACK!
IT'S STUPID, RIGHT?
I KNOW IT IS.
BUT I CAN'T CONTROL MYSELF.
HAAH ...
...FOR REAL?
...KIDO-SENPAI.
IT'S A REAL PAIN.
...HERE.
RINA-SENPAI FORGOT THIS.
I THINK IT'S CHOCOLATE.

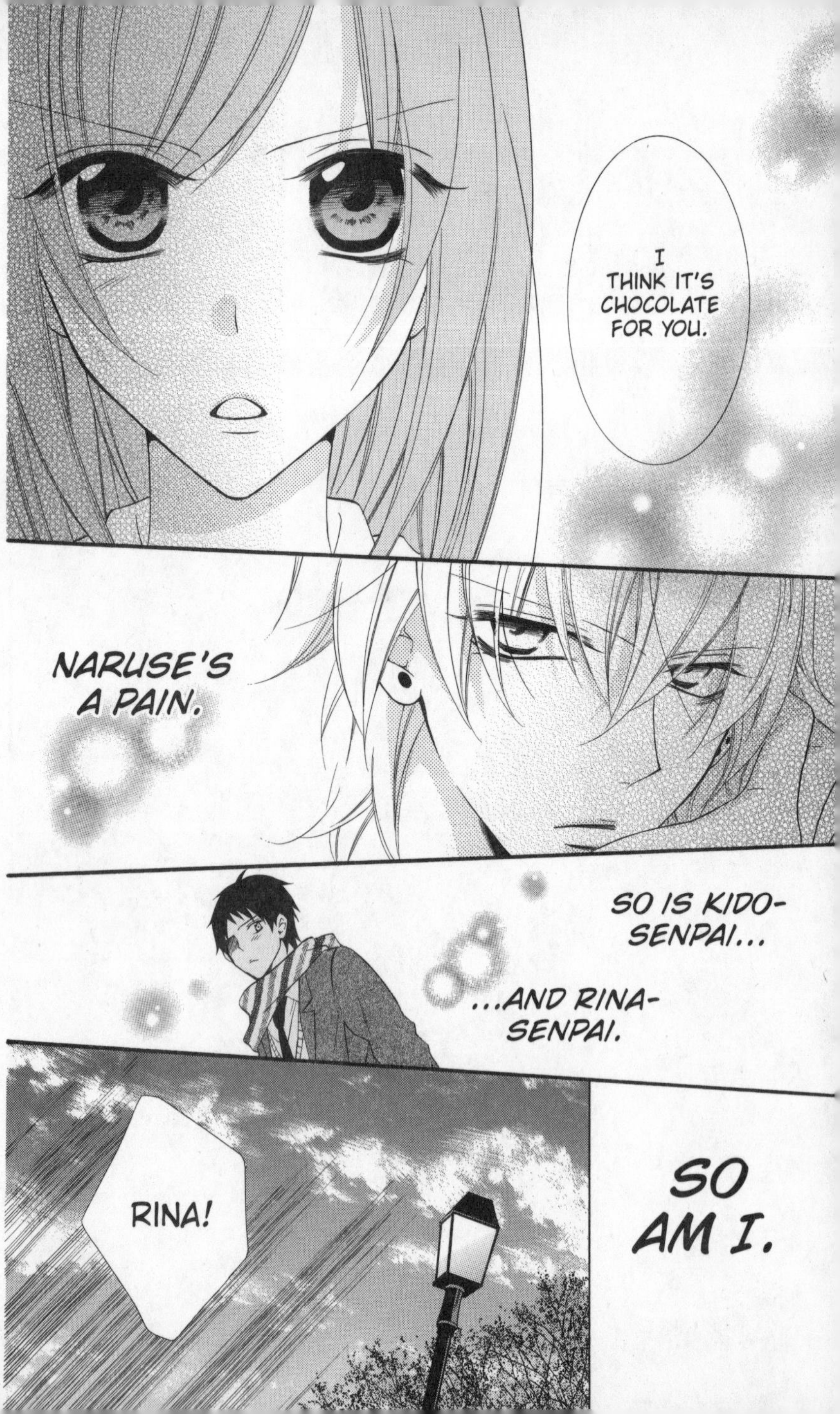
I THINK IT'S CHOCOLATE FOR YOU.
NARUSE'S A PAIN.
SO IS KIDO-SENPAI...
...AND RINA-SENPAI.
SO AM I.
RINA!

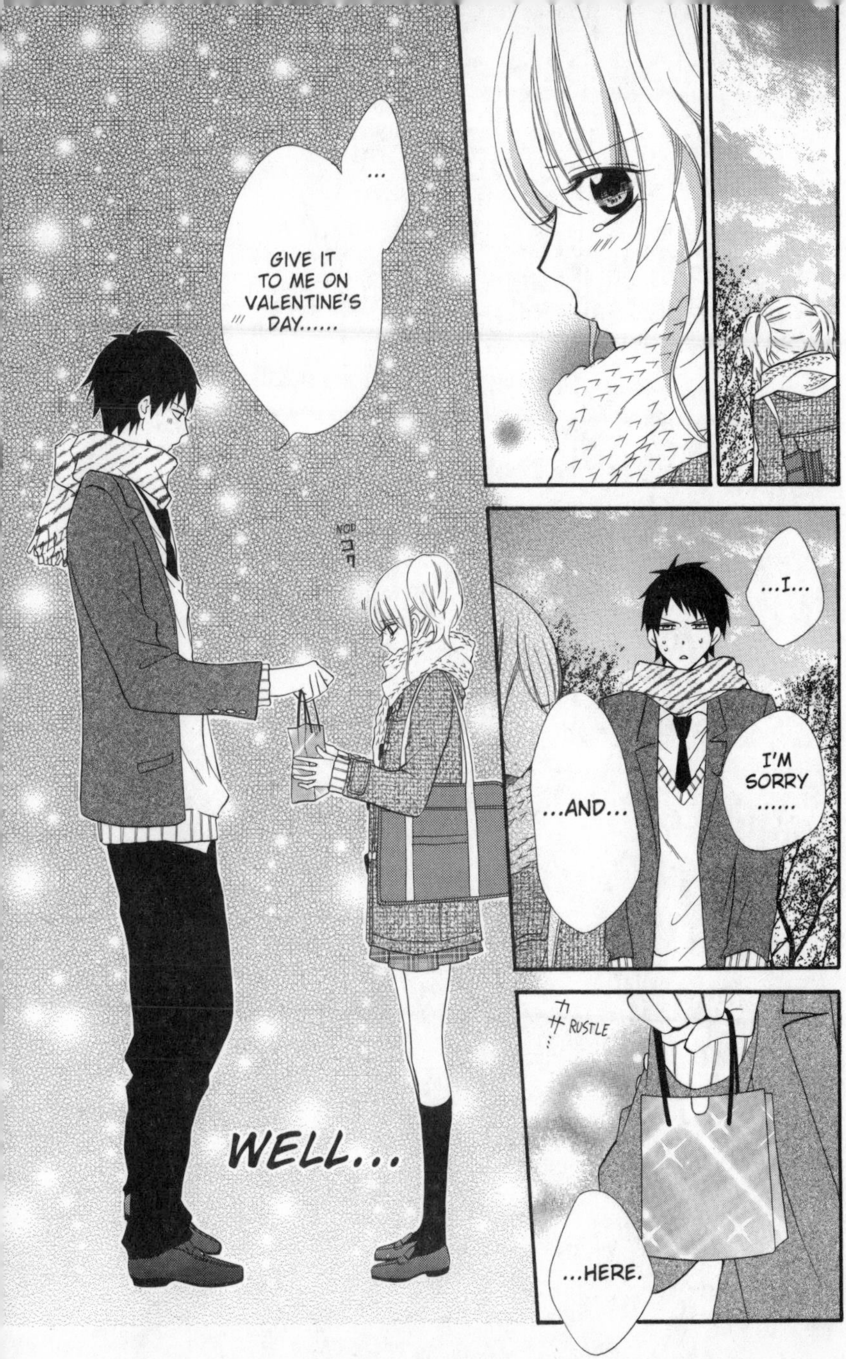
...I...
I'M SORRY ......
...AND...
RUSTLE
...HERE.
...
GIVE IT TO ME ON VALENTINE'S DAY......
NOD
WELL...

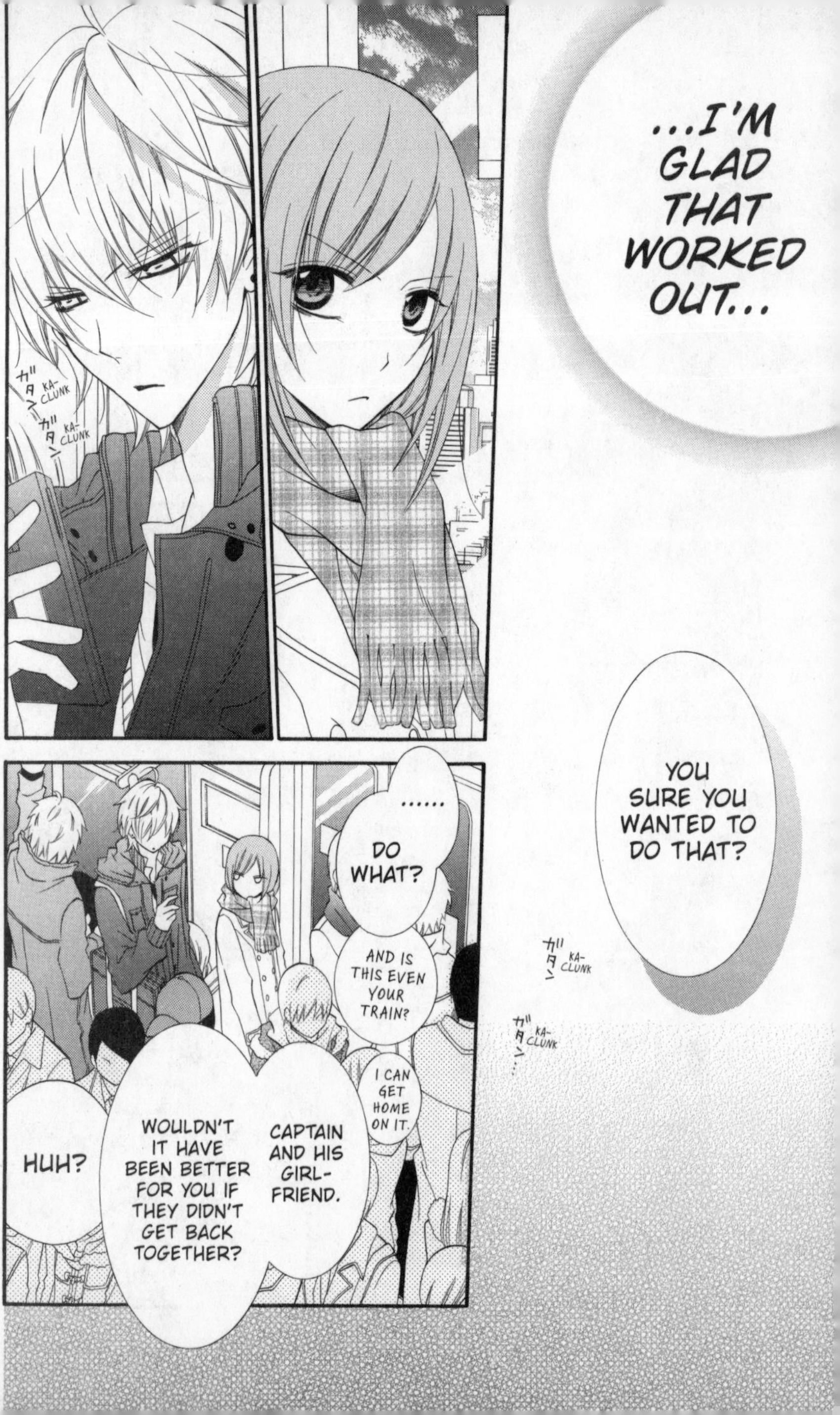
...I'M GLAD THAT WORKED OUT...
ガタン KA-CLUNK
ガタン KA-CLUNK
YOU SURE YOU WANTED TO DO THAT?
ガタン KA-CLUNK
ガタン... KA-CLUNK
......
DO WHAT?
AND IS THIS EVEN YOUR TRAIN?
I CAN GET HOME ON IT.
CAPTAIN AND HIS GIRL-FRIEND.
WOULDN'T IT HAVE BEEN BETTER FOR YOU IF THEY DIDN'T GET BACK TOGETHER?
HUH?

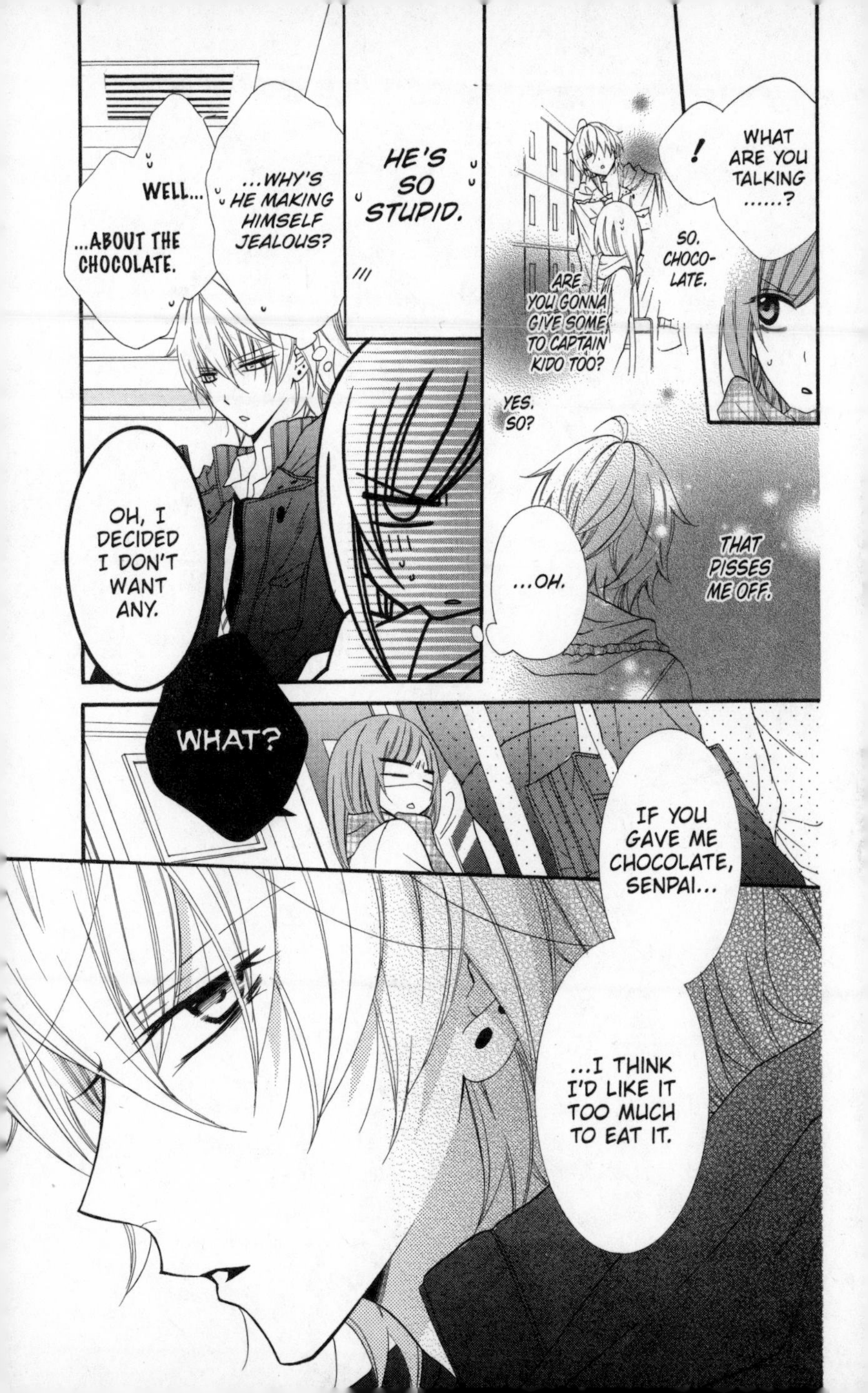

!
WHAT ARE YOU TALKING ......?
SO. CHOCOLATE.
ARE YOU GONNA GIVE SOME TO CAPTAIN KIDO TOO?
YES. SO?
THAT PISSES ME OFF.
...OH.
HE'S SO STUPID.
...WHY'S HE MAKING HIMSELF JEALOUS?
WELL... ...ABOUT THE CHOCOLATE.
OH, I DECIDED I DON'T WANT ANY.
WHAT?
IF YOU GAVE ME CHOCOLATE, SENPAI...
...I THINK I'D LIKE IT TOO MUCH TO EAT IT.

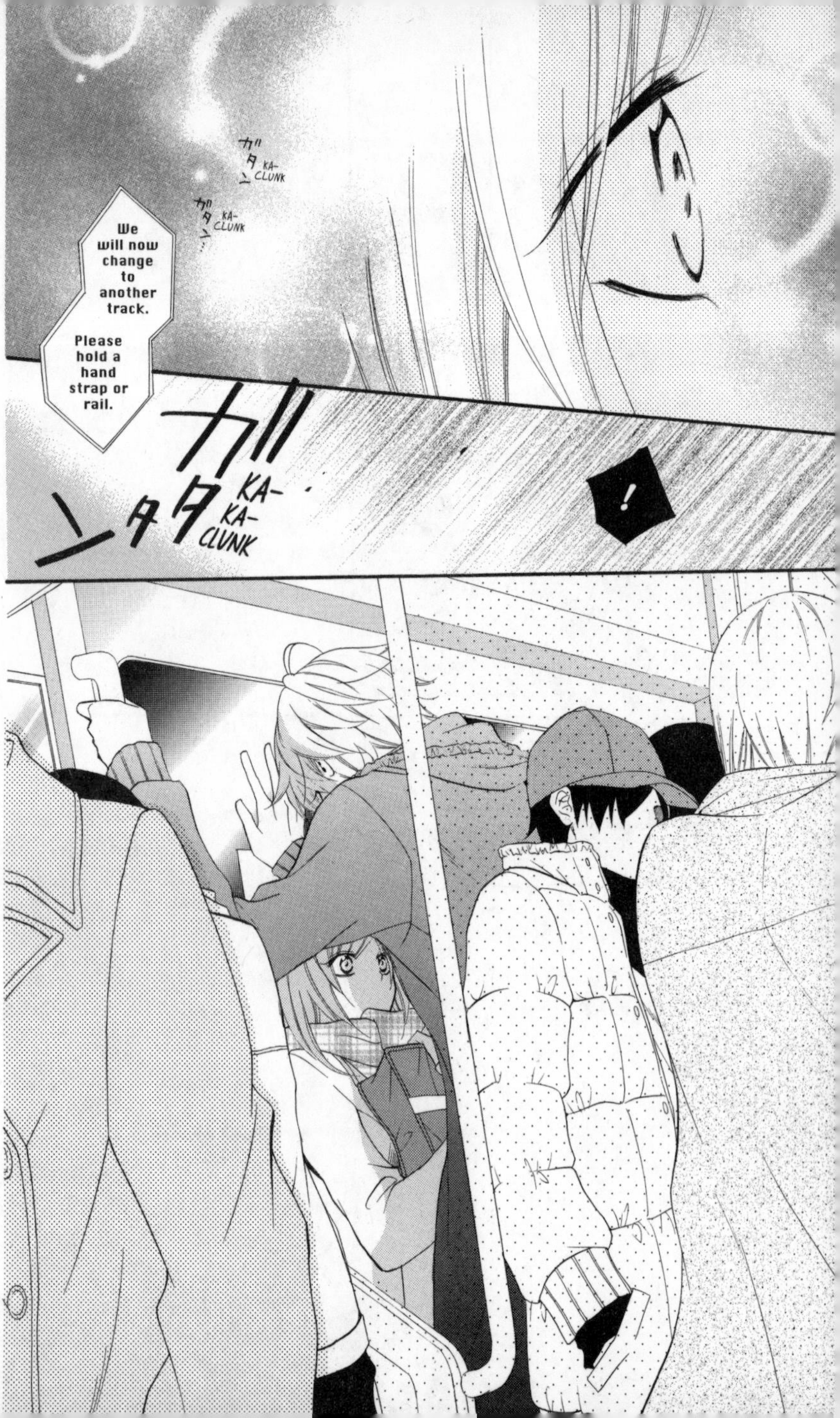

ガタン KA-CLUNK
ガタン KA-CLUNK
We will now change to another track.
Please hold a hand strap or rail.
!
ガタタン KA-KA-CLUNK

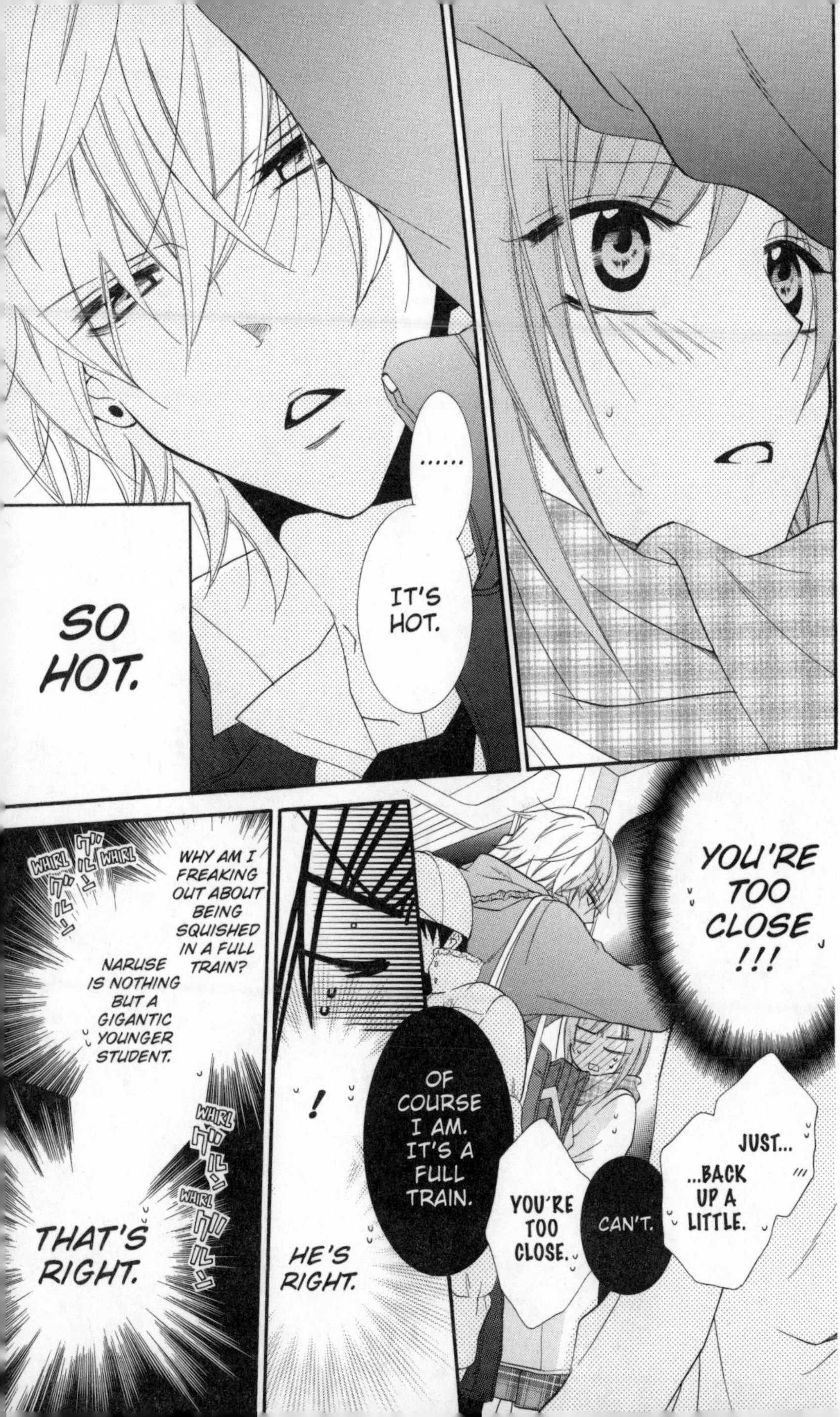
......
IT'S HOT.
SO HOT.
YOU'RE TOO CLOSE!!!
JUST...
...BACK UP A LITTLE.
CAN'T.
YOU'RE TOO CLOSE.
OF COURSE I AM. IT'S A FULL TRAIN.
!
HE'S RIGHT.
WHIRL WHIRL
WHY AM I FREAKING OUT ABOUT BEING SQUISHED IN A FULL TRAIN?
NARUSE IS NOTHING BUT A GIGANTIC YOUNGER STUDENT.
WHIRL
WHIRL
THAT'S RIGHT.

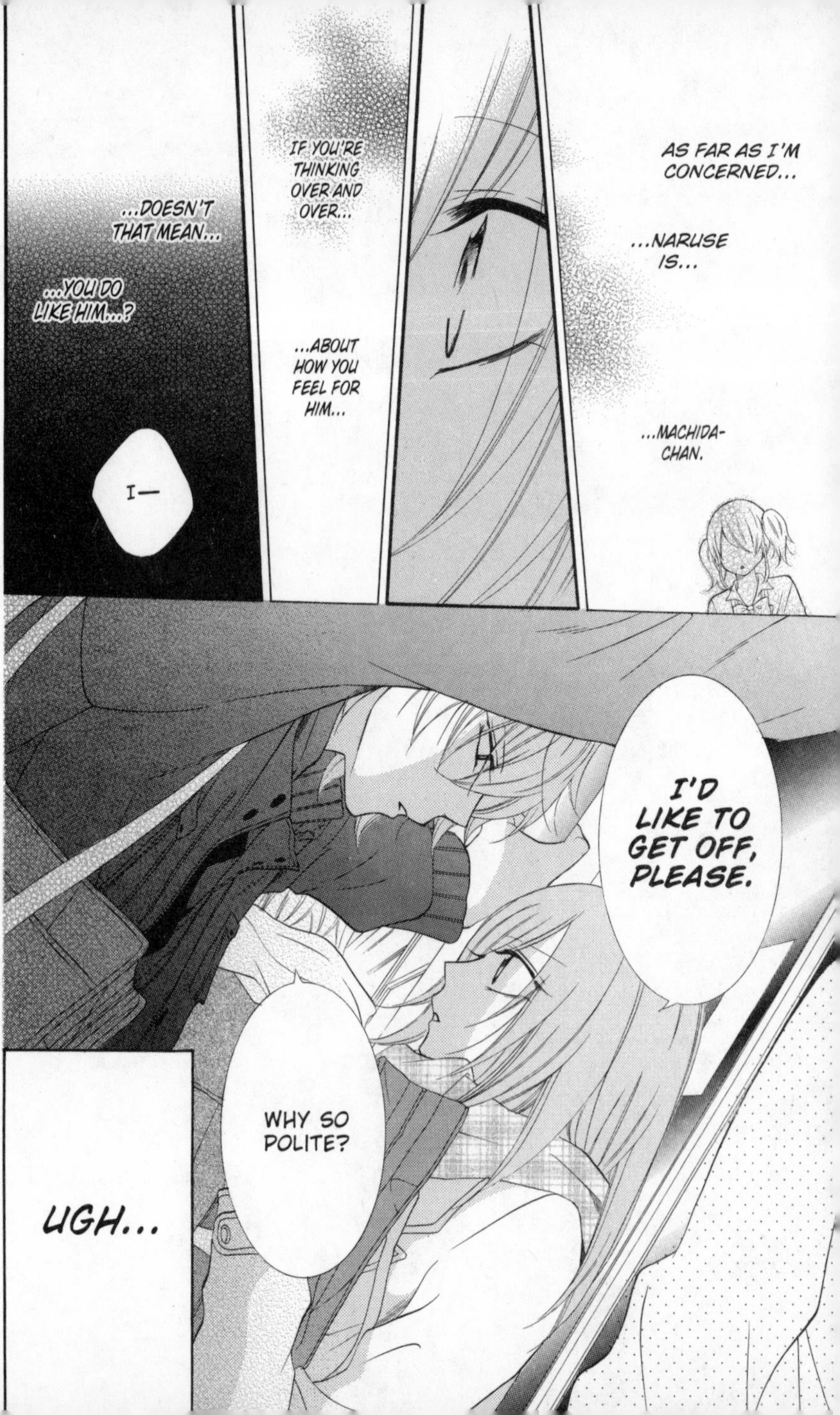
AS FAR AS I'M CONCERNED...
...NARUSE IS...
...MACHIDA-CHAN.
IF YOU'RE THINKING OVER AND OVER...
...ABOUT HOW YOU FEEL FOR HIM...
...DOESN'T THAT MEAN...
...YOU DO LIKE HIM...?
I—
I'D LIKE TO GET OFF, PLEASE.
WHY SO POLITE?
UGH...

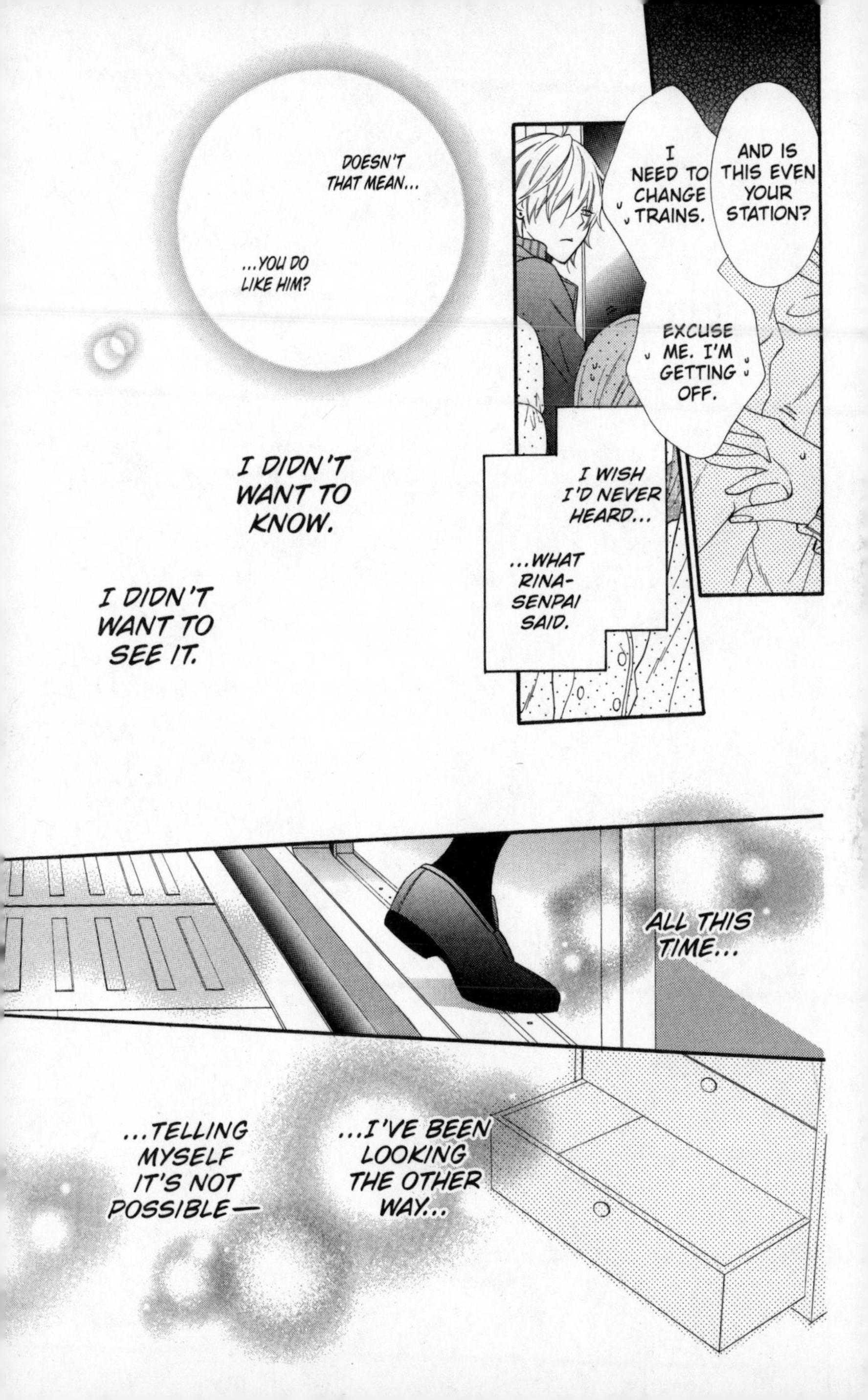
AND IS THIS EVEN YOUR STATION?
I NEED TO CHANGE TRAINS.
EXCUSE ME. I'M GETTING OFF.
I WISH I'D NEVER HEARD...
...WHAT RINA-SENPAI SAID.
DOESN'T THAT MEAN...
...YOU DO LIKE HIM?
I DIDN'T WANT TO KNOW.
I DIDN'T WANT TO SEE IT.
ALL THIS TIME...
...I'VE BEEN LOOKING THE OTHER WAY...
...TELLING MYSELF IT'S NOT POSSIBLE—

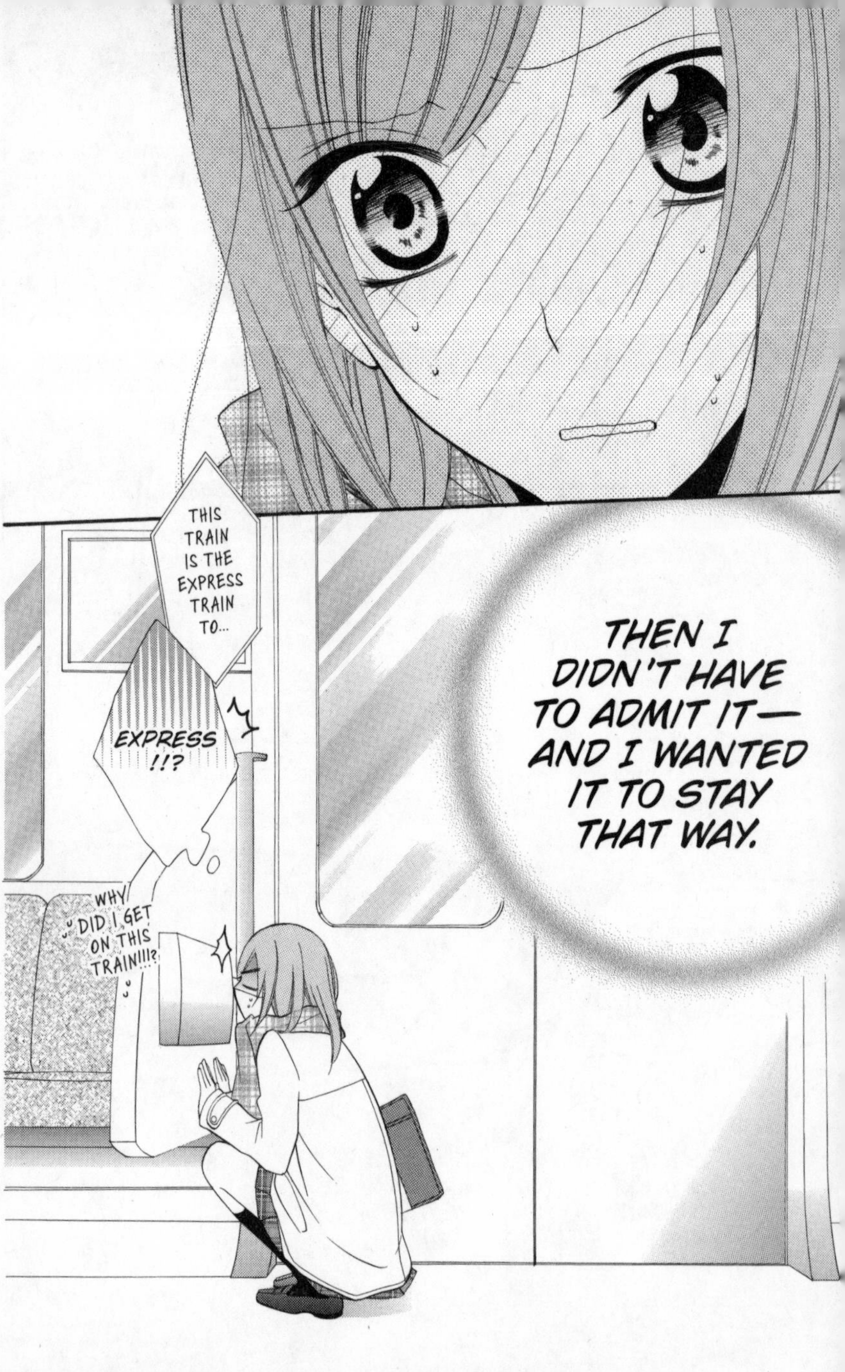
THEN I DIDN'T HAVE TO ADMIT IT—AND I WANTED IT TO STAY THAT WAY.
THIS TRAIN IS THE EXPRESS TRAIN TO...
EXPRESS !!?
WHY DID I GET ON THIS TRAIN!!!?

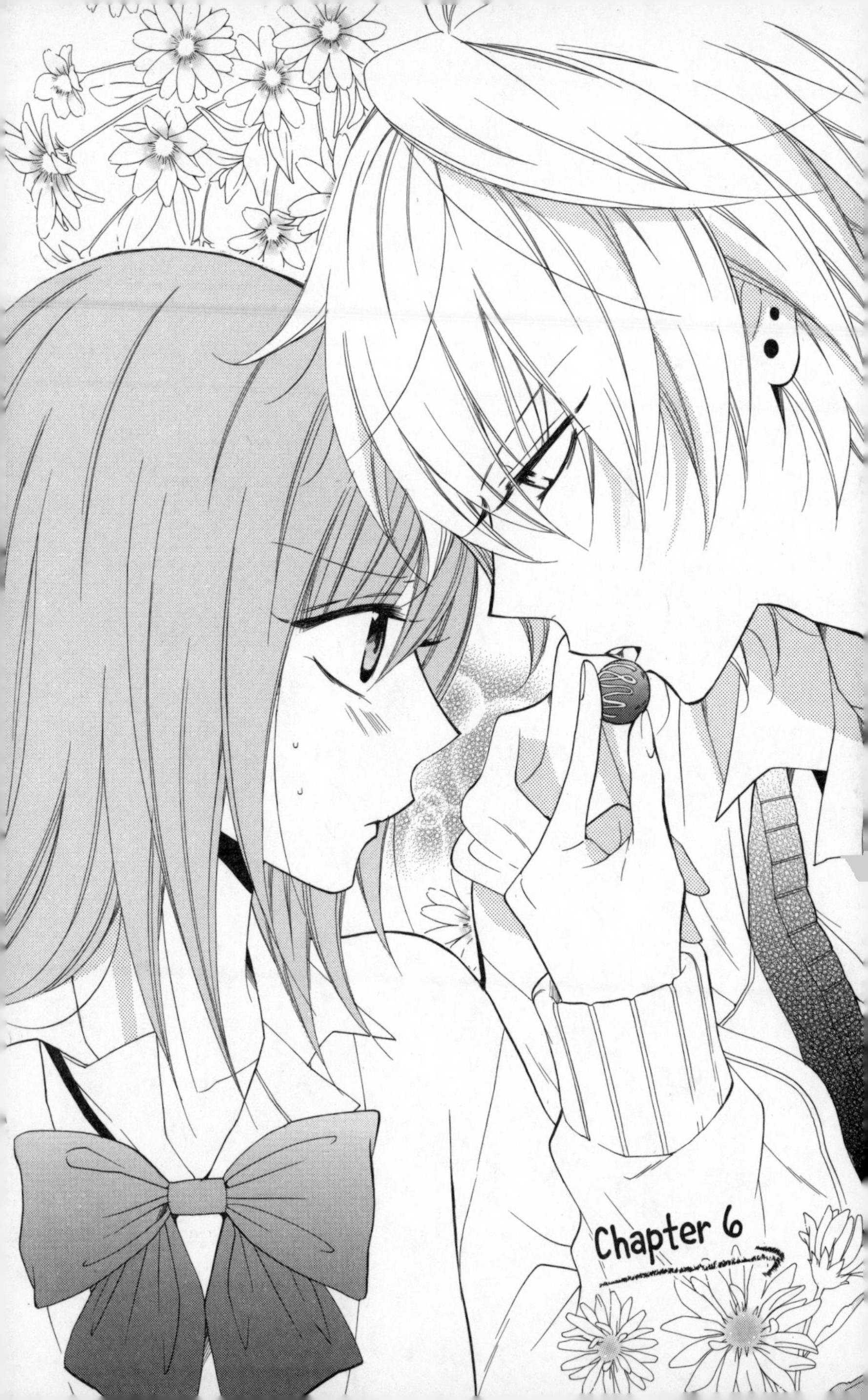
Chapter 6

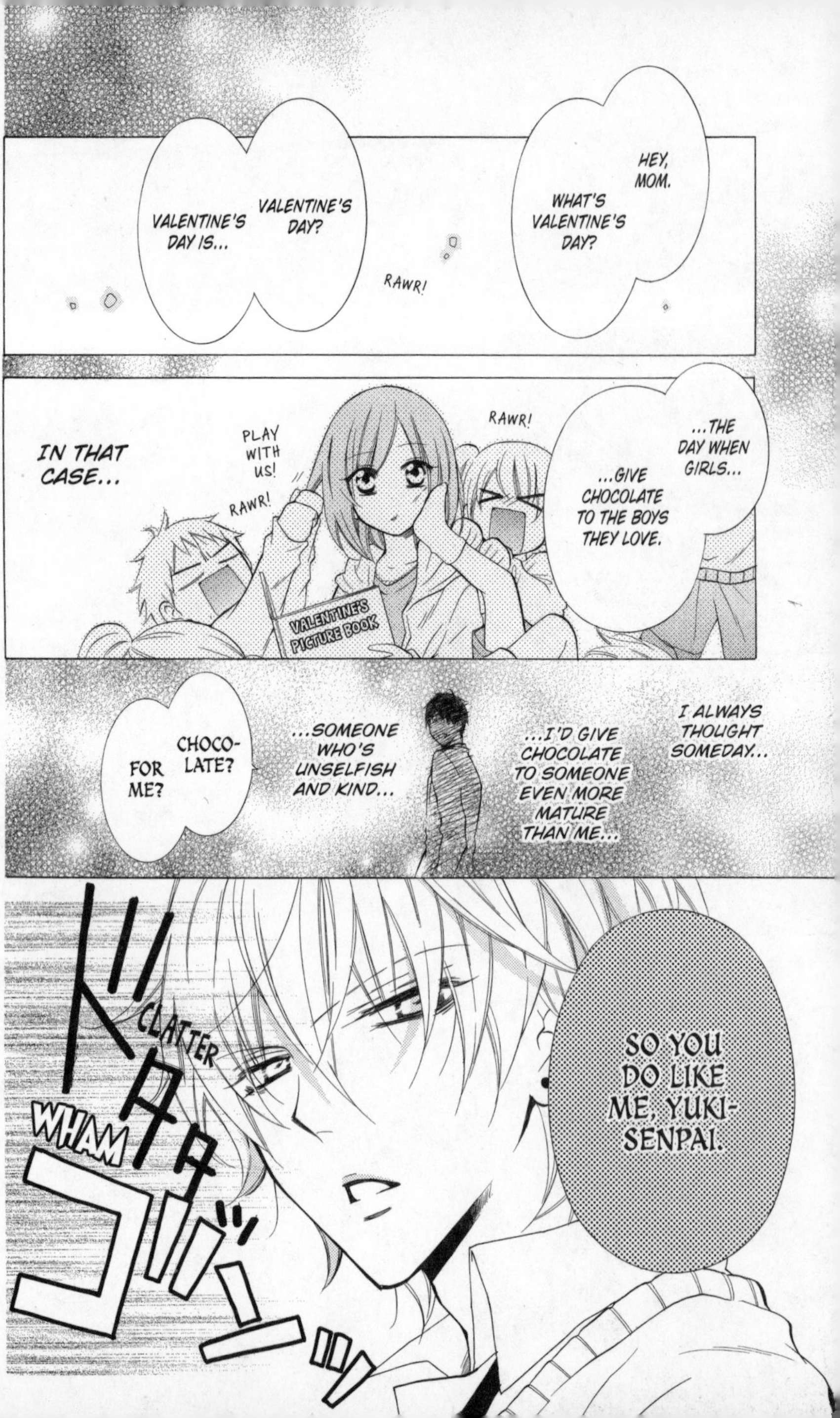
HEY, MOM.
WHAT'S VALENTINE'S DAY?
RAWR!
VALENTINE'S DAY?
VALENTINE'S DAY IS...
...THE DAY WHEN GIRLS...
...GIVE CHOCOLATE TO THE BOYS THEY LOVE.
RAWR!
PLAY WITH US!
RAWR!
VALENTINE'S PICTURE BOOK
IN THAT CASE...
I ALWAYS THOUGHT SOMEDAY...
...I'D GIVE CHOCOLATE TO SOMEONE EVEN MORE MATURE THAN ME...
...SOMEONE WHO'S UNSELFISH AND KIND...
CHOCO-LATE?
FOR ME?
SO YOU DO LIKE ME, YUKI-SENPAI.
CLATTER
WHAM

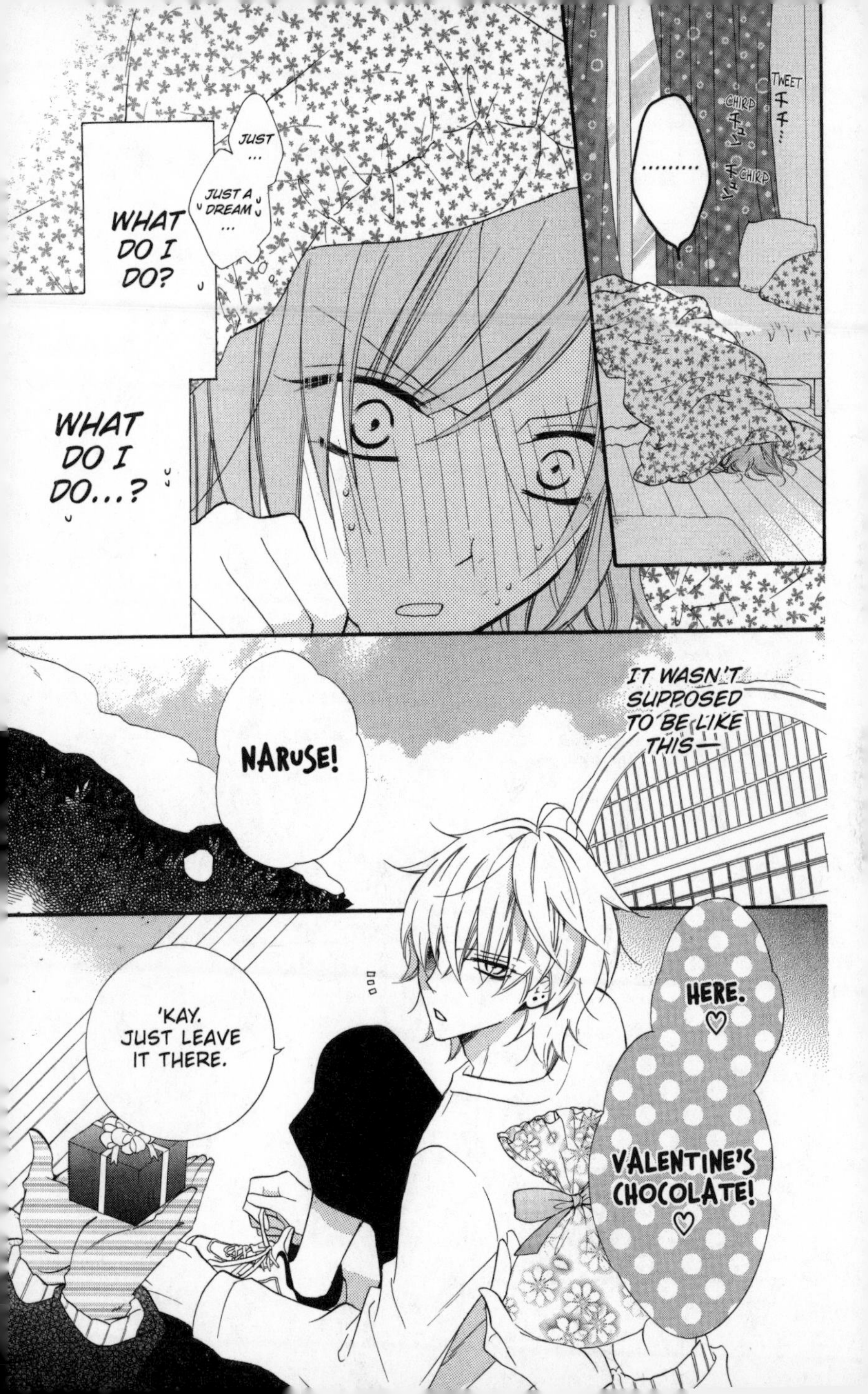
TWEET
チチ…
CHIRP
チュ
チュ
CHIRP
………
JUST
…
JUST A DREAM
…
WHAT DO I DO?
WHAT DO I DO…?
IT WASN'T SUPPOSED TO BE LIKE THIS—
NARUSE!
HERE. ♡
VALENTINE'S CHOCOLATE! ♡
'KAY. JUST LEAVE IT THERE.

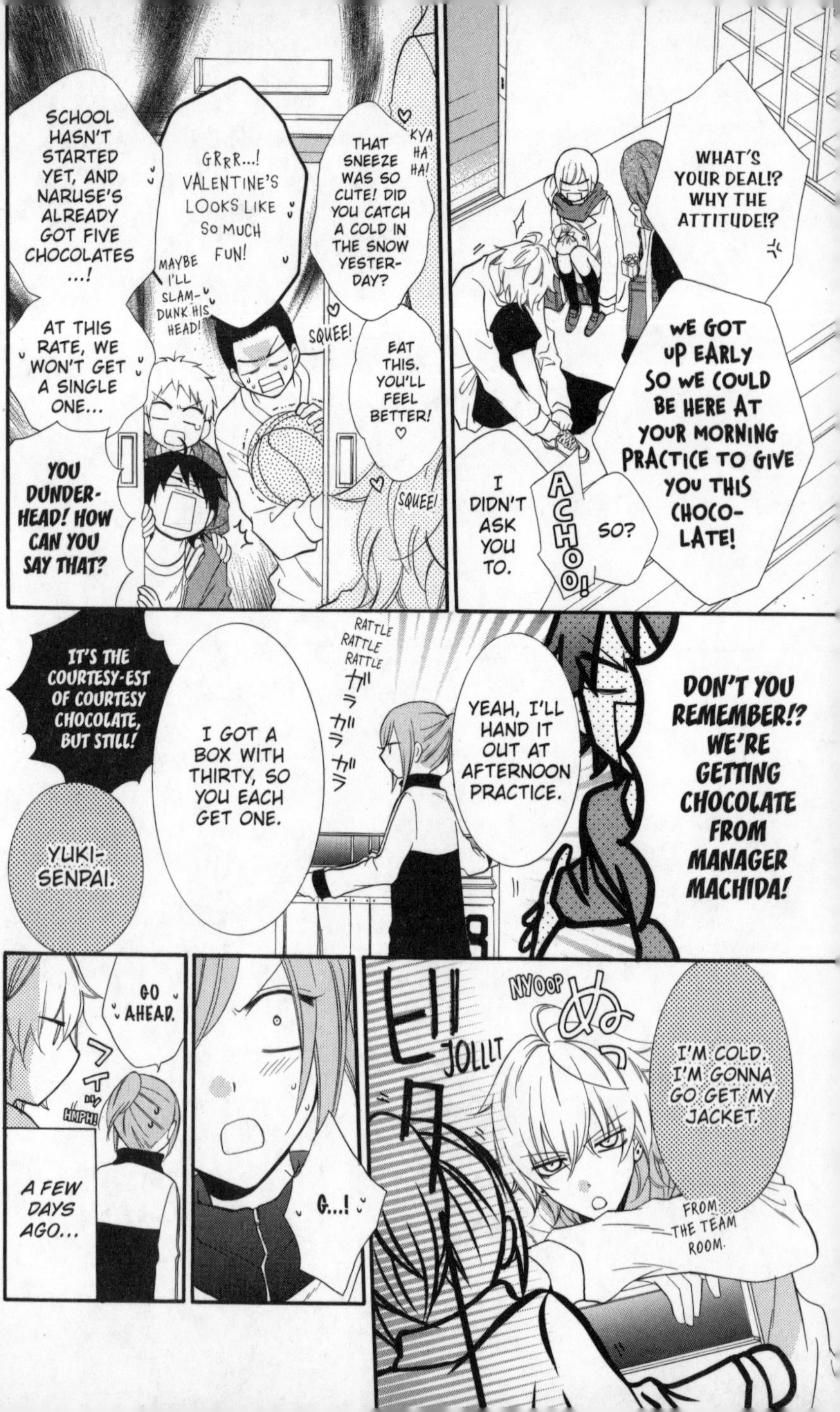
WHAT'S YOUR DEAL!? WHY THE ATTITUDE!?
WE GOT UP EARLY SO WE COULD BE HERE AT YOUR MORNING PRACTICE TO GIVE YOU THIS CHOCOLATE!
SO?
ACHOO!
I DIDN'T ASK YOU TO.
KYA HA HA!
THAT SNEEZE WAS SO CUTE! DID YOU CATCH A COLD IN THE SNOW YESTERDAY?
GRRR...! VALENTINE'S LOOKS LIKE SO MUCH FUN!
SCHOOL HASN'T STARTED YET, AND NARUSE'S ALREADY GOT FIVE CHOCOLATES...!
MAYBE I'LL SLAM-DUNK HIS HEAD!
SQUEE!
EAT THIS. YOU'LL FEEL BETTER!
AT THIS RATE, WE WON'T GET A SINGLE ONE...
SQUEE!
YOU DUNDERHEAD! HOW CAN YOU SAY THAT?
DON'T YOU REMEMBER!? WE'RE GETTING CHOCOLATE FROM MANAGER MACHIDA!
YEAH, I'LL HAND IT OUT AT AFTERNOON PRACTICE.
RATTLE RATTLE RATTLE
I GOT A BOX WITH THIRTY, SO YOU EACH GET ONE.
IT'S THE COURTESY-EST OF COURTESY CHOCOLATE, BUT STILL!
YUKI-SENPAI.
NYOOP
JOLLLT
I'M COLD. I'M GONNA GO GET MY JACKET.
FROM THE TEAM ROOM.
G...!
GO AHEAD.
HMPH!
A FEW DAYS AGO...

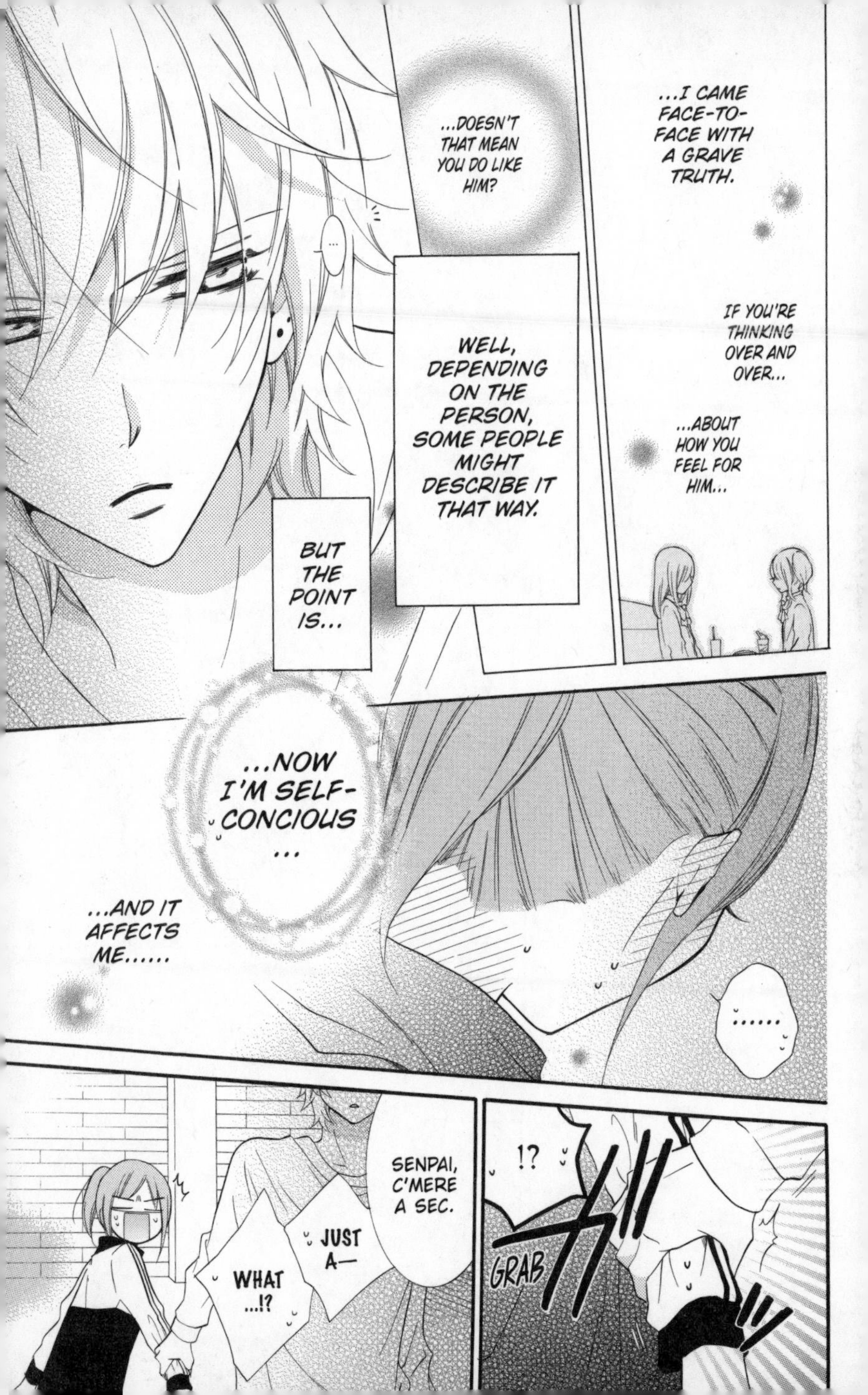
...I CAME FACE-TO-FACE WITH A GRAVE TRUTH.
IF YOU'RE THINKING OVER AND OVER...
...ABOUT HOW YOU FEEL FOR HIM...
...DOESN'T THAT MEAN YOU DO LIKE HIM?
...
WELL, DEPENDING ON THE PERSON, SOME PEOPLE MIGHT DESCRIBE IT THAT WAY.
BUT THE POINT IS...
......
...NOW I'M SELF-CONCIOUS...
...AND IT AFFECTS ME......
!?
GRAB
SENPAI, C'MERE A SEC.
JUST A—
WHAT...!?

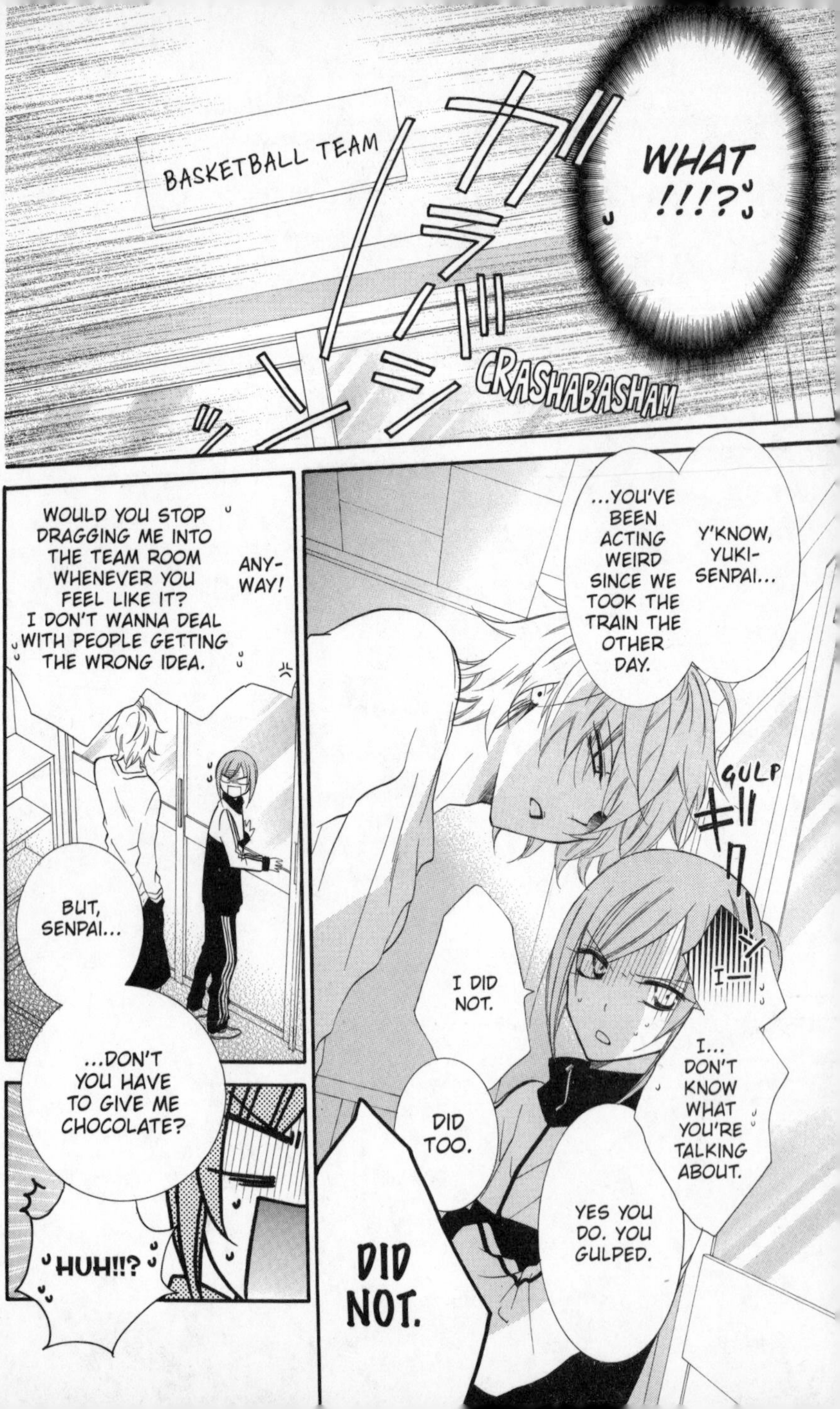
WHAT!!!?
CRASHABASHAM
BASKETBALL TEAM
Y'KNOW, YUKI-SENPAI...
...YOU'VE BEEN ACTING WEIRD SINCE WE TOOK THE TRAIN THE OTHER DAY.
GULP
I—
I DID NOT.
I... DON'T KNOW WHAT YOU'RE TALKING ABOUT.
DID TOO.
YES YOU DO. YOU GULPED.
DID NOT.
ANY-WAY!
WOULD YOU STOP DRAGGING ME INTO THE TEAM ROOM WHENEVER YOU FEEL LIKE IT? I DON'T WANNA DEAL WITH PEOPLE GETTING THE WRONG IDEA.
BUT, SENPAI...
...DON'T YOU HAVE TO GIVE ME CHOCOLATE?
HUH!!?

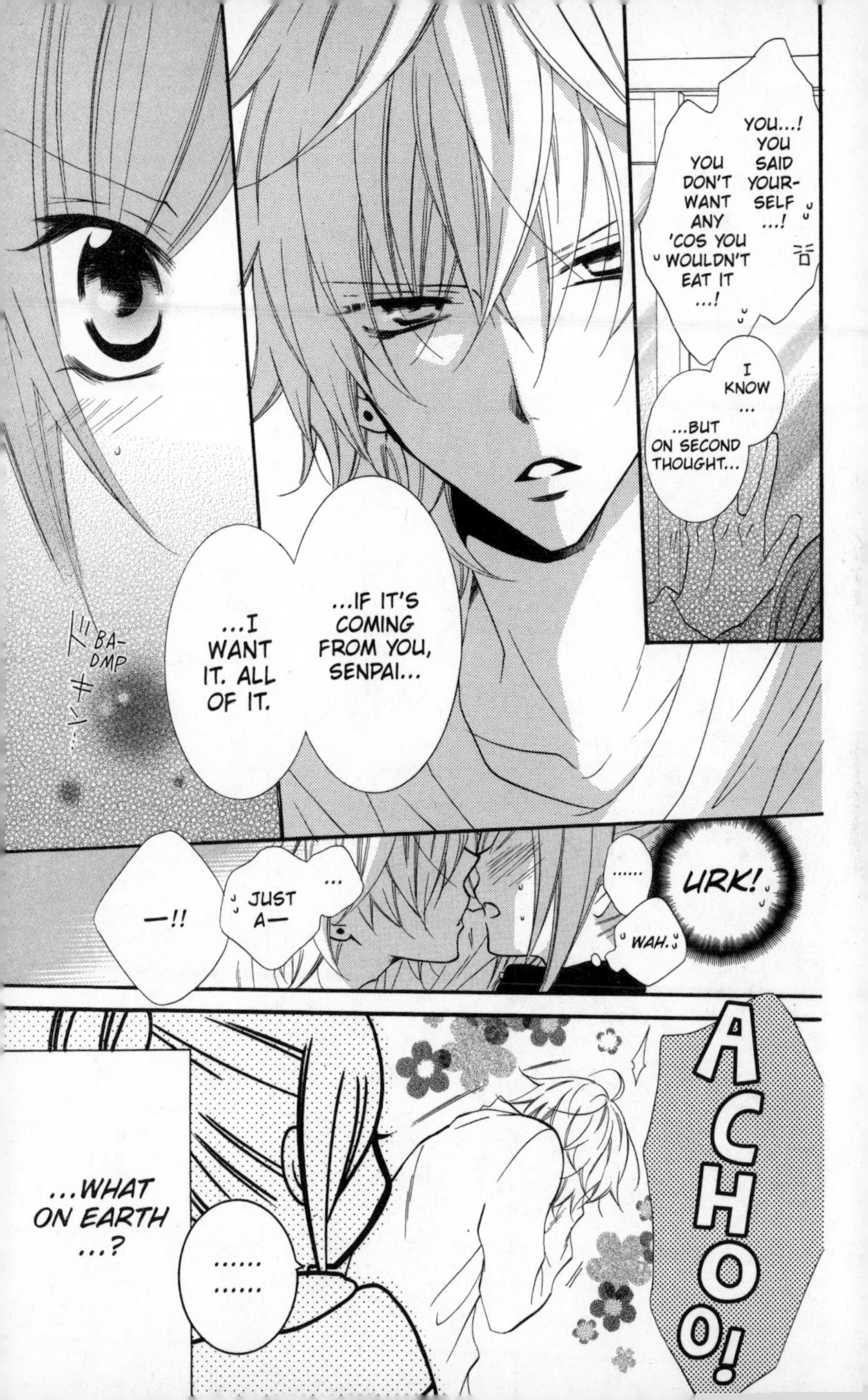
YOU...! YOU SAID YOUR-SELF ...!
YOU DON'T WANT ANY 'COS YOU WOULDN'T EAT IT ...!
I KNOW ...
...BUT ON SECOND THOUGHT...
...IF IT'S COMING FROM YOU, SENPAI...
...I WANT IT. ALL OF IT.
BA-DMP
URK!
WAH.
......
...
JUST A—
—!!
ACHOO!
......
......
...WHAT ON EARTH ...?

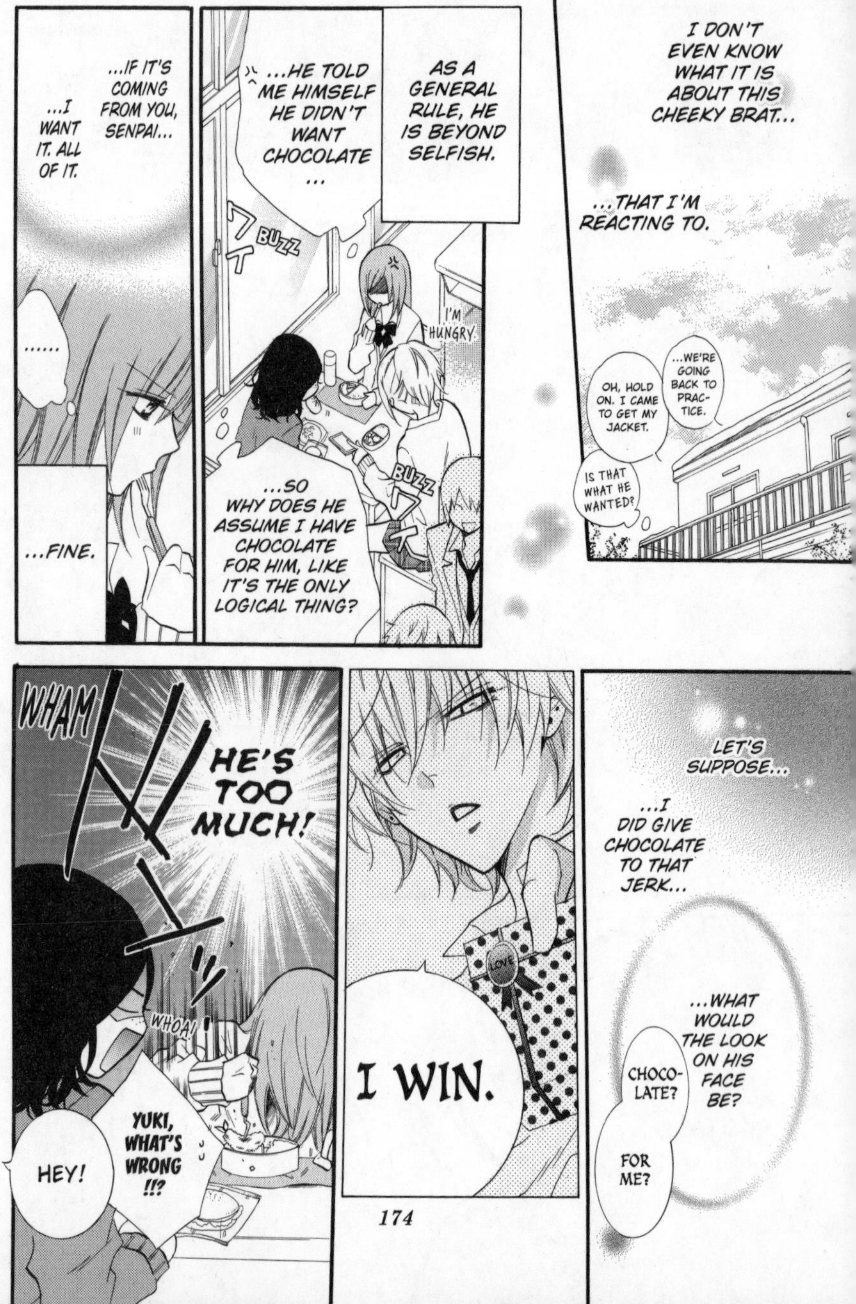
I DON'T EVEN KNOW WHAT IT IS ABOUT THIS CHEEKY BRAT...
...THAT I'M REACTING TO.
...WE'RE GOING BACK TO PRAC-TICE.
OH, HOLD ON. I CAME TO GET MY JACKET.
IS THAT WHAT HE WANTED?
AS A GENERAL RULE, HE IS BEYOND SELFISH.
...HE TOLD ME HIMSELF HE DIDN'T WANT CHOCOLATE...
BUZZ
I'M HUNGRY.
BUZZ
...SO WHY DOES HE ASSUME I HAVE CHOCOLATE FOR HIM, LIKE IT'S THE ONLY LOGICAL THING?
...IF IT'S COMING FROM YOU, SENPAI...
...I WANT IT. ALL OF IT.
......
...FINE.
LET'S SUPPOSE...
...I DID GIVE CHOCOLATE TO THAT JERK...
...WHAT WOULD THE LOOK ON HIS FACE BE?
CHOCO-LATE?
FOR ME?
LOVE
I WIN.
WHAM
HE'S TOO MUCH!
WHOA!
YUKI, WHAT'S WRONG!!?
HEY!

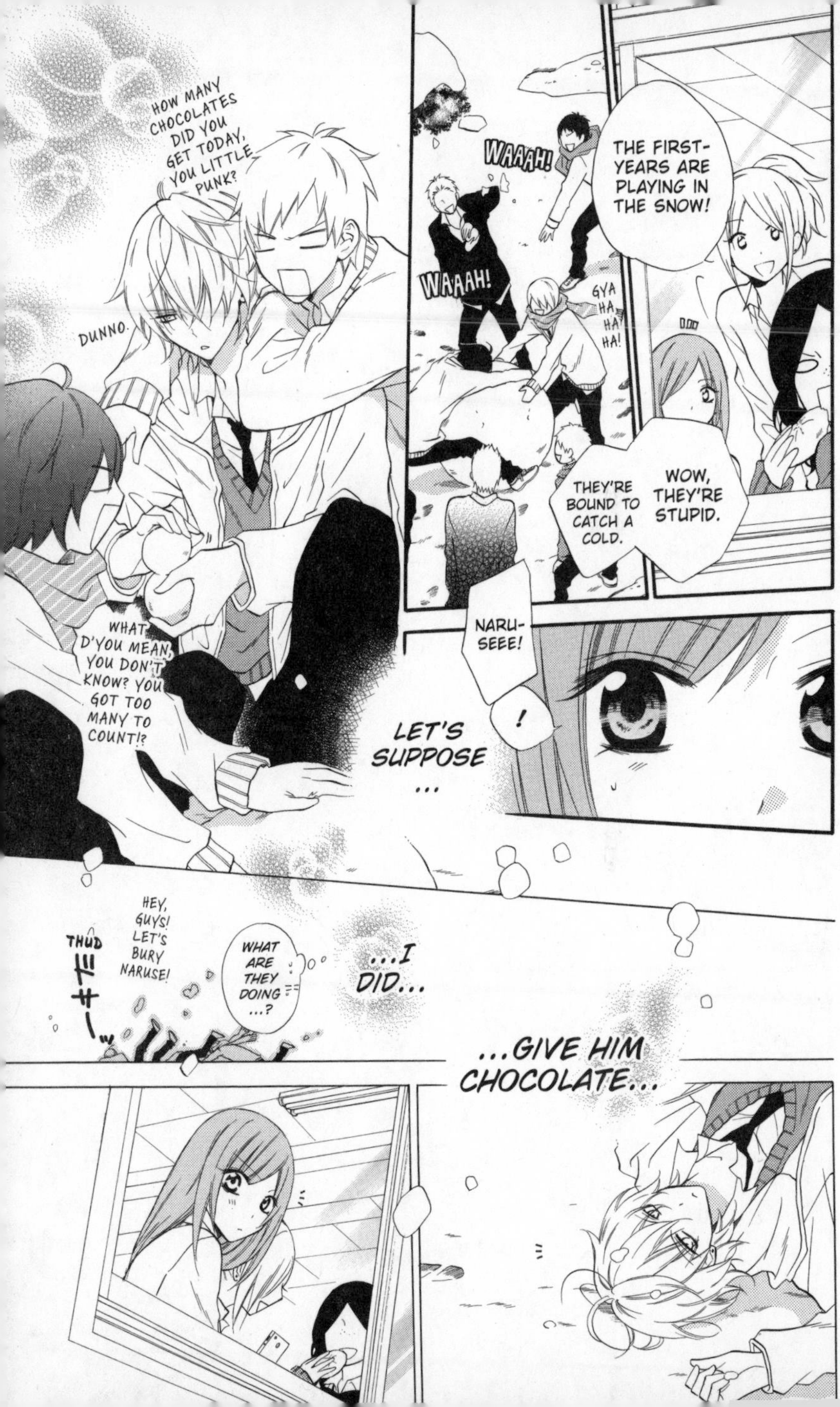
THE FIRST-YEARS ARE PLAYING IN THE SNOW!
WAAAH!
WAAAH!
GYA HA HA HA!
WOW, THEY'RE STUPID.
THEY'RE BOUND TO CATCH A COLD.
NARU-SEEE!
!
LET'S SUPPOSE ...
HOW MANY CHOCOLATES DID YOU GET TODAY, YOU LITTLE PUNK?
DUNNO.
WHAT D'YOU MEAN, YOU DON'T KNOW? YOU GOT TOO MANY TO COUNT!?
...I DID...
WHAT ARE THEY DOING ...?
HEY, GUYS! LET'S BURY NARUSE!
THUD
...GIVE HIM CHOCOLATE...

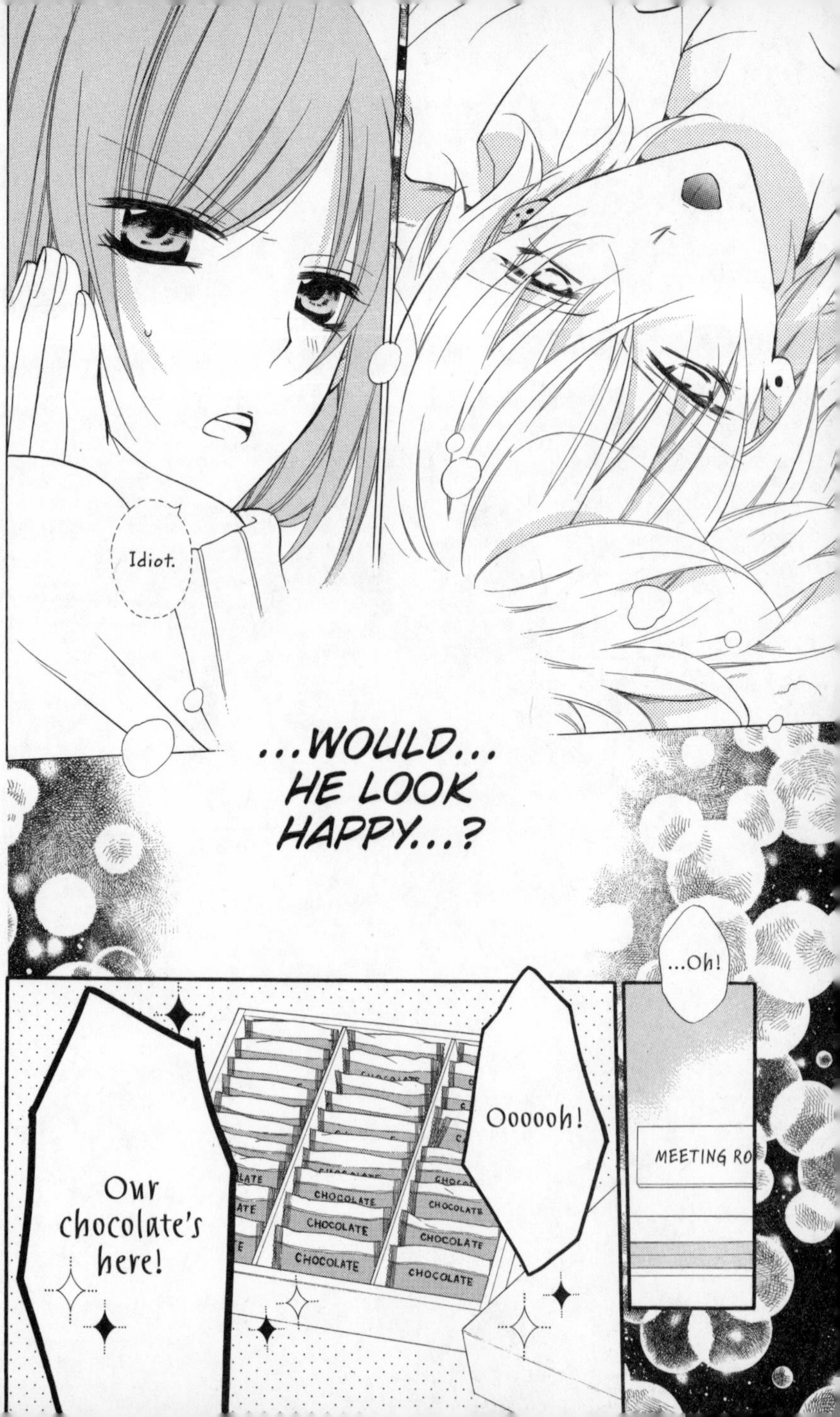
Idiot.
...WOULD... HE LOOK HAPPY...?
...Oh!
MEETING RO
Ooooh!
Our chocolate's here!
CHOCOLATE

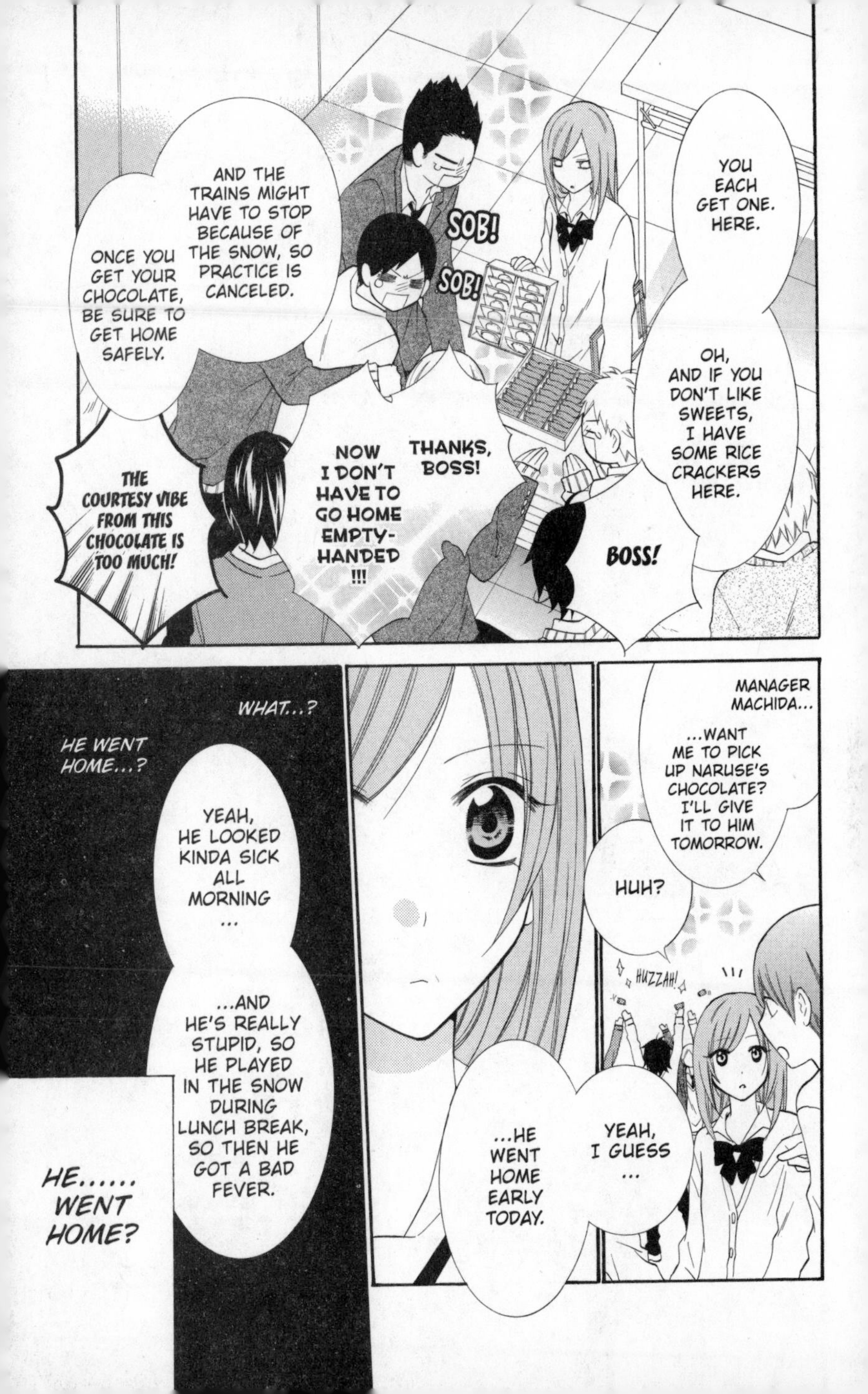
YOU EACH GET ONE. HERE.
OH, AND IF YOU DON'T LIKE SWEETS, I HAVE SOME RICE CRACKERS HERE.
BOSS!
SOB!
SOB!
AND THE TRAINS MIGHT HAVE TO STOP BECAUSE OF THE SNOW, SO PRACTICE IS CANCELED.
ONCE YOU GET YOUR CHOCOLATE, BE SURE TO GET HOME SAFELY.
THANKS, BOSS!
NOW I DON'T HAVE TO GO HOME EMPTY-HANDED !!!
THE COURTESY VIBE FROM THIS CHOCOLATE IS TOO MUCH!
MANAGER MACHIDA...
...WANT ME TO PICK UP NARUSE'S CHOCOLATE? I'LL GIVE IT TO HIM TOMORROW.
HUH?
HUZZAH!
YEAH, I GUESS ...
...HE WENT HOME EARLY TODAY.
WHAT...?
HE WENT HOME...?
YEAH, HE LOOKED KINDA SICK ALL MORNING ...
...AND HE'S REALLY STUPID, SO HE PLAYED IN THE SNOW DURING LUNCH BREAK, SO THEN HE GOT A BAD FEVER.
HE...... WENT HOME?

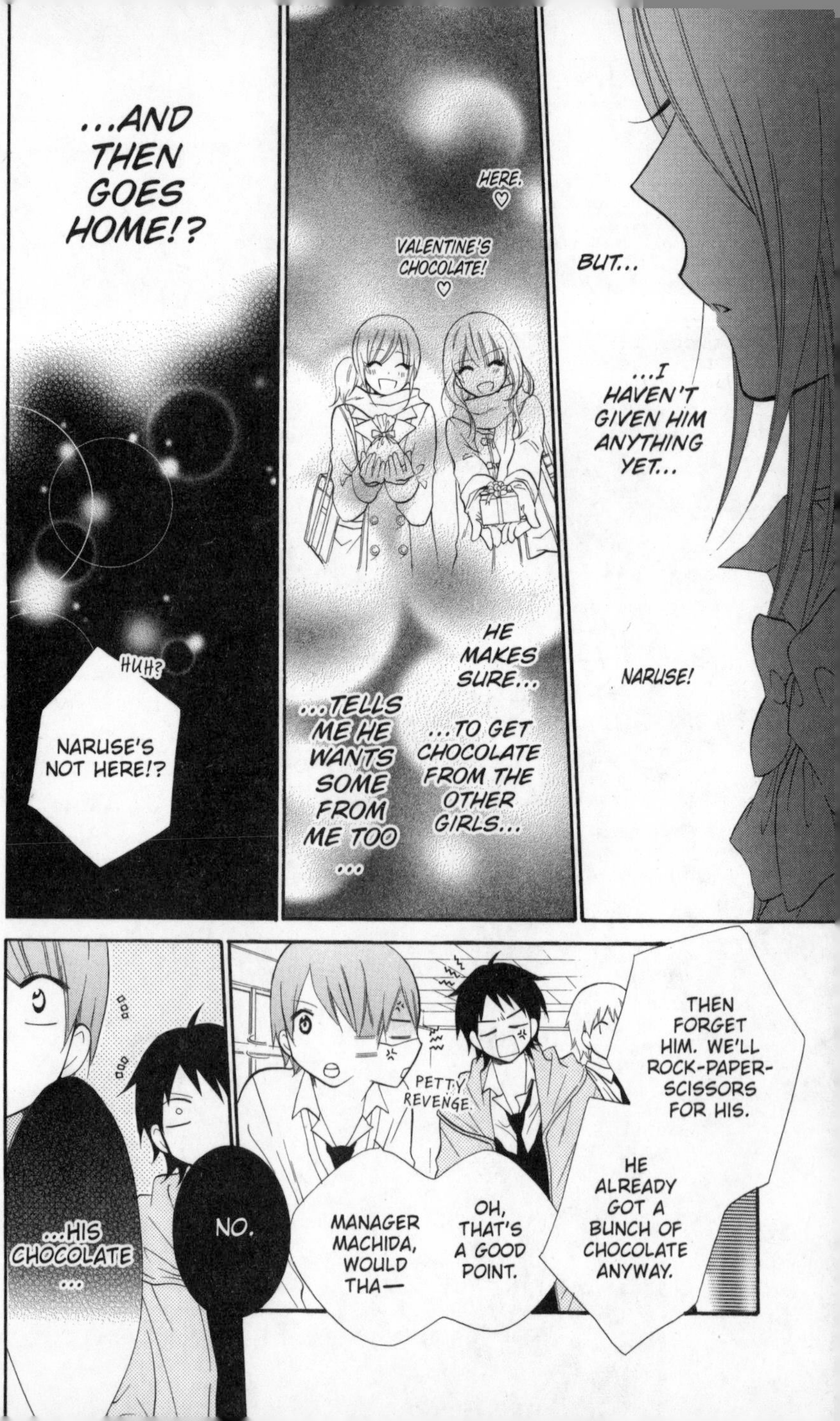
BUT...
...I HAVEN'T GIVEN HIM ANYTHING YET...
NARUSE!
HERE. ♡
VALENTINE'S CHOCOLATE! ♡
HE MAKES SURE...
...TO GET CHOCOLATE FROM THE OTHER GIRLS...
...TELLS ME HE WANTS SOME FROM ME TOO...
...AND THEN GOES HOME!?
HUH?
NARUSE'S NOT HERE!?
THEN FORGET HIM. WE'LL ROCK-PAPER-SCISSORS FOR HIS.
HE ALREADY GOT A BUNCH OF CHOCOLATE ANYWAY.
OH, THAT'S A GOOD POINT.
PETTY REVENGE.
MANAGER MACHIDA, WOULD THA—
NO.
...HIS CHOCOLATE...

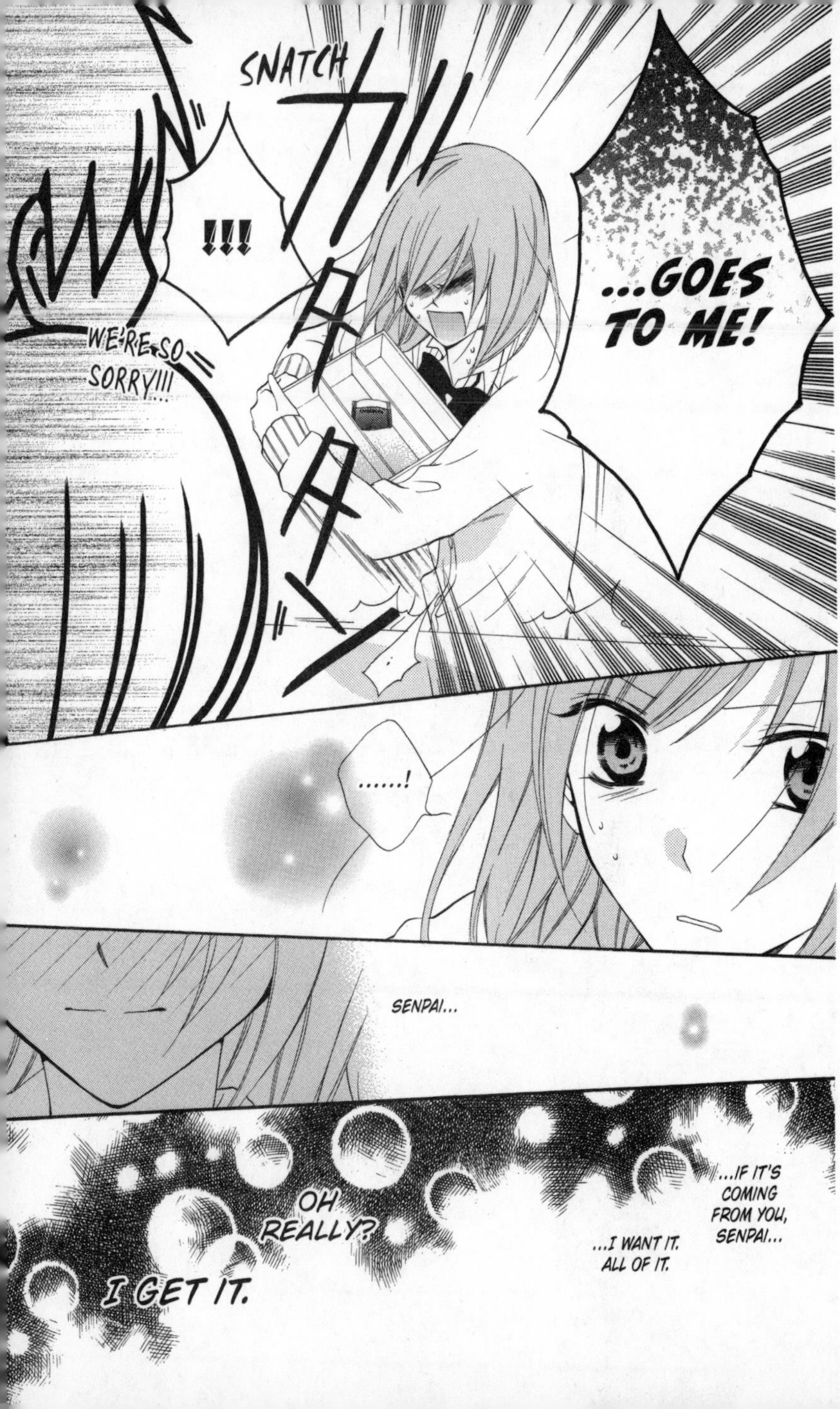
...GOES TO ME!
SNATCH
!!!
WE'RE SO SORRY!!!...
......!
SENPAI...
...IF IT'S COMING FROM YOU, SENPAI...
...I WANT IT. ALL OF IT.
OH REALLY?
I GET IT.

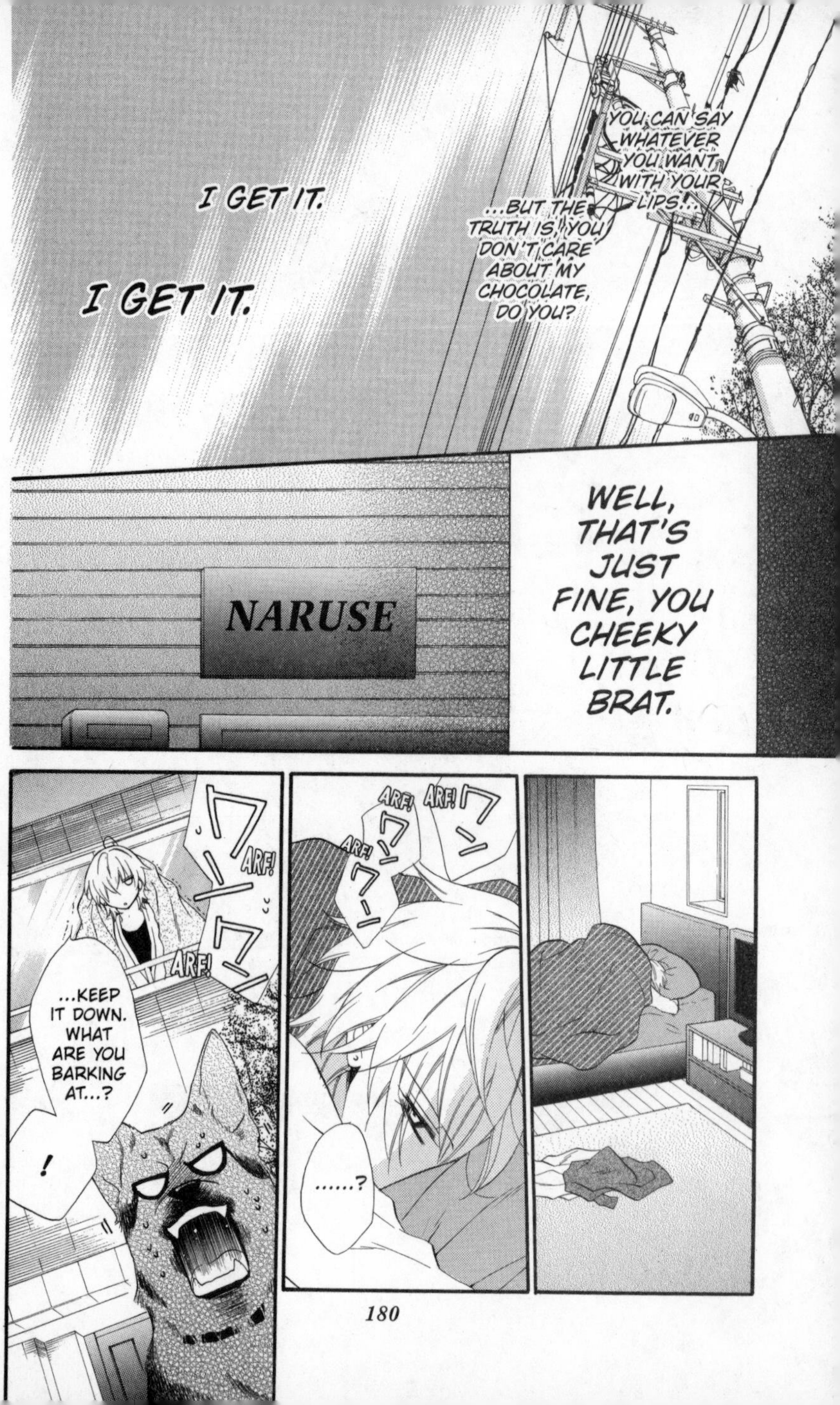
YOU CAN SAY WHATEVER YOU WANT WITH YOUR LIPS...
...BUT THE TRUTH IS, YOU DON'T CARE ABOUT MY CHOCOLATE, DO YOU?
I GET IT.
I GET IT.
WELL, THAT'S JUST FINE, YOU CHEEKY LITTLE BRAT.
NARUSE
ARF!
ARF!
ARF!
......?
ARF!
ARF!
...KEEP IT DOWN. WHAT ARE YOU BARKING AT...?
!

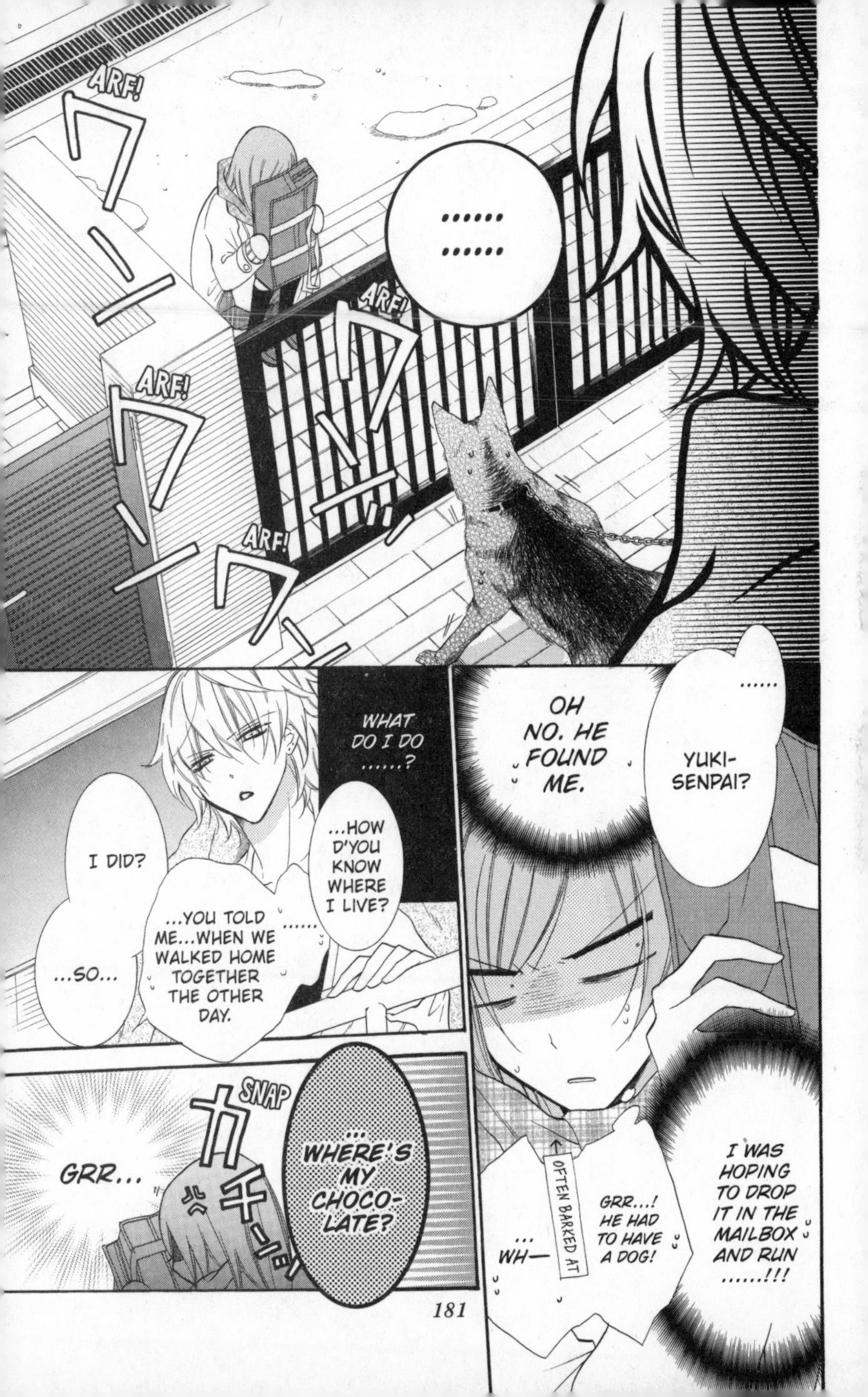

ARF!
ARF!
......
......
ARF!
ARF!
......
YUKI-SENPAI?
OH NO. HE FOUND ME.
I WAS HOPING TO DROP IT IN THE MAILBOX AND RUN ......!!!
GRR...! HE HAD TO HAVE A DOG!
OFTEN BARKED AT
... WH—
WHAT DO I DO ......?
...HOW D'YOU KNOW WHERE I LIVE?
......
...YOU TOLD ME...WHEN WE WALKED HOME TOGETHER THE OTHER DAY.
I DID?
...SO...
... WHERE'S MY CHOCO-LATE?
SNAP
GRR...

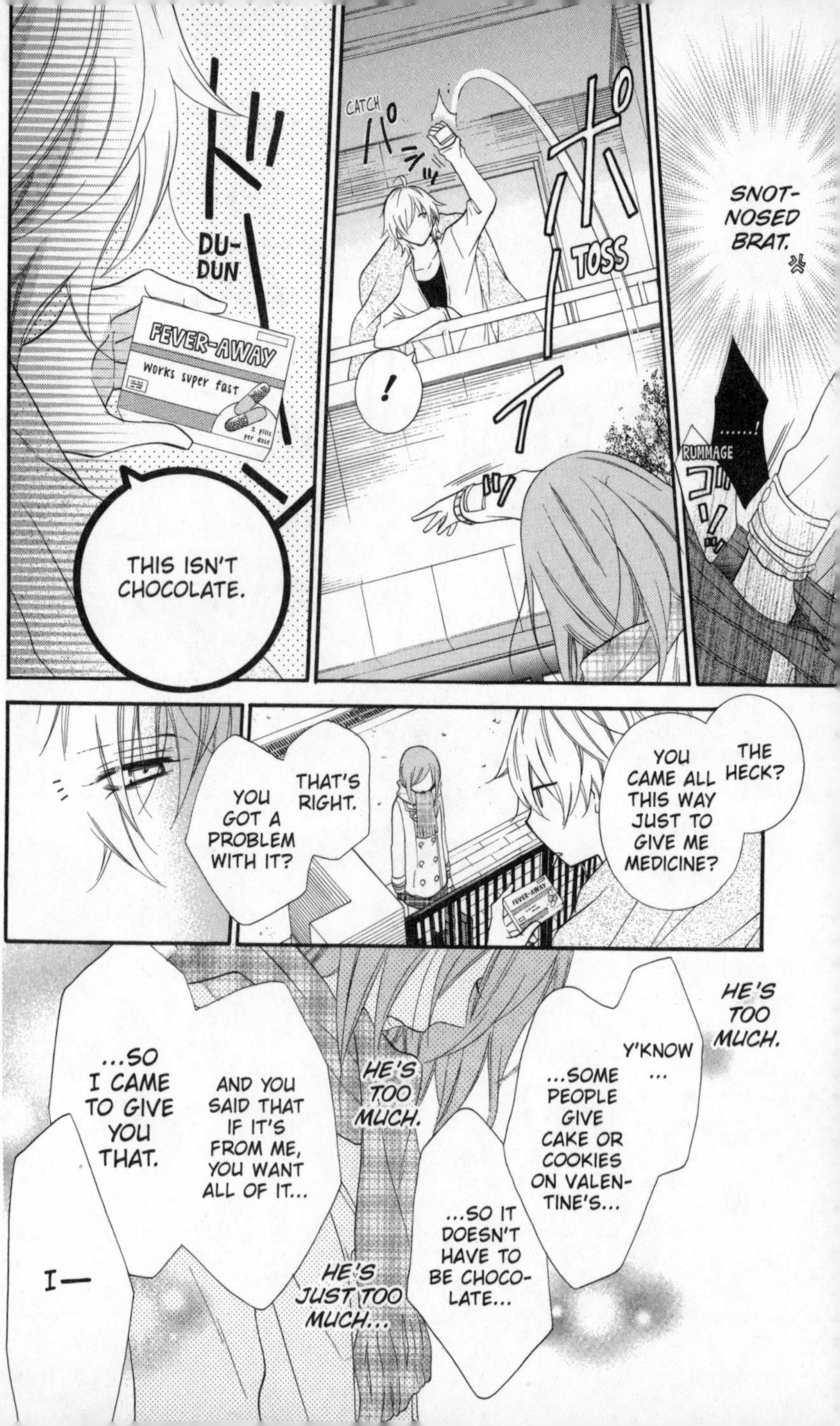
SNOT-NOSED BRAT.
......!
RUMMAGE
TOSS
CATCH
!
DU-DUN
FEVER-AWAY
works super fast
2 pills per dose
THIS ISN'T CHOCOLATE.
THE HECK?
YOU CAME ALL THIS WAY JUST TO GIVE ME MEDICINE?
FEVER-AWAY
THAT'S RIGHT.
YOU GOT A PROBLEM WITH IT?
HE'S TOO MUCH.
Y'KNOW ...
...SOME PEOPLE GIVE CAKE OR COOKIES ON VALEN-TINE'S...
...SO IT DOESN'T HAVE TO BE CHOCO-LATE...
HE'S JUST TOO MUCH...
HE'S TOO MUCH.
AND YOU SAID THAT IF IT'S FROM ME, YOU WANT ALL OF IT...
...SO I CAME TO GIVE YOU THAT.
I—

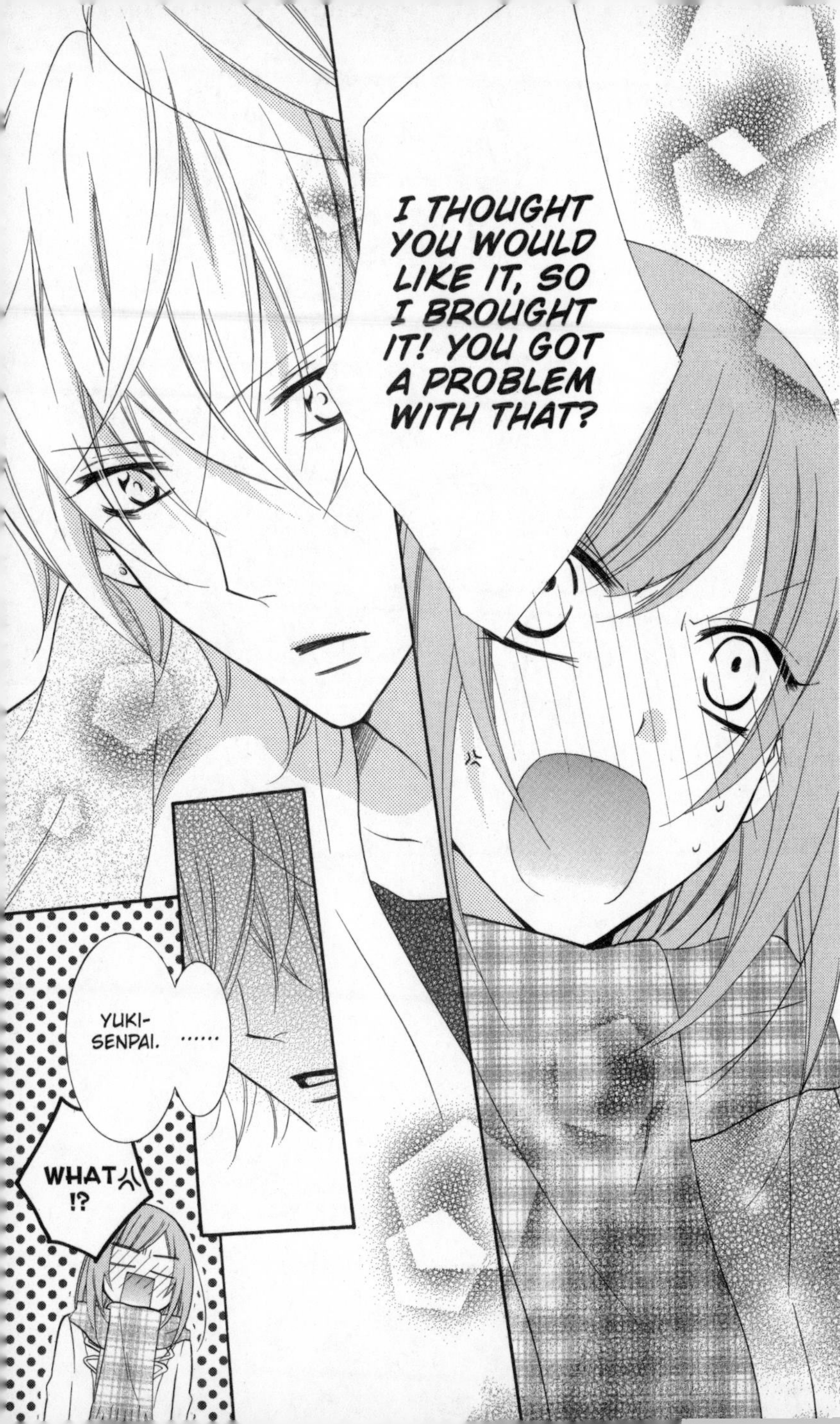
I THOUGHT YOU WOULD LIKE IT, SO I BROUGHT IT! YOU GOT A PROBLEM WITH THAT?
YUKI-SENPAI. ......
WHAT !?

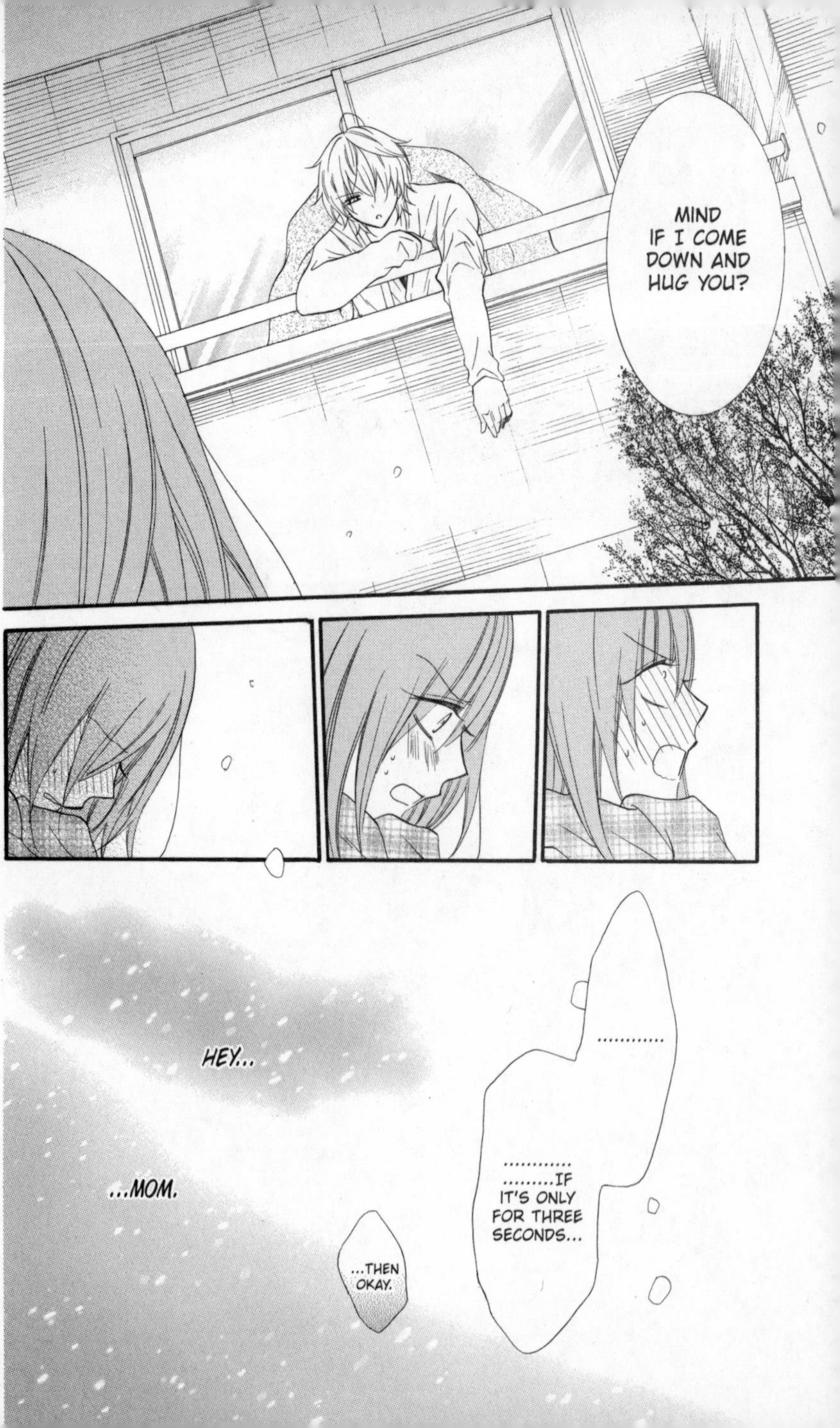
MIND IF I COME DOWN AND HUG YOU?
....
....
.........IF IT'S ONLY FOR THREE SECONDS...
...THEN OKAY.
HEY...
...MOM.

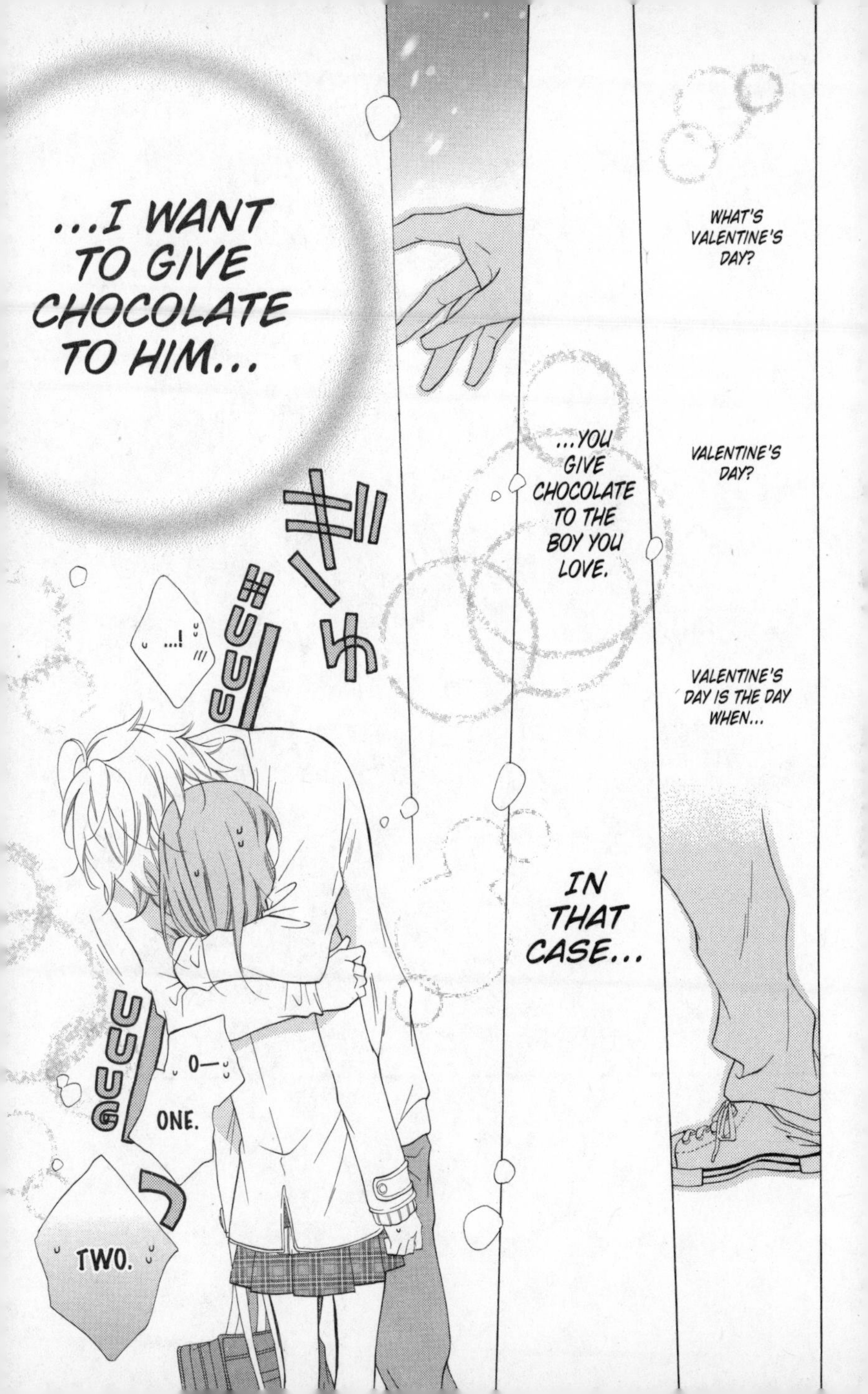
WHAT'S VALENTINE'S DAY?
VALENTINE'S DAY?
VALENTINE'S DAY IS THE DAY WHEN...
...YOU GIVE CHOCOLATE TO THE BOY YOU LOVE.
IN THAT CASE...
...I WANT TO GIVE CHOCOLATE TO HIM...
...!
UUU
O—
ONE.
GUUU
TWO.

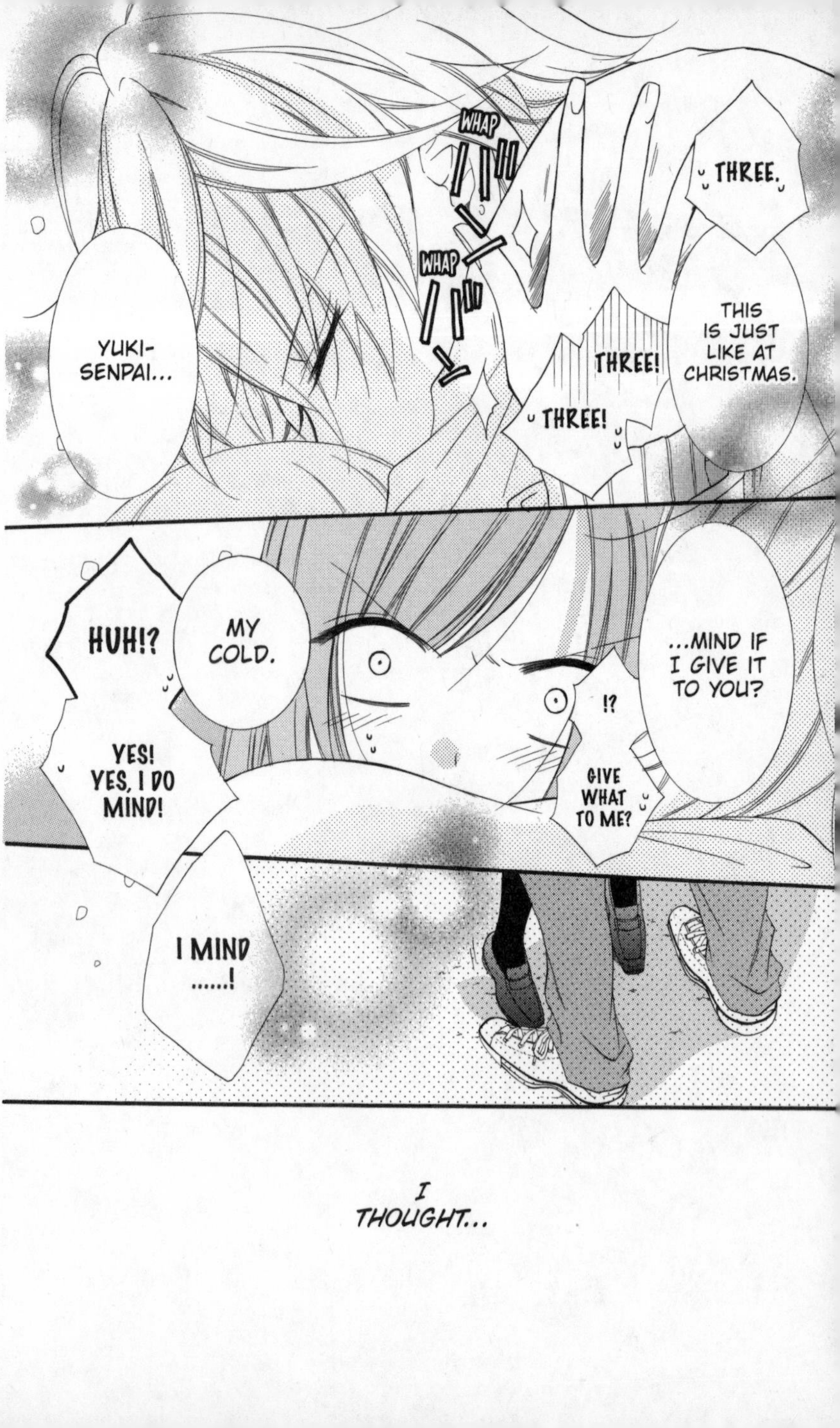
THREE.
THIS IS JUST LIKE AT CHRISTMAS.
WHAP
WHAP
THREE!
THREE!
YUKI-SENPAI...
...MIND IF I GIVE IT TO YOU?
!?
GIVE WHAT TO ME?
MY COLD.
HUH!?
YES! YES, I DO MIND!
I MIND ......!
I THOUGHT...

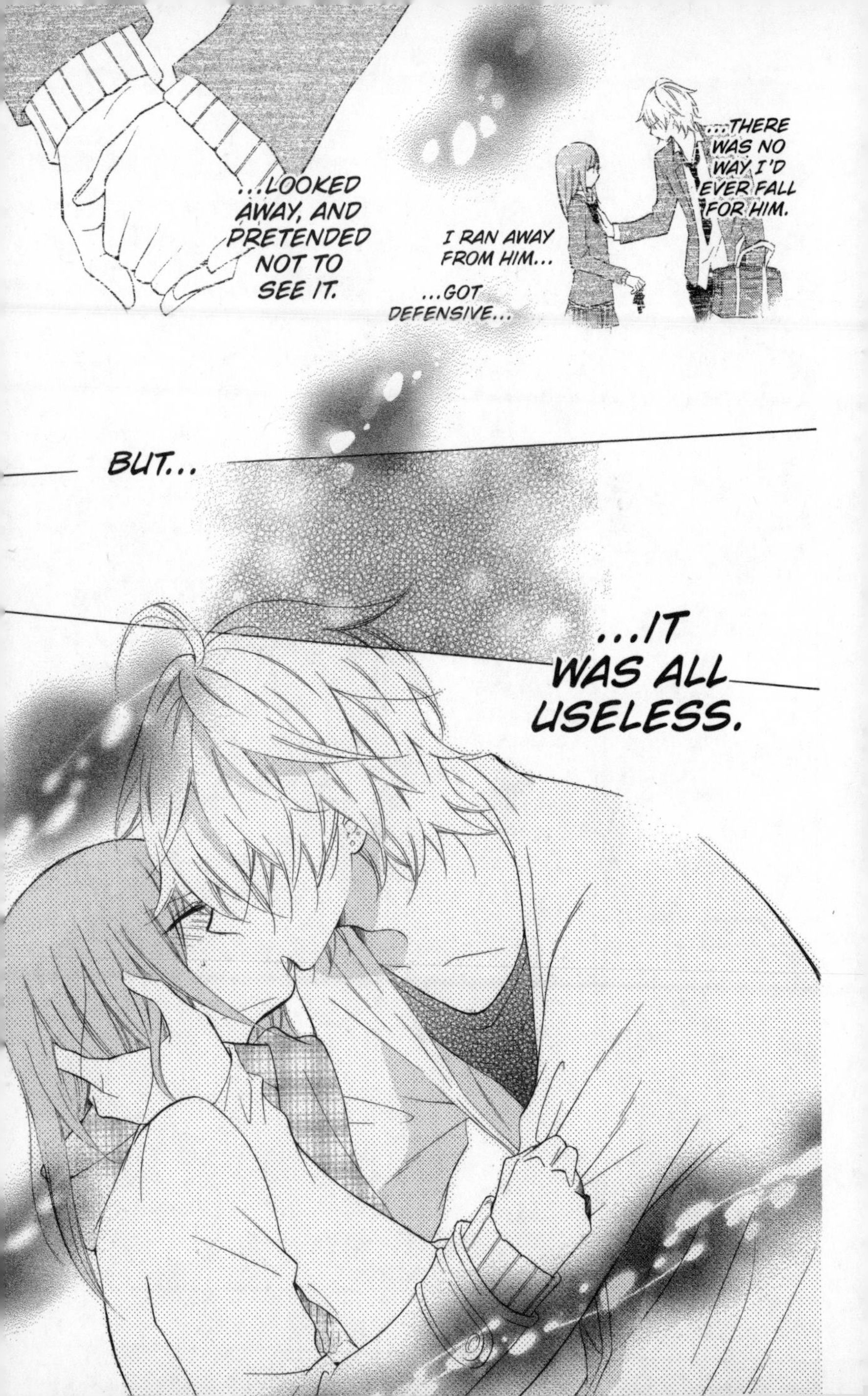
...THERE WAS NO WAY I'D EVER FALL FOR HIM.
I RAN AWAY FROM HIM...
...GOT DEFENSIVE...
...LOOKED AWAY, AND PRETENDED NOT TO SEE IT.
BUT...
...IT WAS ALL USELESS.

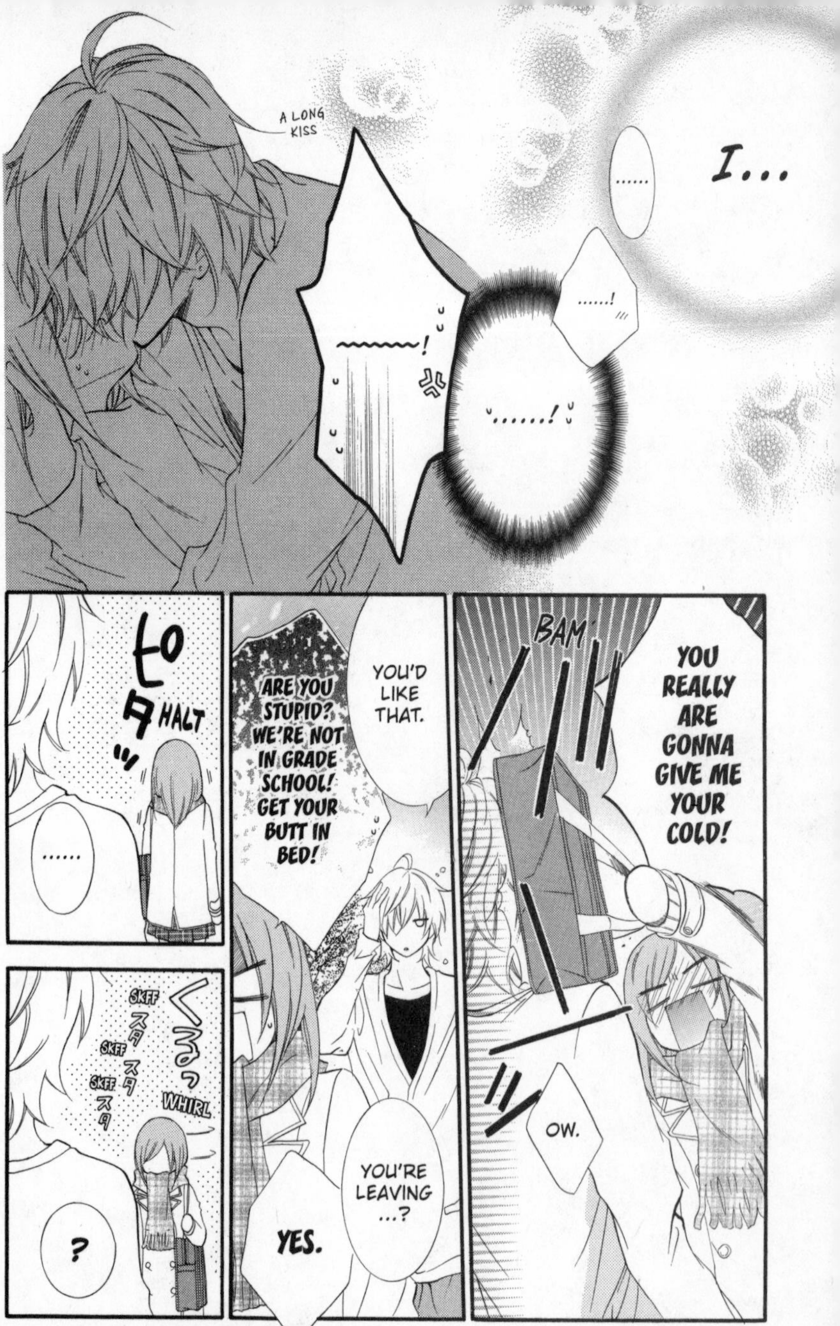
I...
......
......!
......!
~~~~~~!
A LONG KISS
BAM
YOU REALLY ARE GONNA GIVE ME YOUR COLD!
OW.
YOU'D LIKE THAT.
ARE YOU STUPID? WE'RE NOT IN GRADE SCHOOL! GET YOUR BUTT IN BED!
YOU'RE LEAVING ...?
YES.
ピタッ HALT
......
くるっ WHIRL
スタ SKFF
スタ SKFF
スタ SKFF
?
~~~~~~

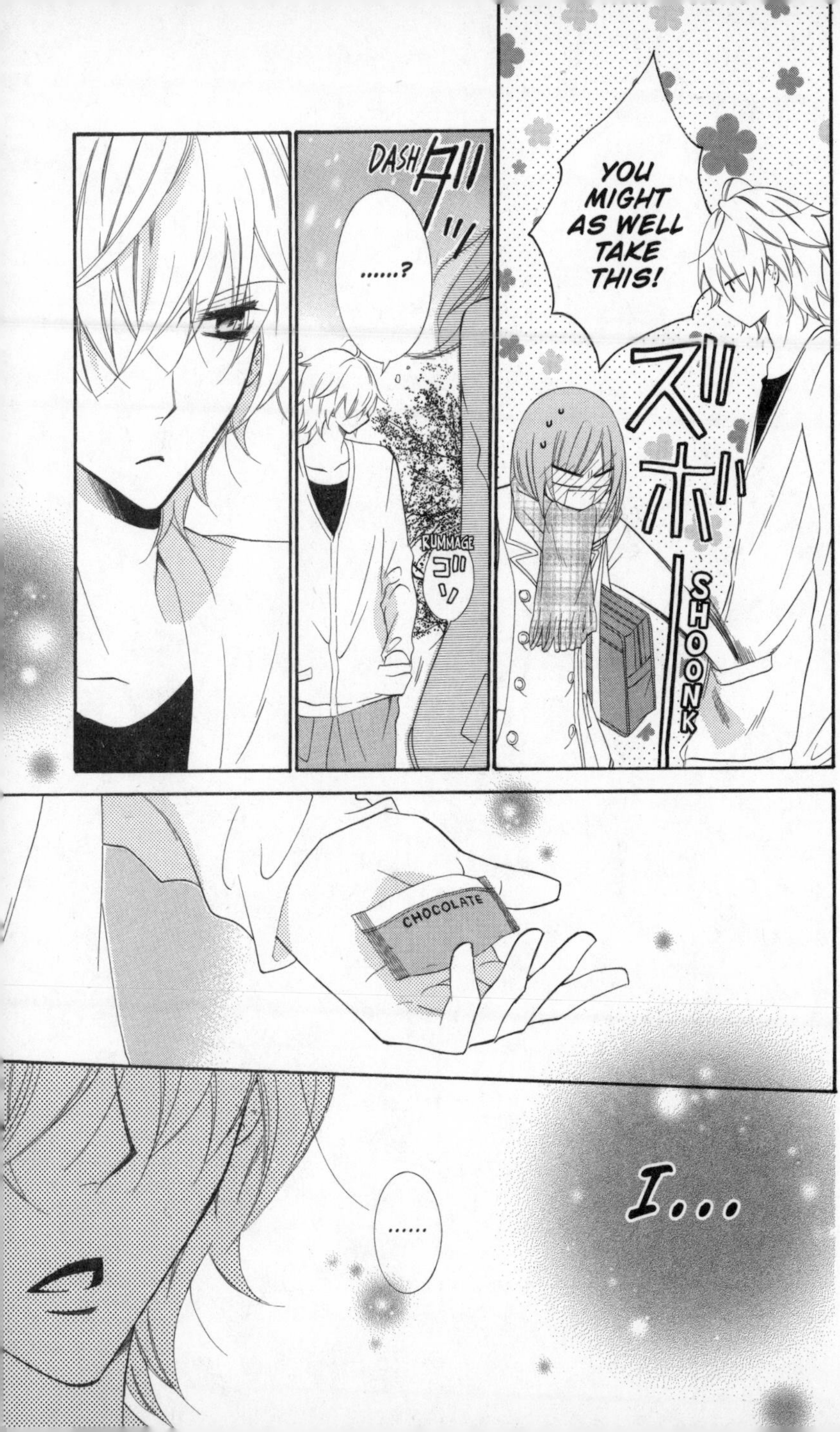
YOU MIGHT AS WELL TAKE THIS!
SHOONK
DASH ダッ
......?
RUMMAGE
CHOCOLATE
I...
......

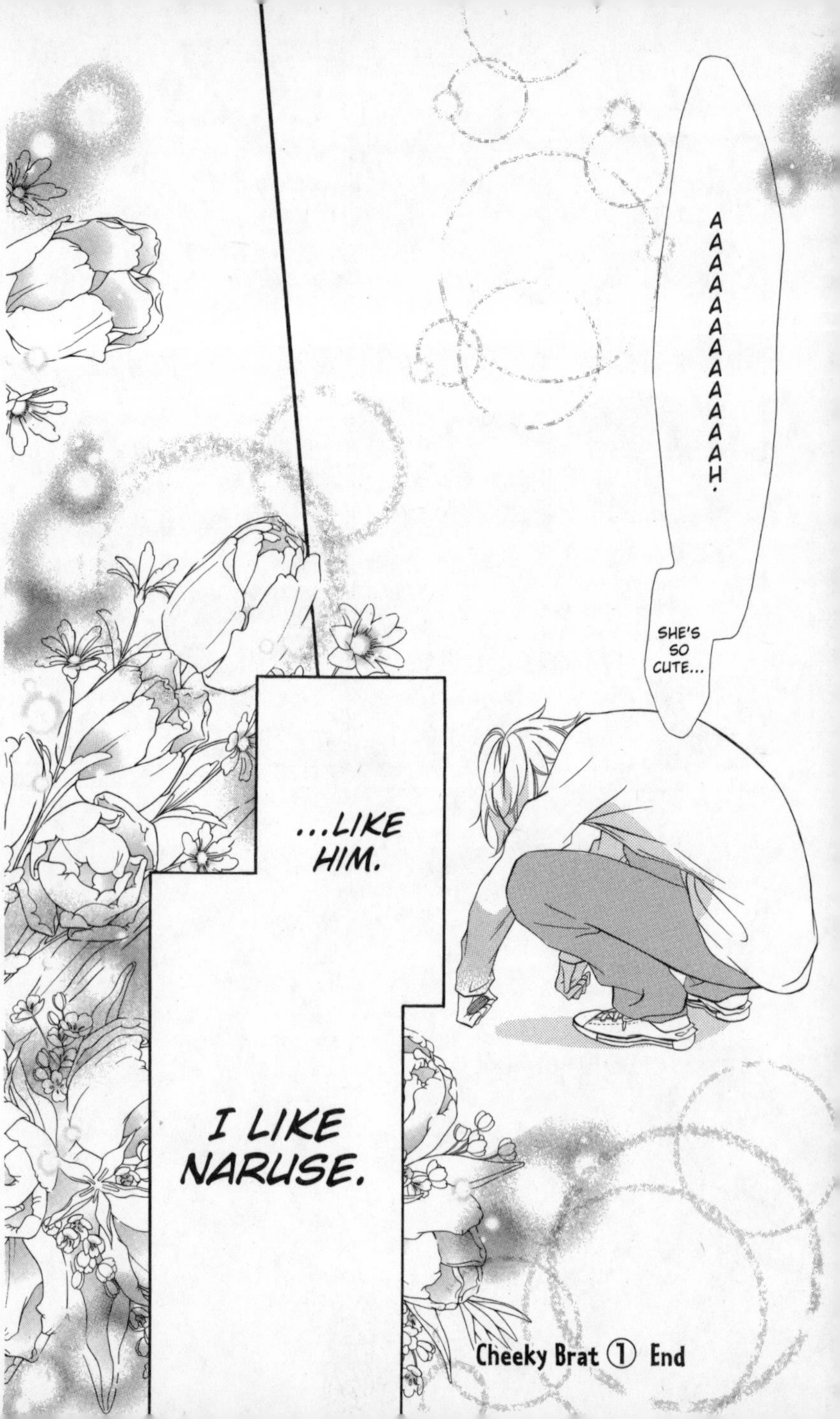
AAAAAAAAAAAAAAH.
SHE'S SO CUTE...
...LIKE HIM.
I LIKE NARUSE.
Cheeky Brat ① End

Translation Notes

PAGE 12

Go-home club: In Japan, almost every student in school is in a club (at some schools, it's required). Usually, the clubs are divided into two categories: *undoubu*, or athletic clubs (including all the sports teams), and *bunkabu*, or culture clubs (including art, music, literature, etc.). There is one final category of clubs, and that's the category for people who haven't joined any club—the *kitakubu*, or "go-home club." Members of this club use their extracurricular time to go home, or, on this particular day, to do odd jobs for their teacher.

Cram school: In Japan, many colleges require their potential students to pass an entrance exam before they can enroll. The more elite the school, the harder the exam. To prepare for these tests, students can attend *juku*, a type of supplementary school specifically geared to help them pass and get into the college of their choice.

Boss: This title is the rough English equivalent of the term *ane-san*, which is a delinquent sort of way of referring to a woman said delinquent respects. It literally means "older sister," but in this series it carries the connotation of "I love you (platonically) and respect you," with perhaps a touch of "Please don't hurt me."

PAGE 19

Show some respect: More specifically, Naruse's teammate tells him to stop using *tameguchi*, which is non-polite speech. He is older than Naruse, and therefore Naruse should speak to him with *teineigo*, or polite speech. Naruse needs constant reminders to use *teineigo* with upperclassmen.

PAGE 63

Hiss-terical Cat: Originally, this was *abuneko*, which is a pun on *abunee*, meaning "Danger!" or "Watch out!" and *neko*, meaning "cat."

PAGE 79

We'll be so lonely on Christmas: In Japan, Christmas Eve is celebrated as a romantic holiday, for people to spend a lovely evening with their significant others. It is also a family holiday with many traditions borrowed from the West (although the turkey is replaced with chicken), so if someone is single they're not necessarily doomed to a miserable night, but in general, the evening is treated very much like Valentine's Day in the West.

PAGE 93

The King Game: A game something like Truth or Dare, without the truth. The players draw lots, which either have a number or the word "king." The king then commands his subjects to do ridiculous things, such as "Number 1 will give Number 3 a hug," or "Number 4 will now dance on the table."

PAGE 145

Valentine's chocolate: The Japanese Valentine's Day tradition is that girls and women give chocolate to the objects of their affection, often as a way to confess their love, or to reaffirm their love to their significant other. It has also become customary to distribute chocolate among male friends, colleagues, etc. to show appreciation for them. This courtesy chocolate is known as *giri choco*, and is often translated literally as "obligation chocolate."

Mitsubachi Miyuki

Translation: Alethea Nibley and Athena Nibley
Lettering: Lys Blakeslee

This book is a work of fiction. Names, characters, places, and incidents are the product of the author's imagination or are used fictitiously. Any resemblance to actual events, locales, or persons, living or dead, is coincidental.

Namaiki Zakari by Mitsubachi Miyuki
© Mitsubachi Miyuki 2014
All rights reserved.
First published in Japan in 2014 by HAKUSENSHA, Inc., Tokyo.
English language translation rights in U.S.A., Canada and U.K.
arranged with HAKUSENSHA, Inc., Tokyo through Tuttle-Mori
Agency, Inc., Tokyo.

English translation © 2021 by Yen Press, LLC

Yen Press
150 West 30th Street, 19th Floor
New York, NY 10001

Visit us at yenpress.com
facebook.com/yenpress
twitter.com/yenpress
yenpress.tumblr.com
instagram.com/yenpress

First Yen Press Edition: November 2021

Yen Press is an imprint of Yen Press, LLC.
The Yen Press name and logo are trademarks of Yen Press, LLC.

The publisher is not responsible for websites (or their content)
that are not owned by the publisher.

Library of Congress Control Number: 2021946316

ISBNs: 978-1-9753-3435-2 (paperback)
978-1-9753-3436-9 (ebook)

10 9 8 7 6 5 4 3 2 1

WOR

Printed in the United States of America